ROUTLEDGE LIBRARY EDITIONS: PSYCHOLOGY OF EDUCATION

Volume 42

PSYCHOLOGY OF EDUCATION

PSYCHOLOGY OF EDUCATION

A pedagogical approach

EDGAR STONES

LONDON AND NEW YORK

First published in 1979 under the title *Psychopedagogy* by
Methuen & Co. Ltd
Reissued with new title and prologue 1984

This edition first published in 2018
by Routledge
2 Park Square, Milton Park, Abingdon, Oxon OX14 4RN

and by Routledge
711 Third Avenue, New York, NY 10017

*Routledge is an imprint of the Taylor & Francis Group, an
informa business*

© 1979 E. Stones; © 1983 E. Stones (Prologue)

All rights reserved. No part of this book may be reprinted or
reproduced or utilised in any form or by any electronic,
mechanical, or other means, now known or hereafter invented,
including photocopying and recording, or in any information
storage or retrieval system, without permission in writing from
the publishers.

Trademark notice: Product or corporate names may be
trademarks or registered trademarks, and are used only for
identification and explanation without intent to infringe.

British Library Cataloguing in Publication Data
A catalogue record for this book is available from the British
Library

ISBN: 978-1-138-24157-2 (Set)
ISBN: 978-1-315-10703-5 (Set) (ebk)
ISBN: 978-1-138-63366-7 (Volume 42) (hbk)
ISBN: 978-1-315-20720-9 (Volume 42) (ebk)

Publisher's Note
The publisher has gone to great lengths to ensure the quality
of this reprint but points out that some imperfections in the
original copies may be apparent.

Disclaimer
The publisher has made every effort to trace copyright holders
and would welcome correspondence from those they have been
unable to trace.

Psychology of Education
A pedagogical approach

Edgar Stones

METHUEN
London and New York

First published in 1979 under the title Psychopedagogy *by
Methuen & Co. Ltd
11 New Fetter Lane London EC4P 4EE
Reissued with new title and prologue 1984*

*Published in the USA by
Methuen & Co. Ltd
a division of Methuen, Inc.
733 Third Avenue, New York, NY 10017*

© *1979 E. Stones
Prologue, 1983* © *E. Stones*

*Printed in Great Britain by
Richard Clay (The Chaucer Press) Ltd,
Bungay, Suffolk*

*All rights reserved. No part of this book may be reprinted
or reproduced or utilized in any form or by any electronic,
mechanical or other means, now known or hereafter invented,
including photocopying and recording, or in any information
storage or retrieval system, without permission in writing
from the publishers.*

British Library Cataloguing in Publication Data
Stones, Edgar
  [*Psychopedagogy*].   *Psychology of education.*
  1. Educational psychology
  I. Title   II. Psychology of education
  371.1′02′019   LB1051
  ISBN 0-416-37660-6

Library of Congress Cataloging in Publication Data
Stones, E.
  Psychology of education.

  *Reprint. Originally published: Psychopedagogy.
London: Methuen, 1979. With new prologue.
  1. Educational psychology. I. Title.
LB1051.S72837 1984   370.15   84-4540*

ISBN 0-416-37660-6

Table of contents

Expanded table of contents vii
List of figures xiv
Prologue xviii

1 Learners, teachers, psychologists 1
2 Learning: foundations 19
3 Language and human learning 47
4 Thought, talk, action 68
5 Teachers talk 104
6 Sorts of talk 122
7 Objectives for teaching 142
8 Analyses for teaching 176
9 Concept teaching 196
10 Teaching psychomotor skills 227
11 Teaching problem solving 251
12 Sustaining learning 277
13 A pattern of teaching skills 308
14 Programming teaching 331

vi *Contents*

15 Evaluating teaching and learning 354
16 Making a test 375
17 Made to measure? 400
18 Learning teaching 434
    Summary 452

    References 466
    Index 478

Expanded table of contents

List of figures xiv
Prologue xviii

1 Learners, teachers, psychologists 1

Victor 2
Washoe 4
Learning and teaching 5
Experimenters and teachers 8
Teaching as problem solving 9
Guiding learning 10
Learners 15
Teachers 17

2 Learning: foundations 19

Reinforcement 19
Schedules of reinforcement 22
Punishment 25

viii *Contents*

Extinction 27
Discrimination 28
Generalization 32
Feedback 34
Learning sets 36
Learning by imitation 39
Affective effects 40
Curiosity 42
The need to achieve 43
Learning motivation 44

3 Language and human learning 47

Signals and symbols 48
Concepts 49
A symbol system 51
Remote reference 53
Cultural accretion 54
Effects of schooling 57
Labels and learning 58
Empty sounds 61
Verbal learning 62
Language and thought 65
Whose world? 66

4 Thought, talk, action 68

The word and the act 68
The acts of thought 71
Sensory-motor intelligence 75
Pre-operational stage 76
Concrete operations 78
Formal operations 79
Teaching and thinking 79
Language and action 81
The process function of language 86
Learning and representation 89
Thinking, acting, teaching: some questions 92
Pedagogical implications 98

Contents ix

5 Teachers talk 104

Language and the guidance of learning 106
Lesson from life: 1 110
Mis-concept-ions 118

6 Sorts of talk 122

Analysing discourse 122
Flanders's interaction category system 123
Lesson from life: 2 126
Lesson from life: 3 127
  Analysis 129
Problems of inference 133
A linguistic view 134
Unstructured approaches 136
Pedagogical implications 137
Non-verbal effects 139

7 Objectives for teaching 142

Do you know where you're going? 142
Theory and practice 143
Getting things clear 145
Getting agreement 147
Analysing objectives 149
The Bloom taxonomy 151
Skills, concepts, feelings 155
Generating objectives 156
Doing 158
Knowing 162
An example 164
An analysis 166
Common sense about objectives 171
Objections, objections 172

8 Analyses for teaching 176

Analysis 178
The learner's task 179
The teacher's task 181

x *Contents*

Task sequence 188
Lesson from life: 4 191
Theory into practice 195

9 Concept teaching 196

Teaching skills 196
Concept teaching: a key teaching skill 199
A teaching schedule 204
Skills in practice 208
Lesson from life: 5 209
Lesson from life: 6 216
Lesson from life: 7 222

10 Teaching psychomotor skills 227

Objectives 230
Task analysis 232
Guiding and cueing 233
Feedback 236
Practice 238
Independent evaluation 239
Norms 240
A teaching schedule 242
Psychomotor skills in practice 243
Lesson 1: Catching a rugby ball 244
Lesson 2: Teaching discrimination
of intervals in music 246

11 Teaching problem solving 251

Problems 253
Algorithms 254
Heuristics 257
Guides to thinking 260
A guide to teaching 262
1 Identify the problem 263
2 Bring to mind the relevant concepts 264

Contents xi

3 Analyse the task 265
4 Give prompted practice 266
5 Give practice with feedback; enhance motivation 266
6 Develop independent activity 266
A heuristic on problem solving 267
A teaching schedule 268
Creativity 267
Creativity and problem solving 270
Problem solving in practice 271
Lesson from life: 8 272
Lesson from life: 9 273

12 Sustaining learning 277

Arranging reinforcement 279
Reinforcers 281
Problems 285
Identifying reinforcers and punishers 290
Feedback 293
A teaching schedule 294
Motivation 297
Reinforcement in practice 298
Lesson from life: 10 299
Lesson from life: 11 303

13 A pattern of teaching skills 308

Some second-order skills 311
Questioning 312
Lesson from life: 12 313
Set induction 317
Lesson from life: 13 318
Lesson from life: 14 319
Closure 321
Other skills 321
A master skill? 322
Synthesis 326

xii *Contents*

14 **Programming teaching 331**

Origins 332
Flexible programming 340
Framing 343
A tested product 344
Monitoring 347
Programming today 349
A teaching system 351
Teachers, programmes, programming 352

15 **Evaluating teaching and learning 354**

Evaluation and guidance 355
The sampling of behaviour 358
Nature of skills tested 361
Test reference 363
Standardized tests 365
Diagnostic evaluation 366
Problems of measurement 367
Validity 369
Reliability 370
Problems of ranking 371
Aspects of evaluation 372

16 **Making a test 375**

The skills tested 376
Essay-type tests 378
Objective tests 381
  Item types 384
  Matching 386
  Completion items 387
  Interpretative items 388
Teachers and tests 391
Tests, institutions, teachers 393
Standardized tests 395
Public examinations 396
Continuous assessment 398

Contents xiii

17 Made to measure? 400

Label and liquidate 402
Salami theories of personality 404
Intelligence? 408
Testing, testing 409
Colour and complex learning 414
   Learning and testing 416
   Black and white pedagogies? 417
Expectations great and small 418
Labelling language 420
Streaming 424
Which differences? 426
Learning difficulties 427
Diagnosis 431
Specific disabilities 432

18 Learning teaching 434

Illusion and reality 435
Mastering the model 436
This is your style 437
Cooperative diagnosis 438
Helping 442
Lesson from life: 15 443
Teaching experiments 450
Envoi 451

Summary 452

References 466
Index 478

List of figures

6.1   Flanders's interaction analysis categories (FIAC) 124

7.1   Bloom's taxonomy of educational objectives 152

7.2   Matrix of skills and concepts involved in specifying objectives 170

8.1   Task analysis 184

8.2   Illustrative analysis of part of the task of teaching pupils that we read from left to right 186

9.1   The relationships between general skills and phases of teaching 198

9.2   Schedule for the teaching of concepts (STOC) 205

10.1   Harrow's taxonomy for teaching psychomotor skills 231

10.2   Illustrative analysis of the task of teaching handwriting 234

10.3   Schedule for the teaching of psychomotor skills (STOPS) 242

10.4   Task analysis of discrimination between ascending intervals of a major scale 248

List of figures xv

11.1 Schedule for the teaching and evaluation of problem solving (STEPS) 268
11.2 Heuristic device for a problem-solving task 276
12.1 Schedule for teacher's use of reinforcement (STUR) 295
13.1 Schedule for evaluating teaching (SET) 327
14.1a Diagrammatic representation of linear programme 339
14.1b Diagrammatic representation of branching programme 339
14.1c Diagrammatic representation of branching programme with sub-sequence 339
14.2 Schematic layout of a programme for relatively unstructured material 342
16.1 Example of matching item using a diagram 387
16.2 Example of interpretative item (1) 389
16.3 Example of interpretative item (2) 390
17.1 Pupil scores on a selection of sub-tests from an intelligence test 411

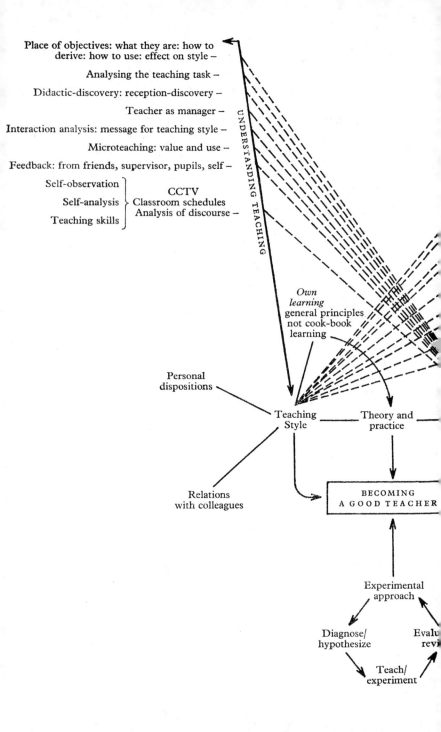

How differs from animal learning
Language-cognition-social influences

Understanding children's learning
 – Cognitive = subjects (learning of) how?
 – Affective = attitudes to subjects,
   school, teacher
 – Psychomotor = learning of skills
 – Solving problems

How these
interpenetrate
Their common
features

Development in learning
 – Growing, learning and teaching: their interrelations

Intervention to enhance learning
 – Diagnosis of present capabilities: how to do this
 – Teaching 'subjects' = concept teaching. Common principles
   across subjects: e.g. from reading, history, maths etc.
 – Written and spoken language

What to do to teach skills
 – Cognitive, psychomotor, problem solving – similarities in approach;
   affective – not 'teach' directly, i.e. not a 'skill' or 'subject' changing
   attitudes and motivation – reciprocal with cognitive and psychomotor.

Assessing learning
 – Testing – criterion-referencing – making a test – item writing

Language and learning
 – Transform learning – helps solve problems.
   Can be counter-productive (labelling)

Differences in learning
 – Effects of class, race, 'intelligence'

Failure in learning
 – What does it mean? Effects of labelling
   Classify problems not pupils

labelling
Human characteristic to classify
Great power but great dangers
Misclassify → mistreat
Problems: label and liquidate
BUT can label and persecute

UNDERSTANDING HUMAN LEARNING

Pupils' learning

A Map of the Terrain

Prologue

Seedlings or cut flowers?

Traditionally courses in the style of *educational psychology* have provided ideas like cut flowers. Carefully plucked and presented they have been stuck in the soil of student teacher studies to flourish briefly and wilt quickly as their sustenance seeped away. Come graduation neophyte teachers rapidly forgot such ephemera or complained at their inutility. What they sought were firm-jointed seedlings that would root strongly in their concern to help children to learn and to like learning, and would be nourished by practical experience.

In recent years many teacher educators have themselves recognized the unsatisfactory nature of the offerings handed to student teachers under the rubric of *educational psychology*. However, there is still far to go. For my part, I have long felt and argued that the way forward for educational psychology is to focus on the act of teaching rather than on education as an academic subject. I have also taken my convictions seriously and, with the help of many practising and student teachers, have explored the applicability and relevance of various aspects of learning theory to actual practical teaching. In the pages which follow I draw on those explorations to outline to readers courses of action that I believe will help them develop insights into practical teaching based on systematic studies of principles that

Prologue xix

help human beings to learn. I believe that those insights will foster the growth, not only of pupil *and teacher* learning, but also of the fresh shoots of pedagogy that have been so long neglected.

Cooperative exploration

Courses that deal with cut-and-dried facts are by nature transitory; lasting growth and development demand openendedness. Thus the general line proposed stresses an exploratory approach to teaching rather than the routine application of predetermined procedures. Teaching is seen as a form of experimental psychology.

Thus I deem it inappropriate merely to present for digestion the findings, thoughts, hypotheses and hunches of psychologists ruminating about education. Instead I have tried to show how teachers can test psychological principles that have been found valuable in their own practice. Not to apply the principles, but to explore their applicability to real teaching with a sceptical cast of mind that sees research findings and currently fashionable procedures as a matter for debate.

In my disquisitions and excursions I take a pluralistic approach and do not espouse any particular school of psychology. The fact that in some places I draw on the work of Skinner as a guide to action does not put me in the 'behaviourist' camp any more than reference to other psychologists puts me in the 'cognitive' camp. Essentially I believe that these categorizations are in the main simplistic and quite unhelpful in discussions of pedagogy and educational psychology. If I must be pigeonholed I think I should be happiest in the 'pedagogic' camp, a location that I think natural for one interested in teaching and teacher training. I hope many readers will feel persuaded to join this select band.

I hasten to add that I do not lay claim to the whole of pedagogy. My concern is with the contribution psychology can make to pedagogy. I am very much aware that in teacher training there are other important aspects of pedagogy, but I do believe that psychology is of central importance and has a great deal to offer teachers with a genuine interest in their profession. Hence the running head in the pages that follow: *Psychopedagogy.*

xx *Prologue*

Perhaps the key contribution the suggested approach offers is the development of a questioning, exploratory turn of mind that does not take as gospel the expositions in textbooks and lectures, but rather sees them as possible guides to be proved (that is, tested) in pedagogic action in practical teaching. I apply the same criteria to what I have written in this book. I feel some confidence, however, since the procedures discussed have, in fact, been tested in practice in various ways. I am well aware, also, that no book can comprise a complete pedagogical system and I discuss the reasons for this. Thus to dedicated pedagogues, all the book can offer is a beginning; only their personal explorations of the validity of the arguments and suggestions can continue the process of their own pedagogical education. Often this may well have to be a bootstrap operation and this point is also taken up in the book.

I have also made clear my own scepticism about some of the constructs and concepts that have influenced teaching in recent years and at times may have been more polemical than is conventionally thought proper. An instance of this may be evidenced in my discussion of current approaches to testing and the classification of people which, I argue, as they are at present, are basically anti-learning and anti-teaching. I think it is justified and important to take such an approach because it makes explicit the controversial nature of many current practices and concepts that at times have been accepted as received truths, with gravely deleterious effects on teaching. It also makes my own prejudices clearer than is usually the case with conventional tests of alleged impartiality. Time alone will tell where truth lies, and naturally I think time is on my side.

Edgar Stones, November 1983

Acknowledgements

I should like to thank Beatrice Nagel and Mike Smith for their helpful comments in the preparation of the book, and all my students who taught me more than they ever suspected. I also wish to thank George Brown and Mary Wills for their help in providing transcripts to lessons.

Acknowledgements

The author and publishers would like to thank the following for permission to reproduce the copyright material which appears in this book: Addison-Wesley Pub. Co. for Fig. 6.1, from N. Flanders, *Analyzing Teacher Behaviour* (1970); Longman Inc. for Fig. 7.1, from *Taxonomy of Educational Objectives, Handbook 1* (1956), ed. B. S. Bloom *et al.*, and *Handbook 2* (1964), ed. D. Krathwohl *et al.*; for Fig. 10.1, Longman Inc., from A. J. Harrow, *A Taxonomy of the Psychomotor Domain* (1972) and McKay Co., Inc., from I. K. Davies, *Objectives in Curriculum Design* (1976); Methuen & Co. for Fig. 7.2, from E. Stones and D. Anderson, *Educational Objectives and the Teaching of Educational Psychology* (1972), for Fig. 14.1a, from E. Stones, *Introduction to Educational Psychology* (1966), and for Figs 14.1c and 14.2, from E. Stones, *Readings in Educational Psychology* (1970); Macmillan, Inc. for Fig. 10.2, from *Encyclopedia of Educational Research* (1969); Ford Teaching Project for Fig. 11.2 and the extracts on pp. 272 and 273–4; Doubleday & Co., Inc. and English Universities Press for the extract on pp. 336–7, from N. A.

xxii *Acknowledgements*

Crowder and G. C. Martin, *Arithmetic of Computers* (1960); Educational Testing Service, Princeton, N.J. for Figs 16.2 and 16.3, from *Multiple-Choice Questions: A Close Look* (1963).

1

Learners, teachers, psychologists

Cast on this globe without physical strength or innate ideas, incapable in himself of obeying the fundamental laws of his nature which call him to the supreme place in the universe, it is only in the heart of society that man can attain the pre-eminent position which is his natural destiny. Without the aid of civilization he would be one of the feeblest and least intelligent of animals . . . man is only what he is made. Necessarily brought up by his own kind, he has acquired from them his habits and his needs; nor are his ideas any longer his own. He has enjoyed the fairest prerogative of his kind, the capacity of developing his understanding by the power of imitation and the influence of society.

JEAN-MARC-GASPARD ITARD, *The Wild Boy of Aveyron* (1801)[1]

This prologue epitomizes my theme. Not original, perhaps, but a view that most of Itard's contemporaries would have rejected

[1] Since this book was written, Harlen Lane's admirable book on Itard has appeared (Lane 1977). In a striking way he traces Itard's influence on the development of psychopedagogy through the work of Montessori to behaviour modification techniques currently in use.

2 *Psychopedagogy*

and about which many of ours would have reservations; but for different reasons. Itard's contemporaries, with a Rousseauesque perspective, saw 'natural man' as the 'noble savage' undefiled by society and liable to corruption if subject to its influence. Some of our contemporaries see civilized man as a 'naked ape' indulging in life-long monkey tricks little affected by society (Morris 1967).

There is proof enough in many places of the absurdity of both these positions. However, I have chosen to refer to Itard's account of his efforts to make human the boy found running wild in the woods for several reasons. One is that his point is proved by the modest success of his efforts. Another is because it illustrates that most important of all aspects of human learning, the fact that human beings alone among the animals can learn from other generations. The chronicle of Itard's endeavours vividly evokes many of the problems with which teachers in all times and places constantly grapple, and strikingly exemplifies modern methods of attacking them. The chronicle also reveals qualities that all teachers might well emulate. Itard combines compassion with intellectual rigour and dedication to his task with a self-critical questioning of his motives and actions. No mean model.

Victor

Itard first saw the wild boy in Paris where he had been brought after being captured in the forest. He was about eleven years old: 'A disgustingly dirty child affected with spasmodic movements and often convulsions who swayed back and forth ceaselessly like certain animals in the menagerie, who bit and scratched those who opposed him, who showed no sort of affection for those who attended him; and who was, in short, indifferent to everything and attentive to nothing.' Pinel, an eminent physician, examined the boy and declared him an incurable idiot 'incapable of any kind of sociability or instruction'. This pronouncement relieved the institute responsible for the boy of a difficult problem. It is a commonly encountered method of dealing with such problems, particularly in teaching. Pinel avoided the problem of socializing the boy by placing him in the category 'idiot', indicating that nothing could be done to help him. This practice is widespread

Learners, teachers, psychologists 3

in education today. Failures in teaching are all too frequently ascribed to deficits in the learners and all too rarely to shortcomings in teaching (see Chapter 17). Difficult problems are evaded in the same way as Pinel evaded the problem of educating Victor. Even the term 'idiot' has been used until relatively recently as a label in much the same way as Pinel used it. This essentially pessimistic approach may well be in part a consequence of our limited knowledge in the field of pedagogy, but it is almost certainly also a cause of that limited knowledge. Until difficult pedagogical problems are tackled, progress is bound to be limited. In the pages that follow I shall be considering different ways in which such problems have been tackled and the way in which the practices of teaching and the work of researchers and experimental psychologists can complement each other in this work.

Itard never accepted Pinel's diagnosis. He believed that the main cause of the boy's condition was his lack of intercourse with other human beings. Whatever the truth may be about the length of time the boy had spent in the woods, it is not the most important thing; the vital thing is Itard's actions after he had established the nature of the problem he took on when he assumed responsibility for the humanizing of the Wild Boy of Aveyron.

Itard took the boy into his own home, where he became known as Victor, and began a programme of systematic socialization and pedagogy. He set out objectives for himself; for example: 'To extend the range of his ideas by giving him new needs and by increasing his social contacts. To lead him to the use of speech by inducing the exercise of imitation through the imperious law of necessity.' Systematically he set about teaching Victor, aiming to achieve these objectives, and then went on to evaluate the success or failure of his efforts. His method is a paradigm for today. Diagnose the pedagogical problem, prescribe the aims and course of action, and evaluate the end result by comparing it with the aims set in the first place.

He did not achieve all his objectives, although in many ways his success was striking. In two years the wild animal had become 'almost a normal child who could not speak'. He was affectionate, lived in the Itard household like any ordinary person and learned to read a little. The stumbling-block was Itard's failure to teach

4 Psychopedagogy

Victor to speak. The reasons for this failure are unknown, but, whatever they were, the lack of speech was the crucial deficit in Victor's development. The basic types of learning common to all animals, including man, presented little problem. But his lack of this vital instrument – which takes learning beyond the level of that of other animals and engenders abstract thinking by the agency of a flexible system of communication by symbols – virtually cut him off from the most characteristically human types of learning. But not entirely. Victor did learn to communicate through the medium of symbols by learning to read a few words; yet this system of communication lacked the flexibility of the spoken word. Had speech or a more flexible symbolling system been available to Victor, the outcome would probably have been much happier for him. Later in life Itard came to recognize the power of signed language, especially in the teaching and learning of the deaf. He also consistently argued for the strong connection between thinking and the use of a language. Lane (1977) speculates that had Victor been discovered thirty years later, when Itard had developed his views on signing, his story would, indeed, have been very different.

The power of speech in human learning and its primacy as a pedagogical instrument are evidenced by Itard's experience with Victor. It is a topic I shall take up repeatedly in a variety of contexts. It relates in a very interesting way to a very different pedagogical problem that exercised the minds of scientists nearly 200 years after Itard and many thousands of miles away.

Washoe

The immediate pedagogical problem was that of teaching language to an infant. The work started in June 1966, and in April 1967 the infant asked its foster parents to 'gimme sweet'. Nothing startling about that perhaps, apart from the fact that the infant was a chimpanzee (Linden 1976).

Rearing chimps in psychologists' families is almost an American tradition. Viki, protégée of the Hayeses (Hayes and Hayes 1951), was an outstanding example. She learned many skills beyond the normal scope of the species. The Hayeses tried to teach her to

Learners, teachers, psychologists 5

speak but failed. An earlier pioneer in the study of chimpanzee learning, Yerkes, suggested that the reason they did not learn to speak was not deficient intellect but lack of ability with the mechanics of oral speech. He thought that an approach to language using a different method of symbolling might enable chimpanzees to develop speech, and suggested gestures.

Allen and Beatrice Gardner tried it with a chimp called Washoe and experienced success which has considerable implications for the way we think about chimp learning and possibly the nature of man's relations to other species. Washoe learned to speak through a system of gestures. The system was Ameslan, the American sign language used by deaf people. It is not merely a collection of unconnected gestures but a true manual language with the attributes of a spoken language. The gestures symbolize either concrete or abstract things, can be combined to make sentences and can express past and future. Washoe learned to converse with the Gardners, with other humans and eventually with other chimps using Ameslan. (Lane (1977) points out the extraordinary fact that Ameslan was developed from a method of signing introduced into America by a deaf Frenchman from Itard's circle of acquaintances.)

The importance of this work is not merely that Washoe learned Ameslan. Because she learned to communicate in symbols, she laid the foundation for the ability to deal with abstract properties. In other words, it enhanced her ability to think. Should it turn out that whole colonies of chimps learn to communicate by signs in this way and teach each other, it will become possible for them to transmit information through the medium of language across generations, so that cultural evolution in chimpanzees is on the cards.

Learning and teaching

The lessons for students of psychopedagogy in the stories of Victor and Washoe are that a social environment is a prerequisite for becoming human, and that the ability to converse using a systematic symbol system, preferably, but not essentially, spoken, is crucial if complex learning involving abstract thinking is to

6 *Psychopedagogy*

take place. Above all, the achievements of both Victor and Washoe are testimony to the importance of planned systematic teaching in complex learning. In the teaching of normal children the systematic pedagogic approach is not only made possible through the agency of speech but enhanced by it.

Victor in the woods and Washoe in the jungle before capture learned enough to keep alive without systematic teaching, but the behaviour of both became much more complex when they were placed in a more complex environment. Had they learned nothing before being introduced to human society, neither would have survived. This is because the behaviour of both chimps and humans is very largely learned. Much simpler animals such as insects depend much less on learning, have very little capacity for it and therefore have extremely predictable patterns of behaviour. A caterpillar left to fend for itself in the woods is much better off than man child or monkey child, provided it happens to be on the appropriate food plant. All it does is to go through a sequence of automatic movements of eating and it survives. On the other hand, no amount of systematic instruction will ever teach a caterpillar to do much more than that. It has little, if any, choice of environment. Higher animals can learn to cope in varied environments; in particular, man and the other primates are extremely adaptable because individuals can learn their own patterns of behaviour – patterns such as may never have appeared before in the history of the species. A simple environment demands little complicated activity to manage it, whereas a complex environment needs correspondingly complex activities. The most complex environments animals of any species are likely to encounter are man-made, and particularly complex are environments involving interactions among people. The important point is that a human social environment is a crucial element in the development in each of us of the complex kinds of behaviour of which average human beings are capable. Crucial, but not sufficient. Coping with the complexities of living in human society today in most parts of the world is dependent upon more than mere exposure to highly complex environments. It depends upon an adequate pedagogy.

Whether or not we would be justified in using the word 'pedagogy' to include the work being done with Washoe and her asso-

Learners, teachers, psychologists 7

ciates depends on one's attitude towards etymology and current language usage. In practice, with this interesting debatable exception, we confine its use to the teaching of humans. I do not imply, however, that there is nothing in common between a system of teaching children and a system of training animals. Many very important principles of learning apply to both. But there is very much more to human learning, as we shall see, although we can get a good deal of insight into some of its important basic features by considering learning in other species as well as in man.

Whatever the type and complexity of learning, it implies change. Change is what learning is all about, and a widely accepted view would equate learning with a change in the behaviour of an organism that persists over time. Temporary states that come and go would not be classified as learning, but those activities that are acquired in order to cope with certain features of the environment, and which become part of the customary pattern of behaviour, do qualify. Changes in behaviour can take place for pathological reasons. Damage to the organism results in changes in the nature of activity because of the damage. These changes would not in themselves be thought of as learning. True, damage to limbs or other parts of the body may lead to one's learning new skills, for example, learning to write with the left hand. The skill of writing with the left hand would be a learned skill, but the actual change from right- to left-hand writing necessitated by damage to the right hand would not be regarded as learning.

Growth can also lead to changes in behaviour. A baby gradually develops the ability to eat solid food not just by learning but through physiological development, the growth of teeth and the development of the digestive organs. Similarly the growth of muscle and bones makes possible the progression from virtual immobility to the ability to walk and run. It would be a mistake to consider these changes as taking place independently from learning; the two interact in a complex way. Change may not be possible without physical development, known as maturation, but in man and other higher animals it is very much dependent upon learning.

8 *Psychopedagogy*

Without learning change would be very limited. Man would be unable to survive without it. Without teaching, the appropriate conditions for learning to take place rarely obtain in human beings. Teaching ideally involves the systematic arrangement of a learning environment using relevant principles of human learning matched with the learner's existing capabilities so as to produce change as economically and effectively as possible. The fact that much teaching is attempted without conscious understanding of the principles of human learning does not, I think, invalidate this view. Whenever anyone tries to teach, he makes a deliberate effort to structure the environment so as to facilitate learning. Lack of knowledge of the optimum ways of doing this will render his efforts less effective and in some cases futile, but I think it reasonable to hope that, as we acquire knowledge about the factors influencing human learning, teaching will become more predictably effective.

Experimenters and teachers

Scientists studying language learning in apes are primarily experimental psychologists. Itard, too, despite the fact that he did his work with Victor before the emergence of psychology as a field of study, seems to have been fired as much by the spirit of scientific inquiry as by dedication to pedagogy. But all were and are willy-nilly both experimenters and teachers. As experimenters they wished to study learning, but in order to accomplish their tasks they had to intervene and do their best to enhance learning. By that action they were assuming the functions of teachers.

The American psychologist B. F. Skinner (1962) gives one of the most explicit accounts of the way in which the experimenter turns teacher to make his investigations possible. In his early work studying the behaviour of pigeons, he was interested on one occasion in the effect of presenting food to a hungry bird when it had carried out a particular action. He waited for the action to occur but the pigeon was not as cooperative as Skinner had hoped and showed no signs of executing the desired manœuvre. Skinner then decided to intervene in the process, realizing there would probably be very little for him to observe if he didn't. He therefore gave the pigeon a little corn when it made a movement re-

Learners, teachers, psychologists 9

sembling the one he had in mind. The animal repeated the activity and was duly rewarded with corn. It had learned the first part of the activity that Skinner had planned. Then the experimenter gave food only when the actions resembled what he had in mind more closely, and when the pigeon was repeating these actions regularly he shifted to actions still closer to the one desired. By this method of 'successive approximations' Skinner was able to observe the learning by pigeons of a wide variety of activities – from turning in figures of eight to playing ping-pong. But he had been able to do this only by having in mind at the beginning what he hoped the learner (the pigeon) was going to be able to do at the end; breaking down the task to be learned into smaller tasks and then actively intervening in the animal's actions to guide them (by presenting food at the appropriate moments) along the desired lines. Finally the experimenter evaluates the results of his experiment by comparing the effectiveness of different procedures in obtaining the same kind of final outcome.

Teaching as problem solving

Experimental psychologists teach in order to study learning. Teachers study learning in order to be able to teach. Both are trying to solve problems. Both create problems – the problems they then attempt to solve. By 'create' I mean that, until the experimenter or the teacher comes along, the problems do not exist. There are two levels of problems in the experimenter's case: the learning problem the learner has to solve and the experimental problem the experimenter has to solve. In studying the former he acquires insight into both. But no animal in the wild ever had to solve the problems of experimental animals. Man's intervention alone results in animals acquiring such improbable behaviours as turning in a figure of eight or playing ping-pong. The same applies to teaching. Until a teacher decides to attempt to so arrange things that a learner will acquire new patterns of behaviour, there is no problem. Once he has so decided, the problems are similar to those of the experimenter. His learners have the problem of acquiring the new behaviour; he has the problem of ensuring that they are able to do just that. No doubt some of the new behaviours teachers through the ages have

10 *Psychopedagogy*

attempted to develop are almost as improbable as those of pigeons learning to play ping-pong. Current agonizing over curriculum is an attempt to ascertain what problems teachers should be setting themselves and their students. This book does not attempt to address itself to that question, although it recognizes that the problem of what to teach is prior to that of how to teach.

The problems of what and how to teach are both determined by society at large. They will vary according to the history and present status of a society, but it is probably mainly in highly developed human society (not necessarily technologically advanced) that the problems are likely to arise. The life of Victor and Washoe in the forests was relatively simple in comparison with that which they learned to live in civilization. They had, we might say, little to learn until they left the forest. Complex human society demands that people acquire new skills to cope with the more complicated demands it makes on them as compared with the simple life of the savage. And the new skills themselves further make possible even more complex developments in society, a theme to which we shall return later.

In human society problems rarely come singly. Experimenters are only able to help explain the behaviour of organisms by devising large numbers of comparable learning situations so as to obtain insight into their enduring common properties. Teachers need these insights when planning their teaching but also need the experience of many attempts to achieve given pedagogical goals. The study of the most simple kinds of learning rapidly move from the single conditional reflex to chains of reflexes and to complex relationships among the reflexes and chains of reflexes. Much of the learning that humans engage in is even more complex.

Guiding learning

Experimental psychologists and teachers investigating or encouraging learning very frequently guide the learners in their efforts to solve their learning problems. In some circumstances they do not do so; experimenters if they are intent on studying activity ethnologically rather than under experimental control, teachers if they subscribe unreservedly to the doctrine of dis-

Learners, teachers, psychologists 11

covery learning. When guidance is given, it commonly takes the form of what might be described as the careful arrangement of rewards. Skinner, in the experiments referred to above, was using corn as a reward to the pigeons when they did what he had in mind, and in fact food is generally used as a reward in experiments concerned with animal learning, although other things have been used, such as water to thirsty animals and the satisfaction of curiosity.

In experimental work, and increasingly in the study of classroom learning, the term *reinforcement* is used for the presentation of a stimulus after a particular activity, leading to the repetition and learning of that activity. In applying concepts of experimental work to teaching we are able to make use of some of the principles derived from animal learning, although in general the form of reinforcement and mode of use are likely to be very different.

Underpinning most of the practices in the use of reinforcement is work such as that carried out by Skinner. In fact one of the first psychologists to apply a rigorous and systematic experimental approach to the study of learning was I. P. Pavlov (1941; 1955). Although the popular stereotype sees Pavlov merely as a man who studied the salivation of dogs, in fact he did much more. In particular, in his study of human learning he consistently drew attention to the importance of language as the agency that transforms and transcends the simpler processes of learning observed in other animals. He also drew attention repeatedly to the way in which man obtains satisfaction (reinforcement) through exploring and manipulating his environment. The importance of language and successful accomplishment of tasks are now firmly established as key factors in human learning. Thus, whereas reinforcement in animals tends to be associated with the satisfaction of needs for such things as food, human activity can be reinforced by a commendatory word from a teacher or the successful achievement of a learning task.

However, neither Pavlov nor any other experimenter was able to produce precise information about the nature and influence of reinforcers in complex learning by animals and humans until the foundations had been laid in very carefully controlled experiments involving quite simple responses. Thus Pavlov worked for many

12 *Psychopedagogy*

years on the salivary response of dogs in order to establish principles that would apply to learning in many different conditions and by many different types of learners.

Pavlov's first steps in the study of learning were taken almost a hundred years ago. They were inspired by observations he made while investigating the digestive processes of dogs: that the animals salivated not only when food was in their mouths but also when they saw the food. Since the function of saliva is to facilitate digestion, it would seem that food in the mouth is the natural stimulus to salivation, and salivating at the sight of food implies a response by the animal to a stimulus other than the one that should naturally evoke it. Whether the two responses are different and, if they are, how they are different are the questions Pavlov set out to investigate. The basic fact soon to emerge from his work was that the responses are different. Salivating to food in the mouth is a natural response which is stable and unchanging. Salivating to a stimulus such as the sight of food is an acquired response which will die away if food in the mouth does not follow.

Under experimental conditions various stimuli were used. The response of salivating was set up to various sights and sounds, bells, metronomes, geometrical shapes, for example. In time, through innumerable experiments ringing the changes on the nature and mode of presentation of many different stimuli and in many different conditions, Pavlov and his colleagues learned to control quite precisely the nature and strength of the responses.

It is useful to consider the value of the new response. Although salivating to the sound of a bell is an unnatural response, it is of definite advantage so long as the natural stimulus of food in the mouth follows. A dog salivating when it hears the bell already has a copious flow of digestive juices when food reaches its mouth: digestion will thus be enhanced. Salivating before food is in the mouth is therefore advantageous. On the other hand, if food never follows the bell, salivation is of no advantage and will not occur.

Because of the instability of the learned response, Pavlov called it a *conditional response* in order to illustrate its dependence upon other factors. He called the natural response of salivating to food in the mouth an *unconditional response*. The natural stimulus – food in the mouth – was called the *unconditional stimulus*. Stimulus

Learners, teachers, psychologists 13

followed by response is called a reflex. Salivating to the presence of food in the mouth is an *unconditional reflex*, since it occurs irrespective of other factors. Salivating to the sound of a bell is a *conditional reflex*, since it is dependent for its appearance and stability on being followed by the unconditional stimulus.

The unconditional stimulus that follows the new, or conditional, behaviour is the reinforcement referred to earlier. Responding by salivation to bells, lights, and so on, is reinforced by the appearance of the 'natural' stimulus for salivation, food.

Once a conditional response is established, it can form the basis for other new responses, so that chains of conditional reflexes can be built up, one thing leading to another. But of course the stability of the chain, like the stability of the individual reflex, is dependent in the last analysis on the occurrence of the unconditional stimulus. The work of animal trainers makes considerable use of such chains of reflexes.

At roughly the same time as Pavlov, the American, E. L. Thorndike, began a study of learning which resembles Pavlov's in its dedication to an experimental approach but which differs in its methods. Unlike Pavlov, Thorndike took a non-interventionist approach (Thorndike 1921). Thorndike's mode of operation was to set a problem to a hungry animal, often a cat, by placing it in a cage with food outside and an escape mechanism which offered access to the food if manipulated appropriately.

When first placed in the cage, the animal engages in apparently random activity, trying to get at the food. Eventually it operates the release mechanism, escapes and obtains the food. Subsequent trials find the animal's activity gradually becoming less random and focusing on that part of the cage which previously led to escape. The time taken to escape decreases until eventually the animal gets out at once.

As may be seen, Thorndike gave little help to his experimental animals, whereas Pavlov exerted considerable control over his during their learning. There is little doubt, however, that they have much in common. Thorndike said, 'Learning is connecting.' Pavlov talked about *temporary connections*, meaning conditional reflexes. Both were referring to the processes of conditioning. To illustrate. A baby soon learns to start sucking when held in the

14 *Psychopedagogy*

feeding position because he has connected this position with the presence of the nipple in the mouth very shortly afterwards. Similarly, if he is fed whenever he cries, crying and feeding become connected, so that hunger pangs are likely to lead to crying, which will in turn lead to his being fed. Both examples are examples of connections being set up between previously unconnected phenomena. There is a difference between the two, however. The first example is of the type that Pavlov studied and is often referred to as *classical conditioning*. Connections of this type are established when one stimulus signals the arrival of another. Being held in a certain position comes to signal to the baby that the nipple will soon be placed in his mouth. The second example is different in that the learner – in this case the baby – has to do something himself before the conditional stimulus arrives. That is, the baby cries and the stimulus (food) arrives and starts off the unconditional (the 'natural') response of sucking. This is learning of the type studied by Thorndike. Captive animals in his experiments had to do something to escape and reach the food. This type of learning is called *instrumental conditioning*.

In general, connections of any type can be set up only when they occur in close temporal and spatial proximity. This applies not only to conditioning but to higher forms of learning such as problem solving and concept formation (which we shall consider later).

On the basis of his experiments Thorndike suggested certain laws which he considered governed learning. The most important one, still thought to be of great importance, is what he called the *law of effect*. In brief this states that the way connections are made and unmade is governed by their effects. If crying produces food, then it will recur when food is needed. Behaviour that does not produce this effect will not be learned. In this way organisms make only those connections that are likely to be beneficial to them. This is the mechanism by which animals select out of the myriads of stimuli from their environments those to which they need to respond by forming new connections.

Of the experiments I have mentioned in developing my theme, few, if any, totally dispense with guidance. Even in the simplest experiments with rote learning in humans – for example, in

Learners, teachers, psychologists 15

paired associate learning such as learning pairs of linked words or nonsense syllables – guidance is provided every time the subject is told he is right or wrong. When this minimum guidance is withheld, learning is very much more difficult. In conditioning experiments it is reasonable to look upon the reinforcement presented in the process of successive approximation as guidance of much greater intensity. The learner is being helped by cues to achieve the learning task much more quickly than he would otherwise do, if he learned at all.

A well-known learning problem involving the learning of fairly complex material with minimum guidance is the work of Bruner on concept attainment (Bruner *et al.* 1956). I do not wish to go into the complexities of concept learning here but merely to refer to the way the experiment was conducted. The subjects were given an array of eighty-one cards with different patterns on them, and they had to find out which combinations of elements formed the patterns the experimenter had in mind. The subjects could choose cards in any order and ask the experimenter whether or not they exemplified the pattern he had decided on. This was a condition of minimum guidance. The experimenter was not mainly interested in the facility with which the subjects solved the problem so much as the way in which they tackled it. It is a simple matter, however, for the experimenter to arrange the order of the cards so as to maximize the amount of information given to the subject, thereby helping him to identify the pattern in question. A teacher interested in enhancing the facility with which the learners acquired the concept would be able to use his knowledge of the way concepts are acquired to speed up their learning considerably. The psychology of concept attainment, together with its practical embodiment in the guiding of learning in this way, is an epitome of the psychopedagogical approach.

Learners

In the discussion so far, I have been talking about the types of learning that are common to most animals. I have also referred at times to learning particularly characteristic of higher mammals and apes. Whatever the nature of the learner, the fundamentals

16 *Psychopedagogy*

of learning are the same. All learning is manifested by a change in the behaviour of the organism in order to cope with new regularities in the environment. The change in behaviour is caused by the changes in the environment and will persist so long as the environment maintains the new state.

But not all species are capable of the same degree of adjustment to change. As I suggested earlier, very simple organisms change little in their behaviour. So it is no good trying to set up identical types of learned activity without taking these species differences into account. In this sense the nature of the learner is an important factor to consider in learning experiments and in teaching. But while we would feel somewhat diffident about attempting to teach an earthworm to ride a bicycle because of obvious species differences that would lead us to prefer teaching the skill to a human being, any differences *within* species should be given a very different kind of scrutiny. Since differences between individuals of the same species cannot by their nature be of the same order as differences *between* species, the main differences between healthy individuals of the same species will almost certainly be the result of the individuals' previous history of learning. Thus, although we should feel reluctant to try to teach a worm to ride a cycle, we should feel no such reluctance in attempting to teach any normal human being. However, we should expect to find differences among the learners, probably connected with their experience of other types of machine which cause comparable types of balancing to develop. We should thus attempt to plan our intervention in the learning of two people to take account of their different experiences before we 'upset their equilibrium' and set them the problem of learning to ride a cycle.

I think there is a great pitfall connected with taking into account differences between individuals of our own species – a pitfall into which very many psychologists and educationists have fallen. They have spent virtually all their time trying to define precisely how the individuals differ and have accounted for differences in learning by referring to the individual differences they have discovered. All too rarely have they looked critically at the way in which the learners have been taught, to see to what extent that could account for differences in learning. In this book the argu-

Learners, teachers, psychologists 17

ment will be that, although we must not lose sight of differences in individual learners from the same species, and although in our own species there is greater scope for variety than in any other, nevertheless we *are* the same species and therefore more alike than we are different. In our search for ways of enhancing human learning we need to scrutinize teaching far more carefully than has been the case hitherto (Glaser 1972).

Teachers

Teaching, not teachers, is what we need to scrutinize. Not that teachers are not interesting; but there is little pedagogical mileage in analysing in fine detail the various characteristics of allegedly different types of teachers. There is a current vogue for this type of activity, manifesting itself in the delineation of various teacher 'types'; among the most fashionable categories are 'progressive' and 'traditional'. Like learners, teachers are more alike than they are different: a fortunate phenomenon. Were it not so, it would be impossible to delineate any general principles of teaching, and there could be no such thing as pedagogy. Each teacher would have his own method of proceeding. As it is, although teachers are undoubtedly different, there is an important basic core of sameness which does enable us, on the one hand, to make some generalizations about the nature of teaching and, on the other (and more important), makes possible the implementing of general principles of teaching by individual teachers who may be of different temperaments and casts of mind (Dunkin and Biddle 1974).

I said earlier that teaching, like experimenting in the field of learning, is a problem-solving activity. Both activities should be directed to descrying new regularities in the form of theoretical principles that will help teacher and experimenter to solve problems themselves. In the process of teaching or experimenting both teacher and experimenter are themselves learners. A theory of teaching is likely to be the future fruit of the joint learning of teachers and professional researchers.

And so our discussion in this book will not focus on the differences between learners or between teachers, although these

18 *Psychopedagogy*

will not be thought irrelevant to teaching. Instead I shall attempt to bring into focus the important general aspects of learning and teaching which different teachers will find useful in teaching learners who differ. I do not suggest that there is a complete body of useful theory ready to hand for any teacher wishing to apply it. Much of what I shall say is tentative and needs the kind of experimentation I have been describing. But this is perhaps an inevitable consequence of the way in which pedagogy has been all too often viewed in the past, whereby a teacher might tend to transfer his teaching attempts to another more promising pupil when difficulty in teaching occurred, rather than trying to improve his teaching of the first learner. Neither Victor nor Washoe would have fared very well with that approach; unfortunately all too many other students have had less perceptive teachers.

2
Learning: foundations

Reinforcement

It may well be that one of the most compelling explanations of the tendency to avoid really difficult pedagogical problems – such as those posed in the teaching of Victor – is the fact that the attempts to deal with them rarely provide much in the way of reinforcement. The same explanation probably applies to the conventional psychological folklore which suggests that experimental psychologists have eschewed classroom experimentation because of its enormous complexity. Reinforcement is a powerful determinant of behaviour in psychologists as well as in other humans and animals. Where an activity offers little chance of success, or where there is a course of action that offers easier rewards, the chances are high that the activity will die away, if ever it starts. So teachers will prefer to concentrate on those pupils who are easier to teach, and many experimenters study learning in rats and other simpler animals in preference to the more problematic organism, man.

This suggestion may be somewhat simplistic since many teachers do teach children who present enormous difficulties, and

20 *Psychopedagogy*

experimenters do study human learning. The apparent contradiction here is an indication of the complexity of the determinants of human behaviour. I have already implicitly alluded to one important complicating factor, the fact that success in activity is itself a reinforcer. This is a particularly human phenomenon, demanding a much more subtle analysis of the parameters of human learning than is applicable to learning in other animals. The fact that humans do, in fact, frequently and deliberately choose difficult tasks when easier alternatives are available is probably connected with the functioning of success as a reinforcer. To some people, the more difficult a task the more rewarding is success. In such cases the considerations that lead to a decision involve the weighing up of alternatives in a complex calculation, perhaps not always consciously realized. In itself the processing of information in this way prior to taking a course of action complicates human activity enormously. But, more than that, it implies that the determinants of human behaviour and the role of reinforcement in human learning operate in different ways from those involved in the learning of other animals. The reason for this difference has been discussed briefly before. It is the fact that, in addition to responding to signals from the physical environment, man also responds to signals from a symbolic environment created by language. This symbolic environment comprises the infinite variety of abstractions from past, present and future, evoked by speech with others. Thought itself is much related to this flow of abstractions, and without social intercourse through speech and the abstractions it generates it would be impossible to conceive of a choice of courses of action. It would be impossible to plan; to prefer to do one thing rather than another. We do not necessarily have to propose a completely different system of operation of reinforcers because of this. The basic mode of operation may well be the same, but the universe of stimuli that can affect our activity is expanded enormously to embrace a world of abstractions as well as a physical world. This is the crucial fact to bear in mind when considering the way in which reinforcement influences how we learn and how we act.

The world of abstractions is, like language itself, a social creation. Thus the abstractions that influence behaviour represent

Learning: foundations 21

social forces. Human actions are reinforced not only by the primary reinforcers such as food but also by such things as the esteem of others, the values and attitudes held to be desirable by society. Reinforcers of this type are likely to be operating in such cases as the one referred to above, where teachers and experimenters choose more difficult tasks rather than those easier to accomplish. To those who make such choices the net effect of reinforcers other than the successful achievement of the task is greater than the success itself. Just how people come to differ in the choices they make is not at all clear. But it is highly likely that the overall determining factor is the previous history of the individual, his learning and those activities that have been previously connected with other reinforcers. Social pressures operating from childhood bring about the acquisition of abstract concepts such as esteem, honesty, politeness, loyalty and approval. Seeing the behaviour of others towards oneself as being influenced by such abstractions leads to one's own behaviour towards others being influenced by them too. By the same token we react to our own behaviour in the same way (Brown and Herrnstein 1975). A person who approves of honesty in others is likely to feel a sense of self-approbation when he makes an honest choice in a moment of temptation. The self-approbation is the reward.

Thus the actual reinforcers that influence behaviour or bring about new learning are a complex amalgam of concrete stimulation from the environment, any symbolic stimulation from other people, and the flow of inner abstractions. The use of reinforcement by a teacher in order to influence learning is therefore clearly a complex matter, but at the same time it has a flexibility that makes possible much more complex learning and teaching than would otherwise be the case.

With this important preamble to remind us that the factors involved in reinforcement in humans are much more complex than in other animals, let us consider some of the ways in which it can influence learning.

22 *Psychopedagogy*

Schedules of reinforcement

Throwing corn to a pigeon every time it does what you want it to do is the quickest way to get it to learn. It is also the best way of guaranteeing that it will continue to carry out the particular activity. However, if you wish to conserve corn and spare the effort, much the same effect can be obtained by throwing corn intermittently (Skinner 1962). A slightly different effect can be obtained by reinforcing (throwing corn) every so often – say, every five minutes – or by reinforcing after the occurrence of a certain number of the activities you are trying to get established.

The different methods of presenting reinforcement are referred to as schedules of reinforcement. Reinforcing every response or every tenth response is an example of a fixed-ratio schedule. Reinforcing every ten minutes is an example of fixed-interval reinforcement. Schedules that differ in intervals or according to ratio also have their typical effects on learning and the sustaining of particular activities. The various schedules have different effects on behaviour. For students of learning and teaching the most important are the fixed ratio of reinforcing every time an activity occurs and the variable ratio where reinforcement is given irregularly. In the former the teacher provides reinforcement every time the learner carries out the behavioural activity that he, the teacher, has planned as part of the learning; this schedule produces the speediest learning. In the latter the teacher provides reinforcement according to no regular pattern: the learner receives reinforcement for 'correct' activity unpredictably, but not for 'incorrect' activity. This schedule is most effective for maintaining in force the behaviour to which it is related.

Although the original investigations of schedules of reinforcement were carried out with non-human learners, there is ample evidence that the same basic processes are applicable to human learning (O'Leary and O'Leary 1977). There is also evidence from the study of animal learning that the way schedules determine the development of learning can account for human activities which on the face of it look too complex for non-humans.

Skinner argues that the contingencies of reinforcement control behaviour in our daily lives and not just in the psychological

Learning: foundations 23

laboratory. He gives many examples in his writings of the nature of this control, and his novel, *Walden Two* (Skinner 1947), depicts a utopia based on the recognition of these contingencies. To illustrate the effect of a fixed-ratio schedule in human affairs, he refers to such things as the high rate of responding characteristic of this form of schedule in the effects of piece-work in industry. A variable schedule is exemplified in the extreme persistence of gamblers in a high level of activity controlled by a low level of reinforcement (winning) on a variable-ratio schedule.

In psychopedagogy, however, we are less interested in keeping up very specific activities such as operating fruit machines or putting checks on bingo cards than with building up new capabilities. Nevertheless it is necessary to be alive to the way in which partial reinforcement works, since we normally expect new capabilities to be applied for some purpose, and unless there is some indication to the learner that these new skills are getting some return when they are exercised they will gradually be dropped. It is therefore incumbent upon teachers to ensure that once a new skill has been learned the learner receives some evidence that it is useful; in other words, teachers should arrange things so that some reinforcement takes place after learning. Reinforcement in school learning is frequently the successful accomplishment of some task. Another potent reinforcer is the approval of the teacher. Consolidating new learning can therefore be enhanced if the teacher arranges for tasks relating to the new learning to be within the scope of the learner to ensure both success and *evidence of success*, or by making sure that learners are encouraged by him when they make use of the new learning. Ideally, of course, the two methods of reinforcement should coincide.

Given the complexity of most human teaching situations, and especially those found in schools with one teacher and many learners, it is difficult to arrange such happy coincidences. It is also extremely difficult to arrange for reinforcement to follow every correct step on the road to new learning. Partial reinforcement makes possible an approach to the solution of these problems. Careful structuring of tasks following new learning so that the learner receives occasional indication of success will help to

24 *Psychopedagogy*

maintain new learning in strength and is more practicable than trying to arrange for reinforcement every time. In the case of new learning as it is taking place, the same principles apply, but there is another important consideration: when a learner is actually engaged in learning it may well be that he makes wrong moves that delay completion of the task; he might still complete the task successfully, but the success could well serve to reinforce the wrong moves as well as the correct ones, causing the learner to persist in error if he does not realize that part of his activity is, in fact, erroneous. A related problem is that of achieving the right answer through the wrong process, for example, guessing in mathematics. The fact that guessing might occasionally produce the right answer acts as a variable-schedule reinforcer (Lunzer 1968). These are difficult problems which permit of no easy answers. Careful analysis of the nature of the learning intended helps to identify such problems, and the careful checking on the actual working out of teaching methods with an experimental approach will help.

Apart from learning what the teacher is trying to teach, pupils learn many other things through their contacts with teachers, other pupils and from their experiences in school generally. McLeish (1976) reports work shedding interesting light on the way in which reinforcement works in group learning. After considerable work investigating the learning of undergraduates in small learning groups, he came to the conclusion that the students were learning precious little of the content of the teaching but a great deal about means of communicating with each other. He also found that this learning was under the control of reinforcement according to the basic principles enunciated by Pavlov and Skinner, although the stimulus and response characteristics of *human beings* learning in a *social* environment are more complex and dynamic.

By the same token, reinforcement, and partial reinforcement in particular, is likely to be potent in the development of attitudes and social behaviour, especially those aspects of behaviour we may refer to as class conduct. Such things as volunteering answers to teachers' questions, participating in class discussion and observing rules of conduct in class are examples of positive be-

Learning: foundations 25

behaviour that might well be kept in force by ensuring it is reinforced from time to time. On the other hand, undesirable classroom behaviour might well be kept in strength by the occasional unthinking reinforcement by the teacher of disruptive activities because it is typical of our reaction to such activities to give them some attention on some occasions.

Punishment

Undesirable classroom behaviour will at some time or other in the professional lives of most teachers result in their attempting to stop it by punishing the troublesome pupils. This is natural enough, given that most teachers will themselves have experienced such treatment as pupils. There is, in addition, the reminder from folk wisdom and current propagandists for law and order that to spare the rod is to spoil the child. There is very good reason to believe, however, that punishment is rarely the best remedy for problems of this nature.

Hard evidence about the effects of punishment on human behaviour is not easy to come by because of the unacceptability of subjecting human beings to painful stimuli, physical or mental, in experiments. Much of our evidence is obtained from work with volunteers in clinical conditions, for example, in attempting to break the habit of smoking (e.g. Hunt and Matarazzo 1973). This work suggests that punishment is far from predictably effective in reducing undesired behaviour and that there are problems attached to its use that are not always realized (Solomon 1964).

If the clinical use of punishment is frequently problematic, how much more uncertain will be its application in the complexities of group life in classrooms? Among the problems involved are that the sufferer of punishment frequently becomes habituated to it, so that the intensity has to be increased. As the misbehavers become inured to punishment, it is increased – only to be followed by the habituation of the pupils to the new level and thus creating a vicious spiral where high levels of punishment coexist with severe problems of disruptive behaviour. Another problem connected with the use of punishment in teaching is that the punishment the teacher inflicts on an individual pupil

26 *Psychopedagogy*

may in fact be acting as a reinforcer. This apparent paradox is explained by the fact that pupils sometimes indulge in behaviour that leads to punishment so as to obtain the attention of the teacher or, frequently, the attention of their peers. The latter result, I suggest, is likely to obtain only in an atmosphere of conflict between pupils and teacher which might itself be generated by the excessive use of punishment.

An atmosphere of conflict is an atmosphere deleterious to learning. Mild anxiety in relation to a learning task may be helpful to learning, but anxiety and negative emotional states implied in an atmosphere of conflict are likely to inhibit learning; the teacher, and possibly the school and the subjects he teaches, may be seen negatively by the pupils as a result of the excessive use of punishment.

One of the associated problems that is not always appreciated is recognizing forms of punishment. Administering electrical shocks in laboratory experiments involves the use of an easily recognized and even quantifiable punisher. Beating pupils is also a relatively easy punishment to identify. But people often punish others without realizing it through ill-considered remarks, facial expressions and other non-verbal signals. Human teachers are subject to human frailties, and no one would expect them to be paragons able to identify all punishers when dealing with pupils. However, it seems reasonable to expect them to study the question to a greater depth than the man in the street, so as to avoid the unintentional use of punishment that could act against the pupils' learning or their receptiveness to the teachers' efforts.

So far I have considered the problems of punishment in relation to those aspects of teaching which are sometimes known as management activities. The question now arises as to what extent it can be useful in teaching content or skills. In essence the problem is the same as teaching acceptable classroom behaviour and the answer is the same. Punishment is intended to extinguish behaviour and, whatever its effectiveness in doing this, it cannot be used to build up responses. Pedagogues of yesteryear applying themselves assiduously to seats of learning were not really beating Latin into their pupils as they thought. They may have been suppressing certain activities connected with the learning, but this

Learning: foundations 27

was essentially a negative action. They might have done better to punish incorrect responses and reward correct ones, a procedure that does seem to have some effect (Rosenshine and Furst 1971).

There are thus many problems connected with the use of punishment in teaching. This is not to say that it is not effective, but that its effects are not clearly understood at present and are certainly more complex than is generally appreciated. In view of these problems and the undesirable side effects discussed earlier, it is better to avoid punishment if at all possible. Other actions by the teacher can help. For example, if the teacher arranges for alternative activities that are incompatible with the undesired ones, the reinforcement of the incompatible activities will encourage their repetition and the elimination of the undesired behaviour. In certain circumstances this may not be possible, and if these circumstances involve danger to the individual himself or to others there may be no alternative but to employ punishment. However, such occasions should be very rare in a teaching situation where the teacher has planned his work with an understanding of the effects of reinforcers, the problems of punishment and the possibilities of other modes of operation.

Extinction

A more satisfactory and more effective method than punishment for ensuring the decrease of undesired behaviour – in connection either with the learning of content or with conduct in class – is available. Earlier, I discussed the way in which reinforcement builds up patterns of behaviour and leads to new learning. By the same token *lack of reinforcement* has the opposite effect: no reinforcement, no new learning, and the gradual disappearance of existing learning that is not reinforced. This process is known as extinction.

Extinction in the classroom is likely to be contingent upon the non-appearance of the teacher's approbation or the lack of signals of success after the behaviour in question. The first procedure involves the teacher's ignoring any activity that he wishes to cease; if the teacher's attention and commendation are seen as reinforcers, then the activity in question will gradually die away.

28 *Psychopedagogy*

The second method attempts to ensure that wrong responses in new learning are not reinforced by indications of success. Both techniques are easy to describe but difficult to implement. Merely ignoring activity will not inevitably result in its going away. And, as I suggested above, wrong responses are sometimes reinforced by the ultimate success of the chain of activity of which they are part, even if there is no reinforcement linked immediately to the wrong responses. In fact the effective operation of techniques of extinction involves more than the simple act of ignoring.

Ignoring, although on the face of it a somewhat negative technique, is a very positive thing. It is necessary to consider what is likely to reinforce undesirable behaviour and try to avoid such reinforcers at the same time as encouraging other activities. It may be that this can be done by reinforcing existing alternative behaviour, or possibly it might be necessary to plan for such behaviour. One problem here is that the teacher might well feel reluctant to reinforce behaviour that is not particularly positive in a pupil who has caused difficulty in the first place. If the problem is to be resolved this reluctance has to be overcome.

In a later chapter I take up the question of the complex relationship of reinforcement, punishment and extinction in connection with practical teaching problems; at this stage, however, I should like to make one important general point. If the problems encountered by a teacher are predominantly related to ineffective learning or misbehaviour in such a way that the teacher feels the need to take action to inhibit behaviour rather than to develop it, this is a clear signal that the whole teaching and learning situation needs careful appraisal in order to identify the reasons for this state of affairs. Some of the principles of psychopedagogy will help to identify the causes and suggest possible solutions to the problems.

Discrimination

In the behavioural calculus that determines the nature of our actions, the complex interplay of different reinforcers and punishers experienced in the past guides our responses to stimuli so that we take the course of action we perceive as best for us at that

Learning: foundations 29

particular time. But our ability to make the appropriate response to a stimulus depends on our being able to identify that stimulus. We have to discriminate between the stimulus in question and all other stimuli. Most discriminations probably present no problems: it may not be difficult to discriminate between a cabbage and a king or between the scent of a rose and the sound of thunder. But it could well prove difficult to discriminate between stimuli that resemble each other.

A vast amount of research has investigated the way in which animals and humans discriminate among stimuli. As I suggested in the previous chapter, this kind of work inevitably involves the experimenters in teaching. Discriminations have been taught to a variety of learners, human and non-human, and among a wide range of stimuli – including lights of different colour, sounds of different intensity, tone and note, and shapes differing in various ways.

Many of these stimuli are of the same nature as some that are involved in school learning. Sound stimuli clearly relate to the learning not only of music but also of spoken sounds. Shapes too have fairly obvious implications for art and craft learning, as well as for such learning as that involved in discriminating between letters in early reading or even between the different shapes signifying different notes on a musical stave.

The limiting factor in the learning of any discrimination is a physiological one. The construction of the sensory organs is such that there is a level of fineness of distinction between stimuli that cannot be detected. Common observation can illustrate this by the way in which people differ in their ability to distinguish between colours or shades or between sounds of different frequencies. Similarly, differences are easily observed in the other senses. At the commonsense level, of course, if we were unable to distinguish between one stimulus and another, life would be impossible. But in teaching, and often in experimenting, we are interested to discover what we can do to enhance discrimination in a productive way.

Teaching pupils to discriminate among stimuli does not involve any change in the physiological limits of the sensory organs, but rather necessitates training the learners to make more precise

30 *Psychopedagogy*

use of their capabilities. In experiences out of school, we learn discriminations by the pay-off from the responses we make to stimuli. For example, we select the correct key out of a bunch because it has fitted the front door on previous occasions. We learn to go to the door when we hear one bell and to the telephone when we hear another bell because these actions in the past have been followed by confirmation that they have signalled, in the first place, someone at the door and, in the second, someone on the phone. The key in the door, the person at the door and the voice on the phone are all reinforcers of the actions we have taken, confirming that our discriminations are correct. Had we made a mistake, our false discrimination would have been punished by our not finding anyone at the door or on the phone or that the key did not fit the lock.

Learning to select the correct key from a bunch is a good example of learning by discovery – that is, unless someone has provided prior means of identification. From a bunch of very similar keys we begin to pay attention to differences we had not noticed at the beginning because they help us to make a correct discrimination. Every time we come to use the key our perceptions are sharpened up, so that eventually we have no difficulty in getting the correct key every time. We have learned to discriminate among the keys through a typical process of stimulus discrimination.

Learning to discriminate like this in activities such as selecting the correct key is perhaps unexceptional. Much learning is of this type. The uninitiated spectator at a ball game will see an undifferentiated flow of activity, whereas the afficionado will see subtleties and refinements that evoke transports of delight. (It may well be that part of the delight is a result of being able to make the fine discrimination.) Similarly the tyro at the orchestral concert will have little hope of making the same discriminations as the devotee. The progress from ignorance to enlightenment in both these fields is heavily dependent upon the learning of fine discriminations, and in both fields the learning of these discriminations is often random and, because of the level of complexity, of an indeterminate level of accuracy.

Psychopedagogy tries to reduce the randomness of learning,

Learning: foundations 31

thereby speeding it up and reducing error. In the case of discrimination, randomness can be reduced by deliberately arranging for the response to the 'correct' stimulus to be reinforced while leaving any responses to 'incorrect' stimuli unreinforced. Coupled with this approach the ideas from the techniques of successive approximations can be of great help. In the case of teaching pupils the discriminations among sounds or shapes of letters when they are beginning to read, it would be necessary to start with discriminations that were easy and gradually increase the difficulty, while all the time reinforcing the correct responses. For example, in teaching to discriminate between the sounds associated with the various letters, it would be sensible to start with those letters whose sounds are very different. Teaching the discrimination between the sound made by the 'n' in 'can' and the sound made by the 'c' in 'cat' would be easier than teaching the difference between the sound of the terminal letters in 'cap' and 'cat'. Teaching the latter discrimination is facilitated by keeping the rest of the word the same so that attention is focused on the last letter. Much the same can be said about teaching visual discrimination among words. Start with the words or letters that look very different and gradually progress to discriminations among words and letters that resemble each other more closely, throughout the process reinforce correct discriminations and ignore the incorrect.

A word of caution may be necessary here. The use of systematic techniques to aid discrimination helps learners to discriminate among stimuli that they had been unable to differentiate before. In the main this is useful and positive. However, under certain conditions this may not be so. Difficulty may be experienced when the learner is being asked to make discriminations that are at the physiological limits of his sensory organs. Pavlov found that dogs manifested symptoms of neurotic behaviour when discriminatory tasks became too difficult. Specifically when they were trained to react in one way to an ellipse and another way to a circle they coped adequately until the ellipses they had to respond to were gradually changed to approximate to circles. Eventually the task became too difficult, the animals showed signs of distress, and their behaviour became disorganized. Human beings have similar

32 *Psychopedagogy*

problems when discriminations are too difficult. At a different level of complexity from this simple stimulus discrimination, similar problems may be observed when decisions have to be made involving a choice from among different courses of action. But in school it is as well to remember that there is a stage when the physiological limits of perception make discriminations impossible and the attempt to discriminate between stimuli at the limits may be distressful. What the limits are is very difficult to say, since they are likely to differ among pupils. The important point is to remember that there may be a problem of this nature when trying to get pupils to make fine discriminations among basic stimuli.

Generalization

If we were unable to discriminate among stimuli the world would be just one great undifferentiated stimulus. If, on the other hand, we discriminated among all stimuli that were not exactly the same we should be overwhelmed by the complexity of the stimulation and destroyed by the effort of reacting to the infinite number of separate stimuli. Fortunately evolution took care of the problem and balanced the development of our ability to discriminate with a compensatory predilection to generalize.

Generalization involves making the same response to similar but not identical stimuli. If this did not happen, learning would be quite impossible since no two stimuli are exactly the same. For example, unless generalization took place, a person who had tasted an apple and found it good would never know what the next one in the barrel would taste like. Every apple tasting would be an experiment, possibly even a dangerous one, since there would be no means of knowing whether the next one might not be poisonous. However, learning does take place because after the first few apples the apple eater's behaviour changes, so that in future, instead of a tentative taste of a novel object, he is able to sink his teeth into a familiar fruit with justified anticipation. Generalization gives him confidence that the flavour will be to his liking.

It should be noted, however, that discrimination is also at work.

Learning: foundations 33

If it were not, the aspirant apple taster might take a bite out of a potato or even a polar bear since these stimuli would be all one to him.

But in apple eating as in all things generalization and discrimination work together to reach a state of equilibrium. At one level a person will learn to discriminate between apples and other kinds of stimuli but react to all apples in much the same way. At another level a person may make the initial discrimination between apples and not apples but will then make finer discriminations. Such a person will react in different ways to a James Grieve apple and to a Laxton Superb. The discerning apple eater will choose a James Grieve from a barrel of mixed fruit in much the same way as a gourmet will go for a vintage wine rather than supermarket plonk.

As with apples and wine, so with stimuli in teaching. In the early learning of most things in school, discrimination is fairly gross to begin with. Before a pupil can learn to discriminate between one word and another he has to learn to discriminate between words and things that are not words. Or, in other fields, between numbers and not numbers, metals and not metals, wind instruments and not wind instruments. The ability to discriminate in this way makes possible the generalizing of the learner's response to all stimuli of the same type but not of others. A learner will react to a word by attempting to read it, but he is unlikely to attempt to read a wind instrument or a piece of metal. Discrimination sets the bounds of generalization.

Teaching recognizes the way discrimination and generalization work and aims to achieve the balance most suitable for a specific type of activity. In the early stages of reading it will be satisfactory if a learner can discriminate between words and other squiggles on paper that are not words and from experience in discriminating among a limited number of examples eventually make a generalized response to all new presentations of words so that he can pick out words from not words at any time. Later the learner will refine his powers of discrimination so that he can distinguish between different words and make different responses to them. At the same time he will be learning to generalize his responses to certain letter combinations by making the same sound when he

34 *Psychopedagogy*

reads the words with the combinations in them. Discrimination here would involve recognizing the difference between words in general, but making the same response. Thus giving the same pronunciation to elements of words that are the same – as, for example, in n*ight*, l*ight*, fr*ight* – is the process of generalization.

The same processes that applied in the case of discrimination learning apply to generalization. When reinforcement follows a 'correct' response the response is likely to be repeated when the same stimulus situation recurs. With apples and wine, generalization will be reinforced by the satisfying taste that follows. Discrimination will be reinforced by the extra satisfaction that follows the choice of particular fruit or wine. In school learning this type of reinforcement rarely occurs, its place being taken by the approval of the teacher or the pleasure of succeeding in the learning task.

Discrimination and generalization are important, as I have suggested, for relatively simple types of learning. But learning to react selectively to different physical stimuli is an important prerequisite for one of the most important types of school learning: the learning of concepts. Concepts are abstractions that we form about the world, but before we can form them we need to be able to identify the regularities in the physical world in a reliable way; this is where discrimination and generalization come in. Just how they operate in concept learning is something we shall consider later.

Feedback

The satisfaction that follows from taking a bite of a favourite apple is reinforcing, and reinforcement is crucial for learning. But in school learning the glow of satisfaction that follows teacher's approval may not be enough. What the learner needs is more precise information about the nature and results of his actions. The nature of this information will be such as to enable the learner to adjust his next response if necessary to approximate more closely to the desired behaviour.

Information about the effects of one's own activities is commonly referred to as *feedback*. An example of feedback with which most

Learning: foundations 35

people are familiar is adjusting one's aim on the strength of the information received from observing whether one has hit above, below, to the left or to the right of a target. A well-known variant of this example is the experiment in which a person is asked to draw a line, say, three inches long, freehand and without looking at the paper. Without feedback the lines may or may not approach three inches in length and are apt to vary quite randomly. The drawer will have no idea whether or not he is approaching the aim of drawing a three-inch line. If, however, he is told after each attempt whether his line is above or below three inches this will soon approximate to the correct length.

As may be seen, there is a difference between feedback and reinforcement although they are sometimes confused and often related. Reinforcement is the term relating to events that increase the probability that an activity will be repeated without necessarily being connected to the task. The gyrating pigeons in experiments on instrumental conditioning are behaving like that because corn follows, but their behaviour is essentially what Skinner called superstitious behaviour – that is, behaviour not intrinsically connected to the production of corn. The appearance of corn is entirely at the whim of the experimenter.

Undoubtedly some school learning is of this nature. Children blindly doing this or that because teacher approves, and not because they apprehend a causal or logical connection between their action and the appearance of reinforcement, are learning superstitiously. Sometimes this kind of learning takes place when the teacher is under the impression that the pupils have really seen connections between their actions and their results. This kind of mistake is likely to take place when the teacher's analysis of the nature of the learning task is faulty. However, he can help himself avoid this error by building into his teaching some form of information-producing device that will give *him* feedback about the results of his own actions; thus he will have clear evidence when the pupils have seen the vital connections.

Feedback, of course, can take the form of punishment. Information that one has failed in an attempted task may well be the opposite of reinforcing, but it is still feedback, even if of a limited nature. Skilful teaching will try to provide maximum feedback

36 *Psychopedagogy*

with maximum reinforcement. In other words, the teacher will give as much information as possible to the learners about the results of their actions so that they will be able to modify their subsequent behaviour if necessary, but at the same time he will do his best to ensure that the actions they engage in will meet with the success that will reinforce those actions. In specific terms – for example, in relation to the writing of English – the task ought to be so devised that the learner has a good chance of being successful in producing a piece of writing of the type demanded and so be reinforced. At the same time the learner should also get feedback informing him as to what specific aspects of his writing were particularly good or what its weaknesses were. An overall comment of *satisfactory* may be reinforcing and does give some information, but the pupil would be helped much more by comments related to the use of vocabulary, the construction of the sentences, the imaginative use of metaphor, and so on.

Sometimes it might be advisable for a teacher to restrict or filter feedback to a learner. Should it happen that a pupil has almost completely failed to cope with a learning task, it might be quite disastrous for the teacher to give him chapter and verse about his failure. And yet it is necessary for the pupil to be provided with information about his efforts. There can be no prescription to solve this dilemma; probably the most useful approach is to reinforce by encouraging the effort, while pointing out the key deficiencies and suggesting ways of overcoming them. It should be said, however, that if it should happen that pupils are in this position frequently, it is a pretty strong indication that there is something wrong with the teaching. Feedback and punishment for the teacher!

Learning sets

In discussing processes of learning I have from time to time made reference to the learner adapting to regularities in his environment. Behaviour that is reinforced is likely to recur because it has regularly been followed by certain events in the environment that are useful to the learner. Should the regularity disappear, new behaviour will be developed as a means of adapting to new regu-

Learning: foundations 37

larities. The regularities I have so far discussed have been fairly basic: corn regularly follows a particular movement, teacher approves when the correct sound is paired with a printed word, a driver brakes when the lights turn red, and so on. But transcending such linkages of stimulus and response are much more complex regularities that take us to the boundaries between learning common to most mammals and those almost exclusively the preserve of man.

The key to the difference is interestingly put in *The Little Red School Book*: 'If you're always taught to do things the same way, you learn only one way of doing things and it becomes harder to cope with all the new things you'll have to face later on' (Hansen and Jensen 1971). That is, the learning that teachers should emphasize is learning which will carry over to novel situations. This is not the same type of carry-over as we might find in stimulus generalization, because it goes beyond stimulus similarity and raises questions about the learning of abstractions. It involves learning to do things in different ways.

Harlow (1949) carried out the investigations that produced some of the first insights into the way in which learning can take account of phenomena more complex than in the simple pairing of stimulus and response. In the experiments he carried out, mainly with monkeys in the first instance and then with children, the learners had to tackle a number of different but related problems and by this means learned to make the correct response to problems of the same general type. He called the ability to solve such problems a *learning set*.

An example of the kind of problem presented to the learners was selecting the odd object out of three. While the shape and colour might differ, the 'correct' object was always the odd one. The odd one was 'correct' because Harlow had so decreed and had secreted a raisin beneath it. Learning to choose the odd one every time took very many trials, as many as two or three hundred, but once it had been learned the learners would respond with more or less perfect accuracy every time they were faced with the problem.

Clearly this type of learning is more complex than acquiring a given response to a particular stimulus. A learner learning to pick

38 *Psychopedagogy*

out the odd one is not responding to any physical stimulus. The size, shape and colour can all change and are disregarded; the learner does not respond to those physical characteristics. What he responds to is an abstraction, the fact that two objects are the same and one is different no matter what their physical appearance. Oddity is not a physical property of any object.

As in other learning discussed earlier, reinforcement plays a key role. 'Right choice' was signalled by a reinforcer – raisins in the case of monkeys, sweets in the experiments with young children. In natural conditions it is most unlikely that the odd one of three would be a source of reinforcement and not the other two. In fact, of course, the chances of three stimuli occurring in a convenient configuration that could be perceived in this way are somewhat remote. Even more remote is the chance that the configuration of stimuli would be repeated the two or three hundred times necessary for a learner to form a learning set that would equip him to single out the odd one whenever he encountered the problem. It is fairly safe to say that oddity is an entirely human creation.

Harlow, the experimenter, was interested in the processes of learning. But, like the other experimenters mentioned earlier, in order to study learning he had to structure the environment for his learners. In other words he had to teach them. The fact that some of the learners were not human does not invalidate the proposition that oddity, or the phenomena underlying learning sets generally, is a human creation. Indeed, in an interesting way it lays emphasis on an important theme of this book: the organization of the learning environment by the teacher is of enormous importance in learning, often outweighing the effects of differences among learners.

Harlow suggested that when a learning set has been acquired the learner has learned to learn. What this means is that, having once learned the rules, as it were, the learner can apply them to different situations almost at once instead of having to go through a new process of learning each time. In the terms of Harlow's experiments, what this amounts to is that the learner needs only one trial to see which rule is operating and will get the right answer thereafter. Faced with a new problem after having acquired a number of learning sets, he would, after one trial, have enough information to make the correct choice whether it involved always choosing the left object or the right or the odd one or the larger of two or whatever the criterion happened to be. In other words, the learning established through the long sequence of trials is transferred to new situations.

Transfer of learning is a particularly (though not exclusively) human phenomenon. It should be pervasive in school learning. There would be no point in a pupil's learning to solve arithmetical problems unless there was a high possibility of his being able to solve other problems later. It stands to common sense that it would be a waste of time to give pupils exactly the same problem of simple addition over and over again, and not many teachers are likely to do so. It may not be so clear to a commonsense view that it is desirable to vary the nature of the problems slightly in different presentations. In the case of simple addition this may involve no more than systematically using different digits in the same position or the same digits in different positions. A more complex example – say, learning to solve problems involving an understanding of base in arithmetic – would suggest that the teacher present problems involving different types of base, not so that the learners would learn to cope with all the bases the teacher used as examples, but so that they would be able to deal with problems using bases they had not previously encountered. There is no suggestion here that pupils should merely be given large numbers of problems without guidance from the teacher. Harlow guided his learners by providing reinforcement each time they made the correct response. This should also be a feature of a teacher's activities, but in addition he has at his disposal an enormously powerful tool to guide learning by explanation and cueing – that is, language.

Learning by imitation

Less powerful than language as an instrument for developing learning, but none the less with its own qualities for guiding the learner, imitation is universally observed but little understood. That humans learn by imitation is beyond dispute, but what

40 *Psychopedagogy*

happens when they do is by no means crystal clear. However, it does seem reasonable to regard learning by imitation as a form of transfer, the learner assimilating to his own behaviour that of the model. The learner thereby acquires a capability comparable to a learning set that will enable him to tackle problems of the same type in the future with success.

Caution needs to be exercised when considering learning by imitation in formal teaching. In general such learning involves a sequence. It is not just a case of copying a single simple action possibly at the same time as the model is performing. The learner has to observe accurately, store in his immediate memory the sequence of actions (to the extent that he has, in fact, clearly observed them) and then reproduce them in much the same way as the model performed them. Perhaps the most appropriate way to use imitation in learning is in the form of cueing. As an aid to guiding various types of motor activity it can speed up learning more than any other approach.

Aspirant teachers need to be particularly conscious of the possible pitfalls in learning by imitation. On the one hand they may assume that pupils can adequately learn entirely by observation complex activities that really need analysis and cueing by the teacher. On the other hand they might well make the same mistake in respect of their own learning to teach. Imitating an experienced teacher is a time-honoured way of training in practical teaching. Since teaching is one of the most complex of human activities, it is highly unrealistic to expect anyone to acquire the necessary skills merely by observation, even if he were able to find a suitable model!

Affective effects

Implicit in the discussion so far is the view that learning is greatly influenced by emotional or 'affective' states in the learner. I have referred to concepts such as satisfaction, approval, enjoyment, distress and other states of feeling, and implied that they act as reinforcers or punishers. I have suggested that they affect general emotional states in the learner and thus impinge upon his learning generally, and that in their association with reinforcers of specific

Learning: foundations 41

aspects of learning situations they enhance discrimination and generalization and in general refine the adjustment of the learner to his environment. I also mentioned the way in which learning problems impinge upon the affective states of the learner. The distress of experimental animals or children when faced with problems too difficult to solve is one aspect of this effect. The other main aspect is the way in which continuous failure to learn inhibits the learner's commitment to learning.

Commitment to learning is usually referred to as 'motivation'. It is possibly an unsatisfactory word because of its generality and the way in which it is often used as a pseudo-explanatory term to describe whatever it is that causes us to act in this way or that: high levels of motivation explain success and low levels explain failure. There is also at times a tendency to talk about 'motivation' as though it were a 'thing' with a real concrete existence, or perhaps to account for a given activity by saying the actor is 'motivated' so to do. Using this approach we can explain why a tree grows towards the light and why a man grows potatoes with equal facility: both are motivated, the one to seek light, the other to grow potatoes. The absurdity of this explanation is matched only by the seriousness with which comparable explanations of human activity are sometimes made.

It is true that trees grow towards the light for perfectly good reasons, although even here we need to beware of the trap of saying that this happens because the tree is phototropic. The causes of men's activities are in general more complicated. Most fundamentally his activities are related to the needs of the human body for such things as air, food, water and the maintenance of body temperature. We may describe but not 'explain' many of man's activities by arguing that he engages in various activities to avoid deficits in these vital requirements. However, since teachers are rarely (if ever), *as teachers*, concerned with such states of basic physical needs, I do not propose to discuss them further here but refer the reader to books on general psychology. Yet because I shall at times refer in later chapters to factors that affect a pupil's attitudes towards learning, teachers and other pupils, and suggest ways in which a teacher might encourage positive attitudes in pupils towards learning (see Chapter 12), at this juncture I shall

42 *Psychopedagogy*

make brief reference to some current hypotheses about motivation as it may affect pupil's learning.

Curiosity

The first one is probably more than a hypothesis. What Pavlov called the 'what is it? reflex' seems to be with little doubt a basic motivator of the behaviour of many animals and man in particular. Pavlov went so far as to say that man's scientific activity is a manifestation of the urge to explore his environment. This seems to be a plausible argument. In the process of evolution this kind of activity would undoubtedly be adaptive for the species and would have developed by the processes of selection. It can be observed in many aspects of life today, from tourism to space research. In various experiments the satisfaction of curiosity has been found to be reinforcing, so that there does really seem to be justification for viewing the need to explore the environment as real and a legitimate reinforcer.

Closely related to curiosity is the need for stimulation. Various experiments have been carried out on human subjects in which they have been placed in environments as stimulus-free as the experimenters have been able to devise (Vernon 1963). Deprived of virtually all external stimulation to the sense organs, the subjects became desperate for stimulation after a day or two and embraced the most boring and mundane activities with enthusiasm when given the opportunity. In animals other than man, stimulus hunger (as it is sometimes called) may be illustrated graphically in the eternal pacing up and down of the caged tiger.

In countless classrooms and lecture halls teachers and lecturers are every day beating down the motivation of their students by ignoring motivators of this kind. Polite adult audiences may doze off after half an hour of stimulus deprivation by a speaker delivering banalities in a voice vibrant with monotony of tone, pitch and tempo. Younger pupils with more energy are likely to react by providing their own stimulation, probably through activities not entirely to the teacher's liking. If learning is to be enhanced and if the conditions for learning are to be made favourable or even, perhaps, tolerable, any teacher needs to take this kind of

Learning: foundations 43

motivation seriously. Curiosity must be aroused and provision made for its satisfaction. Opportunity should be given for pupils to explore and seek out stimulation.

Probably related to the need to explore and grapple with features of the environment, is what has been described as the motivating effect of competence (White 1959). Clearly this is the obverse of the debilitating effect of failure. It is linked with exploratory activity in that a person will actively seek out activities that offer a reasonable chance of a pay-off in terms of success and is not merely a reactive phenomenon with positive effect following success irrespective of the person's own activity. Thus accomplishing too easy a task would not necessarily be seen as success, neither would not coping with too hard a task necessarily be seen as failure. Whether an individual will seek to engage in a particular activity will naturally depend on his history of success or failure on related tasks and on the way other people, particularly those who have attempted to teach him, have treated him as he has attempted those tasks.

The need to achieve

The need to achieve (nAch in the jargon) is a suggested motive resembling that of competence motivation (McClelland *et al.* 1953). The argument is that human activity is motivated by the need to achieve excellence, either in comparison with others or according to one's own views. Naturally one's own ideas and the goals one sets for oneself are socially generated, and so to a great extent do relate to one's comparative performance *vis-à-vis* other people. A form of personality test known as the Thematic Apperception Test (TAT) is used to measure nAch. This test consists of pictures about which the person is asked to tell a story, describing what led up to the situation depicted, what is happening and what is likely to happen. The story is then interpreted by the tester who looks for traces of nAch in the person's reply. This approach to personality testing has been criticized in many places, and it has been suggested that the outcomes often tell us at least as much about the tester as the subject. A moment's thought will suggest that this is not too unjust a suggestion. The

44 *Psychopedagogy*

tester is only doing what he is asking the subject to do. The tester is interpreting an ambiguous situation (the subject's reactions to the stimulus picture) in the same way as he is asking the subject to interpret the ambiguous stimulus (the picture itself); and why should the tester be any better at it than the subject?

This view receives some support in a recent exhaustive review of work on nAch by Fineman (1977) who found that the instruments used to measure it are in general not reliable. The author does not suggest that the notion of nAch should be abandoned but that researchers should continue the search for tests to measure it more reliably and with greater validity. The message for teachers, it seems to me, from such considerations, is that the concept in its current state is of little, if any, practical value to teachers. Its theoretical value for researchers is still subject to debate and may still yield helpful information, but for the present there are more useful concepts that we might focus on.

Learning motivation

The heading is double-edged. We consider what it is that motivates learning and how motivation is learned. The reciprocal nature of the two is typical of many aspects of human behaviour: change the one and the other changes. There is more chance of understanding human learning with this kind of perspective than with the one-way perspective that characterizes the attitudes referred to earlier of viewing motivation as an unexplained energizer of human behaviour.

Thus motivation is not only a stimulator of learning but also a product of the learner's perceptions of the effectiveness of his learning. I use the words 'perceptions of the effectiveness of his learning' advisedly, since these are more important than the accuracy of his perceptions. If he *thinks* he is doing well, the argument is that he is likely to be more enthusiastic in his approach to learning than if he thinks he is doing badly, whatever the objective reality.

There is evidence that pupils' learning is influenced considerably by affective factors. Bloom (1976), surveying the research on the question, argues that attitudes towards specific subjects, to-

Learning: foundations 45

wards the school in general and the learner's own perceptions of himself have a significant effect on learning. Of these three factors pupils' self-perceptions are the most potent. It is important to realize that a pupil's perceptions of himself – his academic self-concept – are not inborn but result from his experiences of school learning. His academic self-concept is an index of how the pupil perceives himself in relation to the achievements of other learners in his group, and is built up from the feedback he receives from peers, teachers, parents and test results. Bloom draws attention to the vast number of learning tasks a pupil encounters in the course of a year. A successful pupil will receive constant confirmation of his success, whereas a failing pupil will be getting feedback constantly informing him of his failure. It is not surprising that the failing student develops negative attitudes towards school and school learning any more than it is that successful pupils in the main have positive attitudes towards school and school learning.

The history of success or failure and the positive or negative affect they engender cast light or shade on future learning. Success may breed success, but failure also breeds failure. Thus part of any teacher's appraisal of a teaching problem should be a consideration of the pupil's previous history of learning and the way it is likely to affect any new learning task. The teacher is more likely to obtain a useful indication of a pupil's motivation in respect of a new learning task by examining his record of success or failure than by administering some form of projective test. Success and positive attitudes towards learning augur well for any new learning task. A history of failure and negative attitudes indicates a much more difficult teaching task.

The crushing weight of years of failure would be enough to squeeze the last drop of motivation out of a pupil were it a substance or quality as it is sometimes referred to. But because it is not that, because it is something less tangible, a disposition that manifests itself in the way a learner behaves in a learning situation and arises from the learner's past experience, it is possible to envisage ways of enhancing it. The ways of enhancing motivation are no more than a particularly sensitive application of techniques that should be the staple of any approach to teaching. The fact

46 *Psychopedagogy*

that they have to be adopted at all is merely a consequence of the failure by teachers to apply them in the past. New learning tasks for failing students with low levels of motivation should be so designed as to optimize success. It may be necessary in order to overcome negative attitudes to certain types of learning to approach the problems in different ways, and in many cases it will be advisable to retrace one's steps and enter the learning tasks at a lower level in order to build up confidence and enthusiasm for learning.

3
Language and human learning

I suggested in the previous chapter that accounts of the conditions of learning appropriate to non-human animals are necessary but not sufficient to explain learning in human beings. It is not merely that the way we learn is influenced by our belonging to the human race, but that our belonging to the human race adds a completely new dimension to our learning and provides a key to teaching that transforms both learning and teaching. I suggested that the crucial aspect of being human that helps bring about this transformation is man's use of language.

It is clear that one way in which learning and teaching are completely refashioned by language is that a teacher can tell the learner what to do when learning an activity that would otherwise have to be learned through conditioning or imitation. Skinner could have saved himself much time and effort had he been able to tell his pigeons to turn in a figure of eight instead of spending hours in shaping their behaviour.

But this is not all, or indeed the main thing. Teachers are not solely concerned with teaching physical skills or activities. Indeed,

48 *Psychopedagogy*

for many teachers such teaching is rare. But practically all teachers are engaged for a considerable amount of their time in teaching their students what for the moment I shall call 'knowledge'. Knowledge may of course range from relatively 'simple' facts of the type 'man is a mammal' to such statements as $E=MC^2$. I use quotation marks with the word 'simple' because, although the statement 'man is a mammal' is indeed relatively simple, it embodies some extremely complex ideas; however, most teachers introducing junior children to the notion are unlikely to stop and ponder long on the implications of this particular combination of words. As for the second statement, I think I need hardly justify the use of the word 'complex'.

The transmission of knowledge may be the most obvious use of language but there is far more to it than that. 'Knowledge' is not a given; something there for us to find. Man creates knowledge, interprets the world and, indeed, makes his world what it is through language. To a great extent much the same can be said about the development of individual human beings, so it is of considerable importance for the student of pedagogy to reflect on the ways in which language bears on human learning.

Signals and symbols

I have no direct proof but I am pretty sure that, save for Washoe and her associates, no non-human animal has ever given evidence of having apprehended the meaning of any one word. I should make it clear that I am not arguing that a particular word may not have significance for an animal. Many kinds of animals have learned to respond in different ways to a variety of words. But the response they make is of a similar nature to the response of Pavlov's dogs to the sound of the metronome: it is a response to a noise. A dog trained to sit when hearing the word pronounced is reacting to the word 'sit' as a signal in much the same way as it might respond to a metronome or a shepherd's whistle. It is quite likely that the animal would respond in the same way to a word such as 'sip' pronounced similarly through the processes of stimulus generalization. A person is unlikely to do this. On the other hand the same dog is unlikely to sit on hearing the words

Language and human learning 49

'be seated' or 'please take a chair', whereas a person is very likely to do so. Other animals almost universally respond to the physical properties of words only; words for them are just noises. For human beings they are much more than that, and what they respond to is not the noise of the words but what the words stand for, or symbolize, the actual sound of a word being relatively unimportant.

Very young children and children with very great learning difficulties respond to words as noises in much the same way as non-human animals (O'Connor and Hermelin 1963). From this extreme there is a spectrum of language apprehension, ranging from an initial reaction to words as noise, through stages in which words gradually acquire the significance of symbols of specific things, to the stage in which they symbolize classes of things. As adults we are likely to be in the first stage when we encounter words in unfamiliar foreign languages or arbitrarily coined nonsense words. A second stage may be identified when, in early language learning, a word comes to stand for a single object only, the spoon a child eats with, for example. With experience and teaching the child gradually comes to realize that the word 'spoon' signifies more than that one object to other people and so gradually acquires a normal human response to that particular word. The normal human response is to regard the word as having generalized significance; that is, it stands for not just the one object but for any object of that nature.

Concepts

The normal human response to a word such as 'spoon' is a reaction not to the physical characteristics of one specific object but to the abstract properties that characterize a class of objects. This is a fact that profoundly affects the course of human learning and makes teaching as we understand it possible. The abstractions to which we react are usually known as concepts. A concept such as is symbolized by the word 'spoon' is relatively simple as concepts go. It is simple because it refers to a class of concrete objects, and other types of concepts refer to more complicated things such as abstract qualities and relationships among phenomena. It is

50 Psychopedagogy

important to note that concepts and words are quite distinct. I was at pains to point out that the word 'spoon' is not itself a concept but is the label for the concept. Learning the word is no guarantee that the concept too is learned.

It is also important to be clear that the generalized response one makes to the sound symbolizing a concept (a word) is quite different from the response generalization found in conditioning. Generalizing through conditioning could transfer from the sight of a lark to the sight of a sparrow because the birds resemble each other, whereas the response would not generalize to the sight of an ostrich because the ostrich bears little resemblance to the lark. Once the concept 'bird' has been acquired, however, it becomes possible to react to the ostrich and the lark in the same way despite the differences in physical appearance of the two animals. Responding to the ostrich and the lark in the same way might involve, for example, understanding that both lay eggs. All a person would need to know in order to make this response would be that both are exemplars of the concept of 'bird' – that is, they are both birds.

To say 'all a person needs to know is that they are both birds' is a gross oversimplification. It seems to impute an unwarranted simplicity to the process of concept learning. It is very difficult for people to avoid this oversimplification when they are talking about familiar concepts. It is most important, however, when teachers are considering concept learning in pupils, to remember that concepts are built on experience, that the chances are high that a teacher will have had much more experience of the concept than the learner, so that the concept he (the teacher) has will be very much more developed than that of a young learner and a pupil could well have difficulty understanding a teacher's discourse purely because of the different levels of understanding of concepts that are symbolized by the same word for the pupil as for the teacher. This can happen with the relatively simple concepts that are abstractions of concrete phenomena; it is all the more likely to happen with concepts relating to abstract qualities and relationships, both of which are common in classroom discourse. It is a central consideration in most teaching since the main object of most teaching is to help learners build up systems

Language and human learning 51

of concepts to enable them to adjust to their environment in more complex ways. The overwhelmingly significant feature of the interaction between teacher and taught in human learning is that it takes place not just in a physical environment but also in an environment of concepts which is the abstract embodiment of the individual's experience of the world. This re-emphasizes the enormous difference between learning in humans and other animals since we have to acquire appropriate reactions not only to the physical world but to other people's abstractions from their experiences using words as go-betweens.

As I have already suggested, the concepts we acquire are the product of our experience. We do not arrive in the world – to adapt Wordsworth – trailing clouds of concepts. Nor do we ever reach a condition when we can, as it were, relax in the knowledge that we have finally attained a fully formed complete concept. Such a state of affairs could exist only if we had no further experiences. However, when this stage is reached, we shall have no concepts whatsoever.

Another point vital to our discussion is that, although the words labelling concepts are shared among a speech community, the concepts are unique to individual members of that community. This follows from the fact that the concepts are products of an individual's experience, and unless two people have exactly the same life experiences their concepts must differ in some way. As the linguist, Sapir, put it, 'experience lodges in an individual consciousness and is, strictly speaking, incommunicable' (Sapir 1963). This is not just a tragic philosophical fact, but has implications for pedagogy which need to be continually borne in mind. The fact that teacher and taught use the same word may mislead the teacher into thinking that the meaning the learner takes from the word is much the same as his own.

A symbol system

The sounds that symbolize concepts may perfectly easily be, and usually are, spoken together with other words. When two words are juxtaposed we bring together two concepts, not just two sounds. But whereas the two sounds are likely to be perceived as

52 *Psychopedagogy*

two sounds, the two concepts interact with each other, most probably to form a third concept. *Red* symbolizes one concept, *rose* another, *red rose* a third and *rose red* a fourth; but there are still only two sounds.

Clearly, then, juxtaposition is important. So is word order. In the example of rose and red, juxtaposing the two words changes the meaning of the sounds but the sounds are still meaningful whichever way round we present them. But this example is not typical of language in general. If you consider the opening sentence of this paragraph you will agree that changing the order of the words not only completely upsets the meaning but in most rearrangements completely destroys the meaning. We have here an illustration of another key aspect of language. As sounds come to symbolize concepts through social convention, so society imposes a system on what would otherwise be a random collection of words. The conventions that decide this word order are those of grammatical usage, usually referred to as syntax.

The sequencing of words (the symbols of concepts) according to syntactical conventions enables us to set up relationships between things, actions and attributes of things which would otherwise be impossible. 'Red roses across the moon' may seem to you nonsense or an appealing poetic conceit according to your cast of mind, but whatever your opinion you would probably accept that the image is meaningful. And yet, without language as a system of symbols arranged in that particular order, such a phenomenon could not exist. More complex if less poetic possibilities arise from the manipulation of word sequence according to grammatical conventions. Such expressions as *if this then that*; *because of this that occurred*; *unless this that will not* are highly abstract concepts utterly dependent upon language. Even relatively simple sentences are capable of generating large numbers of complex meanings (concepts). Sapir illustrates this point when he demonstrates that in the sentence *The farmer kills the duckling* thirteen different concepts are expressed. Some are concrete – *farmer*, *kills* – but there are also ten relational concepts working to produce the exact sense of the sentence. These concepts express such things as subjectivity and objectivity (acting as subject or object), singu-

Language and human learning   53

larity and time (expressed by the form of the verb) (Sapir 1963).
A sentence of a very different kind is discussed by Brown (1973):
The nurse that the cook that the maid met saw heard the butler.
Experiments by Blumenthal and Stolz reported by Brown showed
that, even with unlimited time and with pencil and paper to help,
most college students could not understand sentences of this kind
and averred that they were ungrammatical. In fact, according to
grammatical rules they are acceptable. Whether conventions that
allow of such productions are much use if most of us can't understand them is, as Brown says, unclear. The point of referring to
such sentences here is to exemplify the limitless possibilities for
the generation of complex meanings of an unusual ordering of a
few words familiar to us all and to hint at the possible problems
learners may well have, not because the teacher uses 'long words',
but because he uses grammatical constructions that do not match
the learners' levels of understanding.

The remarkable thing is that children acquire quite early in life
the ability to string together words according to grammatical
conventions. Whether or not this ability is a function of our
genetic make-up, as Chomsky (1965) argues, does not affect the
issue as far as most teachers are concerned. But all of us should
be greatly relieved that children do acquire this ability as they do,
because if they did not there would be precious little time to spend
on other things or little point trying, since communication between adults and children would be, to say the least, at a very
rudimentary level.

Remote reference

Symbolling and syntax working together add a further profound
element to human experience which is quite crucial to teaching.
We can talk to students about things that aren't there. We can
present to learners at the same time and in the same place concepts
which could not otherwise be brought together. We can assemble
in meaningful order concepts such as sea, mountains, clouds,
rivers, lakes, snow, sun, rain and mist. We can also present
stimuli representing concepts which are abstractions very remote
indeed from the concrete physical word. For example, we may

54 Psychopedagogy

use with quite young children stimuli such as 12×12 and with older children $x + y$.

Similarly we can refer to things that are remote in time: we can learn from the thoughts of previous generations of humanity; and we can look to the future. Without language there is no past and no future. Of all the species, only man knows that he is mortal and that there was a time when he did not exist either as an individual or as a species. Thus the learning environment for a child in society is of unimaginable complexity. Not only is he immersed in a complicated technological physical environment, but through the language of adults and other children and through written language and language emanating from electronic media he is bombarded with a continuous flow of concepts arranged in an infinite number of different sequences, some of which refer to concrete observable phenomena, others which refer to abstractions of abstractions; and, as if that were not enough, he has to come to terms with concepts from times past and times to come. It is not surprising that his understanding of these concepts is sometimes very different from adult understanding, or that teachers' realization of his difference of understanding is sometimes deficient. But I hope that by raising these questions here I will alert you to the fact that human learning is completely transformed by man's use of language: that this transformation raises enormous problems for our understanding of human learning and teaching; but that at the same time it presents us with possibilities for development otherwise completely out of the question.

Cultural accretion

I have discussed the three aspects of language that seem to me to be of major importance for human learning: that it has meaning (it symbolizes concepts); that it is a system (the concepts are ordered according to grammatical convention); and that it makes reference to things remote in time and space. These aspects of language profoundly affect the learning and teaching of all of us *as individuals*. But they also have a profound influence on the species. Alone of all the species with which we are familiar, man has the ability to adapt collectively. Not only does each individual

Language and human learning 55

acquire new skills and knowledge through his life experience, but the learning of the individual is absorbed into the culture and contributes to the adaptation of the whole species. The behaviour and development of a child of today is determined not only by the biological adaptations made by the species in the course of evolution and his own experience but also by the accumulated collective experience of the whole of mankind. In part this accumulated experience is embodied in technological developments and in part in forms of social, cultural and political organizations and customs, in ideas, ideologies and all forms of artistic expression. In other species there is little, if any, handing on of skills down the generations. Adaptation in these animals usually results from changes such as that which enabled some reptiles to take to the air, or such as happened when myxomatosis favoured rabbits living above ground. Evolutionary changes of bodily form in species with long life spans is a very slow process. Innate behavioural change in a species is also relatively slow. Thus a species adapted for life in a particular environment is likely to be at risk when there is a rapid change in that environment.

Changes of bodily form or behaviour in other species generally have little permanent effect on the environment. Man, on the other hand, changes his environment profoundly and permanently, partly in an effort to cope with changes in his environment and partly to extend his scope for survival in new and hostile environments. He builds huts, lights fire, wears clothes, constructs boats, aircraft and space vehicles. All these then become part of man's environment and themselves act as further agents of change. None of these developments could take place without men working together and without the use of language. It is not just that language enables men to work cooperatively, but that it also enables them to form concepts that allow them to have ideas about fire, tools or even cooperation.

The crucial implication of social inheritance for human learning is that each new development makes new demands in terms of skills to be learned. I am referring here not only to physical skills but to all kinds of mental and physical abilities. Man is not born with the ability to make boats, to control fire, to pilot an aircraft or even to use a spoon. Technological artefacts are inert and im-

56 *Psychopedagogy*

possible unless we have the skills to construct and use them. Social artefacts such as customs, traditions and philosophies also make their own demands on teachers and taught in all educational encounters. The effects are cumulative and successive generations of children have to learn new types of skills. Driving a car is an example of a skill, recently born of technological development, that is now quite commonplace. The ability to make a critique of the indiscriminate use of the car may well involve much more complex skills of analysis, evaluation and decision making in respect of social needs. Both kinds of skill are new to mankind, and the acquisition of both necessitates some kind of learning and teaching. Both are therefore the legitimate concern of teachers.

But all of us are teachers at some time. A large proportion of us at some time in our lives teach children: our own. If we didn't children would not learn any of the common skills involved in feeding, dressing, and so on. Nor could they learn the use of any of the many common tools of our society: spades, knives, pencils, brushes and other more sophisticated instruments. But more than this. Children are dependent on parents and other adults for learning such skills as reading. And, of course, the most important skill of all, the use of speech, is almost entirely dependent upon adult influence.

In all human societies children are taught by adults the necessary physical and mental skills appropriate to the technological development of the society. In societies at a low level of technological sophistication it is possible for the transmission to be made on a non-specialist basis. Skills can be handed on from parents to children adequately because they are relatively simple and relatively few. But with scientific and technological advance, skills and techniques become increasingly complex, their transmission more and more a specialist job, and professional teachers appear. The job of a teacher itself becomes more complex so that he has to acquire skills and knowledge quite beyond the grasp of earlier generations of teachers.

Effects of schooling

Bringing together teachers and pupils in schools for teaching on a systematic and institutionalized basis has a profound effect on the way children learn. Since teaching in school is rarely of the show-and-tell kind, the predominant pedagogical approach will stress remote reference with children, and the teacher's talking about things that are not present in the classroom and things that have no actual physical existence at all. Children in such situations tend to classify and order the world in different ways from those of their peers not attending school (Greenfield 1966; Cole and Scribner 1974). The main characteristic of this different approach is the search for rules and principles of taxonomic class member-ship, whereas children from rural communities not attending schools often employ other approaches to grouping.

Taxonomic class grouping is essential in school teaching. Once we have learned the defining attributes of a class of phenomena, we are in a position to identify things we have never seen before and apprehend their most important characteristics. A person with a little botanical knowledge would know quite a lot about a plant he had never seen before if he were told or read that it belonged to the species *prunus*. He does not have to learn all about that par-ticular plant from scratch, since he knows from previous ex-perience what its key characteristics are. The *name* of the species to which the plant belongs in this case acts as a key to under-standing but only because the person already has a concept or system of concepts in the relevant field. To the person without this botanical knowledge and not possessing the necessary con-cepts, the name would be no help. It would have no meaning for him, an unfortunate fact of pedagogical life that many teachers in and out of school often forget.

Although taxonomic class grouping can be of enormous help in teaching and learning we need to be alive to the fact that it is not necessarily the most useful way of thinking about the world, and within different types of cultures and subcultures different approaches may be preferable. There should be no implication, however, that these approaches are in some way primitive; they

58 *Psychopedagogy*

are more than likely to be more appropriate to their environment than our ways.

Even within the realm of taxonomic grouping there are no absolute rules of utility. The much-commented-on fact that Eskimos have several different words for snow illustrates this point. So does the well-known story of the teacher who questioned children about animals by holding up a picture of a cow and asking the pupils what it was and got no response. She found it incredible that not one pupil could identify the animal. She eventually discovered that the children, from a farming community, were trying to decide what particular breed of cow it was. In an urban society it is sufficient to know the generic term for the class of animal but this would be of very little use in the rural community. It could be argued that the term 'cow' is more abstract and therefore represents a higher level of thinking, but this view is by no means universally accepted. The point to be aware of is that such differences exist and cannot but influence transactions between teacher and learner.

Labels and learning

Words may reasonably be regarded as labels for concepts. However, few psychologists would argue that that is all they are. There is a considerable body of opinion that they are crucially important in the process of concept formation, and I should like to use the words of one of the most eminent of them, Luria, to illustrate the way language and concept learning interact. He is talking about learning in young children, but it is not difficult to envisage a similar process in older children (Luria 1961).

> When a mother shows a child something and says *cup*, first her pointing and then the name of the object cause an essential modification in the child's perception. By the laws of temporary links (conditional reflexes), the mother's gestures and the word designating the object become secondary signals *causing marked changes in the range of stimuli acting upon the child*. In isolating the object from its environment, the action of pointing strengthens the stimulus making it a figure set in a ground. The word

Language and human learning 59

designating the object delineates its essential functional properties and sets it within the category of other objects with similar properties; it serves a complex task of analysis and synthesis for the child, and later settles into a complex system of links acting on him and conditioning his behaviour.

Luria is here talking about the *process* function of language, as opposed to its labelling function. *Labelling* is the assigning of a name to a learned concept. There is a view which holds that essentially this is what happens in concept learning. We learn through practical experience and then name the concept. As Sapir says of those holding this view, to them 'language is but a garment'. In fact, although the labelling function is important, it is likely that the process function is more important.

Luria's description illustrates some of the ways in which language affects concept formation. More sophisticated learners acquiring new concepts are helped to form them by the manipulation of existing bodies of concepts. It would be impossible to manipulate these abstractions unless they had names. Even at higher levels of learning, words can act similarly to the way the mother uses them in Luria's example. The fact that phenomena which are perceptually dissimilar go by the same name introduces an element of regularity into configurations of stimuli which acts as a cue to the learner signalling to him that the phenomena belong together in some way. You might well be at a loss to grasp what the worm in a watch, the sprocket on a cycle and the rack and pinion on a lock gate on the canal have in common, but if you were informed that they were all gears you would immediately have your attention focused on the essential attributes of the three and would disregard the inessential such as size and material. If you were teaching children about gears, showing them examples such as these would put them in a similar position to the very young child in Luria's illustration. Assuming that you were not going deeply into the theory of gears, probably your first concern would be to help the children identify them when they saw them. It is probably fairly obvious that this would be difficult, if not impossible, without using language. The best way of proceeding is not always so obvious.

60 *Psychopedagogy*

Unless you are an extreme exponent of discovery learning you are likely to want to give the children some guidance in learning what gears are. You could, of course, start by giving them a dictionary-type definition and then explaining the essential characteristics, that is, the criterial attributes. It is extremely unlikely that this entirely verbal approach would be effective with children to whom the whole idea was new. In order to make certain that the children really did grasp the *general idea* of gears it would be necessary to present them with *particular examples* in such a way that they came to realize what the essential characteristics of this general idea are. To put it another way, we aim to help them to learn what the criterial attributes of the concept *gear* are. The process is very similar to the building up of learning sets.

It would be perfectly reasonable to start by explaining that gears are used for the transmission of power or motion and then to go on to present different examples. At first it would be best to show the children examples of gears of different sizes and made of different materials, confirming at the same time that they were all gears. The point of this activity is to vary the non-essential aspects of the concepts (size and material) while at the same time indicating to the learner that these perceptually dissimilar things are examples of the same concept. Other non-criterial attributes such as colour and orientation would have to be varied in similar presentations, while at the same time continuing to confirm that the things were all gears. 'Confirming' to the learner that the things are all gears of course involves the use of language. In all the situations the one thing that remains constant is the word 'gear'. It is possible to envisage other means of confirming the inclusion of things in a particular class but difficult to think of a more flexible and versatile method than using the concept name.

In addition to the teacher's use of language to indicate the invariants in various configurations of stimuli, the learner will also be able to use the name of the concept to indicate his grasp of its defining attributes. For economic learning the teacher will present the various examples of the new concept in a carefully structured progression, moving from examples that are easily identified to examples that are more difficult. The learner will be asked to distinguish between examples and non-examples of the concept;

Language and human learning 61

for instance, between wheels that are acting as gears and others that are not. Eventually the learner should be in a position to identify new examples of the concept when he encounters them.

Let us consider a little further the way in which language in its 'process' function aids the learning of the concept. Clearly my suggestion that the teacher might give a definition pre-empts the discussion. We might, therefore, try to envisage the difference that not having the definition would have made to the learner. I would suggest that, although he would have been able to induce the concept from the various examples presented, it would have been a very much more difficult job. In the process he would have been manipulating concepts such as *motion,* (*gear*) *teeth, turning,* and many others according to the programme of examples the teacher had adopted. It is inconceivable that anyone could do this without the use of language. There seems little point, then, in withholding the original definition. Note, however, that a definition of the type suggested, itself assumes the prior knowledge of concepts such as *power* and *transmission.*

The prior knowledge of the learner is of crucial importance in the learning of any new concepts. In the example being discussed here it is obvious that the definition would have been of no help at all to a person who had no understanding of *power* or *transmission.* Nor, I suggest, would such a person have obtained anything but a very superficial understanding of what a gear was, if indeed he had obtained any understanding at all. The argument, then, is that words do not merely label concepts after they are learned, but that they play a vital role in the whole process of learning.

Empty sounds

Words as labels sometimes positively hinder learning and understanding. Generations of children in schools throughout the world have learned names for countless concepts, and nothing else. Most children of five can be taught the label *psycholinguistics.* Few, I suggest, will have much idea of the concept. This somewhat extreme example illustrates a real problem that has caused some people to emphasize the practical side of learning and

62 *Psychopedagogy*

de-emphasize the role of language. Empty verbalism is an ever-present problem in all learning – which is why concrete exemplars of concepts are so important. At the same time it behoves all teachers to consider the question of the learner's existing know-ledge. No amount of exemplars of the concept will help if the learner's existing level of understanding is deficient in the area of new learning, as in the example of the learner who did not know the meaning of power and transmission and yet was expected to learn what a gear was. More commonplace examples of this empty verbalism can be taken from almost any age and field of study – from the child in primary school from the age of seven up who begins to receive instruction in the rudiments of English grammar, to the student who mugs up model answers for an examination in physics or law without having any grasp of the concepts the words are labelling. If this happens it is not because the teacher and the learner used words, but that either the teacher's teaching was faulty or that factors beyond the teacher's control obstructed the learner's efforts.

Verbal learning

The different aspects of the transforming effect of language on human learning converge in the characteristically human activity of verbal learning. By this is meant the acquisition of concepts through the medium of language without the intercession of the concrete world. Almost uniquely in the animal world humans are able to teach their young by telling. (One has to be cautious in these days of symbolling chimps!) I have already referred to the way language can be used by a teacher to reinstate earlier learning by bringing it to bear on current learning and thereby facilitating such learning. The teacher, for example, talks to the pupils about such things as motion and power when he is explaining about gears. Provided they have acquired these concepts in previous learning, he will be able to explain the way in which gears can be used to apply power and motion most effectively.

Introducing the subject by giving the definition of gears as 'apparatus for the transmission of motion or power' is a very common and perfectly legitimate way of setting the context for

Language and human learning 63

new learning and orienting the learner. But clearly the phrase is much more than the label for a single concept. Juxtaposing the words in that sequence identifies a much more complex concept than the constituent elements. Gagné (1977) refers to concepts of this type as 'defined concepts', and gives a simple example of a defined concept: a saucer is defined as 'a dish (thing-concept) for holding (relational-concept) a cup (thing-concept)' (p. 130). My example of gears is of the type more common in school teaching and learning, involving as it does three defined concepts (apparatus, power and motion). If I were to talk about *gear wheels* I should have a definition 'gear wheels are for transmitting motion or power' which related a thing-concept to two defined concepts by means of a relational concept.

Other aspects of verbal learning which complicate the picture of concept learning are concerned with the teaching of rules or principles. These are produced when several concepts are juxtaposed in a similar way to defined concepts; their important characteristic is that they indicate regularity and predictability. They are generalizations from particular phenomena. Rules of classification in botany, of pronunciation in language learning or of procedure in mathematics are examples of these more complex concepts. It seems reasonable to suppose, with our present state of knowledge, that such rules or principles are themselves capable of being combined in human thinking, and indeed there is strong indication that something like this is happening when one considers the intricate verbalizations of which human beings are capable, either in speech or in writing. With a view like this we conceive of a form of cognitive activity that takes in information at different levels of generality and organizes it hierarchically. The individual concepts, rules and principles combine in increasingly more complex concepts. The most general of these complex concepts constitute the overall principles in particular fields of knowledge. A very large proportion of these concepts, especially the more complex or higher-order ones, are entirely abstract and far removed from the 'thing-concepts' of which Gagné writes. Learning such concepts is very largely an entirely verbal matter since they cannot be apprehended through direct sense experience.

An ever-present problem with learning of this kind is the one I

64 *Psychopedagogy*

have alluded to before – that the learner learns the words but not the concepts they label. This problem has led to many people in education denigrating verbal learning as rote learning, and advocating 'active' methods of learning through direct sense experience. The deprecating of the learning of 'facts' is a particular example of this tendency. Ausubel (1963, 1968) has pointed out the fallacy of taking verbal learning to be, by its nature, rote learning. If the learner *only* learns the words the teacher uses and not the concepts, then the learning is rote, that is, meaningless, and probably of little if any value to the learner. However, if the teacher's expositions are attuned to the learner's levels of understanding, then the words he uses will call to mind the concepts they symbolize and the exposition will thereby be meaningful. By the same token, a learner engaging in direct sense activity without any idea of the concepts and principles relating to this activity could be learning in a rote fashion. The point is that rote learning is more accurately seen as the opposite of meaningful learning, and reception verbal learning as the opposite of learning by direct sense experience (sometimes referred to as discovery learning).

The hallmark of meaningful learning is, then, that any new learning can be related to existing bodies of concepts already learned. Rote learning is when the words only are learned. New learning that can be related meaningfully to existing knowledge is of far greater value than material memorized in a rote fashion. The former is able to be transferred eventually to new situations which are different from the concepts just learned but which are still related to the overall body of concepts in that field. Material learned in a rote fashion will be unrelated and unrelatable to other concepts, and will be useless outside the situation in which it is learned.

With this approach, the learning of facts by the exposition of the teacher and reception by the learner is a perfectly reasonable procedure. It can often be a very economical way of adding to one's concepts in various fields of study, and of course it is the medium of one of the most versatile of teaching devices, the book.

Language and human learning 65

Language and thought

Clearly the whole of this chapter has been concerned in one way or another with the relationship between language and thinking. The argument has been that language has a profound influence on an individual's learning, through the effects of cultural accretion and also through the way it facilitates concept formation by its process function. It is not unreasonable to look upon language as the agent that transmutes the experience of the individual and the species into internal representations of that experience. This is not to say that thinking is entirely dependent upon language. The crucial fact is that language, and particularly speech, constitutes an enormously flexible and versatile system of symbols readily communicable among human beings. Symbols such as diagrams and mathematical symbols may have similar effects but of course are considerably less versatile in their use. Evidence of work with deaf children who do not have access to speech, our normal symbol system, indicates that they do have greater problems in various tests of thinking and tend to perform less well than normal children in such tests (Oleron 1957; Herriot 1970). It is difficult to be sure quite what the position is with such children, however, since one of the difficulties in investigations of this nature is establishing that the children have no system of symbolling at all. Most deaf children brought up in normal circumstances will have some form of symbol system (possibly sign language), even if it is not spoken language, and such symbol systems fulfil the functions of a language system such as normal speech even if they are less effective.

The work with Washoe illustrates the point particularly well. Viki was unable to make progress because the experimenters placed their emphasis on spoken language. Since chimpanzees seem to be lacking in ability to vocalize because of inappropriate vocal anatomy, Viki's problem was probably not an inability to learn a language but an inability to make the sounds that symbolize concepts in English. Washoe, on the other hand, learned language using signs to symbolize concepts and made a good deal more progress almost certainly mainly because chimps are quite dexterous manually.

66 Psychopedagogy

Apart from the use of a symbol system that chimpanzees could master, there was one other crucial factor in these experiments: the role of the experimenter. In fact the experimenters were virtually parents and teachers to Washoe. Without them Washoe would have been no different from other chimps. But the key thing is not merely that someone taught a chimpanzee to use a sign language but that they did this in a particular social environment. The chimpanzee learned to sign for symbols while engaging in activities typical of a child in American society in a pervasive ambience of experimental psychology. So she learned to sign for classes of objects, agents and actions and not just for particular instances. She learned to identify many quite different instances of classes such as *dog*, even using drawings and pictures. In other words she was learning to sign with a middle-class, academic American accent. In a different culture she would have had different experiences, her teachers would have had different hopes and expectations of her, and there is little doubt that language would have helped her to 'think' in different ways. Discussing the question as to whether chimps in the wild use sign language, Brown and Herrnstein (1975) speculate that they may well do, but since they leave no potsherds or other technological artefacts we do not actually know. If they do, however, the activity related to the signing would not be picking out specific examples of taxonomic classes, particularly from picture books; it would be related to the dominant concerns of the species for survival in a very different environment. But the young chimp would not be born with an appropriate mode of thinking; rather he would acquire it mainly from expert members of the species – namely, adult chimps.

Whose world?

Washoe's world was vastly different from that of chimps in the wild. As a consequence she became a different kind of chimp. Victor in the woods was very different from the boy he became after he had lived in the Itard household. These striking examples illustrate a general phenomenon: the world into which one is born has the most profound influence on one's development.

Language and human learning 67

The two examples given relate to cases where individuals were taken from one environment into a vastly different one and radically changed by the experience. Such drastic transpositions are rare but make a point that is often overlooked. People who live in different environments have to make different kinds of adjustments to the worlds they inhabit. People from highly urbanized and industrialized societies have often thought of the way people from isolated and rural communities adjust to their environment as 'primitive'. This view has applied not only to the outward manifestations of the daily lives of people from such rural communities, but also to the way they think, their attitudes to nature and their general conceptions of the world. This view has been particularly held of peoples who have differed very markedly from our own, especially those living in remote places such as the African bush. There has been a considerable shift in outlook in recent years following the realization that ways of looking at the world appropriate to Western urban culture may not be appropriate to life in the African bush, and that 'primitive' ways are frequently more appropriate than 'civilized' ways.

Luria tells a very apposite story about his colleague Vigotsky who went to study psychological processes in a primitive Asiatic tribe. He used conventional Western psychological apparatus including tests of visual perception capable of a variety of interpretations. After some time Luria received a message from Vigotsky to the effect that the tribe 'had no illusions'. This delightful remark makes a profound and double-edged comment on the attitudes of psychologists in Western culture on the relative merits of different ways of looking at the world.

4
Thought, talk, action

The word and the act

For all its power, the speech of adults is not enough in the development of children's thinking. The acquisition of the habits of thought appropriate to a given culture also depends on the learner's own actions. Vigotsky's (1962) argument suggests a plausible way of conceiving the process. Thinking originates in a child's concrete activity, which, thanks to verbalization through social intervention, becomes internalized. The child himself tests the truth of his thinking through this concrete activity. This is ultimately the only way, since the thoughts of adults themselves embody millennia of human accomplishment, itself a product of concrete activity.

In the fairly recent explosion of interest in the role of language in learning, this need for constant checking with practical activity has often been overlooked. Naïve notions that building vocabulary would help thinking were augmented by ideas about the power of syntax or the importance of semantics. It would be no exaggeration to say that many people seemed to hold the view that the thing to do was to spray children with language and ten ideas

Thought, talk, action 69

would grow where one had grown before. More likely to be effective is the involving of children in actively exploring the effects and power of language in connection with practical activities and interactions with other people. Discussion, explanation and argument all demand difficult cognitive activity. They are all intended to influence other people in some way so that the speaker can see the effect of his activity.

Experimental psychologists investigating the interactions between talking, thinking and doing have not been guilty of the simplistic views about the effects of language on thinking just mentioned. Indeed, most of the seminal work in this field of study has taken the view that language, thinking and action are probably inseparable in normal people. The central focus of the work is the way children acquire adults' mental and physical skills and notions about the world. Some of this work is comparable with that mentioned earlier where the experimenter sets tasks for the learner and studies the process whereby the tasks are accomplished. Other experimenters attempt to sample behaviour at different ages to shed light on the progression of young learners in their approach to adult ways. In all the approaches, however, there is a common element. The experimenters present the children with problems based on an adult view of the world, and the experimental finding of interest is the mismatch between children's thinking and actions and adult performance. Thus the focus of these investigations is the developing in children of the ways of looking at the world typical of the culture of a particular time and place. This is a basic fact that teachers and other educationists must consider when applying the findings of the investigations to pedagogy.

Allied to this point is the fact that many of the theoretical expositions relating to the development of language and thinking and their relationship with behaviour are theories in the sense of hypotheses. That is, they are preliminary or tentative and not universally accepted. Even long-established theories related to our understanding of the physical world are subject to challenge and falsification or emendation, and of course this is the way of progress in our understanding of the world. How much more tentative, then, we should be when seeking connections between work

70 *Psychopedagogy*

in the extremely complex and relatively recently developed study of thinking, language and their interrelationships and its practical applicability in the guidance of human learning.

Unfortunately this tentativeness is often lacking in expositions relating the work of key psychologists to the practice of teaching. Pronouncements tend to be made which set forth a model of intellect and action as if it were immutable law, so that a teacher who found in practice that some of the principles of that law did not seem to work out in her classroom would be more likely to worry about her children or her teaching, or think that she had made a mistake of interpretation, than reflect on the nature of the theory itself. Naturally teachers in general do not have the time, facilities or access to research findings which professional experimenters have and they are therefore at a gross disadvantage in examining hypotheses. At the same time they have access to conditions which few experimenters have – namely, large numbers of children of various ages all trying to come to grips with adult ways of seeing the world. Thus if they are aware of the hypotheses of the various researchers they are in a position to try them in probably the most appropriate test bed of all, the classroom.

The argument is much in line with my earlier proposals: that there is much to be gained for a view of teachers as experimenters and experimenters as teachers. Teachers should not be passive recipients of the sayings of the sages but, rather, sceptical inquirers who put the sayings to the test of practice.

The advantage of much of the experimentation on thinking and language and their interrelationships is that it is relatively simple in conception. In fact many students in teacher training do replicate experiments in this field. The crucial point, however, is that these replications should not be carried out just to witness psychological processes in action but to test them. With this approach the focus of interest will be those replications that seem to deviate from the expected. Any systematic deviations could well point to new factors but in any case would help to build up knowledge in the field.

It is likely that most psychologists would support this view. Progress in science is made by the scrutiny of theories, and all theories should be constructed so that they can be tested experi-

Thought, talk, action 71

mentally. Most would probably also agree with the suggestion that the development of a useful pedagogy demands the intervention of educationists and teachers. However, one eminent student of child development, Piaget, believes that it is not up to psychologists to deduce pedagogical theory from his views but that these need to be verified and applied by educationists (Hill 1972).

The acts of thought

Piaget is a Swiss psychologist who has been studying the cognitive development of children for more than half a century. Although he has published books on the subject over the years, his ideas have only recently been taken up by educationists and seen as having relevance to teaching. Once taken up, however, they have been adopted with enthusiasm and often with a great lack of the critical appraisal to which I referred above. Nevertheless the perspectives he has developed on children's thinking have brought new light that cannot but have implications for the development of a psychology of pedagogy, and this applies even if some of his ideas prove to be less well founded than some of his less critical disciples would have us believe.

One of the problems of discussing Piaget's contribution to pedagogy is the sheer enormity of the task of identifying the key elements of his vast output that might have significance (see Flavell 1963; Donaldson 1978). But the all-pervasive insight that comes from this work is that children gradually acquire an understanding of the world like that of adults by a process of experimentation with objects of their environment. The stress is on the action of children, as was suggested at the beginning of the chapter.

Piaget (1961) argues that all we know can be divided into two principal aspects: the formal viewpoint which deals with the state of things to know, for instance, most perceptions and mental images; and the dynamic aspect which deals with transformations, for instance, to disconnect an electric motor in order to understand its functioning. It is the latter that he considers to be the more important and the more difficult to attain. Only the dynamic

72 Psychopedagogy

aspect can make us understand the nature of things. In the course of development children move from a state where the formal – that is, the physical state of things – dominates in their understanding, to a state in which the dynamic – that is, the way the physical state of things is transformed according to certain laws – is dominant. Piaget's argument is that the gradual acquisition of these laws of transformation is the history of the development of thought in children. To him the fundamental genetic problem of the psychology of thought is to explain the formation of these dynamic structures. The problem of psychopedagogy, it seems to me, is to examine these proposed cognitive structures as they may be manifest in teaching and, if they are manifest, see what implications they may have for its theory and practice.

In order to put a little concrete flesh on the abstract bones of the argument and to bring our discussion a little nearer the reality of classrooms, I now consider some of the well-known experiments that exemplify the salient features of Piaget's preoccupation with the development of these dynamic structures of thought. The interesting thing about many of these experiments is that they can be fairly readily replicated, but in addition several of them have fairly obvious areas of application to teaching. In the account which follows I outline Piaget's views with little comment. Later in the chapter I consider other views on the same phenomena which raise questions about their interpretation particularly important for students of pedagogy.

Underlying Piaget's views of cognitive development is a model of adaptation similar to that discussed in earlier chapters. People maintain a state of equilibrium, in part by changing their behaviour to cope with changes in their environment that they cannot control, and in part by changing aspects of their environment that they can control. Piaget has adopted two technical terms for these processes: *accommodation* and *assimilation*. Examples of accommodation are learning to climb stairs since you can't flatten them out and walk normally on them, learning to swim because you can't walk on the water, learning to use a pedestrian crossing because you are unlikely to maintain a state of equilibrium for long if you don't. Examples of assimilation are cutting steps in a cliff so that you don't have to walk five kilometres to get round,

Thought, talk, action 73

and building a boat or a bridge to cross a river. The two processes rarely work independently. When you are cutting your steps you will probably avoid the hard rocks and the loose sandy soil, and when building a bridge you are likely to look for a narrow and probably shallow part of the river even though this involves a detour from your route.

Very young children's early learning will largely consist of adaptation of motor activity. They *accommodate* to the fact that the bars of a playpen prevent them from getting to a toy thrown out. A child may well *assimilate* the environment when he realizes that playpens can be pushed to get near enough to a toy to reach it through the bars. As children's thinking develops through their own activity and the influence of adults and the use of language, the processes of accommodation and assimilation increasingly apply to their mental life. But, of course, the motor activity referred to in the examples given above is a vital part of their developing cognitive abilities. Thought and action develop together and nurture each other. On the cognitive side the two processes are envisaged as contributing to the formation of concepts. Rudimentary concepts are changed (or *restructured*) when they prove to be inadequate in some way as a guide to action. A child finding that the thinking that guides his action does not lead to the result he desired will think again. That is, he will probably modify the concept or concepts that led to the activity. This is accommodation. On the other hand, should his activity be successful, his concept will be confirmed as being serviceable and he will continue to think along those lines. He will not think in exactly the same way, however, since the very act of using a concept successfully in a new situation will enrich the concept in the way I discussed earlier when talking about the nature of concepts. This process of confirmation and minor modification is assimilation. The restructuring that takes place now is much less radical than during accommodation. Assimilation and accommodation working together imply change. Motor actions and concepts enhance their utility in coping with the environment, and the very act of coping leads to environmental change which itself calls for change in the person.

Very early in life motor actions and then cognitive processes

74 *Psychopedagogy*

become coordinated into patterns of activity that act as integrated wholes. Piaget refers to these integrated patterns of motor and mental (or, more likely, psychomotor) activities as *schemas*.

Schemas unify different but related experiences so that when situations comparable to those experiences occur we are able to respond adequately almost automatically. Piaget gives an example of a schema by referring to the development of a simple schema in a baby, related to feeding. Starting with simple reflex actions of sucking, he gradually developed a feeding schema that varied according to whether he was to be fed with a bottle or a spoon. Although the central core of feeding activity was much the same, the grasping activity, mouth movements and bodily orientation were different. Clearly this is much more economical than having to learn a separate form and sequence of activity for each type of feeding.

It is not difficult to think of examples of motor schemas in older children and adults: learning to use different types of eating utensils, learning to drive different types of car or to kick different types of balls, and so on. Cognitive schemas may be considered as higher-level concepts made up of many simpler concepts. It is perhaps fruitful to look upon them as principles that integrate the subordinate concepts. Once a person has acquired a cognitive schema related to a particular body of knowledge, new problems or knowledge related to the schema can be dealt with more easily, because the learner can draw on experience and previous learning in related areas fairly routinely, yet not mechanically since the existing schema provides a frame of understanding for the new learning. This clearly relates to our earlier discussion of rote and meaningful learning.

The process of accommodation and assimilation clearly apply to the development of schemas. In fact, after the very early months of a child's life, schematic activity is likely to predominate. Thus, whereas earlier I referred to the restructuring of concepts, the more usual type of development is likely to be the restructuring of schemas. Schemas change in the course of learning to take in new elements, sometimes to drop others, but in general to become more comprehensive. Piaget suggests that, when faced with a new problem of learning, children bring to bear their past experience

Thought, talk, action 75

in the form of a previously acquired schema. This schema is potentially adequate to cope with the problem. Piaget calls this schema an *anticipatory schema*. If this coincides closely with the demands of the problem, the solution will be easily reached; if there is less common ground, the schema will need to be restructured. The restructuring will be complete when the new learning is mastered. The new schema will be more comprehensive and more relevant to the solution of the new problem as well as to the earlier ones. Thus learning advances by increasing the complexity and comprehensiveness of schemas and, of course, by developing new ones.

Overall, then, Piaget sees the cognitive development of children proceeding from a state where thinking is barely involved in the control of activity, to one where complex concepts and schemas are used to direct activity and to reflect on the world. He has found it useful to suggest that this development can be seen to have four broad *stages*, some of which can be subdivided further. It is important to resist the temptation to think that children step from stage to stage all at once with neat precision. A child may be in one stage for some types of activity and another for others. Indeed, it might be helpful to think of types of behaviour or thinking rather than stages of development. The proposed stages are as follows.

SENSORY-MOTOR INTELLIGENCE (UP TO ABOUT TWO YEARS)

During this period a child gets to know about his environment predominantly through his physical interaction with it. From a state of simple reflexive activity he moves to one in which his actions are more coordinated and organized. In the course of this development he gradually comes to realize that the world comprises phenomena that can be identified as separate objects; that he himself is different from the objects around him; and that these separate objects have permanent existence independent of him, so that if an object is removed from his sight he will continue to look for it, whereas in the early stages he will not. In this period children also come to realize that changing the position of a thing

76 Psychopedagogy

does not change its identity. A cup is a cup is a cup, whether seen from the top, the side or the bottom. As I have already suggested, this is a very important stage for the development of concept formation, but so, also, are the other activities I have mentioned. Since concepts are built on experience, all activities facilitate future, more complex learning. Thus the fact that children seek to prolong interesting experiences at this stage of development is also an important contributory factor in their learning. It is also an interesting example of the close interrelationship between cognitive and affective factors in learning and of aspects of reinforcement and motivation. The child seeks to prolong experiences because he seems to find them interesting; this exemplifies the motivating effects of curiosity with the concomitant reinforcing effects of satisfying that curiosity. The search for satisfaction of curiosity involves the child in activities that contribute to his cognitive development.

PRE-OPERATIONAL STAGE (TWO TO FOUR YEARS)

Perhaps the key development at this stage is the expansion in the use of language for the development of concepts. As I suggested earlier, the use of symbolling, that is, having one thing stand for or represent another, really transforms human learning. However, concepts do not arrive all at once. Over a period of years children move from a stage where their activity is just beginning to include the use of representation and a primitive form of concept development, to one where they use concepts in similar ways to adults. Their ability to use representation is very much tied to activity, their own activity. This tendency is seen clearly in the use of egocentric speech – speech that acts as a sort of running commentary on a child's physical activity.

A very important aspect of Piaget's views is that at this stage of development children find difficulty in seeing the world from any point other than their own; they are egocentric. Not, you might think, a trait solely confined to children of this age. However, children of this age do not choose to see the world in this way, and they have to learn to see it from other points of view. This egocentricity is related to the link between representation

Thought, talk, action 77

and activity. Piaget gives an example from topography to illustrate this. Children shown a model of mountains are unable to select pictures to correspond with the views that would be obtained from different sides of the model. A particularly important aspect of egocentricity is that a child is unable to think about his own thinking. His logic is self-contained. He does not feel it necessary to justify his reasoning, nor can he examine his own chain of thought. Only after long experience of social interaction in which he is forced to discuss and argue with others does he acquire these abilities. This is a point of view which chimes closely with that expressed earlier, illustrating the importance of these kinds of verbal–social interchanges.

Nor, at this stage, do children acquire some pretty important capabilities that are very relevant to early school learning. By the age of seven many children have had at least two years in school and some will have also had experience of nursery school. At some time during this period they are likely to have been introduced to activities related to thinking about number, weight, length and height. We sometimes take for granted their grasp of spatial relationships; and the idea of causality is so much part of our own thinking that we rarely imagine that children may think differently. Piaget argues that this is the case with children at the pre-operational stage, so that we need to be cautious in our expectations and our interpretations of the activity of children at this stage. The main problem seems to be the inability of children at this level of development to consider more than one aspect of a phenomenon at the same time. They seem to focus on the most obvious perceptual aspects of situations rather than on more complex, probably conceptual aspects, as adults do. For example, two sticks of equal length will be accepted as equal so long as they are parallel and in line. If one stick is moved forward a child is likely to say that that one is longer. A child will agree that two identical glasses filled to the same level contain the same amount of liquid, but when the liquid from one glass is poured into a taller, narrower glass he will aver that there is more liquid in the taller glass. Piaget considers that this implies lack of *conservation*. The child does not see that, although the outward form may have changed, the quantities involved are the same (i.e. they are

78 Psychopedagogy

conserved). This experiment relates to conservation of quantity; the experiments with the sticks involves the conservation of length. We meet similar phenomena in experiments dealing with substance, weight, volume and number. Children thinking pre-operationally are likely to lack conservation in all these fields.

CONCRETE OPERATIONS (ABOUT EIGHT TO ELEVEN YEARS)

By *operations* Piaget means actions that are internalized and reversible. That is, children are now able to *think about* actions which previously they could only carry out practically. They also acquire conservation in most fields by the end of this stage. A popular method of investigation in the field of conservation of substance is to show children two balls of modelling clay. They are allowed to handle them and asked if they think them the same size. When they agree that they are the same size one of the balls is rolled out into the shape of a sausage. Children who have learned conservation of substance will say that there is still the same amount of clay in the two lumps. Children not having reached this level will say that the amount has changed. These children seem to be fixated on the visual appearance of the material and do not see that increase in one direction is accompanied by a decrease in the other.

Children at this stage will have no difficulty with the glasses and water problem referred to above. Further, unlike children at earlier stages, they will be able to understand that pouring water back into the original beakers also involves no change in the quantity of liquid. In addition, it is not necessary for children actually to pour the water from one vessel to another; if they are asked what happens when water is poured from one vessel to another of a different shape they will be able to think about the question and answer accurately. Thus children at this stage can think about their activities and understand that, at least in the Piagetian experiment, what's done can be undone. Their actions are internalized and accepted as reversible.

FORMAL OPERATIONS (ABOUT ELEVEN TO FIFTEEN YEARS)

Children at this stage can cope with the problem of reconciling apparently contradictory concepts such as *taller* and *smaller* into a single principle. Instead of reasoning about actions or reality, they are now able to reason with propositions; they are able to manipulate relations between things besides *establishing* those relationships. Piaget gives an example of a problem demanding this type of thinking taken from a contemporary intelligence test. 'Edith is fairer than Susan: Edith is darker than Lily, who is the darkest of the three?' Piaget declares that few children below the age of twelve solve this problem. Before that he suggests the reasoning goes as follows: 'Edith and Susan are fair, Edith and Lily are dark, therefore Lily is the darkest, Susan is the fairest, and Edith is in between.' Children at this stage can reason by hypotheses and work out what would happen if they were true. They might say, for example: if a whale were a fish it wouldn't need to come to the surface.

By the time children have fully developed the capacity for formal thinking and reasoning by hypothesis, they are operating at adult levels of competence. It would be a gross error to think, however, that from then on all their reasoning is likely to be of this nature. Adults and adolescents will often revert to much simpler modes of reasoning, not excluding preconceptual logic, when engaged in argument!

TEACHING AND THINKING

The progressions outlined above from primitive levels of thinking to complex inferential thinking has a bearing on the work of teachers of all ages of children. Piaget has investigated many processes that clearly impinge upon the concerns of teachers in classrooms, and it is therefore important to consider his experimental work. But apart from the intrinsic interest of his work the history of its impact on teaching has a significant bearing on the theme of this book, which sees teaching as a form of psychological experimentation. Piaget drew attention to some probably

80 *Psychopedagogy*

erroneous ideas about the way children think and through a wealth of experiments revealed modes of thinking manifested in children's actions that shed revealing new insights into differences between children's conceptions of the world and those of adults. As the ideas percolated into discussions about educational theory, teachers became sensitized to the fact that aspects of children's understanding of classroom processes were probably discrepant from their own ideas of the same phenomena and their perceptions of pupils' understanding of those phenomena.

This sensitization was undoubtedly a positive development in that it alerted educationists to previously unsuspected factors influencing children's learning which could now be taken into consideration when planning teaching. There were problems, however, that sprang from the fact that Piaget was mainly concerned with non-pedagogical matters. This led to a preoccupation with attempts to reveal underlying structures of cognitive development relatively uninfluenced by its social context.

Other workers have been critical of this approach, holding that it distorts the real-life situation in which children learn and can therefore mislead teachers. In many cases the work that gives rise to this questioning of Piaget's theses has been done in a pedagogical context. That is, the critics have engaged in the experimental teaching I have referred to earlier.

The upshot of these questionings is that the Piagetian view of child development seems to be less well founded than it was a few years ago. The main drift of the reappraisal is to suggest that children are capable of rational thinking at earlier ages than Piagetian theory proposes and that the way problems are presented is of crucial importance for their solution. This is not to say that Piaget's findings are to be rejected. The reverse: their influence will still be considerable. However, the fate of his explanatory theory is a very interesting example of how progress is very often made in our views on the nature of the world. Piaget raised new and very important questions about the nature of human cognitive development. Later workers approach things from a different angle just as Piaget did with earlier theorists. The outcome is likely to be a new, more useful synthesis of ideas to guide our theories and practices.

Thought, talk, action 81

The critical debate about Piaget's work started many years ago, and probably one of the earliest commentators to raise doubts was the Soviet psychologist, Vigotsky. As long ago as the late twenties and early thirties he criticized Piaget's approach on the grounds that the lack of contact between pedagogy and the psychology it espoused gave it an unsatisfactory orientation. He argued that the central focus of researchers should be on the interaction between instruction and development since he believed that 'all the peculiarities of child thought described by Piaget . . . stem from an absence of system in the child's spontaneous (untutored) concepts' (Vigotsky 1962). Piaget, many years later, when he read Vigotsky's critique for the first time, considered that he was closer to Vigotsky's views than the critique suggested. But of course there had been considerable development in Piaget's work since Vigotsky's comment. The important point remains, however, that there is a considerable difference between what tends to be a generally held Soviet view that development and instruction should be investigated together and the type of approach exemplified in Piaget's work and in work in fields such as intelligence testing where they are divorced.

Other experimenters have added knowledge about aspects of Piaget's work on which I shall comment later. For the moment, however, I should like to pursue the work of writers and experimenters who have made important contributions in this field. By so doing I hope to be able to draw some lessons in pedagogy at the end of the chapter.

Language and action

Vigotsky's critique of Piaget was all of a piece with his abiding interest in the role of language in human learning. He was in the tradition of Pavlov in his interest in the second signalling system. But his interest was not in the *signal* function of speech but in its semantic nature. This is the aspect of speech that led Pavlov to hold that the use of speech transformed the learning of humans and the nature of their adjustment to the environment. Language, for Pavlov, not only acts as the main agent of thought; it is the medium which links thought to practical activity, thus increasing

82 *Psychopedagogy*

the complexity and the delicacy of adjustment of human activity. Action and thought interact: as children acquire increasingly complex modes of thinking they acquire more complex patterns of controlling their activity and language is much involved in this process. In early life children have little control over their activities. They learn to sit up, stand and feed themselves, mainly with the help of adults. At first the adults' help involves physical assistance, standing, sitting and feeding. Later, assistance takes the form of guidance by the speech of adults, telling and encouraging the child in its actions. All this is obvious. But what is not so obvious are the processes whereby a helpless child whose activity is controlled physically by adults in his early life develops into a person able to control his own behaviour through complex thought processes.

The two crucial aspects of this development are the transformation of speech from a set of signals to a system of symbols and the gradual internalization of this symbol system as a mechanism of self-regulation.

As has been discussed in previous chapters, the behaviour of animals is controlled by stimuli from their environment. These stimuli are, for animals other than man, nothing more than events in the physical world which, through the processes of conditioning, become linked with certain other events in such a way that the one becomes a signal for the occurrence of the other. Thus the dog salivates when it hears the bell, and the pigeon pecks when the light shows. But no dog trained to a sound ever salivated when the experimenter said 'bell', and no pigeon trained to a light ever pecked when the experimenter said 'light'. On the other hand children who had learned a reaction to the sound of a bell have been found to make a similar reaction to the spoken word 'bell' and the printed word 'bell' (Simon 1957). These children were reacting to the word 'bell' as a symbol of a concept they had learned, a concept that embraced the sound of the bell to which they had learned the initial response. Their activity was thereby rendered very much more complex and versatile through their use of language as a system of concepts than it would otherwise have been.

The significance of this development is considerable. Instead

Thought, talk, action 83

of reacting automatically to a stimulus, the child must, at the very least, appraise the stimulus and match it with an inner representation of classes of stimuli, decide which class if any it belongs to, and then act accordingly. 'Acting accordingly' implies taking action in the light of previous experience of activity related to that class of stimuli. In fact this process takes place in less time than it takes to tell, and it is almost certainly much more complicated than I have described. There is also an implication that the child is responsible for his own actions and is not merely reacting automatically to outside stimulation. This autonomy of action, like the change from signal significance to semantic significance, also has a history of development. As signals gradually acquire meaning and children learn to react to the meaning rather than to the physical properties of speech, they also gradually acquire the ability to generate their own stimuli, language, to control their own activity.

Vigotsky explored this process in experiments investigating the 'egocentric speech' of young children which was commonly held to be a purposeless accompaniment to their activity, and found that such speech was far from purposeless. Children were observed in various activities and their egocentric speech noted. In one method children were drawing and, just as a child would be preparing to draw, he would find the pencil missing. At such moments the amount of egocentric speech almost doubled. The child 'would try to grasp and remedy the situation by talking to himself: "Where's the pencil? I need a blue pencil. Never mind, I'll draw with the red one and wet it with water; it will become dark and look like blue." ' Faced with a difficulty demanding more than the usual effort, the children brought language in to help them think out a solution.

As children grow older, egocentric speech becomes abbreviated and elliptical. In ordinary speech the speaker has to make explicit the subject of his statements; when one is thinking or talking to oneself there is no need to do this. One's speech can be completely predicative, that is, the subject need not be stated. Abbreviated, predicative speech is speech on the way to becoming internalized. Later, egocentric speech disappears to be replaced by inner speech and eventually by thought.

84 *Psychopedagogy*

Inner speech, according to Vigotsky, is by no means the equivalent of social speech. The movement towards the elliptical, seen in late egocentric speech, continues so that inner speech loses its phonetic aspect and becomes entirely semantic. As speech becomes internalized, its functions as a controller of activity are internalized, so that the processes of control started by the speech of adults and continued by the child's egocentric speech are replaced by control through the internal flow of meanings. These, it is suggested, are the mechanisms of self-regulation characteristic of human beings.

A colleague of Vigotsky's, who outlived him by almost half a century, Luria, continued in the same general line of study of the effects of speech on thinking and self-regulation. In many experiments he and his associates investigated the way in which children progress from simple reflexive activity dominated by the signal properties of the environment to more complex self-directed acitivity dominated by the influence of meaningful discourse. An illustration from his experiments will give an idea of the process (Luria 1961).

A child of about eighteen months will usually have made some progress towards responding to the meaning rather than to the physical properties of speech. However, at about this age the physical property is still a powerful influence and tends still to be attached to the stimulus situation. Thus Luria found that if a child of this age is told to take his stockings *off* when he is in the process of putting them *on*, he will be unable to do so. This is because the motor activity of putting on his stockings is a more powerful influence than the significance of the words 'take off'. Similarly, although it is possible to cause a child of about eighteen months to press a bulb on a recording apparatus by telling him, verbal instructions cannot stop him. On the other hand a signal can stop him. If he is told to press when a light appears and his action of pressing puts out the light, he will stop pressing. If the feedback system of the light's going out when the bulb is pressed is disconnected, the earlier lack of clear-cut responses recurs and he presses when he should not. At this stage, although the child is responding to the meaning of the words, the physical stimulus of the light is more powerful than the words telling him not to press.

Thought, talk, action 85

A somewhat older child still has problems. At three and a half, when asked to press for a red light and not for a green, he will still press for all lights. Although he understands the instructions, the light as a signal rather than the meaning of the instructions dominates his activity.

At the same age the motor aspect of speech still seems to prevail over its meaning. A child asked to say 'Press' and 'Don't press' in response to lights of different colours without actually doing anything can cope quite well. He can also cope if he has to press and say 'Press' when he sees the red light and say nothing and do nothing when he sees the green light. If, however, he is asked to respond to the green light by saying 'Don't press' and at the same time to refrain from pressing, we find that the child presses despite himself. Speech impels him to action since the signal aspect of the words is more potent than their semantic significance. Only later, at about five years of age, does this impulsive reaction to speech weaken, to be replaced by behaviour accurately regulated by more developed speech activity. Finally, the stage is reached when the child ceases to use external speech and instead regulates his behaviour by internal speech. At this stage, Luria argues, children orient themselves through signals according to the abstracting and generalizing functions of speech which enable them to formulate rules for themselves through the use of language. The importance of this development lies in the fact that the child moves from a state where his activities are dominated by factors in the environment to which he responds willy-nilly, to a state in which he can plan his activity according to rules he has formulated even when this involves ignoring the physical aspects of stimuli.

Thus language, thought and action develop in complex inter-relationship. It is not just a question of children's activity becoming more complex because they learn more complex words and the concepts they symbolize, which in turn influence their actions, but that the word meanings change with experience. As Vigotsky put it: 'The relation of thought to word is not a thing but a process, a continual movement back and forth from thought to word and from word to thought.'

86 *Psychopedagogy*

The process function of language

When Vigotsky talked about the relation of thought to words being a process, he stressed the reciprocal nature of the relationship between the two. The argument is that language is not merely used as a means of labelling concepts already learned, but that the name and the concept are learned together and the learning of the one facilitates the learning of the other.

His interest in this interrelationship led him to devise a method of investigating the process of concept formation in children in which they had to learn both new concepts and new words. By close observation of their learning he was able to identify various stages on the road to true concept learning which in some ways resemble the findings of Piaget.

In his experiments he used apparatus comprising twenty-two small wooden blocks of five different colours, six different cross-sectional shapes, two different heights or thicknesses and two different cross-sectional areas. Under each block is written one of four nonsense syllables: LAG, BIK, MUR, CEV. The problem is to classify the blocks in four groups so that all the blocks in any one group have common properties which unequivocally mark them off as members of that group and non-members of any other group. The only way of doing this is to group together the tall and fat blocks (LAG), the small and fat (BIK), the small and thin (CEV) and the tall and thin (MUR). The person attempting to group the blocks is shown only the word underneath one block to begin with. After each attempt in which he fails to group correctly, a block is turned over so that he sees the word underneath. Vigotsky's view was that the words would help the person to discover the basis for classification, leading him to realize that the words stood for definite kinds of objects. Once he understood this, he would be able to complete the grouping quickly. At this stage he has learned new concepts and new words that symbolize the concepts.

Vigotsky found that children of different ages set about the problem in different ways and he identified several different types of grouping that regularly emerged. The main feature of the 'incorrect' groupings was that they were, in Vigotsky's terms,

Thought, talk, action 87

complexive. This means that they were grouped together without any conceptual equivalence. Very young children grouped more or less randomly, older children tried to group by colour or shape, but of course it was impossible to produce four groups using these criteria. Frequently, when a child grouping like this was shown a turned-over block with the 'wrong' name, he would remove it from the group and still keep in the group other, similar blocks, not realizing that the one negative instance of his criterion of classification invalidates his grouping rule. He found that in the main children did not consistently classify according to the criteria of height and size of cross-section before adolescence, but even at this stage they did not invariably use conceptual equivalence. A study of English children (Stones and Heslop 1968) found that children up to the age of ten or eleven grouped in a very similar way to those reported by Vigotsky, although no children over the age of six grouped completely randomly. The majority of children of eleven learned to classify correctly and so did some younger children. A similar pattern has been observed in other investigations (Stones 1970, 1975).

Although Vigotsky argued that the most difficult aspect of concept learning is its application to new concrete situations, he gives no information about methods of assessing its transfer in the subjects of his experiments. This aspect of concept learning is quite crucial in the study of psychopedagogy, since this is the main focus of most teaching, particularly at the secondary stage of schooling. The work by Stones and Stones and Heslop, using Vigotsky's approach, introduced the idea of a transfer test of the learning of the concept. This example may serve as an introduction to, and specimen of, the approach to assessing concept learning that I shall be discussing throughout the book.

The rationale behind the approach taken is that, while it is one thing to solve a grouping problem such as the one provided by the Vigotsky apparatus, it is a very different thing to be able to use the same rules of grouping with quite different materials which do not resemble the original apparatus. In order to do this the rules of classification must be fully abstracted from the concrete materials that exemplify them and carried around in one's head, as it were, so that they can be applied to the new circum-

88 *Psychopedagogy*

stances. In the work under discussion children were asked to use the same principles of grouping to sort out a completely different set of objects, small toys and bric-à-brac bearing no perceptual resemblance to the blocks. Unless a person had abstracted the principles of grouping from the blocks, he would have been quite incapable of grouping the different material according to the same criteria. In the experiments children able to transfer in this way were all able to group the original Vigotsky material, but being able to group the blocks did not necessarily guarantee that a child could use the rule when grouping the other material. The children not able to transfer their learning into a new situation seem still to need the perceptual prop of the original materials. It is, indeed, a moot point whether children who cope with the original grouping but who can't apply it in new circumstances can be said to have learned the concept at all.

One other aspect of the work by Stones (1970) relates to the role of language in the process of abstraction. Vigotsky argued that concept formation was guided by the use of words 'as the means of actively centering attention, of abstracting certain traits, synthesizing them, and symbolizing them by a sign'. However, in his reports he makes no reference to comparisons of concept learning by children using words and children not using words. In the investigation in question, two groups of children were compared, one having the use of words under the blocks and one not having the use of words. In the event the children using the blocks with words learned more effectively than those without.

The results of a similar experiment with very young children by Liublinskaya (1957) point in the same direction. She gave children of fifteen months the task of choosing the 'correct' objects from several according to criteria such as height or colour. If the children chose the correct object (i.e. the taller or shorter or the one of the appropriate colour), they were given a sweet. With some of the children the experimenter also said 'tall' or 'short' or 'red' or whatever the criterion of discrimination was. The words thus acted as invariants in the situations which changed every time a new discrimination was asked for. The children who were given the words as well as the sweet as reinforcers learned more quickly than those who received only the sweet.

Thought, talk, action 89

Experiments such as these suggest that the use of words does enhance concept learning. Other work by Semeonoff and Skinner (1971) also supports this suggestion, but more information is needed before we shall be able to say how the use of language operates in the processes of concept learning.

Learning and representation

The process function of language in concept formation hinges on its acting as a form of representation. *Represent* here has the meaning of *stands for*. In the case of language the argument that has been pursued so far in this book is that the key psychological factor that transforms human learning is the ability to let one thing stand for another as in the development of symbol systems and especially in the use of language. Other workers have considered other aspects of representation in relation to cognitive development. In particular the work of Bruner and his associates has looked at the way in which different modes of representation interrelate.

Bruner (1964) suggests that we are able to 'represent' the environment to ourselves in three main ways: by *enactive representation*, by *iconic representation* and by *symbolic representation*. He suggests that human development proceeds by the appearance of the three types of representation in the order given.

Enactive representation, according to Bruner's usage, is the apprehension of aspects of our environment by psychomotor means. Through physical interaction with objects we achieve a heightened level of adaptation with the world around us. Imagery and language play little or no part in this adaptation. In Bruner's words: 'Such segments of our environment – bicycle riding, tying knots, aspects of driving – get represented in our muscles so to speak.' There is clearly much in common in this view with the views of Piaget and others on motor schemas. Through repeated encounters with regularities in the environment we build up patterns of motor activity related to specific phenomena, which we are able to run off when the occasion arises.

This aspect of human learning relates very closely to the learning and teaching of physical skills. While it may be true that little

90 *Psychopedagogy*

imagery and language is involved in the way we remember how to ride a bicycle 'in our muscles' it is certainly not the case that imagery and language play no part in learning and teaching such skills. The point is, however, that very young children have little option but to come to terms with the world by holding, moving, biting, throwing, squeezing, touching, and so on. Older learners can use language and iconic representation to learn motor skills; young children perforce depend upon enactive representation to make progress towards other modes of representation.

Iconic representation involves our building up mental images of things experienced. The memory of things experienced is preserved not only in the muscles but also in the recollection of spatial arrangements, colour patterns, movement and other manifestations of aspects of the environment. There is much in common with Piaget's concept of the early stages of pre-operational thought.

Symbolic representation, in Bruner's terms, has the characteristics I have discussed earlier when considering the influence of language on human learning. He believes, as I have suggested, that language is of crucial importance for human learning and that the activation of language is of fundamental importance in developing children's learning.

One of the experiments carried out by Frank, one of Bruner's associates, illustrates this point. Children aged from four to seven years were presented with the Piaget-type problem of pouring water from one container to another of different cross-section. Although the common finding with young children who lacked conservation was confirmed, there was a striking change when the containers were screened from view except for their tops. Very many of the younger children who had said that there was more water in the container with the smaller cross-section before screening now said that there was the same. When the screens were removed, however, the younger children reverted to their previous opinions, saying that there was more water in the containers with the smaller cross-section. Children at the age of about five still held to their view that the containers held the same amount.

The explanation for these findings seems to be that, when faced

Thought, talk, action 91

with visual displays, children in whom iconic representation is dominant are swayed by the visual appearance of the containers. The level is higher in the narrower container, which they believe indicates more liquid. When they cannot see such a display, as when the containers are screened, they focus on the fact that the act of pouring from one container to the other will not change the amount. Children in whom iconic representation is less dominant are influenced by the discussion about the quantity of liquid when the containers are screened, to such an extent that the symbolic representation (saying that there must be the same because all they did was to pour from one to another) becomes predominant and with many children its effects persist even when the visual display is reinstated.

Symbolic representation itself develops over time. Younger children seem to seek one-step substitutes for direct sense experience. This is illustrated in the experiment by Mosher, quoted by Bruner. Children from eight to eleven were asked if they could find out by yes–no questions what caused a car to go off the road and hit a tree. Two kinds of questions are broadly possible. On the one hand there are the constraint-seeking questions such as 'Was it night-time?' followed up by other appropriate questions. Or, on the other hand, there are questions which test the hypothesis directly, such as 'Did a bee fly in the window and sting the man on the eye and make him go off the road and hit a tree?' The younger children asked the latter type of questions while the older ones asked constraint-seeking questions. Thus younger children tried to solve the problem by guesses which much resembled small snapshots of the incident as if trying out a variety of possible images of the concrete happening, while the older children adopted a systematic approach which gradually builds up and integrates information in a structure that will eventually produce the solution.

This work reported by Bruner bears very much on the aspects of human learning discussed earlier. The use of a symbol system enables man to represent to himself things that are distant in time and place, bring them together and manipulate them internally. He is able to build up rules for the manipulation of the model of the environment that we call reasoning. This is very much the

92 Psychopedagogy

same process as the one I have already discussed when considering the development of self-regulation.

Thinking, acting, teaching: some questions

In this chapter I have presented the views of some of the key contributors to our thinking about the ways in which human beings learn the complex processes we refer to as thought or thinking. I have also paid particular attention to the way language affects the way we act. I suggested that some of the hypotheses advanced to explain certain activities and successes and failure in learning are subject to controversy. I should now like to consider some of the points under debate in a little more detail.

One of the central issues is the question of egocentricity, which I discussed when considering Piaget's views. I referred to the experiment in which a child was asked to describe the view of a model mountain or to select pictures of the view that a doll in a different position from his would have of the model. The fact that young children up to the age of seven or eight are unable as a rule to do this and in general choose the picture that corresponds to their own view is taken by Piaget to signify that they are unable to 'decentre' and see things from the point of view of another person.

This conclusion (not the findings) is challenged by Donaldson (1978) on similar grounds to those taken up by other critics: that the children experience difficulty, not because they are unable to 'decentre' as Piaget suggests, but because they do not comprehend the nature of the problem. She refers to work by Hughes which replicated the basic form of the Piaget problem but presented it in terms that were more meaningful to the children. It involved the use of a model of two walls intersecting to form a cross and two small dolls representing a policeman and a small boy. The boy and the policeman were placed at the ends of two of the walls so that they could see each other but so that each had a view behind a wall that the other could not see. The child was introduced to the task carefully to ensure that the nature of the problem was well understood. He was asked if the policeman could see the boy in the layout described. The policeman was then moved to different positions and the child asked to hide the

Thought, talk, action 93

doll so that the policeman couldn't see him. Any errors were pointed out and the questions repeated until the correct answer was given. Very few errors were made.

The actual test was then introduced. Another policeman was brought in and placed at the adjacent ends of two walls and within sight of the other policeman. The child was then told to hide the boy from both policemen. The task was repeated three times to cover all sections of the model. The ability to hide the doll successfully demanded the coordination of two different points of view, and success would suggest very strongly that the child was quite well able to decentre.

In fact the results with children as young as three and a half were that approximately 90 per cent of responses were successful. More complex problems involving walls with more sections and more policemen also found children operating with high levels of success. Donaldson suggests that the discrepancy between Piaget's findings and those of Hughes is that in the latter case the children understood what they were supposed to do and were helped in this by the fact that the problem was presented in a context of human immediacy and in terms they could comprehend, whereas the Piaget problem was very abstract and outside the child's experience (pp. 21–4).

I believe there is another important point that impinges directly on important questions of psychopedagogy which I discuss in detail later. One of them has already been mooted when I discussed the work of Vigotsky and my extension of his concept-formation problem bringing in transfer material. There is clearly much in common between that approach and the one being discussed here. In both cases children were given preliminary ideas of the problem with feedback, minimal in my experiment but more detailed in the Hughes work, and then asked to tackle more complex examples of the problem. In both cases the transfer of learning is being tested after guided preliminaries by the teacher.

This support by the teacher in the preliminary stages of tackling a problem is very similar to procedures recommended for the teaching of problem solving which I discuss later. A key aspect here is calling to the mind of the learner existing knowledge that bears on the problem to be solved. In the case of Piaget's approach

94 Psychopedagogy

one could argue that the method of presenting the problem obscured its nature rather than bringing to mind the relevant existing understanding of the children. Thus their efforts were frustrated because of his desire to divorce psychology and pedagogy.

Donaldson discusses other research that raises serious doubts about many interpretations of standard Piagetian experiments. Work which presents the same basic problems as Piaget's but in more meaningful form leads to conclusions that children are far less egocentric than Piaget suggests, that they are more adept at conservation, and that they are capable of inferential reasoning at a much earlier age than the results of his approach to experimentation would indicate. The main drift of the reappraisal of Piaget's position that this work inspires is that children are much more capable in many spheres of learning than he would have us believe.

Work carried out by Galperin (Brackbill 1962) also leads to this conclusion. He presented problems to children in a meaningful context and deliberately intervened in the early stages of their learning. He also took up a point made by Vigotsky which I mentioned earlier: that one of children's problems is that the concepts they learn out of school – what Vigotsky called naïve concepts – sometimes hinder learning, because these lack the structure and logic of concepts based on systematic instruction. In one experiment he introduced children to counting and measuring in a different way from the traditional approach. His results, like those reported by Donaldson, indicate that different approaches do have an effect. He argues that one of the reasons young children have difficulty in problems of conservation of number is that the traditional approach to the teaching of number is to build on the children's primitive perceptual ability to distinguish between objects. He thought that a better approach would be to introduce the children to numbers as arbitrary things and that much of the difficulty could be overcome by teaching children measuring before counting so as to divert attention from the perceptual aspect of counting; and that taking this approach would enable them to learn both counting and measuring more easily and more thoroughly.

Thought, talk, action 95

In an experiment to investigate his hypothesis, Galperin found that six-year-old children introduced to counting in the ordinary way by learning to count to ten and then adding the quantity *one* to any number from one to nine learned much less effectively than children who were first taught to measure and then to count. The latter children were introduced to measuring by visiting shops where measuring was going on. They were then given measuring to do in the classroom using unmarked paper strips to help them make comparisons. Some of the strips were then withdrawn so that there were not enough to cover the distance of the things they wanted to measure, and instead they were shown how to use small markers in order that they could, in fact, measure using just one strip. From then on they were introduced to the ideas of *more*, *less* and *equal*. Only then were the children introduced to numbers so that they could count the markers, and then taught to count, add and subtract numbers from one to ten.

There is a resemblance in this approach to that of Frank who forced children's attention away from the perceptual aspect of things in the conservation of liquid problem by masking the containers. This masking forced the children to focus their attention on the process or, in Piagetian terms, on the operational aspect of the problem and to reason about it. Galperin, taking the view that counting should be introduced quite deliberately as a new way of approaching the physical world, from the outset directs the attention of the children away from the process of primitive discrimination between objects and towards the artificial process of enumeration. Moreover, he introduced counting when there was a clearly appreciated function for counting related to the identification of differences in length. Both of these aspects of the instruction take the child's attention far away from simple perception.

There is an implication in these studies that devising instruction quite explicitly to cut across the line of 'normal' development may in some circumstances be productive of learning. Precisely under what circumstances and in what fields of study is by no means clear, for the reasons I have mentioned earlier: the lack of research into the effects of instruction on processes such as the ones we are contemplating at present.

96 *Psychopedagogy*

Among others whose work has cast doubt on some of Piaget's formulations, Bryant (1974) has argued that the reasons advanced by Piaget for some of his findings may well reside in the nature of the investigations rather than in the nature of the children's thinking. In one experiment on children's ability to make inferences he questions Piaget's proposition that children below the age of seven or eight cannot make inferences of the type that if A is longer than B and B is longer than C, then A is longer than C. He does not question that young children generally fail and older ones generally succeed in such tasks; the question at issue is what interpretation should be put on this finding. Is it that children of this age are unable to make this kind of inference under any circumstances because of some cognitive deficiency connected with maturation? Or is it to do with the nature of their experiences in relation to the task? Piaget takes the former position; Bryant investigated the question by manipulating the children's experience prior to the presentation of the problem. He was thus taking an interventionist approach similar to that discussed earlier: the experimenter as teacher.

Whereas Piaget had presented children with the two examples of sticks of different length, A longer than B and B longer than C in two separate presentations, and then asked about the relations between A and C, Bryant introduced a teaching element. The children were taught, using rods of different lengths, that A is longer than B, B than C, C than D, and D than E. A variety of test questions were then given, including a crucial comparison of B with D. Even four-year-old children were able to cope with these test items.

Like the other work discussed above, this finding is of considerable interest to psychopedagogues. Evidence of this nature imputes to teaching a much more central role than is implied in Piaget's attitude that the job of pedagogy is to apply the findings of psychology to teaching. On the contrary, the intervention by teachers (or teacher-experimenters) actually influences psychology. It is *not* enough to take findings of experimental set-ups and *apply* them in teaching. Intervention by the teacher *changes* the set-up and introduces a crucial new factor. The only way in which information can be obtained about the nature of the influences

Thought, talk, action 97

exerted by the teacher's intervention is to carry out experiments 'in the field'. Instead of a one-way traffic from psychologist to teacher we would then have two-way traffic whereby the psychologist learns from the teacher as well as the teacher learning from the psychologist.

A critique by Fodor (1976) relates to theoretical aspects of the idea of stages of development and the role and nature of representation in children's thinking. He criticizes strongly the view of Bruner and Piaget on the role of imagery, and Bruner's notion of iconic representation in children's thinking. He accepts that children do, in fact, go through periods when they pay particular attention first to the manipulation of objects and then to their visual aspect. However, he makes the point that, though this may tell us something about what the children think *about*, it does not tell us anything about what they think with. In other words there is no evidence that, because children pay great attention to the visual, they are therefore *thinking* in images. He develops a lengthy argument that such thinking is impossible, but for our purposes it is perhaps enough to take that point and see it in relation to the experiments just described which could well be seen as lending some support to Fodor's thesis.

Fodor is also critical of Vigotsky's interpretation of the thinking behind the solving of the Vigotsky block problem. He argues that the test merely requires children to learn new names for concepts they already have: LAG means *tall and fat*. He also suggests that children are capable of considerably more complex activities than are involved in sorting the blocks; he instances the development of language and the ability to recognize faces, believing that this type of activity is of more concern than the type involved in solving problems with blocks. He further maintains that the 'lower' types of thinking – that is, complexive thinking – are found not only in children and primitive peoples but also in all of our thinking. This seems to me to be a useful comment on a complex question. Certainly, as Fodor remarks, there are other ways of theorizing about child development which do not accord with a stage theory such as Vigotsky seems to be arguing and which Piaget and his interpreters have so widely disseminated. He suggests that, rather than children progressing from level to level

98 *Psychopedagogy*

as Vigotsky and Piaget suggest, their development could well be uneven, reaching quite high levels of sophistication in some fields while remaining naïve in others. Piagetians very often warn us not to be too rigid in our acceptance of the developmental stages Piaget describes. But it is extremely likely that many people have derived a simplistic view of cognitive development from reading about stages of development that conceive of a situation where a child moves from one stage to another almost at the click of a switch. Whether Fodor is right or not, this mechanical interpretation cannot accord with reality and is extremely likely to lead any teacher of young children astray if she accepts it.

Fodor's other point is useful in that it draws our attention to the fact that the type of concepts studied by Vigotsky were only one of many types and that there are many more complicated concepts than those involved in the Vigotsky test. However, I think there may be more to the Vigotsky test than merely learning that LAG equals tall and fat. The person learning to group correctly may in fact do as Fodor argues and merely use one word where previously he would have used two. But, on the other hand, he learns the basis for grouping the blocks. That is, he learns the rule or principle of grouping and is in a position to use this rule to group other phenomena in the same way. This method of grouping is, of course, extremely unorthodox and would probably be of little use outside the experimental encounter. But the process followed by the children in learning this method of classifying is an interesting illustration of one way they learn to organize the perceptual world and construct rules to help them. Whatever the nature of the underlying process, language seems to help.

Pedagogical implications

It would be a bold act to try to spin out of the work reported in this chapter a thread to guide teachers through the labyrinth of learning which they enter and re-enter daily. As I have said before, it's not merely a question of applying received theory to practice. The theory itself is up for examination. But that doesn't imply that it is of no use. Messy though it is, there is some agreement about the general perspective at the descriptive level, even if there

Thought, talk, action 99

is considerable disagreement at a more fundamental analytical level.

Most experimenters would probably agree that younger children are much more likely to be dependent upon direct contact with phenomena in their attempts at reasoning than are adults, and that the visual aspects of things are likely to exert much greater influence on their learning. If this is not much removed from a commonsense truism, this may well be the way things are. However, the findings of investigations into the detail of children's attempts to grapple with problematic aspects of their environment are far from truisms. They reveal aspects of children's thinking that differ markedly from that of adults in certain fairly consistent ways. Knowledge of these differences will serve to alert a teacher to the likely mismatch between his way and the pupil's way of thinking about the same things.

The complexities revealed through investigations of children's use of language in connection with their thinking and their activity, and the influence of all three on their learning, should be sufficient to make the point that 'spraying with language' (referred to at the beginning of this chapter) is a grotesquely naïve view that will achieve nothing for the children or the teacher. Not that it is possible to give a neat prescription on how to make use of language in the classroom, but we can provide some likely pointers.

Perhaps a key point that emerges from the experiments reported is the importance of the experimenter's approach. The non-interventionist approach typified by Piaget is likely to produce one type of result, whereas different degrees of intervention such as those exemplified by Bryant or Hughes or Galperin will produce another. To some extent the crucial factor seems to be that the problems presented to children need to be set out in familiar terms, to ensure that the disjuncture between their everyday activities and the experimental problem is not unbridgeable. But it also seems that the fact that the type of concepts acquired before schooling differ from many of those taught in formal instruction is important. Going to school involves more than extending the range of the 'naïve' concepts learned earlier; it also involves new methods of thinking. This was the point of Galperin's

100 *Psychopedagogy*

procedure in his approach to teaching counting. It is also an ever-present issue when children begin to learn to read. They have to learn many quite arbitrary conventions that are part and parcel of the ways adults think, and teachers often do not understand the nature of children's problems. Indeed, they very often do not suspect there is a problem (see p. 168). It is most important not only to try to identify such problems but to help children cope with them. Galperin did this through the interesting procedure of 'counterpositioning', where the naïve concepts are deliberately juxtaposed to the 'artificial' ones based on adult conventions.

This deliberate wrenching of children's attention from the most obvious to the most important in a given situation is relevant in connection with the use one might make of visual material in teaching. While it may be useful to take account of children's predilection for the concrete or the visual at certain times, it would be counterproductive not to attempt to intervene. To advise teachers to use a lot of visual aids with younger children may not be the best thing to do if the aim is to develop their powers of reasoning. Fodor's point is very relevant here. We cannot tell anything about the nature of the thinking processes of children from the fact that they are prone to focus on the visual at certain stages. It is far from justified to believe that they think in pictures, as Bruner seems to suggest. Since we don't know, it is unwise to assume that they can think productively only if under the influence of the visual and therefore to present instructional material entirely or even predominantly in an iconic way. Teaching that makes use of language might well focus attention on different approaches and force the use of symbolling, such as seems to have happened in the experiments in which some element of instruction was introduced.

It is important to distinguish between the argument that young children's thinking operates at concrete levels or involves a high emphasis on imagery, and the process of ensuring satisfactory concept learning at whatever age by providing the learner with ample experience of realia when learning new concepts. The former asserts that young children actually think in relation to methods of representation that differ from those of adults, and the use of the concrete is justified mainly on that basis. In the

Thought, talk, action 101

case of concept learning by older learners the argument for the involvement of the learner with realia is to provide him with experience he lacks, so that he is placed in a position where he can abstract the criterial attributes of the concept and not merely the word that symbolizes it. Naturally, in cases where the learner has a good deal of experience of the phenomena to which the concept corresponds, be they concrete or abstract, this going back to the more concrete forms of experience will not be necessary. On the other hand, should a teacher attempt to introduce new concepts quite outside the experience of the learner without involving him in the elementary processes of contact with the things described by any language he uses, then he is likely to do no more than teach the sounds of the symbols – words without meaning which may enable a learner to parrot statements about the phenomena but which will, in the words of Vigotsky, cover a conceptual vacuum.

Thus while it is important to recognize that learners are likely to benefit from experience with the concrete in the early stages of learning – and this is particularly the case with young children – it is just as important to be looking ahead to the next stage and arranging experiences that make demands on the learner to move forward. In the experiments referred to, the common feature that moved the children on to more complex learning was the use of language by the experimenter/teacher and children in questioning and explaining at the same time as the children were grappling with the problem. This interaction between adult and child, which enables the child to cope with problems he cannot solve unaided, resembles what Vigotsky called the 'zone of potential development'. He argued that adults should teach 'to the child's tomorrow'. This perspective is one that makes use of our understanding of the present capabilities and modes of operation of learners but looks ahead to where they are going and arranges learning experiences to ensure that they actually do move ahead and not merely mark time. The teacher's involvement in the process of leading children into and through the zone of potential development is one where he affords considerable assistance at first and gradually tails off as the learner becomes more competent, eventually coping with the problem unaided.

102 *Psychopedagogy*

Work by Galperin (1957) provides a good example of the way systematic intervention by a teacher can help a learner to cope with tasks which are beyond his competence without guidance. He considers that mental actions (thinking or the development of cognitive schemas) are formed in five stages:

1 Creating a preliminary idea of the task
2 Mastering the action using objects
3 Mastering the action on the plane of audible speech
4 Transferring the action to the mental plane
5 Consolidating the mental action

In stage 1, two approaches are possible. In the first the teacher explains the operation to the child and then allows him to make himself familiar with it under the teacher's directions. In the second method the teacher carries out the operation while the child watches and 'helps' by prompting. Galperin found that the second method was superior to the first, a discovery that seemed to him surprising since the first method seems more active. It does, however, tie up with the work of Luria, who found that, at certain stages of learning, the task of acting and speaking – as in the pressing experiment – seemed to be too much for the child. Galperin suggests, in line with this view, that freeing the child from the concrete activity enables him to concentrate on the problem more effectively. Again, this is entirely consistent with aspects of the experiments reported above and the suggestions made in relation to them.

In stage 2 the child manipulates the material himself; the teacher guides, explains and corrects. The teacher's speech directs the child's activities to the manipulation of the material, singling out objects, the goals of the activity, and the methods of achieving the goals. At this stage the child is working things out in the concrete and not abstracting or working things out in his imagination.

At stage 3 the child has mastered the activity using objects. He now moves to the stage where he can *represent* the activity by audible speech, and can now explain or give an account of the way the activity is carried out. What was formerly a practical

Thought, talk, action 103

activity is now a theoretical one. It is still, however, reinforced by the child's own speech.

At stage 4 the child is encouraged to whisper to himself instead of speaking out loud. He is still using language. However, as the activity becomes more habitual it becomes more and more compressed and abbreviated.

At stage 5 the action is completely internalized. It is now extremely compressed and elliptical. The flow of speech of stage 2 has now become a flow of concepts, and the child has transformed what was initially a concrete object action into a mental pheno-menon. Galperin stresses that, if the pupil does go wrong and fails to learn, it is essential to return to an earlier stage and start again. Giving the child practice at the stage where he fails merely reinforces his error.

Galperin's approach brings together several aspects of the work discussed earlier in connection with the complex interactions of thinking, acting and speaking. The active involvement of the learner, and the systematic encouragement to make use of language to represent the concrete, and the guiding of the child along adult lines of thinking and working on problems all contribute to the more effective acquisition by the learner of methods of thinking appropriate to the autonomous solving of the problems. It cannot be denied, however, that this approach, like most approaches discussed in these chapters, demands that the teacher develop in children the modes of thinking current among the adult com-munity. To that extent they are therefore imposing their outlook on the learners. One answer to this charge is, perhaps, 'so what?' – since that has always been the way of the world. A more helpful comment might be that what the teacher is attempting to do is not to foist his view of things on the learner but to help him to learn and think more effectively in order that in the long run he may be better equipped to reflect on adult views and challenge them. It is more difficult to reply to the further charge that, by teaching them *how* to think, teachers teach learners *what* to think, since the one affects the other; for so little is known about the actual processes of thinking. Whether in language and thinking the medium really is the message is a matter for considerably more experimentation.

5
Teachers talk

To judge from the amount of time teachers talk, they do not doubt that the medium is the message. In fact language in some form or other tends to be the dominant feature of classroom life. In most classrooms, despite the trend towards less formal methods of organization, the teacher's speech is ubiquitous. Analyses of classroom activity suggest strongly that two-thirds of all such activity is likely to be taken up by talk, that two-thirds of the talk will be teacher-talk, and that two-thirds of the teacher-talk will be stereotypical teacher activities such as lecturing, giving directions, criticizing children or justifying the teacher's own activity (Flanders 1963). It is sometimes said, because of statistics like these, that teachers talk too much. This may well be the case, but we should recognize that such a statement embodies a point of view about what teaching should be like and what a teacher's role should be.

It is probable that in most cultures teachers are expected to be instructing children orally most of the time and would be considered to be shirking their duty if they were not. To the extent

Teachers talk 105

that such views are formed by influences extraneous to education or pedagogy, there is little to be said here that can affect them. However, I hope that a consideration of the uses and possible misuses of language in teaching will enable readers to make their own assessment of the possibly most useful uses of language in any teaching in which they may be involved.

In the light of the earlier discussion on the way in which language makes the transmission of culture possible and how it facilitates the learning of concepts, it is perhaps not surprising that the teacher's speech is so dominant a part of classroom activity. The argument was that, although interaction with other children and learning of a non-verbal nature is undoubtedly significant, verbal interaction with adults is of prime importance. This is not just because adults 'know more' than children, but also because they have acquired ways of thinking that are more attuned to the world we live in. It is not only that we learn to think about the world *as it is* in whatever society we live in, but that the way we think to a great extent makes the world *what it is*. Customs, beliefs, arts, social and economic organizations and architecture are just some examples of the things influenced by and influencing the way we think. Thus teachers attempting to induct children into their cultural heritage are teaching ways of thinking as well as 'subjects'. There is little doubt that the former is overwhelmingly the more important.

The teacher's talk is the main medium through which he is able to share his ways of thinking with his pupils. It is thus of some importance that his talk should embody thinking that is worth sharing. Analyses of classroom discourse often suggest that this is not universally the case – for a whole variety of reasons, but among them one must loom large, and that is that few of us ever reflect on the question or analyse our own speech when we are trying to teach. Even more rarely do we attempt to relate what we say and how we say it to concepts from psychology that might be relevant.

It is impossible to provide a comprehensive prescription for ways in which language can be used to enhance learning. Apart from the sheer complexity of actually *describing* the flow of speech and the processes involved in using printed materials, we are only

106 *Psychopedagogy*

just beginning to study the subject systematically. But we have some ideas based on experiment and investigation and although these ideas may not have the status of watertight theory they are guides to action; it is only by applying ideas to practice that we can hope to build up more robust theories.

Language and the guidance of learning

Even the simplest types of learning can be enhanced by the use of language. Conditioning, discrimination and imitative learning are all possible without language but may all be drastically affected by its use. Words of approbation or admonition serve as reinforcers or punishers, and as providers of feedback and knowledge of results. It should be noted, however, that even at this level the use of language to aid learning depends on the learner's having learned the conceptual significance of the words. Skinner could have said 'correct' to his pigeons until he was blue in the face without modifying their behaviour in the slightest. One comment of this kind to a child learning the same activity – for example, walking in a figure of eight – would almost certainly have considerable effect because the word would be meaningful to him and would thus act as an indicator of results and a reinforcer.

However, few teachers would be content to wait until a learner had executed the correct movement before taking a hand in the learning. Most would explain what was involved in the new learning. For example, in teaching a physical skill a description of the aimed-for behaviour would drastically curtail the learning time needed. Teaching a figure-of-eight movement in a country dance would in most cases be very simple and could be achieved rapidly merely by telling the learner to walk in a figure of eight. Providing a model by demonstration would probably speed up the learning and make it more precise. On the other hand, providing a model without using language would have no effect at all. One other thing needs to be considered. If the learner did not have the necessary prerequisite abilities, either motor or cognitive, the teaching would be fruitless. If the learner were a young child only just learning to walk, clearly he would have difficulty in coping. Similarly some learners might well be unclear about the

Teachers talk 107

meaning of 'figure of eight' and would thus be unable to take advantage of the description of the activity. In a case like this, it would be necessary to provide a model and pick out the key aspects of the movement by making oral comment, and this could well take longer. Final learning of the movement, however, could not be ensured without the learner's practising it. From his own practice he could obtain feedback and reinforcement from his teacher (again using language).

This is perhaps a very obvious description of the learning of a very simple skill. But it does exemplify some important aspects of all types of learning. Bruner's three types of representation are all involved. Taking the last-mentioned first: the actual carrying out of the movement involves enactive representation. The learner is beginning to 'remember in his muscles'; this is the value of practice. Iconic representation is involved in the teacher's providing a model, either by carrying out the movement himself or by using diagrams or films or other pictures. Symbolic representation occurs when the teacher uses language to structure the situation, to tell what the end result should be, to comment on the effectiveness of specific attempts and give overall feedback and reinforcement.

As may be seen from this relatively simple example, almost all human learning is likely to be a very complex amalgam of different processes, but pervading it all will probably be the influence of language. In most teaching, language is likely to be used to provide a preliminary idea of the task. It will then be used to suggest methods of tackling the job. It can be used to cue the learner as he is actually attempting the task. In the learning of motor skills language will probably be augmented by the use of models as suggested above, since imitation of movement can often take place quite rapidly, whereas a verbal prescription can be quite difficult to follow.

Another example may illustrate the process. A teacher teaching a child to use a file is unlikely to hand him the tool and tell him to get on with it. He will make quicker progress if he starts with some preliminary talk about the way to hold the file, the angle to adopt when using it on metal, the way to make the cutting stroke, and so on. Obviously the teacher will also be very likely to make

108 *Psychopedagogy*

use of modelling techniques for the child to imitate, and naturally a popular model is the teacher's own activity. While he is demonstrating he is likely to use language to draw attention to particular aspects of the skill. This is cueing. Merely to say 'Do like this' is unlikely to be effective even in this relatively simple skill. A child merely observing may well not observe the way the teacher keeps the file horizontal but a few words from the teacher will draw his attention to it. When the learner himself is first practising the skill the teacher's language again comes in to cue the learning. Strong cueing means, for example, that the teacher will tell the learner to keep the handle of the file lower or to make longer strokes, or give other explicit instructions. As the child improves it will suffice to cue much less, for instance, by comments such as 'Is the handle OK?'; later still it will probably be sufficient to make some quite general remark such as 'Are you holding it properly?' In addition, the teacher will be able to give feedback by commenting on the learner's work and drawing connections between his comments and the effects of the learner's activity. For example, he can draw the attention of the learner to the effects on the object being filed if the handle of the file is kept too low or too high. All these verbal activities by the teacher are designed to make the key elements in the learning more prominent or more important to the learner. I shall refer to this process as *increasing the salience* of different aspects of phenomena involved in learning. Eventually, through this process of structuring, cueing and selective feedback, the learner comes to identify for himself the important aspects of the skill and is able to monitor his own performance. It may well be that in some skills he will actually use his own language in the same way that the teacher used his to prompt and cue his activities at the key points as in Galperin's work discussed in Chapter 4. A polished performance eventually follows with practice, and at that stage the self-regulatory function of language (in its external form, at any rate) disappears and the learner really has remembered the skill 'in his muscles'.

Similar processes apply to the teaching of concepts and principles and of complex cognitive skills such as those involved in problem solving. But in addition to cueing, prompting, guiding and providing feedback, in cognitive learning language

Teachers talk 109

can actually establish the learning context. Statements about concepts and principles and bodies of higher-order cognitions actually supply the stimuli and the exemplification of the outcome desired. Modelling is unlikely to be much help in this type of learning since if any imitation takes place it is likely to be of a rote nature. Consider in contrast the learning of a skill such as hopping. An imitation of a skilful hopper here would be satisfactory to the extent to which it approximated to the performance of the model. In the case of the learning of a cognitive skill, copying the final performance may be possible without the learner really understanding what he is doing.

Books and lectures afford outstanding examples of language usage in cognitive learning. If effective, both start with their audience at one level of comprehension of a subject and end with them at a higher level of understanding. The writer attempting to teach is handicapped as compared with a face-to-face teacher, since he is not in a position to observe the student's learning and provide cues and feedback. He should, therefore, be much more alive to the need to establish a pedagogic structure that will carry his audience along without losing them in a fog of symbols with no conceptual significance for them. You will be a fortunate person if you have never had this experience. I only hope it has not happened in reading this book!

In fact this book may be taken as an illustration of the way in which language serves cognitive learning. For many readers it will introduce new concepts in a setting of familiar ones. Statements of concepts, principles, hypotheses, hunches, speculations from the field of pedagogy have been paraded before you, and attempts have been made to relate these to existing 'commonsense' knowledge in the hope that you will gain sufficient clarity about the subjects discussed to make a decision as to how, if at all, you are likely to find them of use in teaching. In all, well over 100,000 symbols will have passed before your eyes before you reach the end. It is true that many of them will appear time and time again. Nevertheless every new appearance is a new performance for the most modest symbol, if only because what has passed since its last appearance influences its current one. This vast network of symbols, whatever its merits, is a learning

110 *Psychopedagogy*

environment of enormous complexity, completely constructed from language.

But a book presents a relatively limited learning environment compared with the linguistic environment of many classrooms. Some classrooms, it is true, resemble books: one person declaims while the rest listen. Other classrooms allow the learner to talk back, some even encourage it. In some there is a completely free flow of talk from teacher to taught and among the pupils themselves. Not only is there declamation, but there is also cueing, questioning, opining, replying, conjecturing, concluding. All exist only through the medium of language in the form of teacher and pupil talk. The potential for human learning in this type of learning environment is barely understood at the moment and our attempts to analyse and describe the infinitely subtle transactions of the language of the classroom are very primitive. Yet they are a beginning and can give us some insight into the way in which this language can help or hinder the learning of those who use it, and this does not only apply to the pupils.

Lesson from life: 1

To give some flavour of the complexity of classroom discourse and an insight into some of the problems and possibilities inherent in its use, I should now like you to look briefly at one or two extracts from actual recorded lessons.[1] The first is taken from a lesson in which children of seven and eight are working from books giving exercises concerned with reading a thermometer. The teacher has just drawn the class to attention and takes up the 'thermometer business' because some children seem to have had difficulties with it. It is important to remember in reading the transcript that we are considering only the verbal part of what is happening in the classroom; no doubt a considerable amount

[1] All the 'lessons from life' are taken from actual recordings, many made using a radio microphone so that there was no observer in the room. Each contribution is numbered consecutively, the source being indicated by (T) for teacher and (P) for pupil contributions, i.e. any pupil. Occasionally different pupil contributions are indicated by numbers e.g. (P1), (P2).

Teachers talk 111

of important non-verbal activity is taking place too. It should also be borne in mind that the transcribed speech conveys hardly any of the affective side of language, since it is virtually impossible to put over any idea of the intonation of the speech which might signal quite clearly, for example, that what appears in a transcript as a question is in fact a fairly direct command.

1 (T) . . . this thermometer business is still getting some people stuck. . . . Now quite a lot of you are doing it or are going to be doing it soon, so let's go over it just once more so that everyone will be clear. Imagine that this is our thermometer, and there's the liquid inside it, it comes down there like that [drawing on board] . . . just the same as our themometer here . . . the red liquid inside showing us what the temperature is, and this thermometer is going to be just the same as ours because it isn't marked [marking on board] . . . for each one, it's got the little marks like that but it doesn't put what each one is, there isn't any room on a small thermometer, it just puts some numbers and then we have to guess or we have to work out the rest, so we start it off at ten. . . . Now what do each of these little marks stand for?

2 (P) Two.

3 (T) Two, yes, each mark means two . . . so that's ten, that's – what?

4 (P) Twelve.

5 (T) Twelve and that's – ?

6 (Ps) [All together] Fourteen . . . sixteen . . . eighteen . . . twenty . . . twenty-two . . . twenty-four . . . twenty-six . . . twenty-eight . . . thirty . . . thirty-two . . . thirty-four . . . thirty-six . . .

7 (T) And so we go right up the thermometer, counting in twos. . . . But where a lot of you seem to come unstuck is when it asks you to find the temperature from A to B. . . . We have to count up in twos, now remember

112 *Psychopedagogy*

> . . . we don't count A, we start on A, so if you count you can put your pencil on there, but you don't say two because we're starting there . . . so when you're counting, start on A, then count up, so from A to B will be?

8 (Ps) [Together] Two, four, six, eight, ten, twelve, fourteen.

9 (T) So, the difference in temperature from A to B is? . . . fourteen. What would it be from A to C? . . . Start on A, altogether . . .

10 (Ps) Two . . . four . . . six . . . eight . . . ten . . . twelve . . . fourteen . . . sixteen . . . eighteen . . . twenty . . . twenty-two . . . twenty-four.

11 (T) Twenty-four would be the difference in temperature. . . . And sometimes you're asked to find it the other way round . . . what's the difference in temperature or what is the fall in temperature because if it's come down it's dropped, hasn't it? . . . colder . . . so what would be the fall in temperature from C to B . . . see if we can do it, from C to B would be – ? . . . we start on C so that isn't two is it, it's – ?

12 (Ps) Two . . . four . . . six . . . eight . . . ten.

13 (T) So the fall in temperature or the drop in temperature would be ten. Would somebody like to tell me what the temperature is in our room at the moment, if they can read this thermometer?

14 (Ps) Miss! Miss! [Volunteering]

15 (T) Adrian . . . [pause] . . . what do you think it is?

16 (P) Erm . . . mmmmm . . . it's harder than I thought it was.

17 (T) It's harder than you thought it was. . . . Well, what's that say?

18 (P) Sixty.

19 (T) Sixty. So that's – ?

20 (P) Sixty-two, sixty-three, sixty-four.

Teachers talk 113

21 (T) Sixty? . . . one more up, isn't it? . . . sixty-two.

22 (P) Sixty-two, sixty-three.

23 (T) No, sixty-two, sixty – ?

24 (P) Four, sixty-six.

25 (T) Sixty-six, yes . . .

26 (T) . . . because we can see, there's sixty, just as we've done on our thermometer, and it's one, two, three marks above, so three marks above will make it six . . . so it's sixty-six in our classroom. You see if it gets right down here. . . . What does it say there, Vivian?

27 (P) Freezing.

28 (T) Freezing . . . that's when it gets down to thirty-two degrees freezing, we hope it's not that cold in our classroom.

29 (P) We'd be ice.

30 (T) You would be a solid block of ice [babble from the children] . . . might keep him quiet anyway. . . . Right, remember you are working at the back of your books because it's primary maths. . . . We haven't got very long before it's time for dancing so see how much work you can get done in the next few minutes.

31 (P) Shall I do that one there?

32 (T) Yes . . . can you put your head down and talk at the same time? Why are you talking then, Scott? Right now, we've just been over that, do you think you can get them right now . . . go and have a try. What have you been doing? . . . Is yours the thermometer too?

33 (P) Yes.

34 (T) . . . you go and have another try with those and see if you can get them right this time. . . . Adrian, do your own work. Never mind what Roger's doing. . . . Copying? . . . that's not work.

In a few pages I shall be describing various systematic approaches to the study of classroom language, but I think that even

114 *Psychopedagogy*

without such an approach you will probably find it quite instructive to look at parts of the transcript in order to identify particular types of pedagogic activities and try to form your own ideas about their value, despite the fact that it is merely a short and fairly simple extract of a lesson.

In the beginning of the extract you will observe the teacher attempting to provide a preliminary structure for the children's learning. She uses iconic representation, the drawing of the thermometer, in conjunction with symbolic representation, her speech. The two complement each other. The drawing short-cuts an explanation of what the thermometer looks like, and a word or two focuses the children's attention on the key aspects of the thermometer. Note in this first extract that the teacher gives complete explanations, and clearly she is referring to the drawing when she tries to get the children to see that the thermometer is marked in steps of two degrees. However, after the first few exchanges where the two-step is discussed fairly explicitly, she then tapers off her own contribution so that in the end she is providing more attenuated cues in the way I discussed earlier in the case of the skill of filing. Note the exchange with Adrian where the teacher has to shift back to more extensive cueing and then works forward again, reducing cueing once more.

It is almost certain that the teacher here was operating intuitively in the sense that she was not working out exactly how she was to decrease the level of cueing, and I think we could probably suggest ways of improving it as no doubt she could herself with the advantage of hindsight. The ability to operate like this, however, is not inborn and like any other skill needs practice and can be helped by examining the principles on which it is based.

An examination of teacher's contribution reveals a very different state of affairs. In the space of a minute or so the teacher makes at least seven verbal moves. She responds to a child's comment from a previous exchange. She comments on the response. She makes a series of managing moves (in the sense of classroom management). Her 'Right, remember you are working at the back of your books' is an order even though it is nicely wrapped up. 'Because it's primary maths' is a justification of her order, obviously referring back to earlier instructions. She refers

Teachers talk 115

ahead to the next lesson and uses its imminence in an attempt to spur on the children to greater efforts. For most of this time there is 'babble from the children'. A complex situation, indeed, and throughout the teacher is attempting to monitor classroom events of various types. Perhaps we might therefore forgive her glaring error when she says, 'You would be a solid block of ice'.

It is impossible now to say whether in fact she was conscious of this error and made a decision not to take up the question at that time, whether she did not notice it, or whether she did not know it was an error. Whatever the case might be she missed one of the very few chances afforded by the discourse of connecting learning to read the thermometer with the children's own experience, since most of them must have been in temperatures below freezing and lived to tell the tale. There is, of course, a greater problem. She may have laid the basis for confusion in some children's minds or provided evidence that what happens in school often has little relevance to real life.

Exchange 32 gives another example of the switching of activity and classroom monitoring. In this case the teacher is switching from child to child and from activity to activity. Her first 'Yes' answers one pupil's query; she then moves to different pupils with management moves, some of which although in the form of questions are basically commands: 'Lift your head up'; 'Stop talking'.

You may find it of interest to contemplate two other aspects of this specimen of classroom discourse. Compare the proportion of time taken by the teacher's talk with that taken by the children's talk. The proportions are not unusual, as I suggested when I referred to the two-thirds rule (see p. 104). What we should consider is whether this ratio of teacher to pupil talk is satisfactory for pupils' learning. If you accept the view expressed in Chapter 4 where it was suggested that discussion, explanation, argument and other verbal exchanges were important in fostering cognitive learning, you are almost bound to conclude that the transcribed extract was not very helpful. All the more so if you consider the fact that only a very few children were involved in individual exchanges with the teacher. The other aspect relating to the efficacy of the teacher's talk is the level of thinking demanded of

116 *Psychopedagogy*

the children through the verbal exchanges. While it is true that the teacher was here basically trying to teach a fairly simple skill, the question we might ask is whether she could have used the children's own talk more effectively. Note that in fact the teacher did virtually all the thinking. The bulk of her questions demanded one-word answers which needed very little cogitation. Moreover, the children seemed to answer most of the time *en masse*. Thus the teacher would have little chance either of gaining feedback about individual children's understanding or of guiding individual children's learning. The latter is, of course, an inevitable problem in all classrooms where one teacher is teaching large numbers of children. It is possible to individualize teaching, and something of this type was going on in this class: while the children were working on books with exercises or tasks of some sort, the teacher would be able to give individual guidance and make individual assessments when she saw specific children's work. It is possible that a method of getting the children to engage in more demanding activity would have been for them to discuss in groups the problem of making a scale when there is little space for the letters and then to make their recommendations to the class. Or the teacher could have led a class discussion on the question and sought ideas from the children individually. Possibly she could have provoked different kinds of solutions to the problem so that the class would have had to weigh one against the other, to compare and contrast, and then come to decisions about how to resolve the problem. This may have been more time-consuming than the method she did adopt, but there is every reason to think that the use of the children's language in this way would be more effective in bringing home to them problems of constructing scales.

The previous extract is a completely random one that I think can be taken as a typical snatch of classroom discourse. At times the teacher was undoubtedly helping the children to form concepts; at other times it is doubtful that she was being of much help, mainly because she was not making enough demands on their own thinking. In the next extract, this time taken from a secondary school by Barnes (1969), the problem is different but related to the pervasive task of building concepts. In this extract

Teachers talk 117

the teacher has used the phrase 'city states' in a history lesson and then pauses to define it. (The children are eleven-year-olds.)

> They were called 'city states' because they were complete in themselves. . . . They were governed by themselves . . . ruled by themselves . . . they supported themselves [short omission]. . . . These states were complete in themselves because the terrain between cities was so difficult that it was hard for them to communicate. . . . Now because their people lived like this in their own cities they tended to be intensely patriotic towards their own city. . . . Now what's 'patriotic' mean?

Barnes suggests that the main problem here lies in what is referred to as the linguistic 'register' the teacher is using. It is not so much that the teacher is using specialist words or jargon, but that the language used to explain the term 'city states' is beyond the grasp of the children, so that one unfamiliar phrase is being explained by a selection of other unfamiliar phrases. Here we have an example of an all too common phenomenon where language does not help concept formation and, indeed, may actually hinder it. The teacher has the concepts and the words and for much of the time seems to think that by relaying the words to the children he is thereby teaching the concepts. In this extract the teacher does not attempt to teach a definition of 'city state' but if he did with the type of language used in his explanation he could finish up teaching the children nothing more than to substitute one set of noises (meaningless words) for another. This is Vigotsky's conceptual vacuum.

There is a similarity between this extract and the first one and, indeed, both exemplify a ubiquitous problem in teaching: the question of the learner's capabilities prior to new learning. In the first extract the teacher backtracks when she realizes that Adrian is not quite at the stage where he can work out the temperature of the room. In effect this is an attempt to bridge the gap between Adrian's existing and inadequate understanding and the level of understanding necessary for learning the new skill. Of course, all teaching in theory demands a monitoring process that continuously takes account of prior competence. In the second extract the teacher takes a different and less useful tack. Clearly he is not

118 Psychopedagogy

too sensitive to the likely gap between his language and the comprehension of the pupils. He becomes aware in particular places, such as when he uses 'city states' and 'patriotism'; however, it would be difficult for this teacher to backtrack since the words he is using to try to explain the concepts need explanation that cannot be covered without considerable explanation themselves. The question this teacher needs to consider is whether he should return to a prior stage and teach the concepts necessary for an understanding of 'city state'. From the specimen of his language that we have considered, it seems that not only has he misjudged the prior competence of the children but also that he is not clear about the concepts that are subordinate to 'city state' but which are crucial to an understanding of 'city state'. He might have achieved a little more clarity had he undertaken some form of analysis of the concepts he wishes to teach, along the lines we shall discuss later (Chapter 9).

Mis-concept-ions

For my next example I turn to research removed somewhat from actual classroom transcripts but which takes further the examination of problems of children's concept formation and problems of teachers' misconceptions of children's understanding of concepts. The problem here is very similar to the one in the second extract and concerns teachers' use of words that mean different things to different people. As you may recall, in my earlier discussion of concept formation I made the point that, since concepts are formed by abstraction from experience, no two persons' concepts can be identical because it is quite impossible for those two people to have had the same experiences. This does not present a problem when the individuals' concepts are not too discrepant, but when they are very discrepant severe teaching and learning problems may arise. The great difficulty, of course, is that sometimes the learning problems will be abundantly clear to the learner and yet be unperceived by the teacher. Sometimes, of course, both teacher and learner may misapprehend and be mutually unaware of the fact that they are talking about different things but using the same words. Consider the learning of complex concepts by

Teachers talk 119

children and teachers. The teachers are adults; they have had extended schooling and have had some form of higher education; they are likely to have read fairly widely in various fields and particularly in their own specialism. The children are younger and have had much less schooling and none of the other experiences the teachers have had (although some will have had experiences their teachers are likely never to have). It is thus obvious that when the teacher discusses some particular field of study with his pupils there is likely to be considerable mismatch between what he means when he uses a word, what the children understand when he uses it and probably what they think he *means* when he uses it.

Take a concept that is commonly used in primary and secondary schools and may be encountered in all kinds of books from fairy stories to books on constitutional law: the concept of 'king'. Peel (1967) reports work which investigated the understanding of this and other concepts by a variety of people from nine years old to nineteen. Learners defined 'king' in various ways, and the definitions could be classified in four categories in ascending order of maturity such as:

1 The king lives in a castle far away.
2 A king is somebody very important and a king is very rich, a famous man out of a royal family.
3 A king is a ruler of the country.
4 A person who may rule his country by himself, may rule it in coordination with advisers or a government, may simply be a figurehead.

Another example, a 'committee', is defined variously as:

1 A place like the town hall could be a committee.
2 A committee is a group of people at a meeting place, is a thing that helps the school.
3 A committee is a party of men who talk and decide things.
4 The committee is the organizing body of a society or similar institution, elected from the members of the same by the members.

Clearly a teacher who was unaware of the different ideas held by

120 *Psychopedagogy*

different learners when he talked about these things would have very great difficulty in planning his teaching effectively.

Other examples to which we return later can be found in other fields of study. Scientific concepts are particularly prone to this kind of misunderstanding, since the words used to label the concepts are frequently words from everyday life. Fleshner (1963) instances severe problems in the learning of physics which in the case of the concept of weight, depending upon the learner's commonsense understanding of weight, led to quite unproductive learning: many children equated weight with measuring on a scale and thought that something too big to put on a scale would have no weight.

These various examples of the use of language in teaching and learning illustrate its two-edged nature. On the one hand a teacher can use language to highlight the key aspects of instances of concepts he is teaching, he can direct attention, he can cue, he can ask questions that help children to direct their thinking along fruitful lines, and he can use it to provide feedback and to assist the learner to solve problems. On the other hand there is the ever-present danger that language may erect invisible barriers between teacher and taught because words are elusive and mean different things to different people, sometimes meaning little or nothing to pupils inexperienced in particular fields of study or in the use of particular linguistic registers. Even when the barrier is breached, when you are convinced you are making real contact with the children and your version of the concepts you are teaching is not too discrepant with theirs, there may be problems. Are you sure that the questions you ask the children are really stimulating their thinking or can they be answered in rote fashion or with the minimum effort of remembering what you told them earlier? Are you sure that your feedback is as useful as it could be or is it so limited in scope and imprecise that they can acquire very little information through it? And if the feedback is designed to indicate that the learner is wrong, is it coloured with negative affect that might well put him off trying? Is what you say when trying to pick out the key aspects of concept exemplars unambiguous?

Any teacher who could answer this catechism and get full marks would be larger than life. But all teachers can benefit from knowing

Teachers talk 121

about these things. *Knowing* at the level of reading from a book may be some help but could suffer from some of the problems I have just been discussing in connection with pupils' learning. A deeper understanding of their use of language in their own teaching can be obtained by recording it and analysing it in ways similar to my analysis of lesson excerpts. The analysis of classroom discourse is being increasingly seen as a fruitful source of information about teaching. It has already shed light on some aspects of teaching and, although we obviously cannot expect it to cover everything in learning and teaching encounters, it is likely to play an increasingly important part in our understanding of the subject, in view of the dominance of language in human learning. At this stage, therefore, I should like to discuss some of the ways in which classroom discourse can be analysed, in the hope that you will thereby obtain greater insight into the pedagogical use of language.

6
Sorts of talk

Analysing discourse

At the moment there are in existence probably hundreds if not thousands of miles of audiotape with recordings of classroom discourse. Some of this has been used very purposefully and systematically by researchers analysing particular aspects of verbal interaction which bear directly on their specific interests. But there is undoubtedly much that has not been analysed because the recordists were unclear about the aims of their investigations and accumulated the tapes with little notion as to how to make best use of them. One of the probable reasons for this state of affairs is that it is possible to slice the classroom cake in several different ways according to one's particular concern. In the extracts I looked at above, my approach was determined by my interest in how different aspects of language usage relate to the ways in which children learn or do not learn, with a specific focus on ideas from the field of psychology. Others have approached the job with orientations from linguistics, from sociology, from

Sorts of talk 123

anthropology and from attempts to delineate job analyses for teachers. The most widely known of all systems of classroom analysis – that of Flanders – has been used by many investigators into classroom transactions; in addition hundreds of workers have produced their own systems based on Flanders's, but with modifications to suit their own purposes. There are, therefore, very many different ways of looking at classrooms. However, all of these ways exemplify the general idea of systematic analysis of classroom discourse. In view of the ideas I have been expounding about the learning of concepts, and bodies of concepts, you should not be surprised if I suggest to you that one of the best ways to build up meaningful ideas about the analysis of classroom transactions is to examine a variety of methods of doing this. I cannot present an exhaustive account here but there are several useful sources of information about the different methods (Simon and Boyer 1967; Stones and Morris 1972; Travers 1973). I shall, however, attempt to give you a preliminary idea by looking at one or two systems and considering their distinctive features.

Flanders's interaction category system

Inevitably I consider Flanders's interaction category system. It is the most widely known and widely used. It is sometimes criticized for doing things it shouldn't and not doing things it should. But these criticisms do not detract from the fact that it has had a seminal influence on the development of classroom studies. I therefore present a straightforward descriptive account of the system, consider some of the criticisms of it and give exemplifications of its use.

The Flanders system divides all talk that takes place in the classroom into ten categories. Seven are devoted to teacher talk, two to pupil talk and a tenth, described as 'silence or confusion', covers all other conditions. Teacher talk is divided into two main categories which are conceived of as exerting indirect or direct influence on the pupils. Pupil talk has the two categories of responding to the teacher and initiating talk. A summary statement about the categories is given in Figure 6.1. It can give only an imperfect outline of the system which is explained in detail in

124 *Psychopedagogy*

Figure 6.1 Flanders's Interaction Analysis Categories* (FIAC)

TEACHER TALK	Response	1 *Accepts feeling.* Accepts and clarifies an attitude or the feeling tone of a pupil in a non-threatening manner. Feelings may be positive or negative. Predicting and recalling feelings are included.
		2 *Praises or encourages.* Praises or encourages pupil action or behaviour. Jokes that release tension (but not at the expense of another individual), nodding head or saying 'Um hm?' or 'go on' are included.
		3 *Accepts or uses ideas of pupils.* Clarifying, building or developing ideas suggested by a pupil. Teacher extensions of pupil ideas are included but, as the teacher brings more of his own ideas into play, shift to category 5.
		4 *Asks questions.* Asking a question about content or procedure, based on teacher ideas, with the intent that a pupil will answer.
	Initiation	5 *Lecturing.* Giving facts or opinions about content or procedures; expressing *his own* ideas, giving *his own* explanation, or citing an authority other than a pupil.
		6 *Giving directions.* Directions, commands or orders to which a pupil is expected to comply.
		7 *Criticizing or justifying authority.* Statements intended to change pupil behaviour from non-acceptable to acceptable pattern; bawling someone out; stating why the teacher is doing what he is doing; extreme self-reference.

Sorts of talk 125

Figure 6.1 – continued

PUPIL TALK	Response	8 *Pupil talk – response.* Talk by pupils in response to teacher. Teacher initiates the contact or solicits pupil statement or structures the situation. Freedom to express own ideas is limited.
	Initiation	9 *Pupil talk – initiation.* Talk by pupils which they initiate. Expressing own ideas; initiating a new topic; freedom to develop opinions and a line of thought, like asking thoughtful questions; going beyond the existing structure.
SILENCE		10 *Silence or confusion.* Pauses, short periods of silence and periods of confusion in which communication cannot be understood by the observer.

* There is *no* scale implied by these numbers. Each number is classificatory; it designates a particular kind of communication event. To write these numbers down during observation is to enumerate, not to judge, a position on a scale.

(Extracted from Flanders (1970), p. 34.)

the handbook on the use of FIAC and in various other publications (see Stones and Morris 1972).

An observer using the Flanders system builds up a picture of a lesson by categorizing classroom talk in the ten classes. He does this by noting every three seconds what particular verbal activity is going on. The idea is that, although only part of the lesson is sampled, it is enough to be reasonably representative of the lesson as a whole. Different ways of arranging the data enable the observer to examine a lesson in several different ways after the record is made. One simple way is just to examine the categories sequentially on a time line (see p. 129). This approach reveals the kinds of activity that develop and die away as the lesson proceeds. Other methods enable one to detect patterns of verbal transactions

126 *Psychopedagogy*

that tend to recur or show cyclical tendencies. One obvious and interesting item of information that such a record can reveal is the proportion of teacher to pupil talk. It is largely the use of the Flanders system that has led to the suggestion of the two-thirds 'rule' referred to earlier (p. 104) – that teachers' talk regularly accounts for two-thirds of all classroom talk.

With a record of this type to work on, one can appraise the teacher's activity in the light of one's understanding of the psychology of learning and teaching. One would consider in this light that the first three categories would be important for enhancing motivation. One would think that categories 6 and 7 would not be very productive in building up concepts in children. Category 5 could be useful but perhaps limited in scope for increasing understanding. Category 4 could be extremely useful if the questions were of a type to make the pupils think and stimulate their own inquiry. The fact that the record does not indicate the nature of the questions falling under category 4 illustrates one of the weaknesses of the system for our purposes. Unless we know the kind of question, our ability to comment on the likely effectiveness of the teacher's activity involving questioning is limited. Nevertheless, any teacher who has not examined his classroom activity in this way will find considerable enlightenment by going through the experience.

To give you a flavour of a Flanders-type analysis of classroom discourse, here are two very short extracts from different types of lesson. I have coded them by using the Flanders categories after each statement made by pupil or teacher. The first extract is taken from an art lesson with nine-year-old children. Numbering is as in lesson 1.

LESSON FROM LIFE: 2

1	(P)	Sir, I can't draw my horse on the paper.	9
2	(T)	Well, just do an outline, I can't draw it for you . . . if you feel you might spoil the painting don't do it . . . think of some way out of it.	6
		The background is so good I'd hate you to spoil it.	2
3	(P)	I'm not going to do a horse because I can't draw one.	9

Sorts of talk 127

4 (T) All right.   1

5 (P) Sir, I can't draw horses.   9

6 (T) Well leave it out altogether.   6
      Most of them are leaving the horses out because
      they can't draw them. Not many people can draw
      them.   1

7 (P) A highwayman . . . I couldn't do it.   9

8 (T) Well draw another part of the poem you see so that
      you can leave the horse out.
      [Noise and interference in the recording.]   10

9 (T) That's – erm – that's very nice, Tina. The – I like
      the man, the back view of the horse.   2
      But it wants something there . . . some bushes here
      or something like that.   6

10 (P) [Inaudible question.]   9

11 (T) Yes, would you go and find it? It's in that book
       called *Discovering Poetry*.   6

12 (P) Sir . . . sir . . . [general babble].   9/10

13 (T) Well it's so nice, Diane,   2
       it's a shame to rush and finish it when adding some-
       thing to it could make it even better. Don't you
       agree?   6

14 (P) Sir, is that enough?   9

15 (T) I think it is enough in that case; actually I think
       you might even spoil it if you tried to do more.   3
       I love the horse and the rider.   2

The second extract comes from a lesson with eleven- to thirteen-
year-old children.

LESSON FROM LIFE: 3

1 (T) We're going to have a lesson about the towns
      which grew up around the new cotton factories.
      Factories that had come up and new machines . . .
      the cotton industry [writes on board] such as
      Cartwright and . . .   5
      who was the final one?   4

128 *Psychopedagogy*

C'mon, for goodness sake. What's the matter with you all? 7

2 (T) Let's go back then to people going to the factories. So you've got thousands of people flocking to the areas of Manchester in the nineteenth century, the first half of the nineteenth century, all looking for work. Well, in the first place then, when you've got all those people you need somewhere to house them all, don't you? 5
Well, what kind of houses did they throw up in a hurry? 4

3 (P) Back-to-back houses. 8

4 (T) Yes, back-to-back houses. 3

5 (T) Now let's see then, whereabouts were the problems then? I've got a model here to show you some of the – erm – conditions in the factories, sorry, showing some of the . . . way these houses were built to give you an idea of some of the conditions made through these types of houses – the bad conditions. Here then is the – erm – house. 5

6 (T) Now what's the first thing you'd say looking at those? 4

7 (P) They've got no back yard. 8

8 (T) They've got no back yard. 3

9 (P) They're not – erm – very well spaced out. 8

10 (T) No. 3

11 (T) What else? 4

12 (P) They'd throw their rubbish out into the streets. 8

13 (T) Yes, in many instances they did, 3
but don't take your mind back to the Tudor days, you know they did have bins of a type – fixed to the wall and they put their rubbish into this area – a great big – erm – bin in a wall and it was called a midden [writes 'midden' on blackboard]. 5

14 (T) So into this midden they throw all their rubbish. 5

15 (T) What would that cause? 4

16 (T) It was open, remember. 5/4?

17 (P) Pollution. 8

Sorts of talk 129

18	(T)	Pollution? I don't think so.	5
19	(T)	Richard?	4
20	(P)	Rats.	8
21	(T)	Rats, yes.	3
22	(T)	What else?	4
23	(P)	Miss, smell.	8
24	(T)	Smell, yes.	3
25	(P)	Diseases	8
26	(T)	Diseases. Yes.	3
27	(T)	Now these houses, then, were very close together.	5
28	(T)	Now what else d'ye think would be caused, then, by these houses being so close together?	4
29	(P)	If anyone had a disease it would spread to everyone else.	8
30	(T)	Yes, it would.	3
31	(T)	D'ye think they spent a long time building them?	4
32	(P)	No, no.	8
33	(T)	No, they didn't take long building them.	3

ANALYSIS

Setting out the categories observed in a simple linear sequence like the time line I referred to earlier gives an easily scanned picture of the pattern of the lesson and provides very clear hints to the user about the nature of the interaction. In the sequences I give now I have merely taken the codings from the two 'lessons from life' and printed them in sequence. I have introduced one additional factor: I have grouped the codings in units of what seem to me to be identifiably discrete exchanges in an attempt to highlight the various pedagogical moves.

Lesson from life: 2
9 6 2   9 1   9 6 1   9 6 10   2 6   9 6   9 2 6   9 3 2

Lesson from life: 3
5 4 7   5 4 8 3   5 4 8 3 8 3   4 8 3   5 5 4 5 8
5 4 8 3   4 8 3   8 3   5 4 8 3   4 8 3

130 *Psychopedagogy*

Extracts like these give rise to a large number of very complex questions. I have no doubt that some expert categorizers would challenge some of my codings. But this is not important. I am not attempting to teach you to categorize Flanders-fashion. But if you are interested it is possible to learn to do this with reasonable accuracy and speed after a few hours' training. Of course, that skill is vastly different from my analysis which examined each separate utterance using a transcript. For our purposes I should like to examine some aspects of the transcripts in the light of some of the ideas I have been discussing.

Almost certainly the first thing to strike you will be the difference between the two lessons. To a great extent this must be attributable to the different subjects being taught. In the art lesson the children are drawing and painting a scene from a poem. Their comments tend to be spontaneous and seem to resemble very much the verbalizing I discussed earlier when referring to the work of Luria and Vigotsky on self-regulation. Note, for example, 3 (P) and 7 (P). Both are remarked on by the teacher but both are very much related to the pupil's decisions about his own activity. The striking thing about this lesson, however, is probably the very supportive and accepting atmosphere recorded by the relatively large proportion of teacher utterances in categories 1 and 2 which I suspect is largely responsible for fostering the climate of spontaneity evidenced by the large number of pupil utterances in category 9. Inspection of one extract cannot prove this connection, of course, but it chimes well with current views on the role of encouragement in learning.

This lesson is a useful example of what Flanders calls 'indirect teaching'. The teacher responds and encourages rather than lecturing and ordering. The second extract exemplifies a 'direct' lesson which gives evidence of the two-thirds rule I mentioned earlier. In this case the teacher's utterances exceed two-thirds of the total (24/34) and if the length of time were computed the teacher talk would exceed this considerably. Here we observe a fairly typical lecture-type lesson. Note the preponderance of utterances in categories 5, 4, 8 and 3.

The teacher in this lesson has a very difficult job, probably more difficult than she imagined. To convey to pupils what life

Sorts of talk 131

was like in the period she was discussing would need more than words since it is most unlikely that the children would have had much personal experience that was directly relevant to the subject of the lesson. In fact she attempted to do something about th s by using a model, which seems to have been of some help since the children were able to identify some of the important aspects of industrial housing of the period. However, if you consider this brief extract in the light of our discussion of concept learning, you will note several important things. The most important point, of course, is that despite the use of the model the teacher presents a very limited array of exemplars of the concept. The model is only one surrogate exemplar. True, the only real exemplar would be a row of back-to-back housing of the period but probably the teacher could have presented other aspects of the concept through the use of a variety of pictures, contemporary accounts from literature and perhaps newspapers or even official reports. As it is, it is unlikely that the children gained much of a picture of housing of the period from the exchanges recorded in the lesson.

Category 4 in the Flanders scheme records questions. Many people have been dissatisfied with this aspect of the system since there is such a wide variety of questions. Recall the account of the twenty-questions game discussed earlier (p. 91). Although the pupils in this extract are giving answers and not asking questions, they could well be thinking at much the same level and doing little else but guessing. The questions asked by the teacher are responsible for this state of affairs. Most are of the type commonly known as 'closed questions' – that is, they almost inevitably invite very short answers that close the exchange between teacher and pupil. There is no cause and often no opportunity to take the matter further. If you examine some of the answers in this extract you may agree with me that they could well be closely akin to guesses. Note how the children dredge up memories of other history lessons that had dealt with housing conditions, so that Tudor housing and early nineteenth-century conditions begin to merge – sufficiently so for the answers given to be more or less equally applicable to either era.

The exchange illustrates very well the potential of classroom

132 *Psychopedagogy*

language. Here is a situation where housing conditions from different ages could have been juxtaposed in order to enhance the children's understanding of both by enlarging their higher-order concepts of the relationships between housing and social and economic conditions. But unless there already existed con-concepts based on a considerable amount of direct experience of non-verbal exemplars, there is a great danger that the children might learn only new connections between words and not enlarge their conceptual understanding at all. The nature of the children's answers in this extract suggests that this is the case here.

You might like to consider the nature of the teacher's questions from other points of view. Note the nature of the question in 6 (T). This is a completely open question and virtually any answer must be 'right', even if it is completely trivial from the teacher's point of view. However, this could be a valuable question and could help to bring the pupils' attention to bear on the problem. But note the follow-up after the first question: 8 (T) and 10 (T) accept but merely repeat the children's answers and then the dialogue is taken further in 11 (T). This question, however, invites another short answer, and there is no probing to disturb the children's existing concepts in such a way as to enlarge them to take in new elements. All that happens is that the pupils come up with answers from their existing repertoire, and very little progress is made.

Note one other of the teacher's utterances connected with questioning: 16 (T) is coded 5/4? to illustrate my difficulty in deciding quite how to classify it. In the light of our earlier discussion (pp. 107–8), you should recognize it as a cue. The fact that it does not have a specific category in the Flanders system illustrates the difficulty different people with different interests in classroom transactions have when they come to use other people's systems. I should, indeed, be very surprised if, when you have studied various systems of classroom interaction analysis, you didn't feel that you would like to introduce your own modifications if you had a particular interest in mind. Thus, although I do not think that this is the place to go into great detail about the various approaches to the analysis of classroom events, I think it likely to be useful to consider some of them briefly and to look

Sorts of talk 133

at some of the reasons why the Flanders-type approach is considered to be unsatisfactory by some people.

Problems of inference

One criticism of the Flanders system is exemplified by the work of Hilsum and Cane (1971), who were interested in recording what teachers did during the course of their working day. They wished to categorize the teachers' activities but rejected approaches such as FIAC since they considered they involved the person doing the coding in *evaluating* the teachers' activities in order to make a classification. For example, they ask – in the case of FIAC category 6 (giving directions: directions, commands or orders to which a pupil is expected to comply) – how the observer knows what the teacher is expecting. In their own system they attempted to avoid inference.

In fact, this is easier said than done. There is evidence that, even in the recording of activities that demand little or no inference such as 'teacher scratches nose', agreement among observers is not automatic, and usually they have to be trained before they are likely to agree on the actual category of the activity observed. But even when you get agreement among observers it seems quite legitimate to ask if this is any more objective in the sense that it 'really' happened like that. For example, in one investigation (Bjorstedt 1968) all the observers had to do was record which part of the classroom the teacher was in. They found a good deal of disagreement about this. Clearly the subject is extremely complex and cannot be considered in any great detail here. I suggest that the best thing for us to do is, while recognizing that any method of analysis in our present state of knowledge can only be very imperfect, to select the method of slicing up classroom discourse most appropriate to our specific purposes at any one time. In the case of a teacher wishing to gain insight into his own teaching, the Flanders system is a useful starting place, but if he wishes to examine his discourse in more detail he would probably wish to make use of a system such as that of Bellack.

Bellack's system is more complex than that of Flanders. It

134 *Psychopedagogy*

demands that the classroom talk be transcribed because each utterance is analysed in several different ways. In the case of a teacher wishing to use this system, it would mean making a recording on a cassette recorder and then writing out the talk while playing back. This is a bit of a chore but small samples of discourse from a few lessons could be quite sufficient to give a good idea of teaching style. Once having made these transcripts, it is possible, of course, to analyse them in a large variety of ways.

The Bellack system is akin to the method I used earlier to look at specimens of discourse. The focus is on the pedagogical significance of the verbal interaction between pupil and teacher. Bellack considers that each utterance has a number of important functions. For example, an utterance could launch a new topic, ask a question or reply to a question at the same time as making reference to the substance of the topic under consideration and involve the interactors in activities at different levels of complexity. To take an example from the last extract, 14 (T), the following aspects would be coded: the fact that the *teacher* is the speaker; the fact that he *structures* the learning situation; the fact that the statement refers to the *problem of refuse disposal* (the substance of the lesson); the fact that the teacher is *stating a fact*. The latter point in this case covers more than one element in the Bellack analysis concerned with different aspects of the instructional function of the utterance. As you can see, the process is complex and more of a research instrument than an easy-to-use indicator of one's own classroom talk. Nevertheless, I hope it serves as one more different exemplar of the general idea of classroom-talk analysis which may suggest some ideas for examining specimens of classroom discourse and thereby shed a little light on the relationship between classroom action and psychological theory.

A linguistic view

Although there are many other approaches to the analysis of classroom talk, I propose to consider only one more here, but one that differs from most others because it focuses particularly on

Sorts of talk 135

the linguistic aspect of talk. It is therefore not central to our discussion of psychopedagogy but makes some interesting points that bear on the other systems and provides a different perspective from which to view them.

The linguistic analysis of Sinclair *et al.* (1972) found the Flanders approach wanting on several counts. Probably the most important was the fact that Flanders took an arbitrary time unit – three-second intervals – as an arbiter of when to make a coding of discourse. They argue that this inevitably leads to the over-looking of valuable and naturally occurring units or sets of related units of discourse. Indeed the three-second-interval method may actually conceal these important linguistic units. They also point out that categories 1, 2 and 3 are all ways in which a teacher may react to a pupil's answer and are all likely to follow a pupil answer that itself will be evoked by a teacher question. Coulthard argues that the two-thirds rule almost automatically follows from this type of analysis and the common classroom convention of teacher asks question, pupil replies, teacher comments. The teacher gets his oar in twice for every once a pupil says something.

The kind of analysis these writers carry out may be exemplified by an examination of the passage on social history discussed earlier (Lesson from life: 3). Referring back to 1 (T) in that extract, the teacher's talk is categorized in several different units. In fact the statement reproduced was preceded by the teacher saying 'So'. This was fulfilling the function of drawing the children to attention and is classified as a 'marker'. Common markers are 'Right', 'OK', 'Well'. The first sentence of the piece reproduced is then coded as a 'metastatement' – a statement designed to help the pupils understand the purpose of the lesson. The sentence that follows is classified 'informative', since its sole function is to give information. The next one is regarded as an 'aside'. The question is coded as an 'elicitation', the function of which is to elicit a linguistic response. The final sentence in 1 (T) is coded as a 'prompt': the teacher is here almost demanding that the children answer. Note the difference between this 'prompt' and the utterances I have classified as cues where the teacher gives the learner some help in order for him to be able to make a particular response. I point this out since sometimes the two

136 *Psychopedagogy*

words are used interchangeably and it is important to be clear about the precise use in a given context.

This brief example of a linguistic approach to the analysis of classroom discourse covers about a third of the categories used by Sinclair *et al.* As you can see, the orientation is perhaps less relevant to a person with mainly pedagogical interests; however, an examination of classroom talk using a system like this can reveal patterns of classroom activity with important implications for the conduct of lessons. Imagine, for example, a lesson in which the teacher uses markers excessively. He would almost certainly be unaware of this without a transcript of his lesson. We could predict that excessive use would make his markers more or less ineffective but it is likely that he would not understand why he was not getting the pupils' attention. Examination of a recording or transcript using a system such as this in the light of some understanding of habituation in the psychological sense would help him to an understanding of the problem and point to a solution (see p. 25) He could not attain the same kind of insight from a Flanders-type analysis.

Unstructured approaches

There is a school of thought that has little time for any approaches of the type I have been considering. They argue that any attempt to analyse classroom events according to a preconceived model such as a Flanders scheme is to look at the classroom with blinkers on. They argue that you should go in and observe and tell it like it is: in other words, not to have preconceived ideas of what you are going to see, but to go and look and record what you see and make sense of it when you have finished. An observer using such an approach would take to the classroom with a blank notebook and not a prepreared schedule such as that of Flanders. Such an observer, according to a recent description (Delamont 1975), is interested in the participants' intentions and feelings as well as what they do. Thus, when she is sitting there with her notebook, she is 'probing, sifting speech for implicit meanings, and *deciding what to record and what to ignore*' (p. 15; my italics). There seems to me to be a curious naïvety about this statement, which suggests

Sorts of talk 137

that there can be such a thing as an observer with no preconceptions to colour her approach and to make her decide what she is going to deem important. It is also interesting to speculate whether, after sitting in a large number of lessons, such an observer would not come to expect certain activities to be thought important and expect to observe and record them in the next classroom she visited. In other words, I rather think that the participant observer is likely to carry a systematic schedule around in her head instead of on a clipboard.

Pedagogical implications

So what can these various schemes offer a beginning teacher who is curious about how ideas from psychology can help him? I suggest that a recording of his own teaching could be listened to or read in transcript similarly to the way I examined transcripts earlier: that is, not necessarily to check every three seconds but to look at every exchange between teacher and pupils. In the first instance this could be done without any particular system in mind but seeing the classroom activities in the light of psychological theories. He might look for uses of reinforcement or feedback or moves intended to build concepts. He might then look at the lesson through the eyes of Bellack or Flanders to shed a different light on it. With a little study of the various systems and the preparation of a few transcripts from different types of lessons he could well attempt an analysis using concepts from a variety of approaches in the way I have done with small excerpts from transcriptions.

Such analyses will not automatically make a better teacher. But they will give some idea about one's own performance that will alert one to possible action to take. In other words, the teacher will be getting feedback and, in view of earlier arguments about the importance of feedback in learning, this kind of information should be of considerable use in learning to teach. Of course teachers do get feedback without analyses of this type. Every time a teacher makes a move in the classroom, he is likely to be observing pupils' reactions and thereby acquiring knowledge of results. It is not easy, however, in the complex and rapidly

138 *Psychopedagogy*

changing conditions of the classroom to note all the reactions of the pupils, and it is even more difficult to assess their significance accurately. A record of some sort provides the opportunity to reflect on what happened and the chance to meet similar situations in future with a little more insight and the expectation of greater success in doing what was intended.

It is not possible to offer a prescription saying do this or that in this way or that way and your teaching will improve. The greatest problem here is the fact that there is by no means universal agreement about what good teaching comprises. I am taking the view, however, that we want above all for the children to learn something and that the aim of teaching is to help them do so. By 'learn something' I do not mean just 'facts', but to learn to think things out for themselves, to learn to be involved in learning, to be curious about the world and want to do something about it, to respect other peoples' points of view but, while being concerned for others, to be able and eager to argue a case. In other words, we are interested in their affective as well as their cognitive learning.

If you take this view of any teaching you may be involved in, you are likely to be interested in doing what you can to help children develop these qualities. On the affective side, it is clear that if you want to enhance motivation and involvement you need to encourage children and give them the opportunity to partici- pate. A recording of a lesson or part of a lesson will soon reveal whether in fact you encouraged the children as much as you thought you did, or whether you gave them opportunity to participate if you had in fact encouraged them. The chances are very high that you will not have encouraged them as much as you thought you had and that you allowed them much less oppor- tunity to participate than you had intended. Next time you will try to do more.

On the cognitive side, you will be particularly interested in the way you tackled the problem of teaching concepts. In the light of earlier discussions you will be looking for such things as the way you presented exemplars, the medium of presentation, the way you gave feedback to the children, and so on. All this information can be compared with your understanding of concept formation,

Sorts of talk 139

and again you can take corrective action next time. In this type of analysis you will also be looking not only for the number of questions you asked (as would be revealed from a Flanders-type analysis) but also the kind of questions asked. You may also be interested in the way you cued the children's learning. Did you just 'prompt' them with a 'Come on then', or did you help by some phrase such as 'Remember it was before the railways were built'? And if you did cue, were your cues appropriate, helpful and graded suitably? Clearly there are very many ways of using records of this kind, but in all cases you would be trying to modify your own teaching activity in the light of feedback from previous efforts and your understanding of factors influencing children's learning.

The kind of feedback I have been discussing is fairly specific. That is, it refers to the way one sets about teaching concepts and is concerned with such things as the type and number of questions asked. I have suggested that you can get this type of feedback from your lessons by making your own recordings and analysing them afterwards. There is no reason, however, why you should not enlist the aid of a colleague or, in the case of a student teacher, of his teaching-practice supervisor. Other people's comments on specific aspects of your teaching will provide the additional benefit of alternative perceptions of your teaching strategies and tactics. This suggestion does not preclude the use of other systems nor, indeed, the obtaining of a general overall assessment; but prior discussion with the person appraising the teaching about the things you are interested in would ensure that you would be more likely to get the feedback you felt was particularly needed at a given time. It might also be interesting to check your mutual perceptions of the lesson observed with a recording!

Non-verbal effects

Although I have been at pains to point out the crucial nature of language in human learning and in teaching, I do not wish to underestimate the importance of communication in the classroom by non-verbal means (Blyth 1976). Non-verbal communication may be silent, as exemplified by facial expression, or paraverbal,

140 *Psychopedagogy*

as exemplified by the inflexion of voice given to words that can make the one word mean several different things. For example, the word 'yes' can be made to serve as the answer to a question or as a question merely by changing the intonation of the voice. Other paraverbal communication may be by such means as sighs, grunts of agreement or of encouragement, usually transcribed as 'Uh uh'.

Silent behaviour that makes a significant contribution to class-room discourse includes signals between members of the group, usually between the teacher and one or more pupils, which sustain the spoken interaction. A teacher will signal to a pupil who is answering a question or making an explanation that he is attend-ing, possibly agreeing with what he is saying and probably encouraging him, by such actions as nodding or smiling. A pupil will indicate to the teacher that he is following an explanation in much the same way. In spoken interactions the speaker needs feedback to let him know that his hearer is in fact listening and following him. He will receive evidence of this from the amount and type of eye contact (Argyle 1969). A teacher's raised eyebrow might well be enough to stop a pupil in the middle of an explana-tion or possibly to make him desist from some activity of which the teacher does not approve. Smiling, frowning, nodding and raising a finger to the lips are all actions of great importance in the interaction between a teacher and the class as a whole. Problems may arise if the non-verbal signals a teacher gives out are in conflict with his verbal ones. Encouraging pupils verbally while at the same time holding up a hand like a policeman stopping traffic is likely to create confusion at the least. Such conflict of signals should be avoided.

The effects of non-verbal aspects of teaching, then, are impor-tant adjuncts to the teacher's use of language. Without them, teaching would be infinitely more difficult, and, when the verbal and the non-verbal messages are in conflict, learning suffers. But while the non-verbal elements are probably crucial, it is the lan-guage of the classroom that nurtures learning. Even when there is silence in the classroom it is almost inevitable that the pupils and the teacher will be using language in some way or other through reading or writing. But although this is activity in which pupils

Sorts of talk 141

are actively engaged in their own learning, the instrument that has structured the learning conditions, established the conceptual setting, and provided cues, links with other learning and guidance for their individual activity is the language of the teacher.

7
Objectives for teaching

Do you know where you're going?

When you read through the lesson transcripts in the earlier chapters I hope you gained some enlightenment about what was going on in the classroom from your reading of the discussion on human learning and teaching. This was the object of the exercise. But although we might be able to get a lot from a thorough analytical examination of a lesson transcript, I think we would get much more had we been informed exactly what the teacher had in mind before he started the lesson. If we had had this information I should have been able to add a further dimension to the examination of the elements of the transcripts. I should have been able to comment on the extent to which the teacher's actions were likely to have helped him achieve his aim. Not having this information I am completely unable to say whether or not what the teacher did at any one point was likely to have been helpful or not. I suggest that our reading of a lesson transcript not knowing the teacher's aims is a similar situation to a teacher

Objectives for teaching 143

teaching with no clear idea of what he is aiming to do. Naturally this statement must be interpreted with common sense. I am not arguing that every tiny action is pre-planned and catered for, but that the overall rationale of the lesson and its key moves are decided beforehand.

One can make decisions about aims beforehand and then work out the details of how to set about achieving them without any reference at all to theory, or one can attempt to base one's actions on some theoretical rationale. It is also possible to operate with different types of theroretical rationale ranging from very general ideas to ideas concerned with highly specific and quite small-scale aims. I believe that the working out of aims at different levels of generality and attempting to work towards these in practical classroom action should be an important concern of pedagogy. My hope is that this approach will facilitate the application to teaching of ideas about human learning and thus enhance both learning and teaching.

Theory and practice

It is probably impossible to operate completely without some hypotheses in mind. Even the most committed practical man does things in this way or that because he thinks doing things this way or that is likely to achieve his desired result. His thinking is obviously a hypothesis. It seems to me preferable to recognize this fact and try to examine the theories or hypotheses upon which our action is based so that we can examine their characteristics, come to understand them better and attempt to improve on them.

This process, it seems to me, is the heart of the matter. It is the way we are likely to improve our teaching, each one of us, but it is also a very close description of the way in which theory can develop. Instead of thinking that theory is something 'out there' in training institutions and that practice is what happens in schools, the two are brought together. Instead of teachers standing apart from theory, they become essential for its development. This follows from the conception of a teacher as a person with a shrewd idea of where he wants to go, a notion of how he hopes to get there and a commitment to checking whether he got where he

144 *Psychopedagogy*

wanted to go and trying to decide what factors led to his arriving where he did. This conception sees the teacher as theorist and practitioner in one. His 'theory' is the body of ideas he brings to the planning of the lesson and its subsequent appraisal, and the practice is what he actually does when teaching. Where a mismatch occurs between intentions and outcomes, he will scrutinize theory and practice to see where adjustment seems to be necessary. Of course he will also continue in his activity if no mismatch occurs. Thus in the process of improving his teaching he is *proving* (in the sense of testing) any theoretical principles he may be using. The proof of the theory is in the teaching.

Unless all teachers have completely different hypotheses about what they are doing when they teach, their collective experiences will have some important common features. It is these common features that hold promise of contributions to a body of general theory. But at the same time we should not forget that teachers take into their planning and teaching ideas from various fields including psychology, ideas which influence theory considerably and can in turn be tried out in practice. We thus have a dialectical relationship between theory and practice, each refining the other. The teacher who adapts his teaching in the light of his appraisal of his success in attaining his goals makes a contribution to theory; the psychologist who develops theoretical insights related to the classroom makes a contribution to practice.

It would be naïve to imagine that what I have just described is widespread practice. Few practitioners or theorists, so far, consciously organize their work with this sort of perspective. Nevertheless developments are taking place, and in my view one of the growth points is likely to be where attempts are made to work out the aims of teaching with some precision and then, on the basis of this analysis, to develop teaching activities to achieve them. I should now like to consider ways of doing this and to give some examples from different fields of teaching in the hope that you will be given some insight into approaches that have been found fruitful by other workers and be able to appraise their value for your own work.

Objectives for teaching 145

Getting things clear

So far I have used the word 'aims' when I have been talking about the problem of knowing where you are going, pedagogically speaking. I used this word because it is in common parlance and because it conveys in very general terms the gist of my argument. But the word 'aims' tends to be used more generally about education rather than about teaching, and aims are often of a very global nature. On the other hand, aims in teaching tend to be more specific and often concerned with only one lesson. In order to distinguish between the very general and the more specific aims, the word 'objectives' is commonly used when referring to the latter. The two are related, however, and in the following pages I try to show the way in which they are related and the way objectives relate to actual classroom activity.

One of the problems facing anyone who looks at objectives as they are often expressed is that they are stated in such vague and general terms that they are virtually devoid of meaning. An example from a college prospectus will give the flavour. One of the aims of the course is 'to provide each student with the opportunity to extend his creative potential to the full'. Who is going to argue with a statement like this? But who knows what it means? I have little doubt that we are all in favour of extending people's creative potential, as we are all against sin. But one man's vice is another man's virtue. And like as not one man's creativity is another man's conformity. And you might ask yourself how you are ever going to know whether you have reached your 'full potential'.

Public-examination syllabuses provide similar examples: 'will have a sound knowledge of', 'will be able to show an awareness of' are recent formulations. Other examples, this time taken from college educational psychology prospectuses, spell out the aims by giving a general heading such as 'Personality Theory' and then give details by listing names of psychologists who have written about the subject, so that students will 'do' Freud, Eysenck and Cattell. 'Doing' Piaget is, of course, a widespread activity of student teachers.

I am not suggesting that I do not think that 'having sound

146 *Psychopedagogy*

knowledge', 'showing awareness' or 'knowing' about Piaget are not important. The problem is knowing what is meant by the expressions. If a teacher has these aims and tries to achieve them, he is going to have difficulty in deciding whether he reaches them. How is he going to decide whether his students have acquired a sound knowledge of? Or if they are aware of? And how will he know whether they have 'done' Piaget properly?

Apart from the problem of imprecision, there is one other common difficulty in the case of aims of the 'doing' type. What is involved in 'doing' Piaget, or fractions, or the metaphysical poets, or the Reformation, or the geography of the Mediterranean? At least the other objectives are stated in terms of what the students should learn. Presumably the intent behind the bald statement of a subject is that the students should 'learn' something about it. But this doesn't help much when one is faced with the enormous scope of some of the subjects. There is, of course, the additional problem of knowing what 'learn' means in the various contexts.

I said earlier that I thought most teachers would agree that their main task is trying to help children to learn something. I have also argued that different types of learning are appropriate in different circumstances. If this is so, and if the objectives are to be of any help, it is necessary to phrase them so that they make clear what kind of learning is aimed for. And if we are interested in fractions or Piaget we should make it clear what aspect of fractions or the work of Piaget interests us.

Since we are interested in children's learning, we must be interested in changes in their abilities, attitudes, feelings and skills which occur as a result of our teaching. You might ask: 'What is the difference between a child who has not had this teaching and one who has?' The answer to this question cannot be in the form of 'fractions' or 'Piaget'; it has to be expressed in terms of the pupil's abilities and feelings. But phrasing it in terms such as 'showing awareness' doesn't get us very far, although it does help. What we must do to make progress is to try to express our objectives in terms precise enough for us to be able to tell when a pupil has 'shown awareness' or 'acquired a sound knowledge' (Mager 1975).

I suggest, therefore, that two crucial points when deciding on

Objectives for teaching 147

objectives are to express them in terms of what you hope the pupils will be able to do when you have finished your teaching and to express them in as precise terms as possible. Having in mind my previous suggestion may help with this task. Writing out how you would distinguish a pupil who had learned what you had tried to teach from one who had not would virtually compel you to set out objectives in the way I suggest.

Think of the 'sound knowledge' formulation and the problems of deciding which of two pupils was blessed with this quality. I think you would have considerable difficulty in deciding merely by looking at them. You may engage them in conversation about the subject, ask them to write something, possibly observe them carrying out some activity. In other words, they would have to *do* something or attempt to do something.

But doing what? Fractions? Piaget? Calculus? Merely to state them exposes their inutility. You would have to decide what you would accept as evidence of learning in the various fields. For example, would you be content with a pupil's ability to state the number of quarters, halves, eighths and sixteenths in a 'whole one' as evidence of a sound knowledge of fractions? Or the ability to write down the names of the main Piagetian stages of cognitive development as proof of having 'done' Piaget? In the light of the earlier discussion about different types of learning and their assessment, I would hope you would want much more evidence.

Whether you do what I hope is up to you. It is a teacher's own decision what objectives to set for himself within the broad framework of a school curriculum. If you believe that being able to recite the various fractions is a suitable objective, or if you have agreed this with your colleagues, then you are perfectly entitled to state it in unequivocal terms. The point about stating the objective in this way is that it makes explicit what is often left vague, so that you and your colleagues are better able to decide whether the objectives are worthwhile or not.

Getting agreement

You will probably find, when it comes to trying to reach agreement on the worthwhileness of objectives, that it is relatively easy as

148 *Psychopedagogy*

long as they are very general. Problems start when people try to agree about more specific objectives. To illustrate this point, consider a general objective that might well be the overall aim of a course of teacher training. Presumably there would be little disagreement with an aim such as 'to produce good teachers'. You would, however, almost certainly run into trouble as soon as you started trying to be explicit about the qualities you hoped students would acquire in order to make them good teachers. There would probably be disagreement about both the knowledge and the skills a good teacher should have. For example, I might think it very important for a teacher to know something about concept formation, while someone else might be quite scornful of this 'irrelevant theorizing'. Similarly some might consider that the ability to administer corporal punishment is a useful skill, whereas I do not. The same difficulties could apply to a wide range of skills and areas of knowledge. The point is that lurking behind different people's adherence to the idea of production of 'good teachers' as being a good aim for a teacher-training course are different models of the 'good teacher'. When the screen of the general statement is removed, the differences between the models are exposed.

The same probably applies to teaching in any field. While it might be possible to reach wide agreement on the desirability of teaching geography or history or literature or religious knowledge, the crunch comes when the constituent skills and knowledge implied by the acceptance of these general areas as objectives are made explicit. Decisions about the nature of the skills and concepts considered desirable for children to acquire under the general headings suggested are rarely for the teacher to make. Social, political, legal, historical, philosophical and other influences besides educational ones bear on the question. All the examples of subject areas given have changed their objectives, in most cases quite radically, in recent years as a result of such pressures. The overridingly important point here is that the crucial decisions about *what* the key skills and concepts in given fields of schooling should be are not made by individual teachers directly. Teachers can, of course, by involvement in the educational, political and social life of the community, make some contribution towards influencing these decisions.

Objectives for teaching 149

In other words there is no way in which the 'true' objectives of any field of teaching can be identified. However, unless teachers adopt some aims it seems to me unlikely that they will achieve much. In fact what usually happens is that, within the social/ educational constraints referred to above, teachers adopt their own aims or accept the aims agreed by a group of peers. This adoption of a set of general aims is the first crucial step that enables individual teachers or groups of teachers to plan their work in relation to explicit outcomes. The further analysis of these general aims, while still involving value judgements, is more of a pedagogical question than the philosophical-political problems of deciding the overall aims.

Analysing objectives

Although reaching agreement on the very general aims is quite crucial, it doesn't get us very far pedagogically. Indeed, it is possible to consider agreement about general aims as a point of departure for the working out of teaching objectives. If teachers are to gain any advantage from the use of objectives as I suggested, these need to be stated with precision and with a level of specificity appropriate to classroom action. The problem of producing objectives of this nature from statements of general aims may be considered as part of the analysis of objectives.

Many writers have considered the question of the analysis of objectives in recent years. But there is little doubt that the most widely known is that produced by Bloom and his associates (Bloom *et al.* 1956). Bloom was the editor of the first volume of the *Taxonomy of Educational Objectives* produced by an American committee of college and university examiners. 'Taxonomy' is a much more familiar word now than it was when the book appeared, and means a system of classification. The authors quote a dictionary definition in the foreword to the book: 'Taxonomy: "Classification, esp. of animals and plants according to their natural relationships . . ."' The authors do not claim that their taxonomy classifies educational objectives according to their 'natural relationships'. It would be a bold man, indeed, to claim to be able to do that in this field. In fact, even in the apparently

150 *Psychopedagogy*

more straightforward matter of classifying plants and animals, today's natural relationship may well be tomorrow's taxonomic howler. The point is that there is no 'correct' system of classification, and taxonomies of educational objectives are by no means the sole prerogative of Bloom *et al.*, a fact that Bloom *et al.* would be the first to acknowledge, whereas many people seem to equate 'taxonomy' with the Bloom system when discussing educational objectives.

The function of any system of classification is to help us cope with complexity. The Dewey Decimal system of classifying books is a familiar example of such a system. It is useful because it helps us to handle very large numbers of books systematically and also gives us, through the Dewey number, an indication as to what a book is about. At the same time the rationale of the system is criticized by many librarians; and in fact many major libraries no longer use the Dewey system and have adopted a system that enables them to do their job more efficiently.

In the same way that some librarians changed to another system when they found the Dewey system lacking in utility, so teachers and other educationists should assess a system of objectives on the basis of its utility. If it cannot meet the demands of practice, then they should look elsewhere – if necessary, develop their own. From personal experience of attempting to use the Bloom approach in a variety of aspects of educational studies, I came to the conclusion that from the point of view of educational psychology it was not very helpful. This is not to say that in the field of curriculum development it might not be extremely useful. But different horses for different courses. And I think one should bear in mind Blake's statement, which I quoted in my book on objectives: 'I must create a system or be enslaved by another man's' (Stones and Anderson 1972). In my opinion, too many have been enslaved by the Bloom system, not because of Bloom but because of their failure to look upon Bloom as a *specific case* and not as the *general rule*. This point is just another variant on the theme that pervades this book: do not be persuaded by the single exemplar. It is not an axiom to appeal to the lazy but if you have read this far you are certainly not one of those.

Objectives for teaching 151

The Bloom taxonomy

With this lengthy, but I think necessary, caveat let us now look at the taxonomies of educational objectives compiled by Bloom and others. There are two taxonomies from the Bloom stable in print: one concerned with objectives relating to the 'cognitive domain', roughly, concerned with 'knowledge'; and one dealing with the 'affective domain', roughly, concerned with 'feelings'. The rationale of the system is hierarchical. Objectives thought to demand behaviour of a high level of complexity subsume – that is, embrace or include – objectives demanding less complex activity. The cognitive analysis has six levels of objectives and the affective has five. Level 6 includes behaviour at level 5, 5 includes 4, and so on. Thus the categories range from simple to complex behaviour and from concrete to abstract behaviour. Each category has a main heading which is broken down into more specific subheadings. The taxonomies themselves are widely available and should be consulted for a detailed picture of their rationale. However, in order to give a flavour of this approach to the classification of objectives, I have reprinted in Figure 7.1 the bare bones of the taxonomy.

In the taxonomy itself each one of these headings has explanatory notes, illustrative examples and also illustrative test items thought to be appropriate to testing knowledge at that particular level. The latter point illustrates the general orientation of the taxonomy. Devised as it was in the heyday of psychometrics, its main value is as a guide to the classification or scrutiny of test questions. Thus, although there is a rationale to the taxonomy, the rationale was devised not as a guide to action in the preparation of teaching objectives but rather as a guide to evaluating them when they have been produced.

In the discussion of methods of testing knowledge the authors make suggestions about the types of test items which are too specific to be helpful in developing an overall systematic approach to the production of a set of objectives related to a given teaching task. One of their comments illustrates a difficulty inherent in the taxonomy. They suggest that, at the level of *Knowledge* (1.00), test items should not assess rote learning but should not be too

152 *Psychopedagogy*

Figure 7.1 *Bloom's taxonomy of educational objectives*

I The cognitive domain

1.00 KNOWLEDGE

    1.10 Knowledge of specifics
        1.11 *Knowledge of terminology*
        1.12 *Knowledge of specific facts*
    1.20 Knowledge of ways and means of dealing with specifics
        1.21 *Knowledge of conventions*
        1.22 *Knowledge of trends and sequences*
        1.23 *Knowledge of classifications and categories*
        1.24 *Knowledge of criteria*
        1.25 *Knowledge of methodology*
    1.30 Knowledge of universals and abstractions in a field
        1.31 *Knowledge of principles and generalizations*
        1.32 *Knowledge of theories and structures*

2.00 COMPREHENSION

    2.10 Translation
    2.20 Interpretation
    2.30 Extrapolation

3.00 APPLICATION

4.00 ANALYSIS

    4.10 Analysis of elements
    4.20 Analysis of relationships
    4.30 Analysis of organizational principles

5.00 SYNTHESIS

    5.10 Production of unique communication
    5.20 Production of a plan or a proposed set of operations
    5.30 Derivation of a set of abstract relations

6.00 EVALUATION

    6.10 Judgement in terms of internal evidence
    6.20 Judgement in terms of external criteria

Objectives for teaching **153**

Figure 7.1 – continued

II The affective domain

1.00 RECEIVING (ATTENDING)

    1.10 Awareness
    1.20 Willingness to receive
    1.30 Controlled or selected attention

2.00 RESPONDING

    2.10 Acquiescence in responding
    2.20 Willingness to respond
    2.30 Satisfaction in response

3.00 VALUING

    3.10 Acceptance of a value
    3.20 Preference for a value
    3.20 Commitment

4.00 ORGANIZATION

    4.10 Conceptualization of a value
    4.20 Organization of a value system

5.00 CHARACTERIZATION BY A VALUE OR VALUE COMPLEX

    5.10 Generalized set
    5.20 Characterization

(Abstracted from Bloom *et al.* (1956), Handbooks I and II.)

different from the examples used in the teaching. They provide examples of test items but leave the method of attacking the writing of the objectives to individual expertise without relating the teaching to the testing or the objectives in any consistent pedagogical way. And yet without this guide to action it is very difficult indeed to know whether what is being tested is rote learning or not. In fact the examples they give of test items at this level of their taxonomy seem to be almost inevitably close to rote learning. Many of them seem also to be very close to word-manipulation tests rather than being tests of the grasp of concepts. For example:

An engineer who designs houses is called: (1) a carpenter,

154 *Psychopedagogy*

(2) a civil engineer, (3) an architect, (4) a draftsman, (5) a mechanical engineer.

One use of the Periodic Table has been to (1) determine the solubility of gases, (2) find the degree of ionization of many compounds, (3) predict undiscovered elements, (4) determine molecular weights of compounds accurately.

This approach is a good deal different from the approach I discuss in Chapter 15 where I talk about testing. This does not mean that this approach is 'wrong' or that I am 'wrong'. Individual teachers or teams of teachers make their own decisions about such matters. The important point is to recognize the nature of the activity, and, if you then consider that asking questions that deal with rote learning is useful, then do it. The danger lies in thinking that you are testing for conceptual learning when in fact you are testing rote learning. The rationale of the Bloom taxonomy is not very helpful here. In my approach to the specification of objectives I consciously attempted to construct a rationale that would take care of this problem. Whether I succeeded or not you may be able to judge after reading the next few pages.

I am sure that you will have noticed one other problem about the Bloom taxonomy: the objectives are not stated in terms of what the learner should be able to do at the end of teaching. Expressions such as '1.11 *Knowledge of terminology*' immediately raise questions about the meaning of words such as 'knowledge' and 'know'. The authors tackle this question to some extent in their explanatory notes but the problem is not altogether dissipated by their explanation. There is thus need for a further operation before the objectives can be translated into terms of actual teaching. One attempt to provide a systematic approach to this problem has been made by Metfessel and others. Their contribution is to take an objective such as the one given above and to 'translate' it into behavioural language. Thus the objective given is 'instrumented' or put into operation by the use of expressions such as *to define, to distinguish, to acquire, to identify, to recall, to recognize*, in relation to *facts, factual information* (sources, names, dates, events, persons, place, time periods, properties, examples, phenomena). (See Stones and Anderson 1972 for full details.)

Objectives for teaching 155

Although this may help, it seems to me that it is a bit of a patching-up operation, whereas what we need is a different approach that takes into account from the beginning the question of stating objectives in terms of student competencies and builds it into the rationale.

In spite of the shortcomings mentioned above, the Bloom taxonomies have been extremely influential – possibly too influential. But it must be recognized that when they appeared they signalled a new development in education that has stimulated work in a variety of fields.

The problem that I and educationists working with me encountered when we tried to use the Bloom approach to generate teaching objectives was that the taxonomies are no more than what they set out to be – namely, classifying devices for pigeon-holing objectives that already exist. What we needed, and what I believe teachers need, is a device to help us generate objectives in particular fields of study according to some logical system that will ensure that our taxonomy is comprehensive and contains no redundancies, and that the objectives produced are related in a logical and, if possible, psychological way. The taxonomic method I looked for would be a guide to pedagogical action without being restrictive of teacher or pupil. Any system should also be dynamic and readily adaptable to new developments.

The approach I evolved is described in detail elsewhere (Stones and Anderson 1972), but I shall discuss its general features here and attempt some exemplification not only in the hope that you will find it helpful in generating your own objectives but also because I think that this type of approach is very useful in making a bridge between pedagogical theory and practical teaching.

Skills, concepts, feelings

It seems to me that teaching has one or two key objectives, whatever is being taught. A teacher will always be trying to help his pupils to acquire certain skills, to learn new concepts and principles, and very likely to develop certain attitudes to life and to learning.

This may appear to be a fairly banal statement, but, since it

156 *Psychopedagogy*

does help to give a useful overall orientation to thinking about objectives, I used it as a guide in devising my method of generating teaching objectives. It does not cater explicitly for the affective (emotional and attitudinal) field; and indeed there is a good case for arguing that attempts to separate thinking and feeling objectives distort the reality of teaching, the two categories being difficult to separate. At the same time there is a very cogent argument that affective objectives are the most important of all. If pupils reject a field of study or school itself as worthless, then no amount of analysis of other objectives is going to help. The development of positive attitudes to learning is frequently advanced as a suitable goal, but this is only a part of a person's total affective life and one might ask if there is any logical reason why teachers should not be concerned with teaching aimed at changing attitudes and feelings in respect of things other than school learning. In addition, one should, perhaps, ask whether teachers should aim to develop positive attitudes towards school and school learning *as such*. I think few people would subscribe to the view that pupils should feel positively towards school no matter what the school was like and no matter what the curriculum or teaching methods. Because of factors like these it seems to me that when we consider affective objectives we are bound to think in terms of discrimination among different types of evidence and in terms of the ability to weigh evidence and come to a decision on the basis of that evidence. In other words, our thoughts tend to relate to skills and to the grasp of bodies of concepts that help one to form attitudes.

Although this fact does not cope with all the problems connected with affective objectives, it may help. I shall return to the question later. In the meantime I should like to continue the account of my approach to producing objectives in general.

Generating objectives

In producing objectives, as opposed to classifying them after they have been produced, I believe it essential to start by identifying very general objectives in a given field of study. Unless the overall teaching aims are agreed on, it seems to me impossible to produce

Objectives for teaching 157

a coherent body of more specific objectives. It is possible, of course, to produce quite specific short-term objectives, such as 'The children will be able to spell "opaque"' or 'The pupils will be able to explain the significance of

> . . . He's here in double trust:
> First, as I am his kinsman and his subject,
> Strong both against the deed; then as his host,
> Who should against his murderer shut the door
> Not bear the knife myself.

or 'The students will be able to calculate a standard deviation using raw scores'. All these are produced without any reference to a body of overall general aims, and I think there are several problems connected with them.

One problem is knowing when to stop. That is, how can you tell when you have produced all the appropriate objectives? There is no end point in this approach to signal to you that you have done all that is necessary. A different problem is knowing whether you have in fact covered the field adequately when you do decide to stop. In this case there is no way of testing that you have not left anything out. A further and perhaps more important problem is that objectives produced in this way are not related to any logical system and could be completely heterogeneous in conceptual significance and in level of importance. In fact, if there is no overall general aim, it is conceivable that the three specific objectives suggested above could be related to one teaching task. Merely to state such a proposition is to expose its absurdity and surely to suggest an explanation: that although there may be no explicit overall objectives in this approach there are implicit ones. We have *hidden objectives*. In the first example the hidden objective may be concerned with systematic or random learning of spelling or it may be related to the 'q'–'u' sequence in English. The second would probably relate to the desire for the pupils to respond sensitively to the Elizabethan world outlook when they read *Macbeth*. Behind the third one could be a general objective that students should be able to cope with simple statistical techniques for use in educational measurement or biology or other fields.

158 *Psychopedagogy*

My argument, then, is that, even when educationists allegedly eschew aims or objectives, they cannot really be aim-less. Even when they are not opposed in principle to adopting overall aims but merely find this difficult, they must still be operating with some sort of implicit, if undefined and amorphous, aims. Far better, in my mind, to face the problem, ask what you are trying to do, and let others know about it – generally your colleagues, but sometimes your pupils, depending upon how you frame your objectives.

Thus for many reasons I believe it better to attempt to devise your objectives at a high level of generality to begin with and then work towards the more specific. These general objectives should be recognized and visible, not unrealized and hidden. They should also be stated as precisely as possible in terms of what the pupils should be able to do when you have finished your teaching.

Doing

As I said earlier, most of us when we set out to teach someone something have in mind that he will be able to do something he couldn't do before and that he will know something he didn't know before. Leaving on one side for a moment the problems of using such expressions, I should like to explain an approach to producing aims that covers these two types of objective.

Let us consider 'doing' in the first place. Even though you may be teaching tables, or spelling, or calculus, or nuclear physics, or Anglo-Saxon, or the law of tort, you are almost certain to have in mind not just the concepts involved in the content or substance of tables, spelling, calculus, and so on, but the kind of thing you expect your pupils to be able to do in order to demonstrate their grasp of the new knowledge. You are going to ask them to recite or write down or answer random questions or use the knowledge to solve problems in the different fields.

If you consider my earlier examples of different kinds of objectives in different fields, you will probably have noticed that I am talking about objectives with two main dimensions. On the one hand they are likely to require pupils to be able to perform tasks at different levels of complexity. For example, chanting the

Objectives for teaching 159

three-times table after you have taught it in that way may be seen as a task of low complexity, whereas using knowledge of tables to work arithmetical problems quickly may be regarded as a task with a much higher level of complexity. The ability to perform either of these may be seen as a perfectly legitimate objective. The fact that there may be disagreement about the value of teaching children to recite the tables merely illustrates the point I tried to make earlier that value judgements inevitably permeate discussions about objectives. However, few people would defend teaching children to chant tables as an end in itself. Most would see it as a prerequisite for more complex arithmetical activity. Viewed in this way it becomes a means to an end and, whether it is or not, to some extent is then amenable to empirical investigation. In other words we can experiment to try to establish if learning to recite the tables is helpful in the acquiring of higher-level skills. At the time of writing it seems that the practice of reciting the tables is being considerably undermined by the rapid and widespread availability of pocket calculators. What, one might ask, is the purpose of having objectives that are only instrumental in helping pupils do more complex things more quickly, when a machine can do it and give us free time for the more complex things? Unless you think that learning tables is good for the soul or a necessary part of the pain of living, then I think you must admit a certain cogency to the argument.

But, of course, if you decide that reciting tables is not for your pupils, you still have the problem of deciding upon objectives that will enable them to cope with the higher levels of objectives. The ability to operate a pocket calculator, then, may become your lower-level objective! The point is, of course, that the general objective is the important thing, but it cannot be achieved without first accomplishing subordinate objectives; it is therefore helpful to identify these sub-objectives before deciding on teaching activities aimed at achieving them. The point about tables or calculators is an illustration that professional judgement is necessary in deciding aims at all levels.

After considering matters such as this for some time, and bearing in mind some of the important ideas in the psychology of learning, I decided that a useful approach to the production

160 *Psychopedagogy*

of objectives would be to focus on three types or levels of skills as desirable outcomes of teaching. I should explain that I am using the word 'skills' in a wide sense as referring not just to motor activity but to any complex activity in any field.

The taxonomic principle adopted classifies skills into three categories. Three types of objectives relate to the teaching of these three types of skills. The most difficult skill is that of using what has been taught and translating it to new situations when performing some novel activity. An example of such a skill would be the ability to get from one place to another on an unfamiliar terrain after instruction in map reading. Objectives of the first type, the type-A objectives, refer to the teaching and learning of such skills, the skills of performance. But these skills themselves depend upon subordinate skills. The argument is that an important preliminary to being able to perform competently oneself is being able to identify competent performance in others. Therefore second-level, type-B objectives are seen as contributory to success in achieving type-A objectives. A teacher setting himself such an objective in map reading would endeavour to teach his pupils to distinguish between competent and incompetent approaches to map reading. The achievement of this objective would demonstrate competence in analysis and evaluation of a specific example of the practical application of a body of general principles. But before he can make this analysis the learner needs to know how. He needs to know what are thought to be the distinguishing features of competent performance. The objective corresponding to this skill, the type-C objective, demands that the pupil be able to recall or remember the distinguishing features of competence in performance. To take our map reading example: a teacher with this objective would hope that his pupils would be able to state or explain how one sets about converting a reading on a map into a direction on the terrain using appropriate instruments.

To take another example. Most schools have a key objective: to teach their pupils to write continuous prose competently. The type-A objective the school sets itself is that the pupils will actually write competently; the skill is one of performance. However, a person is unlikely to be able to write competently himself before he has an idea of what constitutes competent prose. Can

Objectives for teaching 161

he recognize it when he sees it? The skill of recognizing competently written prose is a skill related to a type-B objective – that the pupils should be able to recognize competently written prose when they see it. But the ability to recognize competently written prose is very much dependent upon another skill: knowing what the identifying features of good prose are. An objective specifying that the pupils should be able to state or explain the identifying features of good prose would be a type-C objective.

Carrying out analyses of this type raises several issues in connection with objectives, the curriculum, the relationship of teaching and the learning of different types of skills. I have already touched upon some of these points. One very important one is demonstrated particularly in the example of the objective for teaching the writing of prose. What is good prose? There is no doubt that there are differences of opinion among teachers and even among specialists in English teaching. The formulation, however, allows for such differences. The rub comes when one tries to agree on the meaning of the overall objective. This would be revealed by analysis and discussion with a view to arriving at a consensus. Whatever the final decision as to what is good prose, the objective of being able to write it would be a type-A objective.

A related point is raised by the example of map reading. The value judgement here is of a somewhat different nature. Is the type-A objective valued by the school to be the ability to traverse unfamiliar terrain using map-reading skills? Or is it to be the ability to write about map reading in an examination? Such questions force us to think about the reasons for attempting to teach such skills at all.

These considerations raise another point. Because of the hierarchical nature of the objectives, it is possible to conceive of them at different levels according to the level of difficulty of the skill one is attempting to teach. Thus the skill of answering questions about map reading (type C in my example) might be taken as a performance-skill, type-A objective. The related type-B objective would expect the pupil to be able to assess an explanation of how to read a map, and the type-C objective would expect him to remember discrete facts about map-reading conventions. But

162 *Psychopedagogy*

whatever the level of complexity of the skills the teacher aims to develop, the general idea of the three types of objective should prove useful.

It is not, of course, the only way of doing things, any more than is the Bloom taxonomy. The approach, however, has features that seem to me to be of particular value when considering the objectives related to learning to teach. The type-A objective is to be able to teach effectively, the type-B objective is to be able to recognize an example of competent teaching when one sees one, and the type-C objective is to be able to explain the principles of good teaching. These objectives have many of the features I have just been discussing. They are not very precise, and they imply value judgements (what is good teaching?). Analysis of the objectives would, however, make explicit the criteria on which the objectives are based and would at the same time lend more precision to the objectives. The reason I suggest the approach is particularly useful in learning to teach is that in existing teacher-training programmes students in general learn the facts about competent teaching, observe teachers teaching and then try to teach competently themselves: skills of types A, B and C. That there are many problems with current approaches is a question I shall take up in detail later, but it does not invalidate the argument, as some new developments in teaching practice in training institutions attests.

Knowing

'Remembering' or 'recalling' as called for in type-C skills is what would usually be classed as 'knowing' the facts in a field. I do not wish to enter into a philosophical disquisition on the subject of 'knowing', but am simply taking what I think is a straightforward but not simplistic view of the term as the acquisition of bodies of concepts at different levels of generality in different fields of study. You will no doubt recall, however, that I was not impressed by the use, in the stating of objectives, of expressions such as the student will 'know' this, that or the other at the end of instruction. So, although I think that there may be no harm in using the expression in the original statement of very general aims,

Objectives for teaching **163**

I think it quite important to make clear as soon as possible what is implied by the word.

To some extent I have covered this problem in the discussion of skills. What I now wish to do is to examine the other dimension of student activity that we take as evidence of learning and as an important part of educational objectives. As our skill objectives we hope that our students will be able to *do* something partly as a result of *knowing* something. In the main, I would hope, the 'something' that they know would comprise theoretical understanding related to the skills forming the other aspect of objectives. That is, they would have learned the concepts and principles we consider important in the field of study under question.

A moment's reflection will remind us that concepts come in different shapes and sizes, and that if we hope to tackle the question of specifying objectives at all systematically we need some sort of guide to sorting them out. I have done this by using a method of hierarchical analysis similar to the one used with the skills but with a very important difference in the characteristics of the objectives that are produced. Whereas the skill aspect of the objectives yields three types of objectives which are psychologically distinct and more or less cover the important aspects of learning, the analysis of the 'content' – that is, *what* the students are to learn – is more a logical operation.

The rationale for this approach is to take the overall system of concepts related to learning in the field with which we are concerned and to apply a method of analysis that reveals the subordinate concepts. The process is basically simple. Using your knowledge of the field, you decide what are the very general principles and concepts it contains. You then take each of the main elements in the field and analyse them to see what subordinate concepts they comprise. The general principles depend upon more specific principles and concepts. Each one of these concepts could itself be broken down further into even more specific concepts until we could be talking in terms of highly specific facts. There is, in principle, no limit to this process of analysis. Deciding when to stop is a matter of professional judgement, the question being at what stage the production of more specific concepts is unnecessary. It is worth noting that the levels

164 *Psychopedagogy*

of analysis for different bodies of knowledge are bound to vary: one major concept in one field may yield an analysis that goes down two steps in a hierarchy, whereas another might go down three or more.

Although the method of analysis may be simple in conception, it is by no means easy to identify exhaustively the objectives at each stage in the hierarchy. Obviously the level of difficulty depends on the scope and complexity of the overall objectives being analysed. In my experience of attempting to identify the objectives for a course in educational psychology for teachers I found it extremely difficult at many stages of the analysis to decide what *should* be included, in view both of the differing views of authorities in the field and of the limited time available. Another great difficulty – that of deciding what in fact are the subordinate objectives at each stage – demands the exercise of professional judgement and at some point empirical checking by using the objectives in teaching and thereby testing the validity of one's analysis against the actions of the pupils.

An example

At this juncture it might be useful to provide an illustration of the approach to specifying objectives along the lines I have outlined. I draw the example from a field that will be familiar to all readers, even though some of their memories about the earlier stages may be rather dim. I refer to the learning and teaching of reading; specifically, to the teaching of children just beginning to learn to read – typically, in British schools, around the age of five.

The first step in identifying the objectives in teaching reading is, as you might expect, to clarify what is meant by *learning to read*. I find both in talking to teachers and in reading books about learning to read that the concept is an elusive one. And of course it is possible to take it at many different levels, from the infant school to final degree study. However, if I were to ask you to read the following, you would probably be able to oblige: 'Depop ool fanal bennist natost ol pundin conelup lerset caroon.' You might tell me that it is nonsense but you are unlikely to admit that

Objectives for teaching 165

you couldn't read it. You could even prove that you could read it by reading it aloud. And yet in the world of beginning reading this kind of activity is often scorned as mere 'barking at print'.

The DES report on the teaching of reading had problems too (DES 1975). Discussing 'the reading process' (i.e. reading), it identifies three definitions of reading: 'A response to graphic signals in terms of the words they represent'; this statement plus 'A response to text in terms of the meanings the author intended to set down'; and the first two plus 'A response to the author's meanings in terms of all the relevant previous experience and present judgements of the reader'.

I have no wish, here, to go into an exhaustive discussion of teaching to read, but shall return to that later. However, so that I can use this subject to illustrate my point about objectives and their pedagogical analysis, I must make my position clear and declare that I espouse the first definition of reading. I cannot see, for example, that *any* reader can ever respond to a text 'in terms of the meanings the author intended to set down'. If you think about it for a minute or two you will see that the statement is virtually nonsensical. The reader is not expected to respond to the meanings that were actually set down, but to those meanings the author *intended* to set down. How can a reader ever know what the author intended? I have a fair idea of what I intend when I write these words, but the realization of my intentions is dependent on my experience, my knowledge of the English language and my ability as a writer. Many authors, I am sure, start off with the best of intentions and finish with the worst of expositions.

But if you think a few moments longer you will realize that the statement is doubly nonsensical. In the discussion of concept learning I suggested that all concepts are idiosyncratic. They are private in the sense that they are the product of our personal experience. In normal social intercourse the words we use as go-betweens mean different things to different people. In most cases the differences are probably slight (although we have no means of demonstrating this), but in other cases they could be quite large. All depends on the degree to which people's experiences are similar. Spoken words, however, have their birth in social situations.

166 *Psychopedagogy*

Written words are begotten in private, and there is rarely any contact between author and reader. So the author has to write in such a way as to create a context for his words that will help the reader to realize the interpersonal atmosphere that might have existed if author and reader had been face to face. Sometimes, however, social convention and the author's own life history get in the way of communication. An educational researcher writes in a particular way because that is the convention. A student may have difficulty reading his report, not because the concepts are beyond him, but because the words come between the author and the reader. Many generations of reading books have been similarly flawed. Apart from the tweeness of the language, the concepts behind the words embodied experiences quite different from those of the children they were intended for – different because the author's life experience and outlook were so vastly different from those of his intended readers. With books of this type it is impossible that the children could respond to the text 'in terms of the meanings the author intended to set down'. For my part, this is often a great relief.

An analysis

If you accept my argument about what reading is you will happily go along with me as I attempt to produce objectives for it. If you do not accept my view, then you will probably still be prepared to accompany me, if less happily, since the analysis I propose to attempt will at least try to deal with one aspect of the teaching of reading common to all the definitions. Before starting, however, I should make it clear that I am not against reading 'for meaning' but that I think the 'meanings' are best taught in different circumstances, when the word-concept connection is spoken-word-concept connection rather than written-word. Reading is a difficult enough skill to learn without complicating matters further, and unnecessarily, by trying to teach concepts at the same time (as if that isn't difficult enough on its own!). So the task I hope to examine is that of teaching beginning readers the connections between printed words and spoken words. Thus, for example, according to this criterion, if a child of four could look at the last

Objectives for teaching **167**

ten lines I have written and say the words so that I could understand them, I should consider him able to read.

To begin with, then, I should try to identify the skills and concepts I considered necessary for competence in reading, using the method I outlined earlier. I think that the affective objectives here are very similar to the affective objectives in most teaching. I would want the children to enjoy reading, to wish to read out of school, and actively to seek to read more and more. The skills and concepts can be analysed for subordinate elements, the affective ones being less amenable to this treatment since these are objectives that spill over from subject to subject. However, I think we should keep to the front of our minds that our teaching should embody approaches to all subjects and children which enhance their commitment to the learning of the skills and concepts that we value. In other words, we want them not only to learn what we try to teach them but to like the learning.

One of the problems that makes difficult the analysis of teaching skills and the identification of key concepts in learning to read is that those who attempt the analysis are invariably those who are extremely adept at reading themselves. Not only is there difficulty in identifying the key elements in reading for the new performer, but there is also a difficulty in realizing that the way an adult sophisticated in the skill of reading actually reads is probably quite different from the way a young child does. Practised adult readers are often capable of taking the meaning from a page by very rapid scanning, collecting cues from contexts and reading standard or stereotyped phrases and formulations at a glance; but to attempt to teach a five-year-old this skill would be like trying to teach him to fly before he can crawl.

Until recently many aspects of the beginning skills and fundamental concepts were considerably neglected and, indeed, almost certainly still are in many places. But there are some insights into the question upon which I shall draw when identifying skills and concepts. At this stage I do not propose to make a comprehensive analysis of the objectives of teaching reading but to indicate what I think should be some of the main points.

Analysing the main concept, then – that reading is the ability to respond 'to graphic signals in terms of the words they represent'

168 *Psychopedagogy*

– I would first wish to restate this in what I think are more accurate terms. I would wish to say that reading is a process of symbol substitution. A reader looks at a graphic symbol, the printed word, and reads the aural/oral symbol, the spoken word. Reading, for me, therefore, is responding to graphic symbols in similar ways to the ways in which the reader responds to the equivalent spoken symbols. I do not say 'in the same way' because, as I said before, spoken words have an interpersonal context that printed words do not have, so that it is impossible to obtain an identical response to the two different kinds of symbols.

This statement is virtually a type-A objective, and if we use that approach we can analyse this statement about reading. As in a type-A objective, the reader is actually asked to do something novel: in effect, to read material he has not encountered before. To be more explicit, he is expected when presented with novel combinations of graphic symbols to be able to respond to them as if they were spoken symbols. A type-B objective which could be derived from this overall skill would be to discriminate between correct and incorrect responses to graphic symbols – say, to be able to tell when the teacher or another person has pronounced the correct sound in response to a graphic symbol. The response does not necessarily have to be the pronunciation of the word. If the printed (graphic) symbol asks a question and the reader answers the question as if it were a spoken question, then one might reasonably conclude that he had read the question. A variant on this procedure is actually used in one book of diagnostic reading tests (Daniels and Diack 1958). A type-C objective derivable from the type-B one could be the remembering of rules of pronunciation of certain letter combinations; for example, the modification of vowel sounds by a final 'e'.

Taking, now, the other aspect of the objectives, the body of necessary concepts, we do add an additional dimension. The first overall concept to be learned, clearly, should be the general one that in fact a graphic symbol by convention stands for a spoken symbol. Basically, printed words are symbols of symbols, although in everyday reading we take the printed words as direct symbols of concepts. Astonishingly, until quite recently little if

Objectives for teaching **169**

any attention was given to the need to make children aware of this notion. It was taken for granted that children beginning reading 'knew' (Reid 1966; Downing n.d.; Downing 1970; Merritt 1969). We now 'know' that they don't. Thus the overall level-1 concept is that printed words stand for spoken words.

I now examine this statement of general principle to see what subordinate concepts are implied by it. One springs immediately to mind and may be taken as an example of a level-2 concept. It is that separate words are distinguished in print by the spaces between them. Again, amazingly, there has been little recognition until recently that this secret has to be revealed to young children beginning to learn reading. Another subordinate concept that needs to be learned very early is that in English a left-to-right sequence signifies a temporal sequence in spoken words. Related to this is the fact that words are read from left to right. There are, of course, many other rules and principles about reading that arise from pushing this analysis further and I shall discuss some of these later. At this point, however, I have exemplified the three types of objectives and two levels of concepts.

Let us now consider the way in which the skills aspect and the knowledge aspect of the objectives relate to each other. Figure 7.2 attempts to illustrate the point. It sets out diagrammatically the two hierarchies, and the examples given go down the two hierarchies at once: that is, the objectives are related to lower-level skills and lower-order concepts. The columns A, B and C refer to the types of skills, and the rows 1, 2, 3 . . . X refer to the levels of concepts involved.

The general objective *The learner responds in similar ways to graphic symbols as he does to spoken symbols* is the overall type-A objective and is placed in cell A-1 on the diagram. Cell B-2 with the second example exemplifies the next most complex skill, that of identifying or distinguishing, and its application to a more specific concept, that is, one of the many subordinate concepts of the principle that printed symbols stand for spoken symbols. An example of this type of objective might be *Distinguishes between a reader observing conventional word spacing and one not observing conventional word spacing.* Cell C-3 contains an example of an objective that makes the least demands on the learner. In

170 *Psychopedagogy*

this case he is being asked only to remember facts. A possible example here taken from the same aspect of the overall objectives as B-2 might be *Remembers that print stands for spoken words*.

Figure 7.2. *Matrix of skills and concepts involved in specifying objectives*

Types of skills

		A *Doing*	B *Identifying*	C *Remembering*
Very general	1	First example A-1		
	2		Second example B-2	
	3			Third example C-3
Very specific	X			

Levels of concepts

(N.B. the 'X' level of concepts is given to indicate that there is no reason why the levels should stop at or even reach 3. The number of levels depends upon the nature of the objectives and the teaching.)

(From Stones and Anderson (1972).)

At this level it will be noted that I am now discussing very specific concepts relating to reading. Several of these particular concepts will have been obtained from each level-2 objective including the one I considered. But that level-2 objective, along with several others, will in turn have been derived from the very general principle that printed symbols stand for spoken symbols. Thus by starting from a general statement of objectives in this field it is possible to derive a number of more particular objectives that come very close to actual teaching activities in a network of

Objectives for teaching 171

skills and concepts. In the next chapter I shall consider how this process can be directly related to teacher activities.

Common sense about objectives

You may have thought, when contemplating the number of very specific objectives likely to be generated by an analysis such as the one I described, that a teacher who defined his objectives using this type of approach would have no time for teaching. It is a view that I understand and sympathize with, although I do not entirely agree. It is true that a person could get trapped in the system and go on generating ever more objectives of ever-increasing specificity. This is where one's professional judgement can help. Like other attributes of a good teacher, this needs cultivating. The judgement needed here is knowing when to stop. This can only follow from experience in applying theoretical notions to practice, observing the effects and counting the cost against the pay-off.

Subdividing the field of study and tackling one division at a time makes the task more tractable. The same method of analysis can be applied to the aims of one lesson or a whole course. By the same token it would be possible to apply a comparable method to the curriculum of the whole school. The latter would be a large project embracing many people but its outcome would be different from that of an analysis of objectives in one segment of a field of study, in that the lower levels of objectives would still be fairly general. In fact, of course, one conceives of bodies of objectives nested within each other and related to each other hierarchically according to principles similar to those outlined in connection with the analysis of objectives.

In other words, the size of the task is related to the size and nature of the slice you start with. In relation to class teaching, the slice could be relatively small and tractable. Start in a small way and, if your efforts seem productive, then extend the area of effort using the same approach. In this way you will acquire practice in using the approach and develop the professional judgement I spoke about earlier. Working with objectives in this way can help to give a clear insight into the relationships among the

172 *Psychopedagogy*

concepts and skills you are trying to teach. Even if you do not do a complete analysis of a field of study you will almost certainly see it with much greater clarity when you have attempted one like this. You will also be very much better equipped to prepare your teaching for individual lessons than if you do not attempt an analysis of what you are trying to achieve. If you do, in fact, adopt the approach I have outlined, you will find that this links up very well with the analysis of teaching tasks which brings us right into the classroom and helps us cope with preparing the actual teaching programme. That is, it will simplify the problem of deciding what to do and how to set about doing it when the fat is in the fire and you are standing in front of the class.

In essence, then, although I think that an approach such as I adopt in my own taxonomy can be very helpful, I fully accept that not every teacher will want or perhaps be able to follow through the analysis of objectives in the way I suggest. I would also stress that one should not take the approach to the illogical extreme of particularity and triviality. In other words, use the method but not slavishly or you might be trapped.

Objections, objections

Some educationists are not as enthusiastic as I am about objectives. Among the objections levelled at dedicated specifiers of objectives, especially of objectives stated in terms of student learning (often labelled/libelled 'behavioural'), are that they are only spuriously accurate, that some subjects are not amenable to this type of treatment, that objectives emphasize the trivial, and that objectives restrict freedom and inhibit creativity. My main line of reply to arguments such as these are that all this depends on the outlook and capability of the person who specifies the objectives. There is nothing intrinsic to the activity of declaring objectives that necessarily makes them trivial or restrictive. I think that restrictive teachers will produce restrictive objectives, teachers obsessed with trivia will produce objectives that stress trivial learning outcomes. I suggest, for example, that a perfectly reasonable objective would be to develop creative thinking in children, but it is unlikely that a teacher obsessed with the need

Objectives for teaching 173

to cover a syllabus for some outside examining body would be very enthusiastic about such an objective. Certainly, in the days before creativity became fashionable, an objective of this kind would have been abhorred by many teachers. But whatever the intended nature of the objectives, stating them explicitly in terms of what the learner should be able to do at the end of teaching will help to bring out into the open what lies behind the façade of the global declaration. We should be able to obtain some idea of what is meant by such things as 'creativity' and have some idea of the difference between a creative person and a non-creative person.

This point takes us back to the question of the spuriously accurate objective. From earlier arguments I hope you will have seen the point that it is the lack of analysis that makes consensus spurious rather than that spurious accuracy is a consequence of specifying objectives. I accept that spurious accuracy may occur when one is defining objectives, but argue that this is not an inevitable consequence of the procedure of defining and analysing objectives, whereas I would argue that it is an intrinsic feature of objective-free teaching.

One other important point is sometimes made by those sceptical about objectives. They aver that specifying objectives is constraining in that it does not allow for unforeseen outcomes in teaching. Teaching, it is said, is an opportunistic enterprise and the unpredicted is often the most worthwhile. I, in turn, am sceptical about these claims, not having seen evidence that teaching *in general* is like this. As for unforeseen outcomes, I think that if these loom large in teaching then there is something wrong with its theory and practice. A stance which accorded greater importance to the unexpected outcomes of teaching would be derided in some fields. Consider, for example, the driving instructor or surgeon in a teaching hospital faced with a high proportion of unforeseen outcomes of his teaching. I think you would probably consider with even greater alarm the same outlook in relation to the training of airline pilots. Unforeseen outcomes, it seems to me, are likely to arise in the early days of a person's learning to teach before he has acquired a body of ideas and experience; but, as I said earlier, the actual practice of teaching should

174 *Psychopedagogy*

contribute to the body of ideas about it and thus help the teacher to prepare his teaching with more insight into the way things are likely to go when the lesson starts and, it is hoped, to arrive more or less where he intended.

I think one of the possible reasons for the arguments about unintended outcomes is that the specifying of objectives gets mixed up with deciding how to teach in order to achieve those objectives. Although you decide what you would like the children to be able to do when you have finished your teaching, you do not thereby specify *how* you are going to teach them. For example, two teachers might adopt the same objective: *to increase the number of creative solutions the pupils produce to problems in the field of book design.* One teacher could, given this objective, quite easily teach by dictating notes on book production and design with the conviction that this would be the most economical way of achieving his objective. Another teacher could also just as easily tell the pupils what the problems are, provide materials and tell them to experiment. And there is, of course, an infinite variety of other approaches to the same problem. There is thus no reason why the teacher need ignore unexpected contributions from individual children and not incorporate them into his teaching of the whole class. They could well help him to achieve his main objectives more easily or quickly.

I conclude this discussion of objections to objectives with a reiteration and an example. The activity of specifying objectives is basically neutral. You are like to specify objectives according to your cast of mind rather than because the actual activity forces you one way or the other. If you are a rote teacher, fond of *ex cathedra* teaching and wedded to the idea of covering the syllabus, you are likely to produce objectives stressing convergence, and if you are not then you won't. You cannot but help make objectives in your own image. But, even if you espouse all the ideas of the objectors, I suggest that you can write objectives to cope with these reservations. Your objectives could specify that you intended to increase creativity, to enlarge the learners' freedom to experiment, to focus on the important and eschew the trivial, to take advantage of the unexpected, indeed, an objective could actually intend that none of the learning outcomes should be foreseen.

Objectives for teaching 175

You could even take a leaf out of the anarchists' society's rule-book ('This society will have no rules') and have as your objective: 'In my teaching I shall avoid having any objectives.' But all these flights of fancy come to earth when you try to say what you mean by these objectives and how you can tell if you have achieved them. There is no answer, however, as far as I can see, to the last-ditch rejoinder, 'It doesn't matter whether I achieve what I hoped to achieve, and it doesn't matter whether I know whether I achieved what I hoped to achieve or not', except 'Amen'.

8

Analyses for teaching

Knowing where you are going is no guide to your route. Nor is getting your objectives straight a guide to how to teach so that you will achieve them. But clearly this problem still remains, even if we have specified our objectives in some detail. It may be that you are tempted to avoid the issue by adopting the stratagem used by Mager and Clark (1963) who gave students detailed statements of objectives but no formal instruction. The teacher was available merely to answer the students' questions or to act as a resource. In fact the students learned satisfactorily without the teacher's direct instruction. Is this, you might ask, the lazy teacher's guide to success? I doubt it. The objectives were carefully defined. The necessary materials had been decided upon and provided, and in fact the instructors had a very good idea of the nature of the task they were setting the learners. The point of the experiment was that, if all the requisite materials and objectives were provided, the students would ask questions only about things on which they needed information. They would save time by not being instructed on things at which they were already competent. Since every

Analyses for teaching 177

student would have a different pattern of learning competence in relation to the objectives before the new learning, each student would call for the learning experiences necessary to take him from his own level of competence to the level set out in the objectives, and only those experiences. In other words the students were individualizing their own learning.

In this example the students were implementing a model of learning and teaching I have mentioned before. By prior scrutiny of the objectives they were *diagnosing* their own beginning capabilities using the objectives as a type of pre-test of their competence. On the basis of this diagnosis they *prescribed* for themselves the necessary instruction or information they needed, and the extent to which they achieved the objectives was the *evaluation* of the efficacy of their learning.

An important point about the nature of objectives emerges from this approach to instruction. It is important to clarify for whom the objectives are intended. Objectives are, in general, the objectives of the teacher not the taught, even though they may be written in terms of what the learner may be able to do at the end of the teaching. In some cases the objectives will do for either teacher or taught. But once we get away from objectives dealing with purely conceptual or motor learning, things are less clear-cut. Imagine, for example, an affective objective of this type taken from a set of objectives relating to the teaching of the philosophy of education: 'Commitment to apply philosophical thinking, where appropriate, to educational theory and practice' (Colleges of Education Research Group, Birmingham 1969). This objective would be prefaced by an expression such as 'After instruction the student will have a . . .' This statement is a teacher's objective in the way it is expressed. The question we might ask is: can such an objective be considered appropriate as a student's objective? My view is that it cannot. I cannot conceive of a learning situation where the learner himself is so much in charge of his own learning that he can realistically set himself the objective of *liking* what he is learning, of *being committed* to using his new learning, or *continuing to study* the subject for sheer enjoyment after formal teaching is finished. All three objectives mentioned are commonly instanced in discussions about affective objectives.

178 *Psychopedagogy*

It may be, therefore, that, in some approaches to teaching involving individualized instruction, it would make sense to devise one set of objectives for the learners and one for the teacher himself. In many cases the lists would be very similar, the former being derived from the latter. But, as I have already suggested, although providing students with objectives may be an extremely useful aid to their learning, it is most unlikely that efficacious learning will ensue inevitably merely because they are given these objectives. In this approach to learning, satisfactory outcomes depend on the adequacy of the provision made for coping with the questions and problems of the learners. The ability to make this provision satisfactorily implies that the teacher has a shrewd idea of the nature of the likely needs of the students. But such ideas cannot be plucked out of the air; they demand a good deal of informed thinking about the nature of the learning task the students are presented with. In fact, providing self-instructional experiences for students usually involves the teacher in more thorough planning than conventional face-to-face teaching because of this need to anticipate as many eventualities as possible instead of leaving them to be dealt with *ad hoc* as they arise. I am not suggesting that this sort of anticipation is unnecessary in face-to-face teaching. But since it is not so essential it is honoured more in the breach than in the observance.

Analysis

Honouring the observance of lesson analysis seems to me to be a most desirable pedagogical aim, whatever approach to teaching we take. But a burning commitment to task analysis is not enough. Nothing is simple in teaching, and when a teacher engages in the analysis of a teaching task with a view to getting clarity on the nature of the pedagogical provision necessary for achieving the prescribed objectives, he needs to make a very clear distinction between the analysis of the learner's task and the analysis of his (the teacher's) task.

Naturally, as in the case of the teacher and learner objectives discussed earlier, the former includes the latter. But the latter, although necessary, is not sufficient if teaching is to be consciously

Analyses for teaching 179

planned in the light of insights from psychological theory and previous experience with practice. What is needed is not only the type of analysis of the learner's task commonly referred to in books about instruction under the rubric of task or job analysis, but an analysis of the activities the teacher considers to be necessary for him to help the learner succeed in the task that has been set him. The nature of the task set the learner is obviously of prime importance in discovering the nature of the teacher's task, and many of his activities will be suggested by it quite directly. Others may be less obvious and will depend upon the teacher's appraisal of the learner's task in the light of his understanding of pedagogical theory and may even fly in the face of 'common sense' or natural inclination in some circumstances. In order to explicate the nature of the two aspects of task analysis let us consider them separately in order to examine their characteristics and the relationships between them.

The learner's task

As has been indicated in the discussion of the various types of objectives, all but the very simplest of activities can be broken down into smaller units. In the model of objectives I described, the three types of skills were derived by a process of analysis of the most complex skill into less complex ones, and the analysis of concepts produced an array of conceptual objectives of different levels of generality.

A similar process applies to the analysis of learners' tasks. Indeed it would be very reasonable to consider this form of analysis as an extension of the analysis of objectives. However, whereas objectives focus on the outcomes of teaching and learning, task analysis focuses on the constituent processes of the final outcomes. If we consider the objectives relating to beginning reading discussed in the previous chapter, we shall see an example of this type of analysis. There I referred to some of the sub-skills involved in reading. I mentioned that a learner must respond to graphic symbols in the same way as he does to spoken symbols, that is, he must understand that the printed words stand for the spoken words. Some other constituent skills of reading are the

180 *Psychopedagogy*

ability to discriminate between words and letters, to discriminate between sounds of letters, and to understand that the left-to-right sequence in print corresponds to a temporal sequence in speech. This list is not exhaustive but I hope it conveys a flavour of the way in which learners' tasks may be analysed. Each one of these sub-skills is essential in early reading, and the identification of them makes it possible to devise teaching techniques appropriate to the type of learning involved in the acquisition of these sub-skills. Thus the principles of shaping clearly relate to teaching learners to discriminate between sounds and shapes of letters. Ideas from the field of concept learning would be appropriate to learning that in the reading of English we go from left to right.

Reading is a complex skill and each of the sub-skills is amenable to further analysis. But many other relatively simple skills may be analysed in the same way and frequently turn out to be more complicated than they appeared before analysis. For example, fitting a plug to an electrical appliance involves the combination of various abilities. Among them are such things as:

Being able to discriminate between positive, negative and earth wires
Baring the wires an appropriate amount
Cutting the wires to the correct length
Identifying the positive, negative and earth pins
Twisting the wires to avoid fraying
Fitting the wires to the correct pins
Tightening the securing screws adequately
Tightening the cable clamp screws
Fitting the cover and securing the fixing screws.

Most of these sub-skills probably seem extremely elementary to a person with some experience in fitting plugs. But to a beginner practically each one involves a specific learned capability. Some of these involve what Bruner referred to as enactive representation, in particular, tightening up the screws just the correct amount. Becoming familiar with the layout of electrical plugs could well be seen as an example of iconic representation: one remembers a basic image of the layout of plugs that serves for various specific types. Several of the other sub-tasks involve

Analyses for teaching 181

symbolic representation or concept formation. All of these various skills can be taught by procedures appropriate to the type of learning involved. The analysis of the task gives us an indication of the nature of the learning and from that we can take decisions about the most appropriate approach to teaching.

The teacher's task

Taking decisions about the most appropriate approach to teaching involves us in the analysis of the teacher's task. As I suggested earlier, this also involves us in the analysis of the learner's task – the point of departure for the analysis of the teaching task. I have already indicated how this might apply to the teaching of wiring a plug when I discussed the types of learning involved in the various sub-tasks. In terms of the teacher's task this might be expressed as a sub-task thus: 'Identifies the types of learning involved in the execution of the sub-tasks in the learner's task'.

Identifying the type of learning involved in each of the learner's sub-tasks is the crucial element in the teacher's task analysis. From that flows a variety of related sub-tasks; for example, he would need to make decisions about the way he would structure the learning environment to best cater for the different types of learning. This would demand decisions about the way in which stimuli would be presented, the type and nature of cues and the type and nature of feedback. Stated as sub-tasks they would be couched in terms such as: 'Decides on nature of stimulus material appropriate to the acquisition by the learner of the sub-skills in his learning task'; 'Decides on the nature and mode of presentation of feedback to the learner'.

While some learner tasks may be amenable to very tight prescription in which every sub-task is clearly laid down and allocated a place in a sequence, most are unlikely to be of this nature, and teacher tasks will probably never be like this. A task such as wiring a plug may well be an example of a task that lends itself to tight prescription. A prescribed set of sub-tasks can be identified and if carried out quite rigidly will automatically ensure that the overall task is completed satisfactorily. Such an overall

182 *Psychopedagogy*

prescription may be considered as an algorithm, a term applied to a logical organization of sub-tasks that will inevitably lead to a satisfactory outcome (see pp. 254 ff.). It is a moot point whether one should attempt to teach algorithms. After all, all a person has to do to succeed is to follow the instructions. But one cannot follow an algorithm if one cannot cope with the sequence of actions it comprises. It is therefore necessary to teach the sub-skills in the task unless the learner already has them.

Some school learning may be tackled algorithmically, perhaps particularly in the mechanical operations involved in some arithmetical activities, as in the four rules. But, since most tasks do not lend themselves to this kind of prescription, there may well be a variety of ways of tackling the job of teaching for mastery of these tasks. Indeed, the same is likely to apply to the teaching of the sub-tasks of an algorithmic approach. The point is that it is unlikely that there will be only one correct method of tackling a teaching task even though the various methods are bound to have many common features. Thus, although I now propose to discuss an approach to the analysis of teaching tasks which I have found useful, it can by no means be taken as an algorithm or a blueprint to be followed rigidly but rather a heuristic device or guide to action, an *aide-mémoire* of the things to consider when planning teaching (see pp. 257 ff.).

In this approach I attempt to keep in mind during the process of analysis the idea of the interrelated nature of the various elements. Such tasks are not simple and linear like the simple skills I have discussed so far, but complex and elaborate. Because of this I find it useful, when I analyse the conceptual content of what I am teaching, to have in mind as far as possible all related aspects of the teaching task. Thus, while focusing on the concepts to be taught and trying to decide on what are the key elements, I consider the likely most effective way of teaching them and of evaluating the pupils' learning. I also have in mind other aspects of teaching, so that in the process a teaching plan begins to unfold. To illustrate this approach I reproduce here a scheme that serves as a guide to a systematic attack on the planning of teaching (Figure 8.1).

The headings are intended to bring to mind the things to con-

Analyses for teaching 183

sider and to help relate them to each other more easily than if they are considered one after the other.

The idea is that the scheme should be of general application, but to exemplify I should like to continue the discussion started earlier and examine its application to an objective taken from the teaching of reading. Clearly my example can be only a very limited one, restricted to one small aspect of the teaching of a very complex skill. Were I to attempt to tackle the whole of the teaching of reading, I should be attempting a task in which nobody so far has succeeded and which is held by many people to be impossible anyway.

For purposes of illustration I take the task of teaching children that we read from left to right. This is a sub-skill of the overall skill of learning to read. The conceptual content can be stated in terms such as: 'We read from left to right', I am assuming 'in English'. This overall concept comprises various subordinate concepts, and these are the ones to consider first in an analysis. An exemplification of an analysis of the concept using the approach outlined is given in Figure 8.2.

This example is just one of many possible analyses and I do not claim that it is exhaustive or definitive. Indeed, I have given only a limited number of specific procedures that could be used, although I think that I have covered the main aspects. You will notice that in the 'General content' column I have listed and numbered subordinate concepts in a somewhat different way from how I dealt with subordinate concepts related to the analysis of objectives. When analysing objectives, I worked from the most general concepts to the most particular. In the example given it could be argued that the idea of going from left to right is more general than the idea that words are read from left to right. However, since my concern was to try to decide on the most appropriate teaching approach, I was concerned to sequence the concepts according to what appeared to me the most useful psychological approach. Since the children are only beginning to learn about printed words and syllables, it would be more difficult trying to teach them left to right with actual words than it would with other things. Thus I suggest that we tackle the idea of going from left to right as a general notion and then, when the children are

184 *Psychopedagogy*

Figure 8.1 *Task analysis*

General content	Specific examples	Method of stimulus presentation	Type of learning
Main concepts rules, principles involved	Actual examples to be used in instruction	Pictures Film TV Teachers' speech Actual objects Visits etc.	S–R Concept learning Problem solving etc. (see Gagne)

When analysing the general content of a teaching task it is often useful (sometimes unavoidable) to think about the other aspects of the task as suggested in the other columns (above).

Below is an illustrative example from an analysis of a task to teach area to nine-year-old children.

Concept of surface	Surface of solid object	Actual object	Multiple discrimination and concept learning
	Surface of water	Picture	
	Surface of flat paper	Actual object	
	Surface of pictured object	Drawing	
	Undersurface of object and Top surface of object etc.	}Drawing	

Analyses for teaching 185

Student's response	Feedback	Evaluation

Written communication
Recall of information
Discrimination
Motor activity
	Teachers' verbalizing
	Matching with correct
	   examples, verbal or
	   non-verbal
	Another child's
	   verbalizing
	   etc.
		Germ of items for final
		   test

| Written answer,
   manipulating
   material,
   speaking to
   teacher or peers | Comparison with
   labelled object
Verbal, written
Verbal, written

Verbal, written

Verbal, written | Number of items
   presenting new
   exemplars of the
   concept |

186 *Psychopedagogy*

Figure 8.2 *Illustrative analysis of part of the task of teaching pupils that we read from left to right*

General content	Some specific examples	Type of learning	Method of stimulus presentation
We read from left to right (This is the overall concept)			
Subordinate concepts			
1 The idea of going from left to right.	1 Walking L–R and R–L. Drawing lines L–R/R–L. Passing things L–R/R–L.	All involve concept learning (although they depend on earlier simpler forms of learning). Therefore there is need to provide a programme of positive and negative exemplars to bring out the criterial attributes of going from L to R.	1 Teacher telling, walking, drawing on blackboard, on paper
2 The left to right sequences are analogous to a temporal sequence.	2 Sequence of pictures telling a story. Placing objects left–right according to sequence drawn out of a bag. Placing pupils in sequence L–R according to birthday.		2 Use of pictures, teacher's speech, slides, tape-recording miscellaneous objects.
3 Letter combinations within words are read from left to right.	3 Placing syllables in correct place: E.g. adding 'op' or 'po' to 't' to make 'top' or 'pot'. Specific spoken words to identify last and first letters.		3 Use of cut-out words and syllables, incomplete words on blackboard, spoken words, teacher of tape-recording, playing games like 'I spy' for beginning and end of words.
4 Words within sentences are read from left to right.	4 Placing words in correct sequence.		4 As (3) using complete words.

Notes

*It is assumed that a screening test has established that the pupils do not already have the concept.

†The three types of skill I have referred to are dealt with in the actual teaching by the teacher's asking the pupils to explain about L–R sequencing, to discriminate between correct and incorrect sequencing and actually to perform sequencing correctly. The final evaluation checks whether the type-A skill has, in fact, been learned.

Analyses for teaching **187**

Pupils' responses	Feedback	Evaluation
1 Spoken answer. Holds up L/R hand. Draws line L–R/R–L. Walks L–R/R–L. Passes things L–R/R–L. 2 As (1) plus: Sequences pictures L–R in temporal order. Getting in correct order in line of pupils' L–R according to birthday. Sequencing objects L–R in order of drawing out of bag. 3 Spoken answer to teacher's question. Sequencing of cut-out syllables. Checking teacher's and other pupils' sequencing. Playing 'I spy'. 4 As (3) but using cut-out words.	All could be teacher's speech, other pupils' comments, self-checking devices.	The best method of checking that the pupils had actually learned the concept would be to give them completely new examples to discriminate among and to ask them to arrange things in L–R order according to a temporal sequence. The same activities as in the teaching would be suitable as long as the actual materials were not the same. E.g. drawing different things out of the bag and sequencing them. Arranging different pictures. Lining pupils up according to some other temporal criterion, e.g. bedtimes. Arranging different letters, syllables and words in L–R sequence.

188 *Psychopedagogy*

competent in applying the rule, to employ it to the sequencing of particular things, that is, words and sentences.

Task sequence

Sequence plays an important part in learning to read, as indeed it does in most types of learning. Clearly it is pointless trying to teach pupils to construct paragraphs before they are able to write satisfactory sentences, or to solve quadratic equations before they can solve simple equations. But the sequence implicit in the statement of these skills is one of conceptual or logical comparative complexity. This is a powerful determinant of teaching sequence, but it is not the only one; psychological factors are also of great importance. At the simplest level of learning, it is quite clear that a chain of stimulus-response connections cannot be taught until the individual links are made. In more complex learning, concepts cannot be taught until the learner has learned to discriminate between the criterial attributes of the concepts and those of other phenomena. If the learners do not have the capabilities before teaching starts, then these will have to be taught first. The sequence here is determined by the psychological sophistication of the learner.

As I suggested above, the ways in which one analyses the teaching objectives and then the teaching task may well be in conflict. In the approach to analysis I have outlined, the progression has been from most complex to least complex, whereas in the main the teaching approach is likely to be in the reverse order. Some people suggest that it is useful to give the learner an idea of the nature of the task beforehand so as to orient the learner (Ausubel and Robinson 1969). Galperin (see pp. 102 f) advocates giving the learner an annotated demonstration to create a preliminary idea of the task. But whether or not such approaches are adopted it is more likely than not that the most appropriate teaching sequence will be from the psychologically simple to the complex, and from the simpler concepts to the more complex ones. This procedure can make use of the analysis of objectives discussed in the previous chapter but in this case the progression is from the skills identified in Figure 7.2 (p. 170) from the type-C skills to the type-A skills

Analyses for teaching 189

and from the level-3 concepts to the level-1 concepts. This gives a sequence where the learner learns to recall information, then to identify examples of the application of the information, and finally gives evidence through his own actions that he is capable of applying the concepts and principles himself to new situations.

To apply this approach to the teaching of reading would indicate that one would first teach the pupils to discriminate between different sounds and different printed signs before expecting them to translate lengthy passages of language from the spoken mode to the written and vice versa. In the case of number it would entail the children's learning to distinguish between the various digits before they were asked to perform calculations involving the four rules. Obvious enough, possibly, but the point is that we do not generate our objectives in this way but from the top down. However, there is another point. Discriminating among letters or sounds or digits may not be the best way to start. According to the model, discriminating among different exemplars is a middling-difficulty skill. It might well be that we need to teach pupils that letters stand for sounds before teaching them to discriminate between them. This aspect of teaching reading has not always been recognized and yet it is a quite fundamental prerequisite. According to the model, it is a type-C skill. It involves the learner in *recalling* that printed symbols stand for spoken symbols. Not that we need go into a discussion about symbols, merely to convey the notion that one thing stands for another. It should be noted that in the case neither of number nor of reading am I saying anything about the concepts that the spoken words or digits stand for.

Clearly it is necessary to teach both the concepts and the fact that one thing, a printed shape, is held to stand for another thing, a spoken sound. We should note, however, that when we do this we are assuming that a child has already learned that a written sound (a word) stands for an abstraction (a concept). Teaching that a written word stands for a spoken word is obviously not the most important point. The main thing is that the learner should become able to respond to two stimuli – one spoken, one printed – in much the same way. Whereas in his early learning he probably learned the spoken word and the concept at the same time, now

190 *Psychopedagogy*

that he has the concept all he has to do is to learn to link the printed word with a previously acquired concept, and the spoken word is the agent for this learning. What has not always been made clear to children beginning to read is that printed words stand for spoken words, a fact that is likely to be revealed as soon as one sets about a systematic task analysis of the skill of reading.

As with other aspects of task analysis, it is not possible to provide an authoritative procedure that will meet with universal acceptance. What I have tried to do is to suggest some general lines of attack that will prove of heuristic value in various conditions (see pp. 257 ff.). Dilemmas will still remain when one tries to determine the best sequence for conceptual matter at roughly the same level of generality. In such circumstances the best guidance is likely to be related to the Herbartian dictum, 'from the known to the unknown'. In psychological terms this implies relating new learning to existing bodies of concepts, so that the process is one of gradually extending these concepts rather than having to start from scratch.

I have dwelt on some aspects of the teaching of reading, not to provide an account of recommended practice but to illustrate the general approach to the analysis of teaching tasks. Reading is such a crucial skill for children to acquire that it seems to me an obvious choice when I wish to provide specific examples of general principles of teaching. It seems to me that approaches of this type can be very fruitful in helping one to identify and sequence the crucial elements in most teaching tasks. But it is clear that they are by no means common at present – partly, no doubt, because they are relatively new in the field of school learning, but also, probably, because of the difficulty in implementing them. The difficulty is partly a function of the conceptual complexity but also a function of the time and application needed to produce them. However, in most cases an analysis needs to be made only once, after which it can be a guide to action for some time. This is not the same as saying that a specific lesson plan can be used for ever after its initial preparation, because the analysis is not a precise plan for teaching specific lessons or a series of lessons. It is more of a strategic plan of which individual lessons are tactical manifestations.

Analyses for teaching 191

At this point it might be helpful to consider an example of teaching to see to what extent the ideas expounded in this discussion of task analysis can be related to actual practice. The example I take is one in which the teacher is taking a lesson with seven- to eight-year-old children, many of whom are immigrants. The ultimate aim of the lesson which the teacher announced at the beginning is that the class will compose a poem about a rabbit. The teacher has read them a short poem about a rabbit which she has written, and she has brought a rabbit into the classroom to stimulate interest. When the extract begins she has already discussed various features such as the animal's ears and the way it moves about. She continues in the same vein throughout the extract and then for some time afterwards.

LESSON FROM LIFE: 4

1 (T) What about his nose?

2 (Ps) [Laughter.]

3 (T) What do you know about rabbits' noses?

4 (Ps) I know.

5 (T) Yes, well, what does he do with his nose? Can you all twitch your nose? Can we have a mass nose twitch? Can you twitch your nose?

6 (P) I can.

7 (T) Very good bunch of rabbits. What do you think he's twitching his nose for?

8 (Ps) Smell, Smell.

9 (T) Sniffing, isn't he? What do you think he can smell in this room? Why do you think his nose is going all the time?

10 (P) He's smelling things.

11 (T) He's smelling things. What's he smelling? He's smelling you, isn't he?

12 (Ps) Yes.

192 *Psychopedagogy*

13 (T) These aren't rabbits. That's what he's thinking. Their noses are all twitching because he's just watched your noses twitching but he knows you're not rabbits. Now you know how he couldn't stand up. What do you think he's got on the end of his feet? Yes?

14 (Ps) Paws.

15 (T) Paws. What do you think he's got on the end of his paws?

16 (Ps) Claws.

17 (T) Claws. Long claws or short claws?

18 (Ps) Small claws.

19 (T) Small claws? Where do rabbits live?

20 (Ps) In the ground.

21 (T) Under the ground. How do they get under the ground? Rabbits? Do they have a lift? Do they go down a coal mine do you think?

22 (Ps) No.

23 (T) How do they get under the ground?

24 (Ps) They dig a hole.

25 (T) They dig a hole. Now if you were digging a hole would you want small claws or big claws?

26 (Ps) Big.

27 (T) So what sort of claws do you think a rabbit's got?

28 (Ps) Big. Small.

29 (T) Let's see if I can show you. Look.

30 (Ps) Cor!

31 (T) Can you see how long they are? See that one there.

32 (Ps) Oh!

33 (T) Not little claws at all are they? Don't look at the rabbit, look at the size of that claw. Can you see? Big claws. Big claws on the front feet as well. When he digs . . .

Analyses for teaching 193

> how does he dig? Shovel and spade, do you think? Well how does he dig?

The lesson from which the above was extracted was not based on the method of analysis I have been expounding. It is, therefore, not possible to exemplify each aspect of the mode of analysis by referring to aspects of the teaching. But it is possible to take the mode of analysis and examine the extract in the light of the principles involved to see to what extent we can get clarification of the principles and of the teaching under scrutiny.

In the extract the teacher is grappling with a sub-task in the total teaching task of enlarging the children's concepts about the nature of rabbits. Here her concern is with an important aspect of the concept, that normally rabbits are burrowing animals and that an important attribute of rabbits is the powerful claws, to which she draws attention.

In terms of the analysis of this task, the conceptual content of the extract is that rabbits have sensitive noses and powerful claws. She deals with other criterial attributes elsewhere in the lesson, but in this brief episode we are focusing on just a part of her analysis that may be classified under the heading of 'General content' in the model of analysis discussed above.

When we consider the next heading, 'Specific examples', we see that only one is used. It may be a very effective one but it can still provide only partial information. Other examples differing in various ways would have brought home more clearly the essential rabbitness of the animal. Possibly even more clarity would have been obtained by introducing a non-exemplar – a small mammal that is not a rabbit – to highlight the characteristic features, a small dog, for example.

The type of learning the teacher is trying to encourage is concept learning. Hence the need for a selection of exemplars that rings the changes on the criterial attributes and makes them stand out. The remarks I made about the use of specific examples clearly relates to this point. Further comments that seem relevant here are that the discussion implies some familiarity with claws of small mammals which the pupils may or may not have. One of the types of learning possibly involved here could be multiple

194 Psychopedagogy

discrimination, distinguishing between the 'long' claws of a rabbit and the shorter claws of some other animal. The lack of opportunity for such comparison relates to the points made earlier. The teacher, in this extract, assumes the children have a concept of length in relation to the claws of small mammals that is sufficiently developed for them to be able to say whether in one specific case the claws are long or short. Utterance 28 sheds considerable doubt on the validity of this assumption.

The confusion in item 28 illustrates the problems inherent in the use of the chorused response. To ensure that pupils are responding satisfactorily to the stimuli provided, the teacher needs feedback from the individual learners. Lacking it in this lesson, the teacher is in no position to tell how many pupils are actually following the discussion with understanding. If she were concerned to ensure that all the pupils were acquiring the concept according to her criteria, it would be necessary for her to arrange other ways of observing their responses at an individual level. This problem relates to the question of the evaluation of the pupil's learning and the teacher's teaching. Evaluation will come at the end of the lesson according to the criteria the teacher had set. However, on the road to evaluating the lesson overall, it is valuable to monitor the progress of the pupils towards the achievement of the overall objectives. In this lesson the teacher can really say little more than that *some* of the children seem to have followed the discussion. It is true that *all* of them might have learned the concept very adequately, but the teacher has no evidence to be sure of that.

The remaining heading from the model of task analysis is the feedback the teacher provides the pupils. In this case the teacher's speech is the main agent. This may be perfectly reasonable. As I discussed earlier, the teacher's use of language is a very versatile and effective instrument for guiding learning. On the other hand, there are other important aspects of the use of speech also alluded to earlier. There is, of course, the problem of learning the words without learning the meaning. There is, further, the problem related to the level of the pupils' cognitive development. Children of this age cannot be relied upon to be able to follow the line of logical reasoning implied in utterances 15–28. Much more effec-

Analyses for teaching 195

tive is the action that accompanies utterance 29. This is an example of feedback to the pupils that does not rely on the teacher's speech and may have helped to clear up the problem revealed by utterance 28.

In concluding the scrutiny of this short extract I would say that, although I hope to have made some helpful connections between the ideas of task analysis and practical teaching, I am very much aware that I may have not done justice to the teacher involved. It may be that her overall intention would be perfectly well satisfied if she stimulated the pupils sufficiently to see that particular rabbit more clearly and with more understanding so that when they came to compose the poem their efforts would be enriched by the discussion which had taken place. This possibility seems to me to illustrate the general problem inherent in analysing real-life transcripts of lessons. Unless the teacher's intentions are made quite clear, much misunderstanding of the nature of the pedagogic interaction can take place. Clearly and precisely stated objectives are likely to be the most useful aids to avoiding such misunderstandings.

Theory into practice

The discussion in this chapter has attempted to follow through the analysis of objectives by deriving teaching tasks from those objectives. It seems to me that unless this can be done the aims and objectives we set in teaching are bound to be sterile. Given the complexity of the analysis and the complexity of teaching, it would be unrealistic, to say the least, to expect a smooth transition from theory to practice. Indeed it would be undesirable. Without some sort of tension or mismatch between the ideal working-out of our task analysis and the actual lesson there would be no development. With this in mind, I turn in the next chapter to a discussion of some of the skills in teaching which can help us to achieve our objectives and at the same time yield information that may indicate ways in which our objectives and our teaching may need to be modified.

9

Concept teaching

Teaching skills

There is a current interest in the skills of teaching which takes a similar approach to the one taken in this book. According to this view, skills resemble the type-A skills I have been discussing, but they are not usually related to a particular model of objectives or task analysis. Rather they tend to be seen as *ad hoc* and heterogenous without a clearly identified rationale. At the same time some of them are seen as drawing on psychological principles for their rationale, although this is not always made clear.

Examination of much current writing about skills reveals a very mixed picture. The skills described and taught in work such as microteaching (see p. 309) tend to be somewhat of a rag-bag. This lack of coherence may well result from the lack of a generally agreed taxonomic approach to the identification of such skills. It is common to find skills such as *questioning*, *concept teaching* and *beginning and ending lessons* treated in much the same way as if they were all much the same type of skill. In fact the relationship between such skills is extremely complex and it is most misleading to treat them as if they were all of piece. This is particularly

Concept teaching 197

important when considering how best to teach and learn them and how best to employ them. If you reflect on the skills I have just mentioned, I hope you will see this point. There is a good case for regarding concept teaching as a key skill in a teacher's repertoire and superordinate to most other skills. The other skills relate to concept teaching in different ways. For example, the skill of questioning is desirable if a teacher is going to be able to stimulate children's thinking in such a way as to develop complex bodies of concepts. But it's no good asking questions that demand no cognitive exertion; if you do you may get the 'right' answer from the pupil but his understanding may be quite unchanged. Questions unrelated to any pedagogic plan are of dubious value. Similar remarks can be made about the study of beginning and ending lessons. Getting children's attention and alerting them to the nature of the lesson that is to follow is clearly farcical unless their attention is focused on activities that are calculated to help them learn skills or content of some sort.

My suggestion is, then, that the teaching of concepts is the crucial skill for most teachers. It is, as it were, an overarching skill that many other skills aim to facilitate. Traditional school subjects comprise complex bodies of concepts at different levels of generality, so clearly the skill is one very much deserving of our attention.

This suggestion immediately raises a crucial question in any discussion of teaching skills: to what extent can teaching skills be viewed as being of general application? Specifically, in the context of the present discussion, can knowledge about concept learning be useful to teachers of different subjects or are there specific methods of teaching the content of specific subjects such as maths, painting, English, history, geography, and so on? I think there are aspects of the teaching of different subjects that are particular to them, but I also think that there are elements common to all of them and that these common elements are almost certainly of greater scope than the subject-specific ones. Thus, for example, the same basic principles of learning – say, stimulus discrimination – may be operating in fields as different as the learning of a foreign language (distinguishing between sounds) and woodwork (distinguishing between different types of timber by sight and touch). A knowledge of reinforcement theory and

198 *Psychopedagogy*

the ideas of successive approximation would be helpful to anyone teaching these skills, even though on the one hand aural training is involved while, on the other, visual and tactile are predominant. A glance at the task analysis for the teaching of reading (p. 186) should provide an example of another field in which the same general principle is involved.

Figure 9.1   The relationships between general skills and phases of teaching

Type of skill	Phase of teaching		
	Pre-active	Interactive	Evaluative
A	Analyses task. Ascertains pupils' entry competence.	Teaches employing psychopedagogical principles.	Evaluates pupils' learning.
B	Evaluates an example of task analysis and pupil entry competence.	Evaluates an example of teaching in the light of psychopedagogical principles.	Evaluates an example of the assessment of children's learning.
C	Explains how the principles of task analysis and the ascertainment of entry competence apply to a specific teaching task.	Explains how the principles of psychopedagogy may be applied to a specific teaching task.	Explains how the principles of assessing pupils' learning may be applied to a specific teaching task.

However, it is hardly likely that useful approaches of general application will be identified by an unsystematic, *ad hoc* production of teaching skills. A coherent, interlocking body of skills, it seems to me, can only be devised on the basis of a coherent body of theoretical premises drawn from the study of human learning. The relating of these ideas to the practical activities of teaching by systematic procedures such as those discussed in recent chapters is likely to be the most fruitful means whereby such a body of skills may be produced.

Concept teaching 199

In my attempt to identify such a body of teaching skills, I have made use of the model of general skills discussed in Chapter 7 and applied them to the key aspects of any teaching encounter; its planning, its execution and its evaluation, frequently referred to as the pre-active, interactive and evaluative phases of teaching. In Figure 9.1 I set out a general scheme embodying this approach which is applicable to any aspect of teaching that we might consider important.

As before, the key skill at all phases of the teaching is a type-A skill. The appropriate type-A skill is therefore the planning, execution and evaluation of a piece of teaching. The other skills are contributory to this skill and do not involve the student teacher in actually teaching but in activities closely related to teaching.

Figure 9.1 presents a general scheme relating the suggested three types of skills to the three phases of teaching. In order to derive actual teaching skills from this scheme it is necessary to decide on those aspects of the overall teaching task that seem of crucial importance and apply the procedures set out in the scheme. I have already indicated that I believe the teaching of concepts to be one of the key teaching skills, and I therefore apply the scheme to that skill in order to establish a method of proceeding to teach and to learn the skill. In the pages that follow I shall discuss the application of the procedures to concept teaching, and in later chapters I shall attempt to do the same with other aspects of teaching. However, I do not deal with the full array of activities set out in Figure 9.1, but focus on the type-A skills constituting the top row. The second and third rows comprise contributory skills that would be taught and learned as prerequisite to the type-A skills.

Concept teaching: a key teaching skill

I have already given a fair amount of attention to the way concepts are learned. Among other things I have drawn attention to the vital role of language in concept formation; to the way in which language can also hinder concept teaching when the teacher does not realize that the pupils' ability to use a word does not

200 *Psychopedagogy*

necessarily imply that he has learned the concept; to the need for care in ascertaining that learners do not try to learn new concepts before they have learned the vital prerequisites; to the way in which commonsense understanding of some phenomena is discrepant from specialist concepts; and that at different ages children and adolescents may be unable to learn concepts as adults do. All these points and no doubt others need to be borne in mind by anyone aspiring to teach concepts: that is, I suggest, all teachers. I should now like to draw the various threads together in order to give a synoptic idea of the important aspects of teaching for concept learning as they are presently understood. The marrying of the key ideas about teaching concepts and some of the methods of analysing classroom transactions should give a teacher powerful insights into his teaching not otherwise available and place within his grasp the possibility of planned improvement.

Clearly, one of the most important considerations is the existing knowledge, or entry competence, of the pupils. Evidence from a variety of sources indicates that if the foundations are unsound there is a great possibility that pupils' learning will be very different from that intended by the teacher. I have already given examples from actual classrooms of this kind of problem (pp. 110 ff.). In these examples the teachers seemed to be quite unaware of the great difference between their concepts and those of their pupils. In various fields of study we have seen how teachers attempt to teach new concepts without first making sure that the pupils have a grasp of the subordinate concepts that combine to make the new one. Teachers attempting to teach children to read without ensuring that they know what printed words are, teachers teaching historical ideas such as 'city state' and 'kingship' without making sure that the children had already learned the concepts they used in their attempts to explain, are all courting pedagogical disaster by ignoring or misunderstanding the level of pupils' entry competence.

In a perfect world a teacher would know quite well whether or not his pupils had learned the concepts prerequisite to the new learning he is introducing. His evaluation of his teaching in previous lessons would have given him the necessary feedback about the results of his teaching and his next lesson would take this

Concept teaching 201

feedback into account. Only in completely new departures, or with completely new groups of pupils, would he not have this information. Clearly, some of the lessons I have discussed were being taught by teachers who did not have the necessary information, and it is probably realistic to assume that this is frequently the real-life substance of teaching as opposed to the shadow of the perfect world I mentioned earlier. The question will thus arise for most teachers as to what might be done to ensure that their efforts to teach new conceptual matter will not fail through lack of prerequisite knowledge by the pupils.

Much of the work necessary for coping with this problem lies in the pre-active phase of teaching. Careful task analysis should alert a teacher to the possible difficulties. Recall that one of the elements in the task analysis was the delineation of the specific examples to be used in teaching the new concepts. At this stage it should be possible to identify likely difficulties. Either the teacher decides to avoid using exemplars with which he thinks the pupils might not be familiar or he must incorporate the teaching of these doubtful concepts into his work scheme as a prerequisite to his teaching of the new concepts.

At the interactive stage it is most important to ensure that the new learning can be related to bodies of concepts the learner already possesses. A knowledge of the learner's existing competence will help but care will be needed to ensure that any explanations used in the teaching are also already understood by the learner. This can be done by introducing to the pupils the key terms to be used in labelling new concepts or their attributes and checking that they are acquainted with the words and their meanings.

Obviously the relationship of new learning to existing levels of understanding will vary considerably in different lessons. Teaching which extends the existing knowledge in a particular field will take a different tack from that which introduces pupils to a new field of study. In the former the teacher will be able to make use of existing bodies of higher-level concepts to which they can relate new comparable concepts by direct verbal teaching. In the latter it will be necessary to arrange for direct sense experience if the field of study is completely novel. If it is not possible to

202 Psychopedagogy

arrange for direct sense experience – for example, in teaching the processes involved in volcanic activity – it is imperative to give vicarious experience that resembles as closely as possible the actual phenomena. Recourse will have to be made to aids such as film, slides, pictures and diagrams. Even with these aids, in a very real sense, the concepts learned are bound to be limited but far less so than if the teacher uses only verbal instruction. Extending knowledge in a given field may very often be accomplished verbally by giving a definition. For example, most adults will extend their knowledge of ichtheology, even if only an infinitesimal amount, on being informed that 'a *powan* is a fish of British lakes allied to a trout'. Some people will have their knowledge of psychology extended if they read or are informed that 'a *construct* is a bipolar concept as defined in construct theory'. Obviously 'facts' such as these are at different levels of abstraction and esoterism. The first is generally accessible, the second accessible to a few workers in a particular field. Telling adult learners what a *powan* is will give them at least a rudimentary concept and could be regarded as meaningful learning, whereas telling them what a *construct* is would be meaningless to most people and their learning of the definition would be rote learning. Thus the value of teaching facts depends entirely upon the teacher's competence in analysing the teaching task and teaching in a way that takes into account the learners' existing levels of understanding.

The actual teaching procedures for the teaching of concepts in a new field that depends on direct sense experience or the closest approximation possible have much in common with those involved in teaching by exposition; both draw on the processes of concept learning discussed in Chapter 3. Among the key aspects of such teaching will be the need to call to mind the prerequisite understandings for the new learning, giving the learners a preliminary idea of the learning task, explaining any new terms to be used using concepts the learners already possess, and through careful presentation of exemplars of the new concept to lead the learners, by gradually reducing cueing, to an independent grasp of the concept.

One of the most important considerations in concept teaching is how best to aid the learner to identify the criterial attributes, that

Concept teaching 203

is, those aspects of the concept that are crucial. The trout-like nature is a criterial attribute of a powan but not its weight. To get across the criterial attributes effectively it is desirable to emphasize them in some way; as I said earlier, one tries to increase their salience. This is done by presenting exemplars of the concept in which the criterial attributes are rendered more prominent than the non-criterial attributes. For example, the criterial attributes of the process of shaping behaviour is the progressive approximation, not the nature of the reinforcer or the species of animal. Attention is focused on the criterial attributes of the concept of shaping usually by verbal means, the teacher's explanation or the discussion in a book. In learning concepts involving the use of concrete phenomena the teacher may draw attention to the criterial attributes verbally or through such devices as staining the important features of microscope specimens or exaggerating the vertical scale in diagrams of rock strata to emphasize geological features.

The careful programming of exemplars by the teacher can also considerably speed up the acquisition of concepts. As I suggested in Chapter 1, the random presentation of exemplars of concepts is not the best way to help learning. Systematically ringing the changes on the presentation of exemplars that exemplify the criterial attributes can present the total range of such exemplars and so prepare the learner quickly to identify any new exemplar, whereas random presentation may result in crucial aspects appearing too late to prevent unnecessary errors. For example, a teacher teaching the concept of 'mammal' who omitted to build the whale into his programme of exemplars could be laying up difficulties for his pupils' future learning.

The case of the whale can provide an example of another helpful device in concept teaching: the procedure of counterpositioning (Fleshner 1963). This procedure involves the presenting of exemplars and non-exemplars of concepts in juxtaposition and drawing attention to the factors that make one an exemplar and the other a non-exemplar. Counterpositioning pictures of a whale and a fish of comparable size (say, a shark), and drawing attention to the key characteristics that distinguish the two, helps the development of accurate concepts. Fleshner makes particular

204 *Psychopedagogy*

mention of this in the context of teaching children to distinguish between concepts with 'everyday' meanings such as 'weight' and their scientific meanings.

Throughout the teaching of concepts, language has a powerful influence whether or not the teaching is by verbal exposition. I have made reference to most of its uses, and it is possible to sum them up as the providing of cues and feedback to the learner. Cueing should be faded out as soon as possible; for instance, by encouraging the pupils' own use of language in ways such as describing to themselves or to each other. Verbal feedback from the teacher should also be faded out eventually, but only after ample opportunity to test the grasp of the concept with feedback has been arranged. Successful later use of the concept in other activity will act as continuing confirmatory feedback.

For the teacher, feedback confirming that his teaching has been successful will be provided by his pupils' successful application of the new learning to different situations. For example, he will be reassured if, after he has provided various exemplars to teach the concept of *spinnaker*, his pupils are able to identify new instances of the concept when they see racing yachts running before the wind; or if they successfully identify novel examples of *erratics* in a landscape after instruction on glacial action.

A teaching schedule

I should like now to try to bring together the various aspects of the skill of teaching for concept learning that I have discussed in the last few pages and in previous chapters when I considered the nature of concepts and the role of language in the learning of concepts. I do not suggest that the last word has been said but rather that I have attempted to present the important aspects to be borne in mind according to present views. I shall now attempt to present a synoptic description of the skill of concept teaching by presenting a schedule or guide to the activities a teacher should engage in to ensure satisfactory concept learning. Such a schedule could be used by a teacher as a checklist to remind him of the kind of moves to make, or by an observer trying to assess a teacher's competence in this field. As I said earlier, the schedule

Concept teaching 205

deals only with the type-A skills of teaching as outlined and discussed in previous chapters. This is because the type-A skills are those that characterize the final form of teaching activities, the type-B and type-C skills being contributory to that final form since they would be learned by a student teacher on the way to acquiring the type-A skills.

In drawing up the list of activities I have tried to take a broad view that embraces such things as cognitive schemas, the various types of concepts and rules and also the key aspects of verbal learning.

Figure 9.2   Schedule for the teaching of concepts (STOC)

This schedule sets out in brief the key aspects of teaching activity to ensure satisfactory learning of concepts. It provides a checklist for a student teacher and/or a supervisor to evaluate this aspect of teaching. Teaching performance should be rated in some way; for example, as weak, satisfactory or good in relation to some previously arranged criteria. The student will then have an idea of those aspects of his teaching that need improvement and those areas where he is competent.

A PRE-ACTIVE

1 Make a task analysis of the teaching objectives to identify the key concepts involved, the subordinate concepts, specific examples, methods of presentation, pupils' activities and modes of evaluation.
2 Ascertain pupils' prior knowledge. If this is not possible plan for diagnosis at the interactive stage.

B INTERACTIVE

3 Give a preliminary idea of the nature of the new learning.
4 Explain terms to be used in labelling the new concepts and their attributes and call to mind existing concepts relevant to the new learning.
5 Provide initially a series of simplified exemplars with few attributes to facilitate identification of the criterial attributes.
6 Increase the salience of the criterial attributes to enable pupils to discriminate readily between criterial and non-criterial attributes.

206 *Psychopedagogy*

Figure 9.2 – continued

7 Provide a series of exemplars sequenced to provide a complete range of criterial attributes as economically as possible.
8 Provide non-exemplars in counterposition to exemplars to enhance discrimination between criterial and non-criterial attributes.
9 Provide new exemplars and non-exemplars and ask the pupils to identify the exemplars. Provide feedback for each discrimination.
10 Encourage the pupils to use their own language in explaining the nature of the concepts.
11 Provide suitable cueing throughout to ensure that pupils gradually become independent in their ability to identify novel exemplars of the concepts.

C EVALUATIVE (This process is naturally much the same procedure as would be applied in diagnosing prior level of ability.)

12 Present novel exemplars of the concepts for the pupils to identify and/or discriminate from non-exemplars.

Item 12 on this schedule is the acid test of the understanding of concepts. It would be perfectly reasonable and possibly desirable to ask a learner to give a definition or explain a concept. The thing to watch here, of course, is the non-conceptual response that has been learned by heart. Skilful questioning could take care of this but the ability to identify novel exemplars would be the only real guarantee that the words the learner was using were based on a real grasp of the concept and not mere verbalizings.

This schedule may appear formidable to a beginning teacher; and undoubtedly it represents a very complex activity. However, it is almost certain that this complexity is immensely simpler than the psychological reality underlying teaching and learning in human beings. Teaching *is* an immensely complex activity and it seems to me that the apprehension of this complexity is essential before ever we can hope to improve teaching significantly. But I do not think that the complex nature of the analysis should be seen as an obstacle to approaching teaching analytically. The

Concept teaching 207

schedule I have just presented is my way of coping with a central aspect of teaching and I believe that, subject to the limitations of our present state of knowledge, it is a guide that will have more than specific application. Once understood by a teacher, it should give general guidance in a wide variety of teaching activities, and I would hope it would eventually become a natural part of his activities that would enhance his effectiveness as a teacher. Should he receive feedback from his pupils' performance to suggest that things are not like that, he would need to look critically at what he is doing and attempt to identify his shortcomings. The existence of an analytical guide should help him to pinpoint his problems more effectively than if he worked on general impressions.

I should like to stress that there is nothing in the suggestions I am making about concept teaching that prescribes the kind of 'teaching method' to be adopted. I am thinking here of such dichotomies as 'formal/informal' and 'discovery/didactic'. Indeed, I believe we are barking up the wrong tree by using such expressions. Apart from the fact that their wide generality makes their precise identification impossible, I would argue that a more meaningful division would be between those practising techniques such as I am describing and those who are not, whatever 'method' they adopt for arranging the learning experiences of the pupils. But, of course, even this dichotomy suffers from the problems of the other divisions. It is impossible to draw a meaningful dividing line between those that do and those that don't. In real life there is almost certainly a range of commitments by a variety of teachers to things like formality and informality, and from complete ignorance of the suggested approach to concept teaching to their wholehearted adoption of it. The point I should like to stress is that a knowledge of the suggested approach should benefit any attempt at concept teaching, whatever the 'method' espoused.

I said earlier that the skill of teaching for concept learning is probably one of the most important skills a teacher should acquire. I am not overlooking other skills, for example, those that relate to the teaching of motor activities or those concerned with the affective side of teaching. There are also skills that may be regarded as instrumental. That is, they may be used by the teacher

208 *Psychopedagogy*

not for their own sakes but to achieve more important objectives. A case in point might be the development of questioning skills to enhance concept formation.

Skills in practice

In the world of classroom discourse one thing is certain: reality rarely coincides with theoretical formulations. I do not mean that teacher activity never relates to theoretical principles; rather that teaching in practice is a messy operation compared to the pared-down tidiness of theoretical formulations. Teaching is not unique in this, of course, as anyone who has ever tried to connect the theoretical principles of any sport, industrial process or naturally occurring phenomenon with the actual events will attest. It is not surprising, then, that a search of transcripts of actual lessons for examples of concept teaching is a bit like panning for gold. Nuggets are hard to come by. One thing is quite clear, however, from such a search, and that is that very few teachers deliberately set out to deploy ideas of concept teaching to the teaching of concepts. This is not surprising. These ideas have not been around long and they have not commonly been taught in training institutions. Furthermore, an examination of transcripts reveals that teachers spend much time in management functions – which naturally means time out from pedagogical functions. All the more reason, it seems to me, to strive for an understanding of the principles of concept teaching that will make it possible for a teacher coping with the problems of management and large numbers of children to apply techniques and to deploy skills that are likely to enhance concept learning without having to think things out anew at every teaching encounter.

It is not too difficult to invent examples of classroom discourse to illustrate the ideas of concept learning, and in fact I have used this approach myself on occasions. However, I thought it would probably be more helpful to readers' understanding of the problems of concept teaching if I were to examine actual examples of teaching and point out how they did or did not make use of the principles being enunciated here.

The example that follows is taken from a science lesson given

Concept teaching 209

by an experienced teacher. The teacher in question had recently become familiar with various methods of analysing classroom activities and had recorded the lesson with the intention of analysing the discourse afterwards. He was, thus, not perhaps a typical example of science teachers, but his own appraisal of the lesson makes it clear that the way the lesson went was fairly typical of his usual style. The teacher is introducing the pupils to the Bunsen burner. I cannot say to what extent he carried out the pre-active activities mentioned in the concept-teaching schedule, but we can get some idea of his strategy in teaching a new concept from his recording of the verbal activity of the class and the teacher in the interactive phase.

It is interesting to consider the implications of the commonly used expression 'introducing something to someone' in this type of context. It is clearly a fairly general woolly aim crying out for clarification. We might surmise, however, from past experience that the teacher could have formulated his objectives in terms of acquisition by pupils of the concept of 'Bunsen burner'. We could go further and attempt a task analysis of the job of teaching this concept. We should look for the key attributes of the concept, ways of presenting exemplars, and all the other steps discussed earlier. If we now consider an extract from the lesson we should be able to get a flavour of a teacher's efforts in real life and see to what extent his endeavours approximate to the specification suggested above and perhaps to speculate on what changes might have been desirable.

LESSON FROM LIFE: 5*

Extract from a lesson on the Bunsen burner: junior children aged nine to ten (six children)

Before the extract starts the teacher has demonstrated the burner heating water and melting copper and glass. He has also dismantled the burner, named the various parts and reassembled it. He has told the children that his aim is to teach them to set up

* Parks (1976) *A Small Scale Exploratory Study of Verbal Interaction with Special Regard to Teacher Questioning in Three Selected Middle School Science Sessions. University of Liverpool. Mimeo.*

210 *Psychopedagogy*

and light a Bunsen burner. The extract begins when the teacher asks what they would do just before lighting the burner.

1 (T) . . . usually one gets hold of one of these objects here – which is called an –

2 (P) Asbestos.

3 (T) Oh, yes, fine – you tell me, if you think you know.

4 (P) Asbestos.

5 (T) Asbestos pad, actually, an asbestos pad, that goes on the table there for obvious reasons – can you tell me – what is the obvious reason – can you tell me?

6 (P) The table would burn.

7 (T) It could do, yes. I've seen some very nasty marks on a table caused by leaving a Bunsen burner there for several hours on an experiment, and it's burned the whole of the table, so we have to watch that. Well, now, this is what we do. I assume then that the Bunsen burner is OK, we take it and place it on the asbestos pad, always make sure that the air hole is closed, you'll see why later on, it's closed, then we take the other end of the tubing, and we fasten that on to the gas tap securely like that, OK. Now then, the Bunsen burner is set up and ready for lighting. . . . Well, there, it's lit. I want you to look very carefully at that flame as it stands now. How would you describe it to me? What sort of words can you use to describe that flame to somebody? Imagine that somebody was in the room who was blind, if you like, how would you describe that gas flame to them?

8 (P) Flickering.

9 (T) Flickering, good.

10 (P) Tall.

11 (T) Tall, any others?

12 (P) Orange.

13 (T) Orange.

14 (P) Blue at the bottom.

Concept teaching **211**

15 (T) Blue at the bottom – what sort of shape would you describe it as? Do you think it's got a shape?

16 (P) It hasn't much.

17 (P) It's changing shape.

18 (T) It's changing shape, isn't it? The hint of that, of course, comes in the word flickering, it's moving about, so basically then we've got a flickering, fairly tall, flickering flame – that's a nice expression – tall, flickering flames – and that flame is generally speaking, as you can see, yellow-orangey in colour with a sort of clear, almost transparent bit at the bottom. Incidentally, what does the word transparent mean?

19 (P) See through it.

20 (T) You can see through it, good yes, just like you can see through a window – the window is described and said to be transparent, isn't it? Now supposing I said to you I want us to control that flame a little more and I want first of all to make it smaller, how do you think I could make that flame smaller?

21 (P) Turn the collar.

22 (T) Turn the collar, any other suggestions? To make the flame smaller.

23 (P) Turn the gas.

24 (T) Pardon, son?

25 (P) Turn the gas down.

26 (T) Turn the gas down, so we've had two suggestions, any more? Quite happy about those two?

27 (P) Yes.

28 (T) Well, which order shall we do them, shall we take them in the order I got them?

29 (P) Yes.

30 (T) We said the first one was to . . .

31 (P) Turn the collar.

212 *Psychopedagogy*

32 (T) Turn the collar –

33 (P) It's gone invisible.

34 (P) Faster.

35 (T) We get quite a different flame there, don't we? We'd better talk about this later, but is it really any shorter?

36 (P) No.

37 (T) No, not really, is it? – so that's not really the answer, but we certainly get a different flame, that we must look at in detail soon. Well the other suggestion was that we turn the gas tap down, whoops! Well, we can certainly make the flame . . . ?

38 (P) Smaller.

39 (T) Smaller, by turning the gas down. Now when I turn the gas tap down, what am I in fact controlling? What am I stopping in this case?

40 (P) The gas.

41 (T) Exactly – I'm controlling the amount of gas that's coming through the pipe, aren't I? So if I want to control the height of the flame or the length of it, if you like, then I must use the –?

42 (P) Gas tap.

43 (T) Gas tap. OK. Now, that's fine, but at the moment it's flickering about, yet this one here that's been going for some minutes is certainly not flickering about and it's caused that water to start boiling, and we can see, if you like, and I'll just take that away now and put that side by side – well nearly side by side – anyhow with the gas taps full on, we've got quite a different flame. What is the difference between that Bunsen burner and that Bunsen burner? What do you think is causing the different flame?

44 (P) You've got that air-control column open –

45 (T) Yes.

46 (P) That's facing there.

Concept teaching 213

47 (T) Yes, and so what is open?

48 (P) The chimney.

49 (T) No, not the chimney –

50 (P) Oh, no.

51 (T) The bottom of the chimney is open, but what do we call it?

52 (P) The air.

53 (T) Look at the board if you like, I don't mind you looking at the board.

54 (P) The jet.

55 (T) No, look again – what's the name for that hole at the bottom of the chimney?

56 (P) The air hole.

57 (T) The air hole – the air hole is open. If I close it, I get exactly the same kind of flame.

58 (P) It disappears.

59 (T) Well now, we'd better start thinking about this, hadn't we? Let's try and figure out why this is the case. I'll move that over here, so that we can get them side by side, so that we can remember then that if I open the air hole we notice the flame starts to change, and you told me it's changed simply because obviously I've done something and what I've done is simply opened that air hole by moving the air control column. And we get a different flame just because we open the air hole.

60 (P) Air gets in.

61 (T) The air is getting in, where is the air getting in? Obviously it's getting in through . . .

62 (P) The jet.

63 (P) The air hole.

64 (T) Through the hole. Air from outside here is being sucked in and mixing inside there with the gas, so what in effect is burning there, compared to that one? I'll leave it on,

214 *Psychopedagogy*

then you can do a comparison but concentrate on that first.

65 (P) Blue.

66 (T) Give me a few words to describe that –

67 (P) Blue.

68 (T) Blue.

69 (P) Thin.

70 (T) Thin.

71 (P) Transparent.

72 (T) Yes, it is. I can see you through there. Sorry, I didn't hear that one.

73 (P) Tall.

74 (T) Fairly tall, yes.

75 (P) Fast.

76 (T) Fast yes, what does that suggest? What hint am I trying to give you?

77 (P) You can hear it.

78 (T) You can hear it – can you hear that one?

79 (P) No.

80 (T) I'll soon find out – we've now got a –?

81 (P) Silent.

82 (T) A silent flame, open the air hole and we get a –?

83 (P) Buzz.

84 (T) Buzzing, noisy flame. So we can see quite a difference. I wonder then about one or two things I want to ask you. First of all, if it wasn't necessary to have this air collar and the air hole and we could make do with the flame as it is now, then obviously it wouldn't be there would it? and we would simply make use of it as it is. But they found it better to incorporate that so that we get a mixture of air and gas burning and we get quite a different flame. Can anyone tell me why air makes all that difference, any ideas, any guesses? Why do you

Concept teaching 215

think – try and work it out – why do you think the air seems to make all that difference? Yes?

85 (P) Because the air wants to get out and it's speeding up.

86 (T) I see – no that's not the answer, no.

87 (P) When the air gets in the gas is already going so it shoots up with it and more is being pushed out.

88 (T) It's certainly travelling up with it, yes, but does it travel up, disappear and just go out?

89 (P) Air makes fire go better.

90 (T) Air makes – say it again, son.

91 (P) Fire go better.

92 (T) Air makes fire go better.

In order to keep the extract reasonably short I reported the naming of the parts of the burner rather than quoting verbatim. However, the teacher in this part of the lesson did quite carefully and systematically explain the labels and thus introduce the pupils to the terms to be used. In the extract given the teacher draws attention to some of the key aspects of the apparatus: the intense heat produced, making the burner very hot, and the crucial effect of the introduction of air to the flame. I think you will agree that he fulfilled very reasonably most elements of the schedule for concept teaching. He used his own language to increase the salience of criterial attributes. He used the pupils' own language to help this. He had real exemplars present to demonstrate and he provided feedback to the pupils on the results of their comments. He did not have non-exemplars present and this could be regarded as a weakness. If he had had other forms of burner and had the pupils try melting glass or copper and observing the different types of flame, this would probably have had the effect of sharpening up their understanding of the concept. He did, however, use another Bunsen burner, so that the pupils were able to compare the effects of flame with air and flame without air. This could be regarded as providing an exemplar (the burner with the air turned on) and a non-exemplar (the burner with the air turned off) in counterposition (43).

216 *Psychopedagogy*

I should now like to present a very different approach to the problem of teaching for concept learning. In this case the teacher was attempting to compare two methods of teaching concepts: an inductive method and a deductive method. In the following extract the deductive approach is being used. The teacher indicates to the pupils the criterial attributes of the concept 'immigrant' and helps the pupils to discriminate and classify according to these attributes. The teacher is focusing particularly on the use of positive and negative exemplars of the concept and practising their use.

LESSON FROM LIFE: 6*

1 (T) Now children, today we are going to look at a particu-class of person we call an immigrant . . . see it up there. Can you say that?

2 (Ps) Yes.

3 (T) Say it for me.

4 (Ps) Immigrant.

5 (T) Immigrant. Now, there are three important things that I want you to remember about an immigrant. The first thing is . . . Can you read the first one . . . Margaret?

6 (M) They come into a country.

7 (T) They come into a country. That's the first most important thing about an immigrant . . . they come into a country; and you've got to remember that . . . you've got to remember all three because . . . eh . . . when you're looking at these examples that I'm going to show you, you'll have to remember them because . . . eh . . . each example . . . must have all of these three. Right? Now, the next one is that the purpose is to settle. What does settle mean?

8 (Ps) Stay . . . stay there.

9 (T) It means to stay . . . that they're going to make their home there. And the next one is . . . we've already said

* B. C. J. Devlin (1974), *An Experiment in Concept Thinking*, Liverpool University. Mimeo.

Concept teaching 217

that . . . that they're going to stay. Now remember those three. The first one is . . . [pupils join in] . . . they come into a country. The next one is . . . [pupils join in] . . . the purpose is to settle down . . . they're going to make their home there and they're going to stay.

10 (Ps) Yes . . . Yes.

11 (T) Remember those three now.

12 (Ps) Yes . . . Yes.

13 (T) Well . . . now we're going to look at some examples to see whether these people are immigrants or not. Some of them are immigrants and some of them are not. Right? . . . and we're going to decide which one is an immigrant and which one isn't. . . . Now . . . can anybody read that for me? . . . How about you, Gaynor?

14 (T) . . . Mr Blunt and his family arrived in America to settle in Los Angeles (which is in America). Now, is . . . eh . . . Mr Blunt an immigrant?

15 (Ps) No . . . he's . . .

16 (T) Let's . . . let's look at the three things here . . . he's come into the country . . . right?

17 (Ps) Yes . . . Yes . . . Yes.

18 (T) The purpose is . . . ?

19 (Ps) To settle.

20 (T) It already tells you here . . .

21 (Ps) Yes . . . to settle . . . to settle . . . in Los Angeles.

22 (T) To settle . . . so therefore he must be going to stay. Margaret, is he an immigrant, then?

23 (M) Yes.

24 (T) We all agree with Margaret?

25 (Ps) Yes . . . Yes.

26 (T) Mr Blunt is an immigrant. . . . Now, the next one. . . . Mr Geldwasser . . . that's a funny name, isn't it? He

218 *Psychopedagogy*

has come from Germany . . . he came in 1924, married
an English lady . . . [pupils join in] . . . and he never
returned to Germany. Now again, let's look at our
three points here. He came into the country?

27 (Ps) Yes . . . Yes.

28 (T) . . . from Germany. What was his purpose? Did he
come in to settle?

29 (Ps) Yes . . . Yes.

30 (T) Yes, he must have done . . .

31 (Ps) Yes . . . Yes . . .

32 (T and Ps) . . . because he married an English lady . . .

33 (P) . . . and she made him . . .

34 (T) . . . and did he stay?

35 (Ps) Yes . . . Yes . . .

36 (T) How do we know he stayed?

37 (Ps) Because he never came back to Germany . . . he never
returned to Germany.

38 (T) He never . . . he never came back to Germany. Right.
Very good. . . . The next one. This is a lady this time.
You can't pronounce her name, can you?

39 (Ps) Yes . . . Se . . .

40 (T) Senora . . .

41 (T and Ps) Ravioli. Senora Ravioli . . .

42 (T) That's a nice name for her, isn't it?

43 (Ps) Senora Ravioli . . . Senora Ravioli . . .

44 (T) Now she has come from Italy [pupils join in] . . . to
visit her daughter who lives in Blackpool. . . . So, she
came into the country but . . .

45 (T and Ps) . . . she hasn't settled.

46 (P) . . . she hasn't settled . . . she hasn't settled.

47 (T) She's come into the country, though, hasn't she?

48 (P) Yes.

Concept teaching 219

49 (T) What was her purpose?

50 (Ps) To see her daughter.

51 (T) To see her daughter.

52 (P) She's going back. . . . She lives in Blackpool. . . . She's going back to wherever she lives.

53 (T) She's going back, Margaret . . . good girl . . . she's going back . . . therefore . . .

54 (Ps) She's not an immigrant . . .

55 (T) Is Senora Ravioli an immigrant?

56 (Ps) No . . . No.

57 (T) Are you sure?

58 (Ps) Yes.

59 (T) You're positive?

60 (Ps) Yes.

61 (T) Now, what have we got so far? We've got Mr Blunt . . . which was he?

62 (Ps) An immigrant . . . an immigrant.

63 (T) He was an immigrant. He . . . he's all of these three. Mr Geldwasser? . . .

64 (Ps) . . . an immigrant . . . an immigrant.

65 (T) But the lady . . .

66 (Ps) not . . . not . . .

67 (T and Ps) . . . is not an immigrant.

68 (T) Right?

69 (Ps) Yes. Yes.

70 (T) Now let's look at the next one. . . . We've got two men that were immigrants and a lady that was not an immigrant. . . . We've got another man now . . . and we will see whether or not he's an immigrant . . . because the first two men were immigrants. Now . . . Mr Madu . . .

71 (Ps) M-a-d-u.

220 *Psychopedagogy*

72 (T) He has come to live in Liverpool, right? ... for two years in order to study at the university ...

73 (Ps) University ...

74 (T) ... when he finishes his studies, he intends to teach back home in Nigeria. ... Well? ... what do you think about that?

75 (Ps) He isn't an immigrant ... he isn't.

76 (T) How do you know? He's come into the country, hasn't he?

77 (Ps) Because ... because ...

78 (P) He's going back home.

79 (T) He's going back home.

80 (P) He's going back to Nigeria.

81 (T) Therefore he's not going to make his home here and he's not going to stay.

82 (P1) He's going back ...

83 (P2) He's only going to study for two years, then he's going back.

84 (T) Yes ... so he's not going to stay?

85 (Ps) No ... no ...

86 (T) Right.

87 (P) He's not an immigrant ...

88 (T) So ... which is he then? Is he an immigrant or is he not?

89 (Ps) No ... no he's not an immigrant ... he's not an immigrant.

90 (T) Right ... oh ... we've got these stuck. ... Here's another lady. Now ... the other lady ... Senora Ravioli ... what was she? Was she an immigrant?

91 (Ps) No ... no.

92 (T) No, she wasn't. This is another lady. ... Madame Blanche Mange ...

Concept teaching 221

93 (Ps) Madame Blanche Mange . . . [laughter]

94 (T) That's not an English name, is it?

95 (Ps) No . . . no.

96 (T) No. Can you guess what name that is?

97 (P1) French.

98 (P2) France.

99 (T) A French name. Exactly. Now, she has lived in London for fifty years . . . she was buried yesterday in France the country of her birth. . . . Now, this is a hard one. We've got to think hard about this one. Has she come into the country?

100 (Ps) Yes . . . Yes.

101 (T) She obviously must have done . . . fifty years ago. Right? . . . So she came into the country fifty years ago. Did she make her home in the country?

102 (Ps) Yes . . . Yes.

I think you will agree that the teacher in this lesson was setting about the teaching of the concept in a very systematic and probably fruitful way. My main reservation would be that she might have programmed the exemplars more carefully so as to gradually increase the difficulty of discriminating. However, she did arrange a programme of positive and negative exemplars and she did spell out the criterial attributes and their labels at the beginning. She also dealt quite sensitively with an important non-criterial attribute, colour, when she talked about Mr Madu, a black man who was not an immigrant.

At this stage of the discussion I think you will probably find it useful to consider an extract from a lesson which may be taken as a non-exemplar of concept teaching. I hope that by considering this extract you will clarify your ideas about concept teaching.

I decided that the extract was not an example of concept teaching by examining it in the light of the concept-teaching schedule introduced earlier. I find in the extract that follows none of the attributes that I think are criterial – that is, essential – for concept teaching. The extract deals with an aspect of arithmetic with

222 *Psychopedagogy*

children of about eight to nine years. They are working with blocks on calculations involving the use of different bases. The word 'base' has obviously been introduced in earlier lessons, and the children are now using the apparatus and their previous experience of working with it to carry out new operations. As you will see, in the extract the teacher does not introduce any new terms or present any exemplars herself. The only thing that she does that comes within the purview of the concept-teaching schedule is to provide feedback on the results of children's efforts. It is possible, of course, to argue that the teacher had done the basic teaching of the use of bases and the apparatus in previous lessons and was consolidating in the extract we consider. I do not dispute this; I merely provide the extract as an example of teaching where no new concepts are introduced.

There is a feature of the lesson which gives us an insight into a very important aspect of classroom life. You will note that the teacher spends a considerable amount of time in activities that are not directly connected with the pupils' learning in any formal sense. They are management activities. Very often no new behaviour or understanding is being developed. Pupils are being told what to do or are being helped with their materials, are being given instructions on organizational matters. 'Right, sit up. Right, erm, people working in your books start . . .'; '. . . find some scales and bring them up.' Scrutiny of a random selection of lesson transcriptions convinced me that a very large proportion of class time is spent on these activities. Surveys of the way teachers actually spend their days bears out this unsystematic observation (Duthie 1970; Hilsum and Cane 1971). Now I suggest you consider the extract with an eye to identifying the different types of teacher activity and deciding whether any of it might be seen as contributing to pupils' concept learning.

LESSON FROM LIFE: 7

    1 (T) Right, Margaret, we'll have a base 6 today . . . we'll have a base 4 today . . .

    2 (P) Please Miss my [?] is slipping.

    3 (T) Right, sit up. Right, erm, people working in your books

Concept teaching **223**

start, without any fuss, Christopher – people working on the blocks, remember what I've said – no need for any fuss. First of all people working on the blocks can start building something, using whatever parts you like, then you can work out in a few moments how much you've used and who's used the most. [Pupil murmuring] . . . Right, you can do it today. [Pupil inaudible] . . . No, you can stay with your group today. Now, Hilary. . . . Do you know where the scales are in the stock room, opposite Mrs Read's room? Go down there, the room opposite Mrs Read's, you know, next to the staff room – find some scales and bring them up.

4 (P) I haven't got my book, I've lost my book.

5 (T) It's on my desk, I think, isn't it?

6 (P) Miss, I got . . . [babble]

7 (T) You only need one, never mind, pretend the one isn't. Put them on there, Nicholas. . . . No, you missed a lesson, didn't you, so you can join in with your group today.

8 (P) [Inaudible.]

9 (T) It's on the cupboard there. Come on . . . use, erm . . . have you read this, three figures, one, two and three, you can make six different numbers, they've given you the ones that you can make. Now all you've got to do is write down the biggest of these numbers; that's not difficult is it – which is the biggest? [Pupil inaudible] . . . No, what is that one?

10 (P) 321.

11 (T) That's right, 321 is the biggest.

12 (P) Shall I give them books?

13 (T) No, they don't all need them, just give yours out . . . [babble] . . . someone's got mixed up, haven't they? . . . Have you got base 5?

14 (P) Yes.

224 *Psychopedagogy*

15 (T) That's right, now if you can do the weighing part – are you all right, do you know what you're doing?

16 (P) Yes.

17 (T) What are you doing, Margaret? The first one's done for you, so – sixteen pennies is one and fourpence so now you're going to find out what? [pupils inaudible] . . . that's right – you're doing the same, the same idea – you're doing it opposite, are you? – yes. One and threepence is how many pennies?

18 (P) Fifteen.

19 (T) So now you find out one and ninepence is how many pennies – Right?

20 (P) It's got number three . . .

21 (T) Pardon?

22 (P) What's this one here?

23 (T) What have you got the answer card for, have you finished!

24 (P) I put the word . . .

25 (T) You don't fetch the answer card till you've finished them all – you thought you had. – You've written down the biggest and the smallest, yes – now write the numbers down in order, starting with the smallest, so those in order; put that back till you've finished.

26 (P) Miss Wright, shall I put pence after every sum like that?

27 (T) Well, what's the short way of putting pence? – the short way of writing pennies?

28 (P) P.E.

29 (T) No – just one letter for pennies, what is it?

30 (P) D.

31 (T) So, then – a letter D shows pennies doesn't it – just put a D. Oooh that looks – if I blow on it do you think it will go down. Right, you people start counting now

Concept teaching **225**

> what you've used, right? Count how many of each you've used. I would imagine by looking at it we can see who's used the most but, erm . . . count up and see. [Noise of blocks falling.] No work to do? Erm . . . don't bang them, you'll have all the corners knocked off.

32 (P) Can I go and get? . . .

33 (T) Yes. Right, start taking it down and count what you've used; that's a nice big one. If you have to talk, could you do it in a quiet voice do you think? You could start counting up now what you've used, see who's used the most.

In one sense there is no denying that the teacher's activity contributes to pupils' learning. Sending Hilary for the scales is one tiny element in a complex pattern of activity intended to enhance the pupils' understanding of weight. Whether telling the children to sit up also does this is another and, I suggest, more problematic matter. But in the matter of direct teacher influence in concept formation there is little in the extract that can be so classified. I do not suggest that we condemn the teacher in this extract because she has not made any direct contribution to the children's learning of concepts. I merely provide it as a non-exemplar of concept teaching to help to sharpen up your grasp of the concept of concept teaching by the counterpositioning of exemplars and non-exemplars as set out in the schedule on concept teaching.

Before leaving this extract I should like to comment on the question of management activities. Apart from the fact that some of these activities are essential if teaching is to go on at all (teaching material has to be set out, decisions have to be made about pupils going to the lavatory, windows have to be opened or closed) there is the very important fact that the complexity of teaching and establishing productive relationships with large numbers of children is an exceedingly exacting task which could hardly be sustained for long periods of time. Certainly there can be little disagreement that it would be quite impossible for a teacher to maintain at full pitch for five days a week the teaching activities

226 *Psychopedagogy*

involved in developing new concepts. The time out of teaching afforded by management activities and simple mechanical tasks renders the more exacting tasks more supportable. The pupils are, of course, similarly affected. Although the strain for them may be nothing like that of the teacher, they also need time out from highly focused cognitive activity. With young children there is the additional need for periods of physical activity. It seems to me, therefore, that the time-out type of activities have a vital part to play in learning and teaching. Just how management activities should relate ideally to the more obviously pedagogical activities is a virtually unexplored question. It is also an extremely difficult problem to tackle. The ideal mix of management and pedagogical activities is likely to vary from teacher to teacher and from pupil to pupil. It is also likely to be affected by the nature of the concepts being taught. Apart from the quantitative relationship, the nature of the connections between management factors and affective and cognitive factors is currently obscure. Clearly, management functions can influence concept formation through such things as the arrangement of learning materials. But equally they can influence greatly the affective atmosphere of the classroom. Management by threat is bound to create a different atmosphere from management by encouragement. The atmosphere generated naturally affects the cognitive climate and the interplay of management and pedagogical moves produces a complex network of cognitive and affective influences that interpenetrate and interact. Any consideration of teaching skills should take this into account.

10

Teaching psychomotor skills

Competence in psychomotor skills has an important influence on children's learning, including concept learning. This is because certain basic physical skills are prerequisite to learning in many subjects of the curriculum, perhaps particularly in the learning of younger children. The key subject of reading that many teachers of young children will be teaching depends heavily upon certain psychomotor skills that adults take for granted. A knowledge of perceptual and motor skills will help a teacher of beginning reading considerably. But even older pupils and adults embarking upon new kinds of learning often need to acquire certain basic perceptual and motor skills as prerequisites to the learning of new bodies of theoretical knowledge. Examples of this type of activity are learning to handle apparatus in scientific experiments, and learning to use simple equipment in geography. The teacher himself could well be faced with simple learning of this kind. In order to function efficiently, most teachers need to have a working knowledge of how to operate simple audio-visual aids. A knowledge of skill learning could help them to help themselves if they have not already acquired the skills.

228 *Psychopedagogy*

In other chapters I have used the word 'skill' in relation to general capabilities including intellectual skills. I have, in fact, talked about the skill of reading. Here I am speaking particularly of skills involving perception and motor (physical) activity. There is considerable similarity in the notion of skills of the latter type and the motor schemas discussed earlier. Basically the notion involves the development of complex capabilities over time by a gradual enlargement of existing abilities. A skill does not just involve the chaining of large numbers of discrete responses, but also their smooth integration in a unitary, more complex activity than the constituent elements.

An adult will have a vast repertoire of simple skills that he takes for granted: tying shoelaces or neckties, fastening and unfastening buttons, combing the hair, washing hands and face; walking, standing and swimming are more complex skills that most of us learn by adulthood. A moment's reflection will be enough, however, to remind us that we did not always take them for granted. Observing young children trying to tie laces or carry out other simple skills will bring home to us how difficult these 'simple' skills once were. Such observation will also make clear that what for an adult is a smooth unity is a discrete sequence of actions for a child. Typically the early stages of learning a new skill may be seen as an example of response chaining. One response, e.g. gripping the shoelace, becomes the stimulus for the next response, e.g. crossing one lace over the other; that response in turn becomes the stimulus for the next response, tucking one lace under the other, and so on, until the activity is complete and the lace tied. At each stage in the chain the learner needs a mediator to tell him what to do next. This is likely to be provided by the teacher in the early stages but later comes under the learner's own control and he thinks: 'Now put that lace over the other.' Eventually, of course, this mediator to all intents and purposes disappears.

Unlike the learning of concepts and principles, which in the main tends to be open-ended in the sense that one never reaches a full and final level of understanding, psychomotor skills can be conceived of as having optimum end states of competence. This is not to imply that perfection is reached by all learners but that it is possible to analyse the task and make a description of a

Teaching psychomotor skills 229

response pattern optimally suited to carrying out the activity in question. A further distinction between skills of this type and cognitive learning is that after having mastered the activity at an adequate level, given a particular learner's physical and psychological state, the skill can be polished by repeated practice or overlearning so that it eventually becomes habitual and automatic in performance. Herein lies a potential problem, however. Unless the initial training is satisfactory, it is quite possible for a learner to acquire unsatisfactory response patterns in the learning stage and practise these responses in an overlearning stage so that the bad habits become habitual and the performance is thereby rendered unsatisfactory.

You do not have to look far to find examples of unsatisfactory response learning by adults. Observe a small number of car drivers steering round a corner. The chances are high that a large proportion of them will turn the wheel by pulling with both hands on the same side. All instruction in the subject, however, stresses the importance of passing the wheel through the hands and maintaining a grip on both sides. Holding the wheel like this enables the driver to exert greater force on the wheel if necessary and also to take action should an emergency arise during the course of the manœuvre. The reasons why so many drivers make this mistake are no doubt complex, but probably the main one is the lack of sufficient practice after the skill had been acquired. (The assumption is made here that the driving test has ensured at some time that the correct method of steering was being used.) Similar problems can be found in school. A child who does not learn to hold a pen satisfactorily will continue to practise the wrong actions so much that any later attempt to correct the action will be very difficult to accomplish. It thus behoves teachers to ensure adequate practice that will be resistant to the development of inappropriate responses.

This chapter will, therefore, be concerned with ways in which a teacher can help pupils to acquire the kind of perceptual-motor skills that are instrumental to other learning, and with how to guard against the learning of unsatisfactory responses that are likely to interfere with efficient operation of the skills in question. In fact, much of the approach will be appropriate for skill learning

230 *Psychopedagogy*

in fields more centrally involved with this question, such as the craft subjects and physical education. (For a general discussion of motor skills, see Welford 1968.)

Objectives

Teaching psychomotor skills involves many of the basic techniques discussed in the teaching of content and in developing motivation in the classroom. In the first place an understanding of the nature of the skill involved and an analysis of its key constituents will provide an insight into, and help to provide a rationale for, the teaching approach to be adopted. This would comprise, in the pre-active stage, a prescription for teaching. The implementation of the prescription would comprise the interactive stage of the teaching and the comparison of final performance with the initial specification would provide the grounds for evaluation.

I think it will help our understanding of the nature of motor skills and our attempts to devise a useful schedule for teaching those skills if we consider the type of objectives that we might set up in relation to such skills. Work in the field of psychomotor objectives is not so advanced as in the cognitive field; however, work by Harrow (1972) will give us an indication of some important considerations.

Harrow takes an approach resembling that of the Bloom taxonomy. Her taxonomy goes from level 1, reflex movements, to level 6, which she calls 'non-discursive communication', an example of which would be 'moving expressively to communicate emotions'. Unlike the cognitive taxonomy, the lower levels of the psychomotor taxonomy are matters that the average teacher is unlikely to encounter. Levels 1 and 2 of the taxonomy deal with simple involuntary motor responses to stimuli, at the lowest to such things as crawling, walking and jumping to sliding at level 2. It is true that some children with problems of coordination may well have difficulty with some of the latter activities, but such children should really be given special remedial treatment.

Level 3 takes us into the realm of the more common motor activities. An excerpt from the taxonomy is probably the most

Teaching psychomotor skills 231

useful way of explaining this level (see Figure 10.1). Harrow refers to this level as *perceptual abilities*.

These abilities clearly relate to the kinds of learning that take place in the early years of schooling or before. They underpin some of the basic skills crucial to learning in later stages of school.

Figure 10.1　*Harrow's taxonomy for teaching psychomotor skills*

Level 3 Perceptual abilities	Activities	Examples
Perceptual abilities are really inseparable from motor movements. They help learners to interpret stimuli so that they can adjust to their environment. Superior motor activities depend upon the development of perception. They involve kinesthetic discrimination, visual discrimination, auditory discrimination and coordinated abilities of eye and hand, eye and foot. The skill of discrimination underlies all these abilities, whether they are gross in character or fine in quality. This skill has to be deliberately learned and practised over a wide range of conditions.	Catching Bouncing Eating Writing Balancing Bending Drawing 　from 　memory Distin- 　guishing by 　touching Exploring	Discriminates 　kinesthetically, 　visually, 　tactilely, 　auditorily. Coordinates two 　or more per- 　ceptual abilities 　and movement 　patterns

(Based on Harrow (1972) and Davies (1976).)

Reading is not mentioned in the taxonomy but it depends on the various types of discrimination referred to. Writing, simple drawing and distinguishing by touching are instrumental skills in many, more complex, learning activities. Writing and reading are abilities at this level and are crucial for most higher-level cognitive learning. Both involve most of the attributes referred to in the taxonomy.

As we ascend in the hierarchy, we find that the abilities in

Figure 10.2 *Illustrative analysis of the task of teaching handwriting★*

General content	Method of stimulus presentation	Pupils' responses	Feedback	Evaluation
Writing (This is the overall skill) *Subordinate skills†* The instrument rests between the thumb and index finger and is grasped lightly by the thumb and middle and index finger. The hand slopes so that it rests on the third and fourth fingers. The hand slides across the working surface as the letters are formed. The arm, hand and fingers are all used in forming letters.	Pictures Blackboard Films Teacher explains Teacher demonstrates Teacher guides Teacher cues Video-recordings Other pupils	Pupil *explains* how to carry out the sub-skills and the overall skill. (This is a type-C skill using the categories discussed on pp. 160–2.) Pupil points out or sorts positive and negative exemplars of correct methods in overall skill and subordinate skills. (This is a type-B skill.) Pupil demonstrates writing himself. (Type-A skill.)	Teacher's comments. (Can be used with skills A, B and C.) Comparison with 'model' examples. Comparison with product of own earlier attempts. It would be possible to devise some instrumentation of feedback. Discussed in the text. Kinesthetic. 'Feel' in muscles.	Teacher assessment of sample of handwriting. Pupil's own evaluation on criteria established in teaching phase.

★ In comparison with the analysis for conceptual learning, specific examples are not given, because the general principles are the same throughout. No category of learning type is given, since the learning of motor skills in formal education almost always involves multiple discrimination.

† See *Encyclopedia of Educational Research* ed. R. L. Ebel, Collier-Macmillan, 1969, pp. 571–9.

N.B. This analysis could be continued by examining the finer grain of the movements involved. Only the first column would be affected by the additional entries.

Teaching psychomotor skills 233

level 3 become incorporated in more complex physical movements. Level-5 abilities are those that combine simpler abilities, usually involving the manipulation of tools or apparatus. They are performed smoothly and with apparently little effort or thought. Examples of activities at this level are dancing, sawing, skating, filing, typing, playing the piano.

Finally, at level 6 we find highly sophisticated activities referred to in general in terms such as 'Moves expressively so as to communicate emotions', 'Moves expressively so as to communicate aesthetically or creatively inner feelings'. Examples are 'to smile knowingly', 'to express facially', 'to paint skilfully'.

There is no implication, in using this method of categorizing, that we have a thoroughly substantiated hierarchy of skills. It is best to see the taxonomy as a heuristic device like those I discussed earlier. But I suggest that a teacher working at the pre-active stage in skill teaching could find useful guidance in the scheme, especially by devising objectives and carrying out task analyses.

Task analysis

As in all teaching the identification of the prerequisite capabilities is vital for efficient teaching. What they are will be arrived at by an analysis of the learning task itself. The nature of the teaching task will then be determined by ascertaining the learner's existing abilities and comparing them with those demanded by competent execution of the skill. The Harrow taxonomy will be of help here in suggesting the relationship between different types of abilities. It cannot give all the answers, however, nor can any other system, since our knowledge in the field is far from perfect. But using the approach suggested here will give a teacher some insight into the problem that he would otherwise lack.

It is possible to apply the method of task analysis I discussed earlier (Figure 8.1) to the teaching of psychomotor skills, although some of the categories are not entirely applicable. Under the heading 'General content' one would place the elements of the skill instead of the sub-concepts as in the analysis of content teaching. There are other differences, but over all the method of analysis can act as a useful guide and suggest to us activities to be

234 *Psychopedagogy*

adopted in the interactive stage of teaching. To exemplify the approach, Figure 10.2 applies the analysis to the teaching of writing, a skill that most children have to be taught in school and which is clearly an important instrumental skill for other learning.

Implicit in the analysis in Figure 10.2 is the mode of operation at the interactive stage of teaching. The actual working out of the teaching activities will depend on a knowledge of other teaching skills such as explaining and demonstrating which we shall consider later. One other thing about Figure 10.2 may need a little more explanation. I have referred to the types of skills A, B and C which I previously discussed. I suggest that even in the teaching of psychomotor skills these categories have their place. Before being able to write fluently himself, a learner will benefit from an explanation of how to set about the task. He should be able to explain this to someone else. This is a type-C skill. Next he should be able to look at someone attempting to carry out the activity and say whether the correct procedure was being used. This is a type-B skill. Finally the learner demonstrates his capability by carrying out the activity himself. This is a type-A skill. All these can be applied to the example of handwriting, but also to other skills, some of which I shall discuss later.

Guiding and cueing

A pupil learning a new motor skill will have difficulty if the teacher just demonstrates the activity and says 'Do as I do'. Writing is a particularly good example of this problem. A teacher demonstrating writing on the blackboard could well be creating difficulties for his pupils. Merely demonstrating the finished product is of little help. It may be of some help for the pupils who are already adept at handling pen or pencil but it could be confusing for others. Writing on the blackboard involves quite different techniques from writing on paper. The chalk is held differently, the arm moves differently, the whole body posture is different. The only real resemblance it has to writing on paper is the product, the writing. But, apart from this, a skilled performance will be a smooth and unified whole and will afford little guidance to a new learner. Thus although demonstration has an

Teaching psychomotor skills 235

important part in the teaching of skills it is important to use it carefully.

The first step in teaching a new skill is to explain what the finished performance involves, what the subordinate parts of the skill are and how they link together. Teacher talk can be augmented by examples in pictures, films, drawings on the blackboard and by the teacher demonstrating the individual subordinate parts. By these means the pupils will learn simple concepts about the correct movements and their interrelations. They can demonstrate their grasp of these concepts by explaining to the teacher or by discriminating between examples of correct and incorrect activities.

The next stage shades into the first. Using much the same methods of presenting the task, the teacher now involves the learner in his own activity. The learner imitates the actions of the teacher or uses other stimulus materials as models of technique. The variation on this method developed by P. Y. Galperin has proved effective (see p. 102). Instead of the learner manipulating the instrument himself, the teacher carries out the activity under directions and prompting from the pupil. This is an interesting procedure which should be investigated more widely. The argument is that by being freed of the concrete activity the learner is more able to concentrate on the elements in the task and organize his own learning more effectively.

Whichever method is used – and there are probably good grounds for using both – the learner progresses at this stage to making his own attempts at carrying out the activity. Now the teacher needs to prompt and guide, probably mainly orally, but possibly by actually guiding the learner's activity physically. In the case of handwriting the teacher might actually guide the learner's hand and fingers to enable him to experience something like correct muscular tensions.

At the beginning of this activity the constituent elements should be tackled first. This simplifies the learning and helps accuracy. In the case of handwriting, if a beginner has to attempt to cope with all four of the subordinate skills at the same time, it is quite likely that some of them will go amiss, so that he could well grip the pencil properly but make difficulties for himself by

236 *Psychopedagogy*

bearing down on the working surface rather than having a light sliding action. Concentrating on one thing at a time at the start helps avoid this.

Once the sub-skills are mastered they are keyed together. The completion of the first element becomes the stimulus for the beginning of the second. Taking the correct grip on the pencil becomes the stimulus for resting the hand on the writing surface in the manner described, and this itself sparks off the activity of forming the letters, which in turn leads to the sliding motion across the paper. Throughout the activity the teacher will prompt and guide as necessary. The prompting should be kept to the absolute minimum, the aim being gradually to fade it out and allow the learner to assume responsibility for his own actions. It will probably be helpful at this stage to encourage the learner to take over his own cueing and guiding. In the same way as he cued and guided the teacher earlier, he now attempts to do the same for himself. At first this could well be by speaking aloud, but this should gradually fade away into internal speech and then into thoughts about the procedure.

Feedback

I have, of course, been talking about feedback throughout this section: the cueing and guiding I mention is precisely that. As in most learning, the teacher's voice is a most versatile and effective medium of feedback for the reasons I have discussed earlier. By its use he is able to help the learner to perceive subtle differences in technique that would be difficult to convey otherwise. It is particularly important in the early stages to provide feedback promptly; lacking it, the learner would be doubtful about his performance which could well go wildly astray. In teaching involving one teacher and many learners, providing feedback like this is very difficult. In the case of handwriting, much thought is needed if the teacher has many pupils. Providing a model for the whole class, then asking them to imitate it and providing feedback on a class basis could lead to some very unsatisfactory learning. It would be apparently much slower to see each pupil in turn but in the long run it could well be more economical and almost

Teaching psychomotor skills 237

certainly produce more competent writers. It is, of course, basically impossible to provide satisfactory feedback on a class basis.

In my task analysis I suggest that it might be possible to devise instrumentation to provide feedback. I am not aware that this has been done but it would be possible to monitor electronically virtually all the elements in the skill of handwriting; it would, however, probably be prohibitively expensive. Videotape feedback, on the other hand, while not providing the same immediacy, could well be used to give some idea of performance in the intermediate stages. In other skill learning, much use has been made of instrumentation to provide feedback. At its most sophisticated the simulators for teaching aeroplane pilots or astronauts provide feedback in safe conditions during training. A much earlier if somewhat cruder device was the quintain which was used to train jousters in medieval times. The jouster charged a shield mounted on a pivot with his lance. If he smote it at the wrong speed or in the wrong place, the pivot swung in such a way as to bring round a sack of sand to give him a buffet. The trouble with this device was that although it gave the jouster overall feedback (he'd got it wrong) it didn't tell him how he had gone wrong. Effective feedback must do just that. Similarly, if we wish to use videotape feedback in the classroom it is important to do more than let the pupils see the error of their ways; we have either to draw their attention to the key factors making for their errors or, better still, give them adequate teaching to enable them to scrutinize their own performance critically.

Scrutinizing one's own performance critically is a type-B skill in my taxonomy. The difference between the operation and the earlier description of its use is that here one is bringing to bear one's knowledge of an activity to analyse one's own performance and thereby enhance not only one's understanding of the process but also one's own practice in future attempts.

These various methods of providing feedback will themselves be contributing to one of the most important sources of continuing feedback once instruction is ended. The learner gradually comes to associate particular muscular tensions with the successful accomplishment of the task. As Bruner put it, 'he remembers

238 *Psychopedagogy*

in his muscles'. This remembering is kinesthetic feedback. Muscle tension tells the learner whether he is right or not. It is clearly of extreme importance in skill learning because it is an internal source of feedback.

Practice

Achieving a criterion level of performance of a skill is a demonstration of learning. However, for the skill to be useful it is necessary for it to be part of the learner's permanent behavioural repertoire. If a learner is content to achieve competence and take no further steps, this is not likely to happen. In the example of incorrect steering in car driving mentioned earlier in this chapter, being charitable to driving instructors, I suggested that the drivers had achieved a level of competence sufficient to get them through the driving test but had not practised the skill sufficiently for it to become a permanent piece of behaviour. Reasons for this are probably not far to seek. Most of us have to pay for driving lessons and are highly motivated to take the test after as few lessons as possible. We reach criterion, the driving test, and thereafter our driving is a more or less private affair. We receive little feedback on our performance and even if something goes wrong we are unlikely to be able to analyse the reasons any more than was the jouster using the quintain. If, on the other hand, nothing goes wrong it is possible to drift from the correct exercise of the skill until we are doing many things incorrectly and placing ourselves and others at greater risk should an emergency arise.

In order to prevent this state of affairs in any motorskill learning, it is necessary to provide for practice with feedback. In the case of handwriting the pupil needs to practise writing over a period of time not only with the feedback of being able to see the results of his activities by the words he writes, but also with corrective feedback from the teacher on the elements of the skill. The question might be asked: why bother with this corrective feedback if the product is satisfactory? If the motorist gets to his destination, if the cyclist does not fall off, if the skater gets along swiftly without falling down, if the writer produces legible handwriting, why worry about the constituent elements of the skill?

Teaching psychomotor skills 239

I have already tried to answer the first point. To a degree the same can be said about the other skills. Questions of safety, fatigue or in some cases avoiding damage to apparatus are all possible considerations to favour a satisfactory level of practice. The one common element to all skills that argues for a satisfactory level of practice is that, given an accurate task analysis and suitable training procedures, the adoption of sub-skills deviant from the ones recommended will almost certainly result in the learner doing less well than he would were he to use the correct techniques.

In order for the skill to be maximally useful it should be capable of application in a variety of conditions. Learning to drive one particular type of car along quiet country lanes in bright sunny weather is a useful but limited skill if the learner is to be faced with motorway driving on a dark snowy winter night or through London traffic in the rush hour. The same applies to learning other skills. A pupil needs to be able to write with different writing instruments on different kinds of surfaces of different heights and in different light conditions. What I am talking about here is akin to a complex motor schema such as I discussed earlier. It is a smoothly operable comprehensive skill which automatically adjusts to different conditions to produce the same level of competent performance. In teaching motor skills this factor needs to be taken into account and the learner exposed to a variety of realistic conditions that will expand his schemas against all likely eventualities. In arranging for this variety of experiences a teacher should bear in mind the principles rehearsed more than once in earlier discussions: introduce the learner gradually to the more complicated conditions. Do not throw him in at the deep end. Do not send him off on the motorway on a snowy night the first time he drives. Do not ask him to paint the ceiling of the Sistine Chapel before he has practised on an easel.

Independent evaluation

In the end, of course, the teacher withdraws. If he does this too early the learner will be in danger of practising incorrect sub-skills until they become fixed. But he has to remove himself from the

240 *Psychopedagogy*

scene as soon as possible without incurring this danger. The methods I have suggested above should help a teacher to do this in a controlled and satisfactory manner. The gradual fading of cueing and prompting at the early stage, the gradual tapering off of feedback at the practice stage, involving the learner in directing his own attempts through verbal commentary at different stages of his learning, and coupling all these methods of providing feedback through means other than the teacher: all these will contribute to the learner's becoming able to monitor his own exercise of his newly learned skill.

Norms

Throughout this discussion of motor skills I have made no reference to norms of performance. Such norms are often given in connection with skill training but for reasons I spell out in detail elsewhere (Chapter 15) I think that they are in general frequently unhelpful. I believe this is particularly the case when we talk about motor skill training. My reasons for this belief are that norms, even those that are unsystematic, serve to signal to the unsuccessful that they are failing, which in turn exacerbates the problem because of the negative emotions generated. The unsystematic norms I referred to are the expectations that teachers and pupils have about average levels of performance in common physical skills such as running, jumping, hopping, kicking or throwing a ball. Most children have little difficulty in achieving a reasonable level of competence in such activities but others have a great deal of difficulty. The reasons for this frequently lie in poor coordination of hand and eye and foot and eye. Such children are sometimes referred to as 'clumsy'. They have disabilities that are less than totally incapacitating but are less than normal. The activities where most youngsters find no trouble give great difficulty to children with this problem. But the greatest problem of children like this is almost certainly that teachers and children tend to be unsympathetic. The derision of their peers and the impatience of their teachers creates a vicious circle from which few of them escape. Such children need special consideration rather than condemnation.

Teaching psychomotor skills 241

Taking the approach I have outlined here enables a teacher to give consideration to children with learning difficulties, since the method of task analysis and approach to teaching takes into account the learning capabilities of different children. If a child has a problem with any of the sub-tasks, there is a good chance that this can be traced to an underlying contributory ability that is insufficiently developed. A systematic attack on the deficiency may go some way to solving the problem, whereas to attempt to teach the higher-level skill without remedying the deficiency may create further problems since it is then likely that failure will ensue and depress even more the pupil's self-confidence and motivation.

Much the same can be said about learning in other fields, of course. The problem is the general expectation of 'normal' levels of performance. Such 'normal' expectations spill over into other subjects. Teachers in general expect pupils to be able to sketch reasonably well, to write legibly and neatly, and to use simple instruments and equipment adequately. Most have no trouble. Pupils with problems of coordination will, on the other hand, have a good deal of trouble. Failure to recognize this could lead to inaccurate assessment of the pupil's capabilities in the subjects under discussion. Should work in geography, history or a science subject demand a certain standard in drawing, for example? The teacher should bear in mind, if faced with a child with problems of coordination, that his indifferent performance in drawing should not be held against him when his ability is being assessed in relation to the subject of study. In fact, of course, this comment is relevant to learning in any field. And in all cases a suitable task analysis would indicate to the teacher which elements of the new learning are central and which instrumental to the achievement of his objectives. If he decides that the pupils need to draw men in armour in history, he should ask himself if the ability to draw in this case is a necessary demonstration of skills and knowledge pertinent to learning history. For children with difficulties in motor coordination, a lot depends on the answer he gives.

242 *Psychopedagogy*

A teaching schedule

Here I bring together the key elements in teaching psychomotor skills. The schedule given below provides a checklist for a teacher attempting to monitor his own teaching of skills. It can also form the basis for a supervisor of student teachers to guide and evaluate their learning. It provides an explicit rationale for tutor and student to identify the key elements in such teaching which both will be concerned to monitor.

Figure 10.3

Schedule for the teaching of psychomotor skills (STOPS) This schedule sets out in brief the key aspects of teaching activity to ensure satisfactory learning of psychomotor skills. It provides a checklist for a student teacher and/or his supervisor to evaluate this aspect of teaching. Teaching performance should be rated in some way, for example, as weak, satisfactory or good. The student will then have an idea of those aspects of his teaching that need improvement and those areas where he is competent.

A PRE-ACTIVE

1 Make a task analysis of teaching objectives to identify the key subordinate skills, to decide on methods of presentation, the nature of pupil activities, the provision of feedback, the evaluation of performance and the arrangements for monitored practice.
2 Ascertain the pupils' existing levels of competence. Pupils lacking the prerequisite motor abilities to perform the subordinate skills should not be admitted to the main programme of teaching but should be given remedial teaching to bring them up to scratch.

B INTERACTIVE

3 Establish a preliminary idea of the task by explaining and demonstrating.
4 Identify for the learner the subordinate skills and show their relationship to the overall task as in (3).
5 Involve the learner in describing the activity himself, possibly

Figure 10.3 – continued

by guiding the teacher in performing the activity and in the use of subordinate skills.

6 Prompt and guide the learner in carrying out the subdivisions of the task.

7 Prompt and guide the learner in making a smooth transition from one division of the task to the next. Use counter-positioning in areas of difficulty.

8 Fade the prompts and guidance gradually to ensure the learner assumes responsibility for his own prompting.

9 Provide feedback at all stages and for all responses if possible.

10 Arrange for practice to ensure that the learner consolidates his new skill.

11 Monitor the practice from time to time but gradually fade the monitoring.

12 Arrange for practice to take place in varying circumstances.

C Evaluative

13 Assess the level of success of the learner's performance against the objectives set out in the pre-active stage.

14 Encourage the learner to assess his own practice against the criteria established in the interactive stage, particularly (3), (4) and (5).

Psychomotor skills in practice

I have tried to show that there are certain basic principles related to the learning of perceptual motor skills that may be applied to a wide range of such skills. I have also suggested that in many cases, probably all, an element of concept learning is involved. Establishing a preliminary idea of the task often involves the learner in acquiring new concepts. Even learning to tie a shoelace can involve such learning since it is unlikely that the concept of a knot held by a child who has not yet learned to tie a lace will be more than rudimentary. By the methods of task analysis, I have suggested ways in which the teaching of motor skills can be tackled and have made reference to certain conditions in school where these methods might be used. I should now like to illustrate

244 *Psychopedagogy*

the procedures I have discussed by referring to two lessons devised for the teaching of skills in two fields: in rugby football and in music. These lessons are not reported verbatim but the skill analysis on which they are based is presented as an illustration of the way in which the same basic approach can be applied to two very dissimilar subjects. In both cases the performance of the learner at the end of instruction was extremely satisfactory even though instruction time had been very limited.

LESSON I: CATCHING A RUGBY BALL*

In this lesson the teacher carried out an analysis of rugby football to ascertain the component skills of the game. He defined two broad areas of individual and team skills. Taking the individual skills area, he identified a number of separate individual skills and from these skills selected the skill of catching the ball under certain conditions. These conditions were set out in a teaching objective which read as follows.

> At the end of instruction the pupil will be able to demonstrate his ability to catch and shield a rugby ball descending from a height of 20–25 feet while under pressure from an opponent following up at speed. The above to be carried out under normal ground and weather conditions and with a minimum standard of 80 per cent efficiency.

Next the teacher made an analysis of the sub-skills involved, taking them to form a chain of responses.

	Stimulus	*Response*
1	Sight of ball being kicked or thrown	Getting into position to receive the ball
2	Ball approaching	Raising hands, palms upwards
3	Ball touches hands	Draws ball to chest
4	Ball in body/arm contact	Body relaxes to cushion impact
5	Safe gathering of the ball	Need to protect ball from opponent
6	Approach of opponent	Presentation of hip and thigh

* J. R. Martland (1977) *The Application of Learning Theory to the Teaching of a Perceptual Motor Skill.* School of Education. Liverpool University Mimeo.

Teaching psychomotor skills **245**

Before starting to teach, the teacher tested the pupil to ensure that he could not already fulfil the objectives and that he had the prerequisite subordinate abilities. The instruction then proceeded as follows.

1 The teacher demonstrates catching, emphasizing link 2 in the chain (raising the arms above head height, palms upward, fingers outstretched).

2 The rugby ball is thrown directly to the pupil. Verbal prompts and instructions are given and as success is gained the ball is thrown to increasing heights.

3 Teacher demonstrates link 3 (taking the ball on the chest and cradling with the forearms).

4 Sequence 2 is repeated.

5 Teacher demonstrates link 4 (cushioning the ball).

6 The ball is now thrown to the pupil at a consistent height of 25 feet.

7 The trials are repeated with the pupil receiving the ball anywhere within a predetermined area marked by a grid.

8 Protection of the ball is demonstrated and an explanation of hip-and-thigh technique is given, also the need to avoid the 'knock on', which may lead to the kicker or player following up regaining possession of the ball.

9 Practice is continued with the pupil.

10 A first test of proficiency in catching the ball in a relatively stationary position is given. The minimum acceptable level of success is 80 per cent.

11 The pupil now practises the skill, running into the grid to receive the ball.

12 Opposition, in the form of another pupil, is introduced. The opposition runs at the catcher on a given signal. The run is timed initially to allow the catcher ample time. As success is gained, the time lag is reduced.

In order to maximize the efficiency of the feedback the teacher prepared a diagnostic table of likely faults and the methods of

246 *Psychopedagogy*

correcting them. This enabled him to identify and correct errors quickly and effectively.

Finally the teacher gave a test to the pupil to assess the extent to which he had achieved his objective. As I sugggested earlier, he did in fact achieve his objective and the pupil caught the ball satisfactorily five times out of five.

In this example of skill teaching, competence was acquired in a relatively short space of time (about half an hour). But, of course, for the skill to become part of the pupil's habitual repertoire he would have to practise it over a period of time and in different conditions. It would be helpful, during the early stages of practising, if the teacher were able to give occasional feedback as confirmation to the pupil that he was continuing to carry out the actions correctly.

LESSON 2: TEACHING DISCRIMINATION OF INTERVALS IN MUSIC*

Like the lesson on rugby, this lesson takes one small task from the whole of a field, in this case music. The skill is that of discriminating between notes that are different in certain ways. The difference may be simply defined as 'the distance apart of two notes on a scale'.

As I have suggested is the case with most skill learning, a pupil facing the task of learning to discriminate intervals needs to acquire or have acquired some related concepts. In the case we are considering, the teacher decided he would need to teach the concept of an interval and the principle which is used to name the intervals as well as teaching the actual discrimination of the notes. This dual purpose is reflected in his task analysis. His objective was:

> The pupil shall be able to identify aurally and name the intervals of a major scale when played consecutively, ascending from the tonic note, on a piano in any key.

The analysis the teacher developed working from this objective is set out in Figure 10.4. As you can see, both concepts and motor skills are involved in this learning and are therefore included in

* D. Evans (1977) *The Teaching of Aural Discrimination between the Intervals of a Major Scale*. School of Education. Liverpool University Mimeo.

Teaching psychomotor skills 247

the analysis. The concept is that of an interval, and the principle or rule is that 'an interval is named by the number of notes between the two notes being played'.

In order to test the grasp of concepts and principles, the pupil was asked to demonstrate on the piano keyboard. Then the procedure was as follows.

The teacher arranged a series of discrimination tasks of ascending difficulty. One of the problems in doing this was that there seemed to be no generally agreed sequence of difficulty among musicians. This is an interesting fact that may be suggestive for the teaching of this aspect of musical skills. In this example intervals were introduced by playing the two notes on the piano in ascending order of difficulty as determined by the teacher.

Each time a new interval was introduced it was played three times in different keys and then played at least twice in different keys together with the previously learned intervals. The object of this procedure was to teach the pupil a skill that would be of general application and not just confined to one key.

When the pupil had difficulty in distinguishing between intervals, the method of counterpositioning was introduced. This involves playing the intervals contiguously and attempting to highlight the differences. Verbal mediators were also introduced to assist some of the more difficult discriminations. Feedback was given to the pupil after each attempt at a discrimination.

The method of teaching achieved the objective with 79 per cent success in the final test. This is perhaps not satisfactory, since 100 per cent is really desirable. However, the lesson was very short and, given more time, there seems little doubt that 100 per cent would have been achieved. As with the rugby lesson, however, the initial learning is not enough on its own. It needs to be supplemented and consolidated with more practice, preferably with monitoring by a teacher in the early stages.

The two lessons discussed are taken from subjects commonly taught in schools and give an indication of the application and efficacy of the approach to skill training discussed here. Neither of the teachers had made a previous specialism of psychopedagogy applied to this kind of teaching. Knowledge of its principles helped

248 *Psychopedagogy*

Figure 10.4 *Task analysis of discrimination between ascending intervals of a major scale*

General content	Specific examples	Type of learning	Method of stimulus presentation
The ability to name the ascending intervals of a major scale from aural examples			
Subordinate tasks			
1 Concept of an interval	Various intervals of major scales	Concept by definition	Teacher telling. Examples of intervals played on the piano.
2 Naming intervals	Second to eighth, ascending from tonic note	Rule (or principle) learning	Teacher tells rule. Plays examples on piano in various keys.
3 Aural discrimination between intervals	As above (2)	Multiple discrimination	Teacher plays examples on piano (unseen). Teacher suggests suitable mediators verbally.

Teaching psychomotor skills 249

Pupil's response	Feedback	Evaluation
Pupil distinguishes between examples and non-examples. Pupil plays examples on piano.	Teacher's speech	Correct playing of examples
Pupil names other examples. Pupil plays intervals on request.	Teacher's speech	Correct playing oi intervals
Pupil writes intervals played, then answers verbally.	Teacher tells correct answer. Pupil corrects on response sheet.	Test section of all seven intervals. Procedure as for teaching section. Written responses analysed.

250 *Psychopedagogy*

them to an understanding of the nature of specific teaching tasks and suggested guidelines for effective teaching. In the process of preparing and teaching the lessons, both teachers acquired a new insight into the nature of the skills. A related fact of much interest to all who attempt to teach motor skills is that many of these skills have not been analysed in any systematic way. In the case of musical intervals, although learners are expected to be competent in identifying intervals there seems to be little, if any, systematic analysis that would be of help to a teacher adopting the kind of approach discussed in this chapter. There is little doubt that there is a great need for such analyses in a variety of fields. They would be of considerable value to teachers. However, any teacher faced with the problem of teaching psychomotor skills would be well advised to attempt his own analytical approach along the lines outlined above rather than to rely on demonstration and imitation augmented by exhortation. By attempting such analyses, individual teachers can make their own contribution to the application of psychological principles to teaching practice and possibly add in a small way to our understanding of those principles.

11

Teaching problem solving

In the last few chapters I have been putting in fine focus the question of how one applies the ideas from the psychology of human learning to teaching. I have discussed a model of objectives relating to pedagogy and suggested a variety of skills and concepts which, taken in conjunction, should help to improve the quality of one's teaching. At the same time, I have been conscious of the fact that the suggestions I make may have no utility at all if they are merely memorized for whatever reason. In an attempt to help the reader who is also interested in avoiding this outcome, I presented teaching schedules and suggestions for their use so that an interested reader could try them out in practice.

I have not at any stage told such a reader *exactly* how to put the ideas into practice in teaching. I have, however, tried to give him as much help as is possible in a text, so that when he faces a problem that demands the deployment of a type-A teaching skill he will be able to tackle it with a fair degree of success. I have not told him exactly how for the simple reason that it is impossible. As I have said more than once, teaching is enormously complex

252 *Psychopedagogy*

and the idea of there being identical lessons is so farfetched as to be not worthy of consideration. So every teaching problem, on this view, is unique. And, naturally, every answer must also be unique. That is, the plan and execution of every lesson will differ, if only slightly, from all others.

Apart from the uniqueness of each teaching problem, there are other factors that preclude the teaching of solutions at a distance. Obviously it is impossible for an author to prompt and guide his reader as he grapples with particular problems or to give corrective feedback when he goes astray or even give confirmatory feedback when he goes the right way. And yet these are crucial activities for any learner faced with applying the concepts and principles he has learned in the practice of a type-B or type-A skill. In the case of the psychological principles underlying teaching activities, type-B skills demand that the student teacher apply his knowledge to the analysis of an example of teaching to see if he can identify and evaluate key elements. In order for him to do this, the student teacher needs information as to whether he is on the right lines. The schedules I have presented could help a good deal, but the help of an experienced tutor would be most desirable. Similarly with type-A skills: using a schedule to evaluate one's own efforts is helpful, but a tutor working with the same schedules could not only give one a more objective appraisal but also should be more perceptive about the teaching and give guidance that would help in future.

In my attempts to help you to tackle problems of teaching I have been exemplifying some of the activities a teacher must adopt when teaching pupils to apply the knowledge he has taught them to the solution of problems. In just the same way as a student teacher might apply his knowledge to a teaching problem, the pupils would apply their knowledge to problems in the appropriate fields of study. I have already made some mention of this point when I referred to the type-A, -B and -C skills in relation to the learning of young children, and should now like to take up the general question in the hope that it will provide a little more insight into how to help pupils to learn.

Problems

When Archimedes jumped out of the bath in elation at having solved a key problem relating to the theory of flotation, his leap wasn't entirely out of the blue. His mind had for some time been just as immersed in cogitation about the theoretical principles related to the problem as his body had been in water just prior to his historic leap. In other words, people don't solve problems in areas of knowledge they know nothing about. The best qualification for successful problem solving is an extensive knowledge of the appropriate field of study.

In these pages I am doing my best to provide the basic knowledge that will enable you to solve particular teaching problems as they arise. When I use the word 'problem' I am not implying that every teaching encounter is likely to present great difficulties. But any teacher worth his salt is going to regard the lesson to be given as something of a challenge, even if only a small one. The challenge will be to make decisions to tackle the teaching in an interesting and effective way. Recall that every lesson will be a new one, so that there is really no question of 'using the notes you used last year' unless you wish to join the ranks of the partly living and not of the living teachers. Thus in each lesson there will be a demand for a novel application of principles; this is what is implied in the expression 'problem solving'.

The means I have employed to acquaint the reader with the knowledge requisite to teaching exemplify the way a teacher could tackle the job of providing his pupils with the foundation abilities to cope with the problems they encounter. In addition, the schedules and the discussion related to them indicate methods of proceeding so as to build up the necessary foundations. These procedures should go a long way towards helping the pupils cope with the new and unusual. The question might then arise as to whether there is any other action a teacher might take to help pupils use their knowledge more effectively.

The answer is, yes; up to a point. Again, I have foreshadowed the question when I discussed the setting of objectives and the carrying out of task analyses. Not that I am suggesting pupils should be expected to carry out operations of great complexity

254 *Psychopedagogy*

similar to those in the preceding chapters. But an essential, and perhaps obvious, prerequisite to problem solving, is to know what the problem is. I should warn you, however, that there are those on the fringe of discovery learning who are so committed to the ideas of self-actualization and independent discovery that they have considerable difficulty in bringing themselves to reveal what the problem is. I believe that we should let the pupils into the secret.

Letting the pupils into the secret means informing them of the performance expected of them. Clearly this is much the same formulation as the objectives I discussed earlier. And similar methods of attack can be explained to the pupils to help them to get to grips with the problem. Methods of analysing what the problem holds in the way of sub-problems, or what principles are relevant to its solution, will all be helpful. As in the learning of concepts and psychomotor skills, prompting by the teacher will help pupils to solve the problems. In fact, many of the items on the schedules for evaluating aspects of teaching will be laying a foundation for helping pupils to solve problems. Let us consider one of the simpler ones.

Algorithms

Landa, a Russian psychologist, asked a number of teachers the question: 'We are constantly being called upon to demonstrate something in our daily lives. What must be done to prove that some object X belongs to class Y, or, conversely, that it does not belong to class Y?' (Landa 1976). This is clearly a problem in the application of learning about concepts. It links with the schedule on concept formation when it refers to the provision of exemplars of the concept sufficient to cover the criterial attributes, and the cueing of children in a structured sequence of exemplars and non-exemplars. The teachers were unable to answer satisfactorily. Examples of the answers were as follows. (1) 'Can't answer this question. It depends on what must be proven.' (2) 'You must analyse X, then Y, compare them, and do your proof.' (3) 'Find all the attributes of X, all the attributes of Y, compare them and draw your conclusion.' (4) 'To demonstrate that X is Y, you must:

Teaching problem solving 255

(a) list the attributes of X; (b) list the attributes of Y; (c) compare them; (d) if all the attributes coincide you conclude that X is Y, if they do not, then X is not Y.' It is my fervent hope that by now you can see the inadequacies and misunderstandings in the replies to the question. But lest you think the explanation for the lack of understanding lies in Russian backwardness, I invite you to try the same question on friends not privy to the line of argument developed in this book.

Landa then took the proposed solution (4) and applied it to a specific case. He looked at the window and wrote down its attributes.

1 Opening in the wall of the building.
2 Lets in light and air.
3 The lattice divides the surface into four sections.
4 The frame is 2 × 2 metres.
5 The frame is white.
6 There is a large scratch on the right side of the frame.

The teacher agreed that this was a reasonable statement. Landa then took a dictionary and wrote down what it said about *window*, namely: 'An opening in the wall of a building to let in light and air'. Comparing the two lists as teacher (4) had suggested leads to the conclusion that the window with the six attributes listed which he was looking at was not a window according to the dictionary definition because it had too many attributes. Clearly the difficulty here is that the teacher was far from clear about the processes of concept formation. I hope that the account in earlier chapters of these processes and in more recent chapters of the teaching of concepts will ensure that you do not make the same mistakes.

Landa takes things a step further. He is here primarily concerned not to teach about concept learning and teaching, but to present the processes of explaining to learners how to set about deciding whether a thing is an exemplar of a given concept or not. He regards this as a problem that can be solved by recourse to what he refers to as an algorithm. In this case the algorithm is straightforward and relatively simple to express. Landa's formulation is as follows.

256 *Psychopedagogy*

To show that X is Y we must:

1 Ascertain the attributes of Y.
2 Check to see if X has these attributes of Y.
3 Draw a conclusion according to the following rules:
   - If X has all the attributes of Y, X is Y.
   - If X does not have all the attributes of Y, it is not Y.

When we apply this to the window problem, it is easy to see that the method works. One needs to take account of *only* the criterial attributes of the concept and one disregards the non-criterial attributes. This, of course, has been the burden of all my discussion of concept learning and teaching.

Landa refers to this logical sequence of steps for checking the inclusion of a phenomenon in a given class as an algorithm because it provides a method of operation that will always lead to a correct solution. It is, therefore, eminently sensible to acquaint pupils with the idea. And one can, of course, devise algorithms for a variety of problems. The terms of an algorithm are completely clear and unambiguous and set out in detail exactly how to solve the problem to which they are addressed. Everyone following the instruction in an algorithm will, given the same starting material, perform the same operations, take the same route and arrive at the same answer. However, algorithms do not just apply to specific problems but to all problems of the same type. The algorithm for identifying exemplars of concepts can be applied to all concepts.

Much classroom teaching and learning uses algorithmic methods: in particular, work in number and mathematics. A simple example commonly found is the rule of division in early stages of number learning (Landa 1976, p. 30).

To divide one positive integer by another (e.g. 243 by 3) we must:
1 Take the first digit of the dividend.
2 Determine if it is divisible by the divisor. If yes, perform the division and go to instruction 3. If not, take the next figure and repeat instruction 2.
3 Write the quotient obtained in parentheses.

Teaching problem solving 257

4 Multiply the quotient by the divisor and write the product under the digits of the dividend.
5 Subtract the product from the original number and write the result. And so on.

Clearly this type of approach resembles the analytical methods discussed above in relation to the analysis of objectives and teaching tasks. But there is an important difference. As I have said before, the methods outlined in relation to the analyses of teaching tasks *will not* produce identical solutions, and *will not* determine that the route to the solution will be the same for everybody. Landa puts this type of approach to problem solving at the other end of a continuum of problem-solving procedures from algorithms. On the one end the completely determined and predictable algorithm, on the other end the structured and analytical approach but one that is indeterminate in its outcome and the route to it. This approach is called the heuristic approach by Landa and, of course, this is a commonly used term that I have employed earlier.

Heuristics

Whether a method should be classified as heuristic or not is a matter that cannot be decided by inspection. It follows from my remarks about problem-solving ability being dependent upon the knowledge of the individual concerned that one man's heuristic could well be another man's algorithm. This is the case when one problem solver's understanding in the field is sufficiently developed for him to see aspects of the problem as non-problematic because of his existing knowledge, whereas another person with less understanding would not be capable of seeing things in this way. The first could well see the problem as algorithmic or nearly so – that is, more or less readily solvable by the application of certain set procedures. The second, not having the basic knowledge of these procedures or their constituent elements, would find the operation completely problematic and would not be able to carry out the points specified in the method for solution of the problem. The first would proceed from point to point in the method, one point being the cue for the next point.

258 *Psychopedagogy*

To exemplify this I should like to take an example from a commonly used type of algorithm in botany: the dichotomous key to classification of flora. In this case I am referring to the classification of fungi. The problem I have is a real one: to identify edible fungi from among a multitude of plants, some edible and some very poisonous. The key may be regarded as an algorithm when used by a person with a certain level of knowledge in the field, who will invariably identify the fungus he is interested in and, by consulting a list of poisonous and non-poisonous, and possibly tasty or uninteresting fungi, will be able to make a decision as to whether he should bother to cook it or throw it away. People with this level of knowledge will always follow the same route through the key and will always reach the same conclusion when presented with the problem of classifying a given fungus. In my case this is by no means true. Presented with a fungus and the key on different occasions, I am quite likely to follow different paths through the key and arrive at different conclusions. Not a comforting thought when one is genuinely interested in the culinary properties of fungi. A brief extract may make the point.

In this key the fungi are classified in six main divisions or genera, A to F (Lange and Hora 1963). The first step in using the algorithm is to consult the list of attributes of the different genera and compare them with the specimen you are trying to classify. Here is the list of genera with their attributes. The numbers following the attributes refer to pages in the key where more detailed information about the various genera is to be found.

A Fruit-body a cap with gills on the underside, typically with central stipe, 20.
B Fruit-body with stipe and cap or head but without gills on the underside, 25.
C Fruit-body cup-shaped or turbinate, with or without stipe, 26.
D Fruit-body globulose, tuberous, pear-shaped or star-shaped (stellate), 27.
E Fruit-body $\pm$ club-shaped, branched or not, 28.

Teaching problem solving 259

F Fruit-body bracket-like; irregularly lobed or forming a crust; on wood, 29

If you have survived that experience and are sure that the specimen you are contemplating belongs to class B, say, the next step is to proceed to the appropriate page, in this case, 26. On page 26 we find a list of attributes of fungi in this genus. To continue the search to establish the classification of the specimen one starts at 1 and proceeds to the number indicated after one has made the appropriate decision demanded by 1.

1 Cap with pores or tubes on underside, 2. [i.e. go to number 2 if the specimen has these attributes.]
1 Cap underside smooth, ribbed or veined or with pointed peg-like teeth, 4. [i.e. go to number 4 if the specimen has these attributes.]
2 Flesh $\pm$ hard; usually 'brackets' on wood, *Polyporaceae*, 62. [i.e. the specimen is identified as *polyporaceae* and is illustrated on page 62.]
2 Flesh $\pm$ soft; stipe central; on soil, 3. [i.e. go to number 3.]
3 Cap smooth or minutely and softly scaly, *Boletus*, 186.
3 Cap with $\pm$ overlapping coarse scales; blackish grey; flesh turns reddish, *Strobilomyces*, 194.
4 Underside of cap with pointed, peg-like 'teeth', *Hydnaceae*, 58.
4 No 'teeth', 5.
5 Fruit-body funnel-shaped; underside smooth, hairy or with veins or ribs, 6.
5 Otherwise, 8.

This section of the key goes on to number 19, but I imagine that the details given above will be sufficient for you to have a rudimentary grasp of the method if you have not encountered it before. Clearly what happens is that the guide makes a systematic and gradual approach to the identification of all the fungi commonly found. The person with some knowledge in the field would have an infallible guide to the classification of those fungi. For such a person the guide would be an algorithm. For me it is a heuristic device.

260 Pyschopedagogy

The reasons for the difference are to be found in my lack of training in the field. My understanding of some of the terms is extremely hazy, but in addition I am far from competent at making consistently accurate discriminations of the criterial attributes of various fungi. I may scrutinize the cap or the stipe or the fruit-body of a specimen and still be unsure as to whether it has a veined cap or a central stipe, or a funnel-shaped fruit-body. Thus when I use the key I find it useful as a guide but I always need a very clear picture of the fungus against which to match the specimen before I am likely to feel convinced that my classification is correct. On the other hand, a skilled person would be able to make the classification without the need to see a picture.

My use of the key to the classification of fungi was heuristic because it is possible for me to get the wrong answer. The fault, however, does not lie in the method, but in me. To persons with the necessary prior knowledge and skills it is an infallible way of identification. The question could well be posed: 'Is it possible to produce algorithms for all problems so that all those with the necessary prerequisite competence would be guaranteed success?' The answer is that this is not possible. In the case of teaching, for example, our current state of knowledge of psychopedagy is insufficiently developed for us to envisage anything like this. We could well conjecture that the problem of teaching optimally is so difficult and enormously complex that it will *never* be possible to produce an algorithm applicable to problems in teaching. But this can only be speculation.

Guides to thinking

Algorithms and heuristic devices are both extremely useful devices for problem solving. But there is no suggestion that all we need to do is to teach a given set of both for pupils to be able to tackle all problems. In some cases, of course, it will be useful to adopt a ready-made algorithm or heuristic guide and apply it to the problem. But the most useful way of proceeding is to introduce pupils to a variety of both applied to a variety of problems and to guide them in the use of both approaches. By having explained

Teaching problem solving 261

the way the two approaches work in such varied circumstances, the pupils will acquire a *general idea* of these approaches to solving problems. When we teach pupils using such approaches we are in fact teaching them to think in ways directed to the solving of problems generally, so that when they are faced with a problem they will bring an analytical approach to bear and possibly discover an algorithm that fits the problem, either by making one up or finding one to fit. Thus there is no suggestion that all pupils should be equipped with a set of algorithms that will be put into operation automatically when a problem arises. As Landa says, when we teach pupils the use of algorithms and heuristics, 'we are simultaneously engaged in two processes: we are teaching pupils the methods of both algorithmic and heuristic thinking' (Landa 1976, p. 62).

Such learning supplements a pupil's conceptual knowledge. Without that knowledge, as we have seen, no one can solve problems. On the other hand, having lots of knowledge is no guarantee that one is going to solve problems effectively. This is why the important thing is not to provide specific guides to solving this problem or that, but to develop higher methods of thought that will enable a pupil to think about his thinking and choose the right approach to fit problems as they arise.

Many of the devices mentioned in the schedules related to different aspects of teaching are useful in helping a pupil to become more proficient in solving problems. In particular, the teacher's language, used to cue his moves as he tackles the problem, can help him to move from stage to stage and provide the vital feedback necessary to confirm that he is on the right lines. If we adopt the approach I have used above when discussing the three general types of skill, we would look upon what the pupil learned about different approaches to problem solving as learning at the level of type-C skills. Type-B skills could well form the crucial link in developing problem-solving ability because here the learner would be discriminating between different approaches and evaluating them. In the teaching that led up to the practice of this skill the teacher might adopt Galperin's approach and gradually let the pupil move from observing the teacher's activity while solving the problem, through describing what the teacher is doing, to

262 *Psychopedagogy*

describing what he is doing himself. This approach is useful because the pupil would first see the teacher analysing the problem, identifying the key elements, calling to mind the necessary concepts and principles for tackling the problem, and then applying a systematic approach to solving it. Describing these actions is a useful way of instilling them in the learner's consciousness. Moving from type-B to type-A skill, that is, carrying out the operation himself, would involve the learner's attempting other problems of the same general type.

In fact there is much in the schedule on psychomotor skills that would be useful in problem solving. Although the emphasis in the discussion in Chapter 10 was on the motor aspect of the skill, the cognitive side is also involved. The cueing by the teacher, the establishing of the problem (establishing a preliminary idea of the task), the involving of the learner himself in the activity, the provision of feedback, then the arranging for practice and finally weaning the learner so that he becomes independent in the activity – all contribute to helping a pupil to develop his problem-solving skills.

The last point is crucial. There is a view which holds that problem solving is very much like the learning of concepts and principles except that, when solving problems, the learner has to assume more responsibility for his learning than in other forms (Gagné 1977). In other words, the gap between his present level of competence and the task to be mastered is greater than in the other type of learning.

A guide to teaching

Here I will try to draw together the main features of teaching activity likely to help pupils to develop the ability to solve problems. However, before coming to the specific details I should like to make one or two general comments. First to say that problem solving can quite usefully be viewed as a particular form of learning. Undoubtedly it is more complex than the other types of learning I have discussed so far, but many of the teaching activities described in relation to other aspects of teaching are applicable when helping pupils to solve problems. Another

Teaching problem solving **263**

relevant point is the opinion that little help should be given in problem solving and that pupils are better left to find their own solutions to problems because they thereby learn more effectively. This is the view held by many supporters of discovery learning. I think it is mistaken and believe that pure discovery learning, if it ever existed, would mean the abdication of the teacher. However, I do not wish to caricature the ideas of discovery learning but suggest to you that the two most likely outcomes of this approach will probably be the inability to solve the problem, or the solving of the problem by trial and error which would leave the learner very little better off if he met a similar problem later. In fact, of course, most teachers do give guidance of some sort. Guidance of the kind I have been discussing here would avoid the two dangers just mentioned and prepare a pupil for new problems. Let us now consider the things to have in mind when trying to foster problem solving ability.

I IDENTIFY THE PROBLEM

All too frequently this is not done. The nature of the problem is left obscure. In some cases, through faulty analysis of the topic being taught, the teacher himself has failed to identify the problem confronting the learners. An interesting example of this is the investigation by Reid into the problems faced by children beginning to learn to read (Reid 1966). Whereas the teacher thought the problems were of the nature of distinguishing between different words, the problems the children were actually trying to solve were of the nature of what a printed word actually is. Some guidance here would have helped enormously with the solving of the problem the teacher had in mind.

If there is no problem of this nature, the learners should be helped to obtain a clear idea of the nature of the task, if possible expressed in terms of what they would be able to do when the problem is solved. You will no doubt recognize familiar phraseology here. It is, indeed, much the same as setting learning objectives, except that when a teacher defines his objectives they are *his* objectives and not the pupils', even if they may be expressed in terms of learner capabilities at the end of instruction.

264 *Psychopedagogy*

2 BRING TO MIND THE RELEVANT CONCEPTS

All the historic problem solvers from Archimedes to Einstein have been noted for their feats of bringing to bear, on difficult problems, concepts and principles from apparently disparate fields of knowledge. Their feats are so impressive precisely because of this unexpected yoking together of existing ideas into a new synthesis. But, as I have already said, nobody accomplishes this kind of feat from a position of ignorance. One can't solve problems by bringing ideas from various fields together unless one has some ideas. Like other kinds of learning it is necessary to ensure that the learners have the prerequisite capabilities.

Once it has been established that the learners have the necessary capabilities, if at all possible *before posing the problem* (see the various teaching-skill schedules), every effort should be made to help the pupils to bring them to mind. Only by so doing can one reasonably expect them to see links that might lead to a solution. The bringing together of ideas in this way – ideas that have been acquired at different times and in very different circumstances – is an interesting illustration of the power of language, to which I Ireferred in the earlier chapters. Other animals are willy-nilly forced to attempt to solve their problems by trial and error.

A teacher can help pupils remember ideas that might be useful by cueing them about aspects of the problem that might be helpful. Reminding them of the properties of some of the elements of the problem will give them a useful focus rather than lead to a blind alley. It is important, too, to encourage the learners not to be too restrictive in their thought. Encouragement to range wide in their thinking about the problem may help them to see connections they might otherwise have missed. Too narrow a focus may get them stuck in cognitive tramlines and make them blind to other routes to the solution (see Luchins 1942). In the approach to task analysis I discussed earlier (Chapter 8) I recommended that the person doing the analysis should let his mind range over all the aspects involved in the analysis so that he might more easily see links between the different elements. What I am talking about here is the scrutiny of different aspects in the analysis such

Teaching problem solving 265

as the type of principles involved, the method of assessment, specific instances of concepts, the type of learning involved, etc. The teacher planning instruction in tackling a pedagogical problem and working through the different aspects involved in tackling it more or less simultaneously enhances his chances of seeing connections that he would not otherwise notice. This approach to analysis is what I have referred to above as a heuristic and, as I have also suggested, such devices could be useful for pupils as well as for teachers. Let us therefore now consider how they might be used by pupils.

3 ANALYSE THE TASK

As I have suggested, this activity is very closely linked with the one of bringing to the front of one's mind ideas that relate to the problem. A heuristic such as the one I suggest for task analysis is a method of self-cueing to accomplish this end. Young pupils may have difficulty in implementing an approach as sophisticated as this, but, of course, it is unlikely that we should be posing problems that needed such a sophisticated approach. However, the general principle is still valid. Explaining to pupils that problems can be analysed, demonstrating how this can be done with a variety of problems and giving them guided exercises in practising this method will equip them to tackle things on their own later. Obviously the heuristic I described above is specifically related to teaching tasks and would for the most part be inappropriate for young learners. However, the idea of trying to think of principles relating to the problems and of concrete instances of the principles are two elements that will naturally be useful for any learner.

I mentioned the heuristic approach, but there is also the algorithmic method, and pupils who have been acquainted with this would be additionally equipped to cope with problems amenable to algorithmic attack. Again, as I stressed in the discussion of algorithms, giving the pupils an idea of the way algorithms are constructed and used, followed by guided practice in their use, will enhance their ability to cope with a variety of problems. No claim is being made that teaching about heuristics

266 *Psychopedagogy*

and algorithms will guarantee solution of problems, but they will be useful contributory factors in making solutions possible.

4 GIVE PROMPTED PRACTICE

I refer to this section as prompted practice. But of course it is not practice for the problem under consideration, so the prompting is two-edged: it helps the pupil to solve one problem and adds a little to his ability to cope with the next problem of related type. Prompting can take different forms and has been discussed fully in connection with other aspects of teaching. Suffice it to say here that the teacher's and *the pupil*'s use of language are both key aids to prompting. In particular, the pupil's own use of language will help him towards greater independence in problem solving since it will encourage in him the habit and ability of providing his own cues, probably in relation to his thinking about the concepts and principles evoked by the activity of calling things to mind and attempting to analyse the problem.

5 GIVE PRACTICE WITH FEEDBACK; ENHANCE MOTIVATION

Having coped with problems of a particular type with prompting from the teacher, the pupils should be given the opportunity to work on other problems of similar types. As in the teaching of psychomotor skills, this form of prompted practice should be faded gradually so that the learners become independent in their approach to new problems of the same type. Careful planning by the teacher with regard to prompted practice and practice with feedback should be aimed at enhancing motivation by ensuring that the learners experience a fair degree of success in solving the problems. This is not to say that they should be given practice by endless repetition of the same kind of problem once they have mastered the method. The items on the reinforcement schedule (p. 296) will be applicable here.

6 DEVELOP INDEPENDENT ACTIVITY

All the preceding items have had this aim. Discussing with learners the various elements in problem solving outlined here

Teaching problem solving 267

and elsewhere should help them tackle problems on their own with assurance. This item is the capstone to the whole operation for helping children to solve problems.

A heuristic on problem solving

My description and suggestions on the subject of problem solving themselves exemplify the concept of heuristic. Clearly they do not provide an algorithm, or you would be guaranteed success with every lesson if you followed the set of instructions. Nor is the language couched in completely unambiguous terms. All that I have been able to do is propose a plan of action that will help a teacher to ensure that his efforts to teach his pupils will have a greater degree of success than if he did not use such a plan. He will interpret the suggestions of the heuristic in his own way, but the foundations of his activity will be the proposals of the heuristic. Naturally, there is no prescription to use this particular heuristic: he may use the one proposed or a modified version; or he could take something quite different, although I doubt that such an approach would prove effective since the method described here is closely related to our present knowledge about problem solving. If anyone were to reject the approach entirely, the most likely reason would be a fundamental objection to systematic approaches to encouraging pupils in their problem-solving activity. In such a case the whole concept of heuristics would be rejected, not merely the approach proposed here.

A teaching schedule

I will now bring together the key aspects of the teaching of problem solving that I have rehearsed above in the form of a schedule of the same type as those presented earlier. It should be used in the context of the preceding discussion on the question of problem solving.

Figure 11.1. Schedule for the teaching and evaluation of problem solving (STEPS)

A PRE-ACTIVE

1 Analyse the task to clarify the nature of the problem to be solved.

268 *Psychopedagogy*

  2 Ascertain that the pupils have the necessary prerequisite capabilities.

B INTERACTIVE

  3 Explain the nature of the problem to the pupils.

  4 Encourage pupils to range widely in their approaches to solving the problem.

  5 Remind pupils of properties of the elements of the problem that might be useful.

  6 Encourage the pupils to make an analysis of the problem.

  7 Prompt the pupils judiciously without solving the problem for them.

  8 Provide for feedback at key points.

  9 Encourage an independent approach to problem solving by explaining methods of tackling problems.

C EVALUATION

10 Present pupils with new problems of the same general type.

In addition to item 10 a teacher might present different *types* of problems to evaluate the pupils' more general approach to problem solving. The object of scrutiny would then not be so much whether the problems were solved but whether the activities likely to enhance problem solving were employed. It would be useless attempting this, however, without having carried out steps 1 and 2 first.

Creativity

Creativity is one of those OK words like *virtue*. Nobody is agin it. But rather like virtue it is not too easy to agree on what it is. For my part it has acquired a faint odour of pretentiousness through my reading about the subject in the years that it has become fashionable. This may be because of the tendency of some educationists to elevate the concept into an almost mystical quality that evades the grasp of writers like me trying to find rational explanations of what takes place when one person tries to teach others and to bring some order into our understanding of the pedagogical

Teaching problem solving **269**

interactions. So you see, I am somewhat prejudiced in my appraisal of the concept; nevertheless I shall try to explain what seem to be the most widely held views on the question and how it is perceived to fit into our scheme of human learning.

Creativity for most authorities implies the production of something original. For most of us that production may be original for us but not particularly new for anyone else. The original productions of an outstanding genius are such that they are strikingly new to everyone else. It seems reasonable to assume that there is a range of productions between these two extremes. How one conceives of that range seems to me to be an interesting question.

One answer to the question has been proposed by the production of tests of creativity. These tests take a view of creativity that has attracted a wide following. The basic tenet of this view is that a creative act is one that exemplifies what has been referred to as 'divergent thinking' (Guilford 1967). Divergent thinking is characterized by such things as flexibility, originality and fluency. Problems presented to a divergent thinker will tend to be solved in unusual ways when several solutions are possible and equally acceptable. A convergent thinker, on the other hand, is likely to come up with solutions that give little if any evidence of thinking outside the obvious confines of the problem.

Tests constructed to assess the two styles make use of items geared to the three qualities referred to above, among other things. Flexibility is tested by such things as asking the person to suggest uses for common objects such as a brick. Answers that list uses predominantly related to building (of houses, schools, churches, etc.) are taken to show little flexibility. Answers that depart from this by suggesting such things as a bookend, plumbline, bed warmer, drainage, hammer or shot putting exemplify flexibility. Originality is assessed by, among other things, finding unusual titles for short stories. Titles that merely provide a synoptic heading for the content of the story are described as convergent, those that depart from this kind of title but still make the point, perhaps by a play on words, are described as divergent. Fluency refers to the amount of ideas produced in response to given questions.

The interesting question I referred to above arises from a

270 *Psychopedagogy*

consideration of the way in which tests of this kind are scored. Should a person's divergent score be arrived at by comparison with other people's performance? Or is there some way of determining divergence without reference to the performance of one's peers? To consider the latter first: it is clearly impossible to assess divergent thinking by reference to an outside objective criterion. Divergent thinking is a construct of the intellect of men, a concept of a high degree of abstraction. It has in itself no objective referent, and can have no existence outside the minds of men. It is thus at best dependent upon consensus views for a yardstick against which to measure any specific performance. In itself this is a reasonable proposition but there is something bizarre in the idea of competence in divergent thinking being assessed by the convergence of views about what divergence is!

The same difficulty applies to using the performance of others as the yardstick of competence. Apart from any other difficulties we still have the same problem of finding a criterion. And again at best we must make use of consensus views of what comprises competence in divergence. In addition, merely comparing one person's performance with a group performance may be doing nothing more than distinguishing between different levels of mediocrity.

However one tests, and however one obtains a criterion for the assessment of divergent thinking, the crucial link is still missing. There is no general consensus that divergent thinking and creativity are the same thing. Or even that divergent thinking is a main element in creativity.

Creativity and problem solving

Many people think there is a good case for considering creativity as a form of problem solving. The discussion earlier in this chapter relating to problem solving may have suggested to you some of the elements that can reasonably be held to resemble the concepts frequently discussed under the heading of creativity. In the discussion, you may recall the suggestion that in attempting to foster problem-solving activity the teacher should encourage pupils to keep open minds and avoid getting stuck in cognitive tramlines.

Teaching problem solving 271

This is clearly the same type of outlook as that underlying the ideas of divergent thinking. I would suggest that looking upon creative thinking or creative activity as belonging to the same genre as problem solving is helpful. It is problem solving at the stage of independence when the learner is not receiving help from a teacher. Much the same considerations obtain, and much the same procedures are applicable if one is trying to foster creativity in the classroom, as apply in fostering problem solving. The unexpected solution that brings together disparate phenomena in new synthesis cannot be a guaranteed outcome of the suggested activities but, provided we do not have unrealistically romantic notions about the levels of creativity pupils are capable of, it is likely that they will be of some help.

Problem solving in practice

It might be helpful here to look at one or two examples of children tackling problems. As with the other extracts of lessons in this book, the ones I am about to consider are pieces from genuine lessons, unstaged and unrehearsed. They are not models of the teaching of problem solving. Because of this I am unable to provide neat illustrations of the points I have made above in relation to problem-solving activities in teaching. But I hope the extracts will give you a flavour of real classroom interactions where problems are being tackled and perhaps provide you with material for a type-B skill exercise. One of the things I have discovered is that inspecting transcripts of lessons is a very unrewarding exercise for providing illustrative material related to problem solving. In the search I have carried out I find relatively few examples of pupils grappling with problems of any magnitude. In the main the problems seem to be of the type that takes the learner just a little bit further than his current level of competence, and sometimes they do not take him any further. I have no quantitative evidence on the subject, but I suspect that the picture I get from my investigations is fairly typical of what takes place generally. The teachers concerned were not practising the principles outlined in any of the sections in this book; in fact, I suspect that, in the main, they are probably unaware of them.

272 *Psychopedagogy*

LESSON FROM LIFE: 8

The first extract provides an interesting illustration of the teacher's perception of the importance of the pupil's identifying the nature of the problem in order to be able to tackle it effectively (Ford Teaching Project, Unit 3, p. 31).

1 Teacher   What was the problem?

2 Girl   Give some reasons why early varieties of potatoes aren't grown in large quantities in the Fens.

3 Teacher   In the Fens, that is the question near the bottom of the page?

4 Pupil   21.

5 Teacher   Now what was the problem. Now how are we going to set about tackling this – what is the clue? How can we set about it? – What is the first thing you think we have to be quite sure about? Even if we don't know any answers we must be sure of something. What must we be certain of before we start; before we make any progress? What must we be sure of? Let's put it this way. I am a stranger in the town and I walk up to you and say: 'Please I took the station'. What would you do?

6 Boy   Say I don't understand.

7 Teacher   Thank you. Now then what is the first thing then in order to help this stranger; what have you got to be clear about? You don't understand, so what have you got to do before you can help him?

8 Girl   Try and understand what he means.

9 Teacher   You have got to try and understand what he means. Now let's go back to the question now. Is it the same situation; haven't we to be sure of something? What have you to be sure of?

10 Boy   The question, what it means.

11 Teacher   That's spot on, isn't it?

Teaching problem solving **273**

Here you see the teacher grappling with the problem of getting the children to apprehend that grasping the implications of the problem is of prime importance. In utterance 5 he attempts to assess the success of his efforts. He then proceeds to take action on the strength of his assessment and finally concludes the exchange in utterance 11. You may care to consider whether he was justified in doing so. It is impossible to be certain, of course, by looking at a transcript shorn of all the non-verbal elements, and the nuances of tone and emphases in the teacher's and pupils' voices. The main thing to consider that bears on the question is that the teacher's utterances were very heavily cueing the pupils' thinking. Did the pupil in utterance 10 fully grasp the point? Or was he merely giving the teacher back what he had just received fairly explicitly? If the teacher was mistaken, his next move would provide feedback indicating his mistake and his next action would be a backtracking to try once again to get the point clear. This extract does not, of course, provide an example of *how* to decide what the implications of problems are, merely that ascertaining the nature of the problem is, in fact, of crucial importance in problem solving.

LESSON FROM LIFE: 9

The next item illustrates a teacher's use of prompts. She is trying to remind pupils of some of the key considerations to be borne in mind when measuring distance (Ford Teaching Project, Unit 1, pp. 2–4).

1 Teacher If you are doing distance in the playground, what have you got to think about? . . . Is one of you going to walk a certain distance and then the other one do it?

2 Girl Yes.

3 Teacher How are you going to be certain what distance you are going?

4 Girl Well we will walk down from the trees to the bottom and then walk up again.

274 *Psychopedagogy*

5 Teacher What I mean to say is if you are going to be walking distances you want to be sure you are all walking the same distances. She might cut the corner or something you see – she might cheat – in which case you couldn't really compare them. And how many times are you going to walk this particular distance?

6 Girl Once.

7 Girl And then afterwards we are going to see if we can . . .

8 Teacher If you walk them just once would you be able to say that would be the definite time you would take to walk that distance? Do you think that would be a fair test?

9 Girls No.

10 Teacher So what are you going to do?

11 Girl We are going to do it again.

12 Teacher That's right, I would do it twice. Three or four times really.

13 Girls Yes.

14 Teacher What could you do with your results?

15 Girl See how far it is . . .

Several commonly observed classroom phenomena occur in this extract. The teacher starts with a question that may be construed as an alerting device. She creates a condition of uncertainty: 'what have you got to think about?' She goes on to try to make the pupils recall some of the factors to be borne in mind when one is using imprecise measures such as length of stride. She suggests rather indirectly the lines along which they should be thinking. However, note at the end of utterance 8 a question that is not a question. I have no direct evidence but I think the context makes it fairly clear that it is one of those questions where the pupils have little difficulty in knowing what answer is expected, even if they don't really understand the reason.

Teaching problem solving 275

Utterance 9 seems to me a typical example of pupils giving teacher the answer she wants, irrespective of their level of comprehension. This hypothesis is given support by the answer to the teacher's utterance 14. The pupil who answers this one gives every indication of not having understood the reason for repeating measures when the measuring instrument is imprecise. The teacher is back at square one or, if you like, utterance 1 in this transcript, so far as this pupil is concerned. She really should re-enter her own problem-solving cycle for this girl at the first utterance.

The final extract is not a transcript but an account of an approach to a lesson which illustrates a method of analysing a problem and calling to mind important things related to the problem. A discovery approach was planned on the topic of *castles* with a group of eight- to nine-year-old pupils. After various approaches by the teacher involving very little guidance of the pupils, he felt in the fifth session that the 'proceedings were grinding to a halt': 'Instead of the children pursuing their own lines of enquiry they were singularly lacking in ideas and could only produce drawing after drawing of the same type.' 'The children were lost and needed guidance.' This seems a very good example of pupils lacking the experience of tackling problems. In the teacher's account of his approach to solving his teaching problem and helping the pupils solve their problem, he does not tell them all they need to know, nor does he get them merely to rearrange their already existing concepts. Instead he suggests a way of proceeding and provides a method of calling things to mind in what might be reasonably considered a form of task analysis. It is very likely that the experience of this method of tackling the problem will be of help to the pupils when they encounter other problems (Figure 11.2).

Here we have a heuristic device giving the pupils a plan of action which does not provide the answers but which draws on their present knowledge, involves their use of skills of investigation in seeking answers to the questions, and which subsequent experience indicated was successful in breaking the impasse that had arisen.

I suggest that in addition to giving an insight into the way in which teachers adopt some of the tactics that help problem solving, the extracts suggest strongly that a more systematic study and application of the various elements in enhancing problem-solving activity would be of considerable use to these teachers and, I suggest, by implication to teachers generally.

Figure 11.2   Heuristic device for a problem-solving task (From Ford Teaching Project, Unit 4)

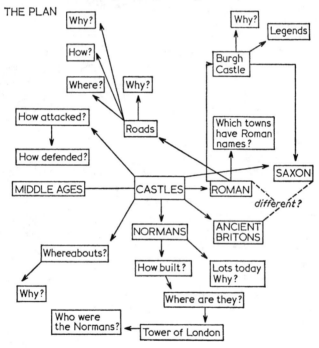

12
Sustaining learning

I have suggested that the teaching of concepts is the prime concern of most teachers. I have also suggested that a knowledge of the teaching of psychomotor skills and problem solving is important. However, I am quite aware that there is eloquent testimony in many places which argues a prior condition for all teaching and learning: the existence of a relationship between teacher and learner that is humane and based on mutual respect (Kohl 1969, 1977; School of Barbiana 1970). I accept this viewpoint and count myself as one of that party. The most satisfactory approach, it seems to me, is not to make an issue of which is the most important but to accept that all are necessary.

It helps to clarify the relationships among the various suggested teaching skills if we consider them as contributing to the creation of classroom 'climate'. By climate I mean the type of learning conditions existing in the classroom. These conditions include those that are predominantly cognitive and those that are predominantly affective. Classroom climate is obviously affected by phenomena completely outside the control of teachers. Social,

278 *Psychopedagogy*

political and economic forces can aid or hinder and in some circumstances completely negate the work of teachers. Bombing, urban violence, economic and cultural deprivation, political repression could well make a mockery of any attempts to apply the skills I am discussing. Therefore I make the initial assumption that external circumstances are not too hostile to the development of desirable classroom atmospheres. With this premiss I suggest a development of the relationship among teaching skills discussed earlier. This view sees the creation of a desirable classroom climate as largely dependent on the teacher's ability to sustain the pupils' learning, to motivate them, and to build up positive attitudes towards new learning. These aims are likely to be achieved by arranging satisfying learning experiences for the pupils in an atmosphere of positive affect. The most powerful influence in producing such conditions is the reinforcement provided by the learning environment, either directly from the teacher or indirectly through his arrangement of learning tasks that offer good opportunities for successful outcomes and progress in learning. The skill of providing reinforcement is therefore seen as one of the crucial teaching skills. I should now like to examine this skill and attempt to bring out the contribution made by related instrumental skills as I did when I examined the cognitive skill of concept teaching. When this examination is complete we should have a fairly clear indication of what the second-order or instrumental skills might be.

I make an assumption in the discussion that follows, of a similar nature to the one I made in the discussion of classroom climate. I assume that the pupils we are concerned with have their basic needs for food, shelter, warmth, and so on, satisfied, and that praise, attention and encouragement, together with such things as satisfaction of curiosity and the competent execution of tasks, will act as reinforcers in the classroom. I think this is not an unreasonable assumption so far as most readers are concerned, although it is not impossible that even in affluent societies schools will have among their pupils some whose basic needs are not fulfilled. Children from such backgrounds need different prescriptions from those this book can offer, but they are not pedagogical ones.

Sustaining learning 279

Arranging reinforcement

In the light of earlier discussions I suggest that we can focus on two main aspects of reinforcement and see in what way they can be applied to the classroom. They are the scheduling of reinforcement and the process of shaping. Let us take the latter first. I have already touched on a similar process when I discussed teaching for concept formation. Then I referred to the careful grading of exemplars and non-exemplars of the concept so as to build up new concepts more economically than is likely with the usual experimental practice of random presentation. The systematic reinforcing of behaviour according to the principles of successive approximation demands a similar understanding and skill of the teacher. In the shaping of behaviour in animal experimentation, the procedure is usually to reinforce in the first instance behaviour which only grossly resembles the desired behaviour and by steps gradually make reinforcement contingent upon behaviour which increasingly approximates to the desired behaviour. When Skinner moved into the education field from animal work, specifically into programmed learning, he took with him this idea. I believe, however, that the gradual progression in learning made by a learner working through a carefully graded sequence of teaching steps is usually not the same as the procedures in animal experiments, since what teachers are usually concerned with is the teaching of concepts and not completely arbitrary patterns of behaviour, as is the case in almost all animal learning.

There are some very important exceptions, however. Some early learning such as learning the connections between sight and sound in beginning reading is, in fact, arbitrary, and a teacher would be well advised to adopt methods similar to those used in animal experiments, the crucial difference, of course, being that in school we would use reinforcers other than food. Other types of learning where these techniques would be appropriate are learning to read music, learning discrimination in sounds in music, discrimination in speech (as in reading), discrimination of colours and tones in painting, of textures in design, of symbols in mathematics, and of conventions in map work. In the field

280 *Psychopedagogy*

of skill training the application of these techniques is widespread.

In all approaches to teaching, however, at whatever level and with whatever type of learning a teacher is concerned, a central problem will be deciding on how to structure the learning environment so as to facilitate the implementation of the principles of reinforcement under discussion. In the learning of concepts the important thing will be the careful sequencing of the presentation of exemplars and non-exemplars and in varying the salience of the criterial attributes so that the pupils will experience success at all stages of the learning. In non-conceptual learning the task will be to present the stimuli to be paired, discriminated among or generalized from in a similar gradient of difficulty, again to ensure that the learner experiences success regularly but that the difficulty of giving the correct response increases as competence increases. A very important element in the skill of reinforcing may thus be seen to be a pre-active skill: the skill of deciding beforehand how to present the learning material so as to enhance the likelihood of a successful progression through the learning sub-tasks. And, of course, this raises immediately the question of task analysis.

Earlier discussion of task analysis has, in fact, raised one of the key issues in arranging the gradient of learning. The notion of entry capability – that is, what the learner is capable of before starting new learning – clearly relates to this question. If the prerequisite skills and concepts have been adequately learned, then the next step should not prove too difficult and the chances of success will be high. If the steps are too steep, failure is almost inevitable. Apart from the cognitive gain from carefully graded progression through the sub-tasks of new learning that we have discussed in earlier sections, the affective consequences are clearly crucial and, equally clearly, the two interact. A learner failing is not only not equipped cognitively for the next stage, he is also impeded by the negative emotion resulting from failure. Which is just another way of saying that success breeds success.

Sustaining learning 281

Reinforcers

So far I have been talking about reinforcers, as distinct from reinforcement, by implication rather than explicitly. But I imagine it will be fairly clear that the reinforcers I have in mind are the approbation of the teacher and the satisfaction of successful learning. The two are bound to be closely linked, although at first blush it seems to be possible to separate them. They must be closely linked in the thoughts of any teacher trying to implement reinforcement techniques effectively because if they were not he could well be in the predicament of wishing to encourage children who were not succeeding in the learning tasks he had set for them. It would not be impossible to do this, of course. Thousands of teachers are doing it every day. But every one of those teachers is faced with the problem of encouraging and at the same time avoiding reinforcing pupils' activity that is irrelevant or deleterious to the learning he is trying to develop. The more failure there is, the more difficult the teacher's task.

Thus it seems to me that the preliminary planning of learning activities is a crucial element in the teaching skill of reinforcing. If this is done competently, the implementing of suitable procedures when the teaching is actually going on will be considerably simpler, whereas it may well not be possible if the mismatch between the teacher's activities and the pupils' state of expertise is extreme.

In the interactive phase of teaching, the actual deployment of reinforcement skills is still complex, even if the pre-active planning has been appropriate. In new learning it will be necessary to identify and react to all responses if possible. In most teaching situations it is impossible to do this on a one-to-one basis – a fact which lies behind Skinner's view that as a reinforcing agent the teacher is out of date (Skinner 1954). Nevertheless there are still a lot of teachers about and since mechanization of teaching seems no nearer than it did when Skinner couched that apophthegm I think it important that we examine the problem to see what can be done to cope with Skinner's syndrome.

Skinner himself made an important contribution when he began to apply his ideas to teaching. In the early sixties he

282 *Psychopedagogy*

applied his work in operant conditioning to human instruction through the media of teaching machines and programmed learning. Skinner had the vision of improving teaching through the principles which he applied in experimental conditions with animals, and he based his teaching programmes on these principles.

Although programmed learning had a phenomenal vogue during the sixties, Skinner's position was continually under attack from those who thought his attempt to apply principles developed from the study of the learning of rats and pigeons to human teaching and learning was far too simplistic. To my mind the main error was to attempt to apply the principles to all types of human learning. As I suggested above, some of the earlier stages in learning certainly rely on principles such as those proposed by Skinner, but much of human learning, being conceptual and dependent on symbols, cannot be explained or controlled in the same way. However, the crucial thing that Skinner brought to pedagogical thinking was his insistence on the careful preparation and pre-testing of the instructional material. The object of this careful structuring was to keep the level of success of the learner at a very high level and thereby keep reinforcement too at a high level.

Time has shown that the prototypical Skinnerian unit of instruction, just a sentence or two, has been unpopular with learners and teachers. It has also shown that writing programmes is an unpopular activity with instructors and authors. It is so much more difficult than arranging schedules of reinforcement for pigeons. Ideas about the nature of concept learning have also undermined the purist Skinnerian position. However, there is little doubt that the notion of careful structuring to facilitate reinforcement has permeated much of the thinking in the field of human instruction. And this, of course, takes us back to our discussion of pre-active preparation.

But it also points a way forward. A teacher skilled at reinforcing will have in mind the factors discussed above. He will have taken the necessary pre-active steps to ensure a high rate of success by his pupils in the intermediate stages of learning, and he will reinforce by approval or other means, such as making the facts of

Sustaining learning 283

success clear to the learner or giving him the opportunity of other activity the teacher knows is reinforcing to the learner. In the process of new learning the teacher will do his best to reinforce *every correct step on the road to mastery.* When mastery of the new learning has taken place it will be sufficient for him to reinforce occasionally using a random schedule. The latter will ensure that degree of overlearning which will consolidate the mastery of the new task. The variable schedule, it is clear, resembles what happens in many classrooms fortuitously. Many teachers knowing nothing at all of reinforcement theory will encourage pupils randomly by commending correct work when mastery has been achieved. It is a different matter in the intermediate stages of learning new concepts or activities. With the average size of class it is obviously quite impossible for a teacher to reinforce every correct step of every pupil on the road to mastery. However, in addition to taking the steps mentioned above, related to the careful structuring of the learning milieu, there is another powerful means of reinforcing open to the teacher. I refer here to the potentiality of the group in reinforcing.

The class group can contribute to individual learning in at least two important ways. It can be used as a reinforcing agent itself, and it can be used by the teacher to provide vicarious reinforcement for individual actions. A teacher making use of the potentialities of the class group for reinforcement would so arrange his lessons that individual effort would work to the benefit of the group, thus providing support and approbation not only from the teacher but also from other pupils. Linked with this approach is the practice of pupils providing other pupils with feedback. Groups of pupils working cooperatively hold the potential for providing feedback to individuals. Pupils within groups are likely to differ in their current levels of capability and interests so that pupils would be able to help each other by checking on each other's efforts without the continual intercession of the teacher. Small-group work in beginning reading is a good example of this.

Teachers can, and often do, use the class to provide vicarious reinforcement for individual pupils. An obvious example of this is when a teacher commends the whole class for some piece of behaviour. Another might be discussing with the class the 'correct'

284 *Psychopedagogy*

outcome of some piece of learning and commending those who had successfully completed the task. There are obvious dangers here, of course. Unless all the pupils had succeeded, commendation of the *rights* could involve the condemnation of the *wrongs*. This is the perpetual dilemma in teaching large numbers of pupils. The problem is acute and difficult to circumvent. However, being aware of it is a help, and being persuaded that it is worth trying to do something about it is even better. Unfortunately all too often teachers are unaware that there is a problem. A teacher skilled in reinforcement techniques will be aware of the problem and give evidence of trying to cope with it.

The instances I have provided so far, in relation to the class group in reinforcement, have referred to reinforcement of specific learning tasks. And this is the way reinforcement in learning usually operates. There is another more global form of reinforcement that has minimal cognitive content so far as school learning is concerned. I am referring to the effect of reinforcement on the affective atmosphere of the class generally. Chances are that this influence will be exerted in connection with the management tasks I referred to earlier. In the process the pupils and the teacher will be learning about each other rather than about academic subjects. The skilful teacher will ensure that the atmosphere generated in this process will be conducive to the cognitive learning he is seeking to foster. He will do this by the same methods he would use with individuals but, in addition, he will be most careful never to make one pupil's success contingent on another pupil's failure.

There is, however, an important difference between the way reinforcement can be used in these circumstances and in those relating to new learning. Much of what goes on in the classroom has to do with organizational matters; these are the activities that draw on the teacher's management skills referred to above. In the main no new learning is involved here. There is some, of course: when starting school, or moving to a new class, or meeting a new teacher. But, once the initial learning in connection with the new situation is accomplished, class activity of this type is essentially concerned with the same procedures; that is, with the same patterns of behaviour, unlike the progression of pupils'

Sustaining learning 285

learning in school subjects. In other words, once the pupils know what is expected of them in the way class activities are organized, and actually operate those procedures, then the amount of new learning likely to be needed is fairly small. In these conditions reinforcement needs only be at a high level of regularity at the beginning of the period when pupils and teacher come together for the first time, or when the class conditions change drastically. In the normal day-to-day running of class activities, once the learning has taken place, the teacher could well rely on intermittent reinforcement of a random kind to maintain the pupils' behaviour according to the conventions previously established. It would be as well to remember, however, that some reinforcement is necessary for optimal results. Ceasing to reinforce when patterns of behaviour have been set up might well result in their eventual disappearance.

In concrete terms it would be important to encourage and commend pupils who followed classroom routines connected with setting out equipment in laboratory work, or in games periods, extremely frequently in the early stages of introducing them to the routines. Once the pupils were operating the procedures satisfactorily, it would be sufficient to commend them from time to time. But it would be highly desirable not to neglect this continuing intermittent reinforcement if the desired routines are to be carried out consistently. If reinforcement is not given at a high level in the early stages, the learning of the routines will take longer or not take place at all. If they are not reinforced at all once the learning has taken place, they might well die away.

Problems

The best-laid schemes of mice and men and even teachers go agley from time to time. The suggestions I have made for the building up of a classroom atmosphere that will sustain learning will, I hope, help in pointing the way to keeping a teacher on track, but it would be unrealistic not to expect the question to arise: what happens if a pupil transgresses the normal conventions? What if a pupil engages in undesirable behaviour? The suggestion

286 *Psychopedagogy*

that I made in my earlier discussion on the role of reinforcement in learning – that the most effective way to change this state of affairs is almost always to ignore the undesired behaviour – is sometimes greeted with derision by practising teachers. The difficulties of ignoring are obvious. Some of them relate to possible disruption of the classroom routine but I think it likely that some also relate to the teacher's *amour propre*. To people brought up in a society in which the ideas of punishment and retribution are deeply embedded, it takes considerable conviction and determination to carry out procedures that seem so contrary to normal methods of proceeding. To be sure, there may be circumstances where ignoring undesirable behaviour is impossible but there is little doubt that principles of extinction are effective in many cases where punishment has failed.

Consistently ignoring behaviour is much more difficult than it would appear. It is not just a question of not reinforcing, it may involve not giving any attention to a misbehaving pupil. Even looks or comments of disapproval may be reinforcing if the child is seeking to deflect the teacher's attention. Examples of teacher activity that are likely to lead to extinction if carried out systematically are turning away from the pupil, walking away, and paying attention to a pupil who is behaving correctly even when the troublesome pupil is behaving undesirably. A teacher should remember that any attention given to undesirable behaviour almost certainly has the effect of reinforcing that behaviour. If the teacher attends to a misbehaving pupil even very occasionally he will probably reinforce the behaviour and the schedule of reinforcement would be intermittent which would keep the undesirable behaviour in strength instead of extinguishing it. The message is, then, no matter how difficult, that it is far better to continue to ignore undesirable behaviour with extreme consistency. It may be difficult to do this since it takes time for the patterns of behaviour to change, but persistence is almost certain to be reinforcing to the teacher and well worth the effort.

In addition to the danger of giving intermittent reinforcement mentioned above, there are other problems connected with the control of the procedure in attempting to extinguish undesired behaviour (Drabman *et al.* 1976). Among these problems are the

Sustaining learning 287

failure by the teacher to ascertain definitely that it is his attention that is providing the reinforcement for a particular pupil activity. If it is not – for example, if the pupil's peers are the source of reinforcement – the teacher's ignoring of the activity will have precious little effect. In such circumstance the best thing to do might be to reinforce the pupil's peers for ignoring his behaviour or possibly removing him from the scene using time-out procedures (see p. 289).

The main likely cause for the teacher's making a mistake as to the source of reinforcement of misbehaviour is the failure to establish a *base line* for the procedure. Base line refers to the establishment before starting the deliberate ignoring of the actual frequency of occurrence of the behaviour in question. In order to do this it is necessary to be quite precise about the nature of the undesired activity. What exactly is the pupil doing? What happens when he does it: i.e. how does the teacher react? And how frequently does the behaviour take place? With this information the teacher can start the process of extinction in an informed way with some hope of establishing whether the procedure is succeeding.

A great problem with teachers trying out extinction techniques is the fact that initially the undesired behaviour will almost certainly increase. This is probably because the pupil is trying harder to get the response from the teacher that he obtained previously. This is obviously a crucial stage in the process. A teacher thinking that just ignoring will be immediately effective will be disappointed and may well think that the method does not work, whereas in fact there is a good deal of evidence that it does (Axelrod 1977; Drabman *et al.* 1976; O'Leary and O'Leary 1977). This *response burst*, as it is called, will eventually cease and the undesired behaviour will gradually die away, but clearly this stage demands the teacher's care and determination. If the teacher reacts to the response burst by attending to the pupil, he will reinforce the increased level of activity and will be worse off than before.

Ignoring in order to extinguish undesired behaviour must not be seen in isolation. I have referred to the need to be sensitive to the role of peers in reinforcing behaviour and suggested that

288 *Psychopedagogy*

action needs to be taken to ensure that they do not do this. Engaging their attention in more interesting activities and encouraging them in those activities will help greatly. But the same thing applies to the pupil who is behaving undesirably. It is important to be on the lookout for any scrap of desirable behaviour and to reinforce it at once. Even a small action is a step in the right direction and should be seized upon. So the two things work together. Ignore the undesirable and reinforce the desirable no matter how small.

In my own work I have found that reinforcing for small steps in the right direction causes many people difficulties. Teachers seem to be reluctant to reward pupils unless there is a substantial action to reward. But if they do not, they are likely to have Skinner's experience when he waited for the pigeon to perform a fairly complicated manœuvre before reinforcing. Only by reinforcing the small steps does the final hoped-for outcome result. Probably the teacher's reluctance is influenced by a feeling that the pupil should do something that demonstrates effort and is worth while rewarding. The trouble is that it is impossible to set a value on actions to determine whether they are 'worth' rewarding. Each person will have his own notions and probably there are cultural differences too. For example, at a subjective level I would think that American teachers are generally more ready to praise their pupils than English teachers. The problem is complicated by the fact that most teachers have little idea how much they actually do reinforce pupils. I have found that most teachers overestimate the amount of reinforcement they use. Viewing videorecordings of their lessons almost invariably demonstrates that their actual use of reinforcers is much lower than their own estimated use. This is a subject that needs much more investigation than it has had so far. It could well be that a little less reluctance to reinforce, coupled with a systematic approach to extinction, could effect great positive changes in schools. Use of baseline techniques for both could enable teachers to act as experimenters to test these procedures and, as I have suggested earlier, so add to our store of knowledge about teaching.

In certain circumstances it may not be practical to ignore behaviour for the purpose of extinguishing undesired activity.

Sustaining learning 289

Activity that disrupts the work of others or causes danger has to be dealt with quickly. In such cases punishment may be used but used with care. Removing the offender from the scene as suggested above is a useful technique for dealing with many problems of this nature. It may be necessary only to send the pupil to the back of the room or to exclude him from some activity. More serious difficulties might necessitate removal from the classroom. But as with reinforcement it is necessary to be systematic about the course of action one takes and to make it clear to the pupil why the action is being taken, how long the 'time out' is to last and whether there are any conditions for remission; for example, for going as soon as he is told he earns five minutes' remission of the time out of class. The obvious problem with the use of time out as a punisher is that in some circumstances it will be more of a reinforcer than a punisher. If the teacher, or the class, or the subject being studied is disliked by the pupil, the time out will be a relief. If there is any reason to believe this is the case, the problem does not lie merely with that particular child but with the whole teaching situation including inappropriate actions by the teacher.

Perhaps the most common punisher used by teachers is the verbal reprimand. The advantages of this punisher are its flexibility, and the ease of usage. They might also be its disadvantages leading teachers to use it with less thought and discrimination than is desirable. One aspect of this form of punishment frequently overlooked is the fact that when used publicly, as is almost invariably the case, the intensity of the punishment is likely to be enhanced by the mere fact of its being public. There seems to be a virtue in using verbal reprimands that are only audible to the individual concerned (O'Leary and O'Leary 1977).

I discussed earlier some of the undesirable side effects of using punishment, and these should be borne in mind in any consideration of its role in teaching. The important thing is to see the question of maintaining a positive emotional and pedagogical atmosphere as involving a complex interrelationship between reinforcement and extinction procedures, with recourse to punishment only in the extreme case. In other words none of the uses of teacher attention should be seen in isolation.

290 *Psychopedagogy*

Nor should questions relating to classroom affective climate be seen separately from questions of cognitive learning. Reinforcement will build up a climate receptive to learning; the anxiety generated by a punitive classroom atmosphere might well inhibit cognitive learning altogether.

Apart from these considerations *vis-à-vis* classroom climate and the inhibitory effects of punishment on cognitive learning, its use could well have powerful social learning effects on pupils. Pupils' learning is not restricted to classrooms, and a school that relies heavily on punishment to conduct its affairs provides a model for the pupils' social learning. The institutionalization of punishment cannot but help signal to pupils that this is an acceptable form of social regime. In schools where corporal punishment is used – and at the time of writing this included the majority of British schools – the effect is to institutionalize violence. So pupils learn that punishment is an accepted way of ensuring social conformity and that physical violence is also an acceptable means of social control. A teacher skilled in reinforcing techniques will avoid punishment altogether and emphasize reinforcement by encouraging the socially and pedagogically positive activity and ignoring the negative.

Identifying reinforcers and punishers

A teacher may be eager to accentuate the positive and eliminate the negative and yet fall far short of his aim because of his lack of understanding of the varied and subtle nature of reinforcers and punishers in school life. The unconscious assumptions of adults and society at large that school is an unpleasant place to be in, and that absence from school is a reward, is proclaimed every time a distinguished visitor makes the traditional request that the school be given a day or half a day off to celebrate his visit. This is perhaps a gross example of many comparable attitudes. Setting written work as a punishment is the obverse of the day-off type of reward. If writing an essay is meted out as a punishment on Monday, why should a pupil be expected to consider it a pleasure on Tuesday? Punishers are often used unintentionally. A teacher who rejects a pupil's work by speaking deprecatingly about it or

Sustaining learning 291

by his actions is going to discourage him and probably make it less likely that he will try so hard next time or be so willing to be kindly disposed towards the teacher. It would be impossible to list all the subtle punishers that are used in schools, very often without conscious intent. But to illustrate: the teacher who makes a remark such as 'Have you *only* got three right?' is not asking a question, he is inflicting punishment, even if only in a small way. In the general case the criterion to apply in deciding whether a teacher activity is a punisher or not must be an estimation of whether the activity can in any way generate negative emotional states in the learner. Teacher disapproval, rejection, reproof, rejection of work, continuous experience of failure are all categories likely to diminish the self-esteem and positive emotions of pupils because of their effects as punishers. It is difficult, probably impossible, to identify every instance of punishers while teaching, or even observing teaching. The difficulties of observing and classifying accurately are enormous. Ideally teachers in training would get the opportunity to observe classroom life or recordings of it in order for them to develop their ability to identify categories of teacher behaviour and, in this specific case, to sensitize them to the type of punishers used by teachers, wittingly or unwittingly. Acquiring this capability of identifying punishers is the essential prerequisite to learning how to control their use and, it is hoped, how to avoid them. The ability to identify punishers is a type-B skill in the category system discussed earlier. Controlling their use consciously when teaching is a type-A skill. Avoiding them altogether is a type-A skill with a personal value judgement built in. I would support the latter course for reasons advanced above, and in devising a schedule for reinforcement in the classroom I should adopt that course while recognizing that conscious control is a prior ability.

Avoiding punishment is not a line that appeals to all teachers. For example, British teachers as a group seem to have a touching faith in the efficacy of corporal punishment as a pedagogical prop and have resisted attempts to have it banned over the years. At the time of writing, Britain is one of the few industrialized countries where it is allowed. In some countries inflicting physical violence on a child is as much of a crime as

292 Psychopedagogy

assault on another adult. Schools in such countries do not seem to have terrible problems with 'discipline' which seems to be the main fear of its supporters in Britain.

It may be that fears of this type give a clue to the main problem of 'discipline'. The attitudes they reflect are essentially negative. Instead of the focus of attention being on how to make life in classrooms more agreeable and enjoyable to the learners, the emphasis is on how to contain the threat to the teacher's authority. In view of the phenomenon of teacher expectations, this attitude is likely to be a potent influence in encouraging problems. This point seems to be supported by the fact that frequently discipline problems are associated with individual teachers within schools rather than with classes of pupils.

The appropriate emphasis, therefore, is on the prevention of difficulties rather than on working out what to do when they happen. Good and Brophy (1973) have provided a most useful exposition of this approach. They suggest specific teacher activities aimed at overcoming some of the more common problems, and the reader is referred to the book for full details. One point that was originally described by Kounin (1970) as 'with-it-ness' is worth particular mention; this is the importance of the teacher's continually monitoring the classroom. This continuous scanning enables the teacher to keep track of all the events of the classroom and so deal with any difficulties as they arise. But as Good and Brophy point out, all the specific techniques in the world aren't going to be of much help if the teacher's attitude is basically antipathetic to children and teaching. Assuming this is not the case, then much of the success in classroom management depends on good planning and good motivating strategies.

One other aspect of Kounin's work has important implications for the development of a positive classroom atmosphere. He observed that the whole group of pupils is affected by the tenor of the teacher's interactions with individuals. In particular, the punishment of one pupil led to negative affective states in other pupils. Kounin referred to this phenomenon as a 'ripple' effect. By the same token positive teacher–pupil interactions may help to establish a positive atmosphere more conducive to learning. The best ways of coping with the effects of a spread of negative

Sustaining learning 293

affect is to try to avoid punishment of individuals in public (by reprimands for example).

Feedback

Throughout this discussion of reinforcement the concept of feedback has been lurking in the background. Feedback gives the learner knowledge of the results of his actions and is, of course, indispensable for learning to take place. In all cases of reinforcement or punishment that I have discussed, feedback has been implicit. The information from the teacher that a given activity, either in conduct about the classroom or in specific learning responses, is correct will increase the likelihood of its being repeated. If the teacher signifies approval as well, the effect will be increased. Feedback and reinforcement are here working together. Information that he has failed in a sub-task of learning, coupled with the teacher's displeasure and criticism, will act as a double punisher for a pupil. A skilful teacher will arrange things so that even if a pupil fails to cope with a given piece of learning he is given encouragement, so that the teacher's reinforcement acts against the punishing effect of failure. There is no question of reinforcing the mistake. The skill lies in giving accurate feedback which helps the learner to diagnose his problem and do better next time, while at the same time encouraging him in his efforts. Knowing that the teacher does not think any the less of him because he has failed in a piece of learning is obviously more likely to enhance a pupil's learning than piling punishment on top of failure. Sadly, however, schools all over the world operate this double-barrelled system of punishment daily.

I have discussed feedback when talking about cognitive skills and, of course, it is a phenomenon that provides a good example of the fact that the cognitive and the affective interpenetrate all the time. Economical learning necessitates careful structuring of the learning experiences of the pupil. Optimally the structuring should be such that a learner would have a range of experiences that would enable him to cope in any situations that necessitated the new learning. Errorless learning would be the ideal case here. It is also extremely unlikely to happen. But the ideal coincides

294 *Psychopedagogy*

with the ideal state of reinforcement and feedback. All feedback would inform the learner that he was succeeding and should therefore continue along the same lines. At the same time he would be acquiring confidence through the reinforcing effect of success. In other words the affective and the cognitive effects of the optimally structured learning conditions would coincide. A superbly skilful teacher would approach this ideal state. However, in devising a schedule for the guidances of lesser mortals we should still be advised to look for this capability.

There is little doubt that the idea of errorless learning is likely to raise a few eyebrows. As is well known, we learn by our mistakes. Like many folk sayings there is a good deal of truth in this one. The point is, of course, that it relates to learning and not teaching. Or, if you prefer, learning without a teacher and learning with a teacher. In the latter case the learning environment is quite deliberately structured; in the former no such structuring takes place. This structuring does not keep the learner from error only to expose him to more error when the teacher's aid is withdrawn. The skill of the teacher lies in arranging the maximum feedback for the learner, and this will embrace the feedback that he might have obtained by making mistakes. He could well be better prepared for novel circumstances than the pupil who had 'learned through his mistakes'.

A teaching schedule

I should now like to draw together the threads of this discussion of the teaching skill of reinforcement. What I hope to do is to set out briefly a simple catalogue of the desirable teacher activities for helping pupils to learn and to like learning. I hope that the discussion of reinforcement has enabled you to see the implications behind the relatively bald statements of desirable teaching attributes in the schedule, so that you will be able to apply the method of appraisal in a variety of situations. If you are a student teacher, viewing recordings of your own teaching with these ideas in mind should provide you with helpful feedback about your efforts. However, it is as well to remember that the ability to examine a piece of teaching, even your own, is a

Sustaining learning **295**

complex skill in itself (type B in my taxonomy) which needs training to accomplish. It is advisable, therefore, in the early stages of your learning to teach, to have comment from a supervisor who, one trusts, would give you the necessary support should you not fare as well as you hoped when you planned the lesson. Since it would clearly be highly desirable to have the supervisor focus on specific teaching activities in order to give you the maximum information, it would be best to talk to him about the modes of observation before embarking on the teaching.

Figure 12.1   *Schedule for teacher's use of reinforcement (STUR)*

This schedule sets out in brief the key aspects of a teacher's use of reinforcement to enhance learning and motivation and create a positive classroom environment. It provides a checklist for a student teacher and/or a supervisor to evaluate this aspect of teaching. Teaching performance should be rated in some way; for example, as weak, satisfactory or good. The student will then have an idea of those aspects of his teaching that need improvement and those areas where he is competent.

A PRE-ACTIVE

1 Make task analysis of the teaching objectives to arrange a learning gradient sufficiently gentle to ensure that pupils achieve high levels of success.
2 Plan for feedback to follow pupil's activities at a very high level. This would probably involve the use of methods other than the teacher's own actions or words.

B INTERACTIVE

3 In all new learning reinforce every correct response at first. When learning is established shift to a random variable schedule. (Basically this boils down to taking care to reinforce each time at the beginning and remembering to reinforce from time to time later.)
4 Arrange to reinforce by methods other than the teacher himself; e.g. peer approval, experience of success, satisfaction of curiosity. (This could well be a consequence of good planning at 1 and 2.)

296 *Psychopedagogy*

Figure 12.1 – continued

5 Involve the whole group in reinforcement by encouraging cooperative work.
6 Provide for vicarious reinforcement by including a whole group in encouragement of effort and correct (or near-correct) attempts.
7 Reinforce management activities every time in the first stages of learning the routines, and reward occasionally when the routines are learned.
8 Recognize punishers and ideally avoid them altogether. Never punish for mistakes in learning; instead examine your teaching.
9 Ignore undesirable behaviour consistently and engage other pupils in activities to deflect their attention from misbehaving pupils.
10 Reinforce any positive behaviour on the part of pupils acting generally negatively.
11 Ensure that feedback planned in item 2 is reinforcing.

C EVALUATIVE (much more rarely done than in content teaching)

12 Attempt to assess pupils' enthusiasm for the activities involved in the teaching. (Difficult, but careful observation of class activities, involvement in the work, and extent to which the pupils maintain an interest outside the class are possible indications.)

The acid test of a good affective classroom climate would be to allow the pupils free choice as to whether they would attend or not. But this test itself depends on other considerations prior to the planning or execution of the teaching. The best teaching in the world would not inspire and motivate pupils who thought that what the teacher was trying to teach them was completely irrelevant. It can be argued that part of a teacher's job is to help pupils to see the relevance of their studies, but it could hardly be thought that this should apply in all circumstances. The question of 'relevance' takes us outside the realm of psychopedagogy into the fields of philosophy and curriculum studies, but what can be said here is that a young teacher trammelled by the constraints of what has been called 'the sabre-toothed curriculum' (i.e.

relevant to Stone Age man) (Benjamin 1939) may well have to make the best of a bad job and do what he can to make his teaching interesting to his pupils, recognizing that he is almost certain to achieve less than a hundred per cent success.

Motivation

Some educationists make a fuss about the use of what they call 'extrinsic motivation'. By this is meant the use of reinforcers outside the individual. A teacher's approval and the use of tangible rewards such as sweets are examples of extrinsic motivators. It is argued that these methods of reinforcement should be avoided and that instead teachers should make use of 'intrinsic motivation'. This approach lays the stress on engaging the interest of the learner so that the fulfilment of the task or the acquisition of new skills would be motivating in itself.

It is unlikely that anyone would argue against intrinsic motivation. I think, however, that some of its supporters fail to understand the case for extrinsic motivation. While there seems to be strong evidence for curiosity as a motivator and the competent fulfilment of tasks as a reinforcer, there is little doubt that they could not stand on their own. Thus, while it is clearly desirable to encourage the development of intrinsic motivation, it is as well to realize that it is unlikely to be enough in itself, and also that extrinsic reinforcement itself contributes to the development of intrinsic motivation. The point of this comment is that the life story of an individual, willy-nilly, in school or out of school, will include countless occurrences of activity reinforced extrinsically, and these reinforcements will interact in very complex ways with motivators such as 'the joy of learning'. In fact, I would suggest that it is impossible to avoid the use of extrinsic motivation in teaching.

An allied objection to the use of extrinsic motivators is the view that the teacher using approaches of this nature is 'manipulating' the pupils. By use of techniques akin to brainwashing he is imposing his view of the world on his pupils. This may be an extreme position but people do hold it. Some people are worried that reinforcement techniques will be used to produce pupils like robots conforming to the teacher's requirements. The questions

298 *Psychopedagogy*

of what is desirable behaviour and what we mean by classroom control are raised very sharply when we see the possibility of actually influencing pupils' behaviour systematically. Questions of this type are not psychological questions; they are questions to be faced when deciding on educational aims and objectives and, as I have said earlier, these are value judgements based essentially on the consensus of workers in the field and ultimately on society at large. Teachers cannot avoid such questions of value but it seems to me that the achieving by teachers of the hoped-for outcomes of their actions through an understanding of the processes of reinforcement can only have dire consequences if the teacher is destructively disposed towards the pupils. There is nothing in the technique itself that inevitably leads to brainwashing. It could be used to encourage independence of thought and action and the development of self-control. The pedagogical techniques should be the stock-in-trade of teachers, but they will not tell him *what* attitudes and *what* type of activities should be fostered. For my part I would hope that most teachers would wish to use the techniques to optimize learning in their pupils based as much as possible on intrinsic motivation and cooperation with peers, a view that I hope most readers would support.

Reinforcement in practice

In all classroom discourse much is lost when the words are transcribed into print. All non-verbal material is lost and the verbal loses a great deal when it is shorn of intonation and nuance of facial expression. Any attempt to examine such discourse for its relevance to our discussion of reinforcement in the classroom therefore needs to be handled very carefully. It would be very easy, for example, for a stranger to classroom life to look at a transcript and interpret a string of 'good's as a high level of reinforcement, whereas in fact the teacher could well be using the word as a punctuation mark with little, if any, commendation built into it. Or the same word could be being employed as a 'marker' delineating the beginning or end of a conversation. In the case of the latter our stranger would possibly be able to deduce the significance of the word 'good' from the context, but in the

Sustaining learning 299

former this would be more difficult. With these cautions in mind I should now like to examine some material transcribed from classrooms to see how in real life teachers tend to make use of reinforcers.

One of the difficulties in using such material is the enormous amount one has to go through in order to provide examples in a full classroom context of the kind of thing I have been discussing. In fact the striking thing one observes after viewing and listening to lessons is the relatively small amount of reinforcement that actually takes place. When things go badly wrong, one is likely to observe a large number of punishers or intended punishers, but in other classrooms the incidence of reward is in general quite low. Therefore in the material that follows I have selected from various lessons aspects that exemplify the use of reinforcement and punishment in settings that have themselves been taken from complete lessons. It is thus not possible to get the full flavour of the episodes, but as I have already suggested, there are other problems that make such excerpts less than real. The excerpts can, however, help us to see the reality of reinforcement in teaching even though they may not tell the whole story.

LESSON FROM LIFE: 10

The extract that follows is a sad example of a teacher unconsciously demonstrating several of the points I made earlier about punishment. It takes place at the beginning of the lesson. The pupils aged around thirteen or fourteen are entering a classroom rather noisily but there is by no means uproar. The teacher tries to get them to sit quietly. In the episode only the teacher's voice is reported since there is no actual dialogue with any pupil and the pupils' talk is noise or confusion, as Flanders would have it. Some of the pupils' contributions are, in fact, reactions to the teacher's remarks, in general protests about what she is saying, but in the general hubbub it is very difficult to discern specific contributions. The general level of the teacher's discourse is very loud. At times she shouts extremely loudly. These shouts are shown in capitals and in one place I have indicated where the teacher's voice rose to a particularly high level.

300 *Psychopedagogy*

Teacher

1 'Right' – Quiet – Sit down and shut UP. NOW!

2 Rodney. Come here. No one else. Come here. Henry where Michael is sitting. Vanessa where Henry is sitting.

3 Chewing gum in the waste-paper basket. No – YOU may NOT.

4 You left it on the floor?

5 Martha, Joan, Bridget, Frank, Michael.

6 Just shut up.

7 Good afternoon Helen. Nice to see you.

8 Helen Stephens. Over here.

9 [Shouts] QUIET – ALL RIGHT. [Protests from pupils.]

10 You may all change places when you are reasonable persons which I think will be in the year 2000.

11 Then you'll behave won't you?

12 Tomorrow afternoon the detention will be [pause] twelve minutes.

13 That is to say twelve minutes after you have complete silence. Tomorrow afternoon.

14 Do I have you tomorrow afternoon?

15 That's right.

16 You were late.

17 David.

18 Paul White, where are you?

19 Tomorrow's detention is now fifteen minutes.

20 That's right *fifteen minutes*.

21 David! Put your chewing gum in the waste-paper basket. NOW.

22 NO I can't read to you today because I am thoroughly annoyed and FED UP WITH YOU!!!

23 Tomorrow's detention is now *twenty minutes*. [Diminution of noise.]

Sustaining learning 301

24 At last. All right. We have detention tomorrow afternoon for the whole class.
Twenty minutes. [Protests by pupils.]

25 *TWENTY MINUTES here at 3.30 tomorrow afternoon.*

26 Thank you.

27 Open your exercise books, please, to the page that you did yesterday while I was not here. I was having a lovely time. I was somewhere else. I wasn't with you, was I?

28 OK. Helen Stephens.

29 Read me your answer to the question 'How many items of food laid out on the breakfast table can you remember?' without referring to the passage.

30 Helen Stephens, HELEN STEPHENS, HELEN.

31 Naturally.

32 Why do you do what Bridget says? Bridget's not teaching you. *I AM.* No. No.

33 Michael! Look at the worksheet.

34 Put the date at the top of the work.

35 David!

36 Right – you then, Michael. Copy what's at the top of the worksheet into your book.

37 No. The whole thing.

38 The vowels are 'a' comma, 'e' comma, 'i' comma, 'o' comma and 'u' full stop. That is what it says.

39 Yes, that's what I have said. How many times?

40 Four. I excuse myself.

41 Do number two which says 'Make two new columns in your book'. Look at the list again.

42 Put the words which end in vowels in the left-hand column and the words which end in consonants in the right-hand column.

43 Right. In two columns. Vowels on the left, consonants on the right.

302 *Psychopedagogy*

44 Helen!

(Extract transcribed from BBC TV recording of part of a school lesson 1977)

As I said earlier, the printed word conveys only a very limited idea of the nature of the transaction. Taking utterances 7 and 26 at their face value would give a very misleading picture. In both the teacher's tone was one of extreme sarcasm belying the surface meaning of the words and giving more or less the opposite meaning to the pupils. Throughout the passage the message that comes over loud and clear is that the teacher is not interested in the pupils and probably doesn't like them. Utterance 27, particularly, rubs it in: 'I was having a lovely time. I was somewhere else. I wasn't with you, was I?'

The extent to which the pupils took the teacher's diatribe as punishing is problematic. A snapshot of classroom life like this one does not give any idea of the events of the weeks and months before in the lives either of the pupils or the teacher, or of the story of their lives together. It is probable, however, that the pupils were thoroughly habituated to the situation and the sarcasm and hectoring probably was not perceived as particularly hurtful. At the same time the emotional atmosphere of the class could hardly be expected to be good for learning.

The nature of the learning task in which the teacher sought to engage the pupils is not likely to have been helpful either. I do not know quite what the task was, but on the face of it it seems supremely unimaginative, trivial and boring and is hardly likely to have been thought of by the pupils as relevant to their lives.

The threat of detention some time in the future seems to have limited effect, although from among the sounds of noise and confusion one could detect a certain amount of hushing and eventually the noise does diminish. The unhappy thing is that there is nothing positive at all in the teacher's words, and on the non-verbal side all the signals she gave off were also negative.

Thus this extract is presented as a non-exemplar of reinforcement, and despite, or more appositely because of, its apparent ineffectiveness, as an exemplar of punishment. However, since it is impossible to teach concepts by the exclusive use of non-

Sustaining learning 303

exemplars, let us now consider some positive instances of the concept of reinforcement.

Easier said than done. Scrutiny of any number of transcripts of lessons reveals that teachers in general use verbal reinforcement rather infrequently. This does not imply that they do not reinforce. Non-verbal factors are clearly important, as I have suggested. One problem with non-verbal reinforcers, however, is that they are sometimes, perhaps frequently, misunderstood. The same applies to verbal reinforcement but with probably less force since it is the medium of overt interaction in the classroom and also the main channel of feedback to pupils about the effectiveness of their learning. Thus, while I am aware of the danger of underestimating the amount of reinforcement when one omits the non-verbal, I take the view that the record of the verbal transactions is a useful and reliable index of teachers' use of reinforcement. And the record suggests to me that many teachers reinforce their pupils sparingly.

A big problem, then, when one searches through lesson transcripts for examples of reinforcement, is that one scans acres of print to find a few examples. The reader, not having had this experience, might well imagine not only that the items presented to him exemplify reinforcement, but that the number of reinforcers in the extracts is an indication of the density of reinforcers in the teachers' usual discourse. This assumption should be resisted and the extracts that follow should be seen only as indicating some types of reinforcers teachers use.

The next extract comes from a lesson to eleven- to twelve-year-old pupils. It is much the same lesson as that reported in Chapter 6 except that it is given to a different class.

LESSON FROM LIFE: II

1 (T) I'm going to show you a little model to start off with, of these back-to-back houses. Now, em, if I show you this here. That is one street there and that is another, so that is their front door, and the man who lives here, where's his front door going to be? You show me Stephen.

304 *Psychopedagogy*

2 (P) Here [points].

3 (T) That's right.

4 (T) So. You'd have in other words, you'd have, em, Anne, Annette living here and at the back of her Sandra. And that would be two completely different families and two houses.

5 (T) Now what have you got on either side of them?

6 (T) On either side of Annette and Sandra's house. What have you got?

7 (P) Ground.

8 (T) Oh no, no.

9 (T) What do you think this is?

10 (P) Ground.

11 (T) No.

12 (P) Alleyways.

13 (T) No.

14 (P) Another house.

15 (T) Yes, yes. In that road there, that would be about twenty houses all in one long strip.

16 (T) So that, em, in your house where you lived there's someone at the back of you and someone else on either side.

17 (T) Now what, em, would you get a lot of?

18 (P) Disease.

19 (T) Yes, disease.

20 (T) And something else?

21 (T) Something that can be very irritating besides disease.

22 (P) Lots of arguments.

23 (T) Well.

24 (T) What do you mean, arguments?

25 (P) Noise, em, noises from babies crying and things like this.

Sustaining learning 305

26 (T) Yes a lot of noise. Yes.

27 (T) Perhaps with some of them they were so jerry-built that you could hear a conversation practically. Especially if there was someone having an argument.

28 (P) They could hear how much ground they had or how much they earned.

29 (P) There weren't any gardens.

30 (P) Their gardens were streets.

31 (P) Dampness.

32 (T) Pardon?

33 (P) Dampness.

34 (T) Yes, there was a lot of dampness.

35 (T) What do you think causes dampness? John.

36 (P) Steam.

37 (T) Yes, steam.

38 (T) What else?

39 (T) Come on.

40 (T) Come on, Susan. What do you think?

41 (T) We're thinking what caused dampness.

42 (T) Angela.

43 (P) The weather.

44 (T) The weather, yes.

45 (T) In what way would it cause dampness in there though?

46 (P) Because it went straight through the roof.

47 (T) Oh, yes. It might have done.

48 (T) But go on.

49 (P) Miss, the, er, materials they used wasn't strong enough.

50 (T) That's a very good answer.

An obvious problem with this kind of discourse is that there is not very much opportunity for the teacher to reinforce pupil activity since the pupils' share is so limited. Having this problem in mind, as I suggest in the schedule, may help to increase the

306 *Psychopedagogy*

amount of reinforcement since the teacher would plan for a pattern of interaction which he would hope would involve pupils more and provide more feedback with a consequent increase in possibilities for reinforcement.

However, in a short transcript it would be unrealistic and probably unreasonable to expect large numbers of reinforcers. A high frequency in a short transcript would imply a very large occurrence of reinforcers over all. Fears are sometimes expressed that such ubiquitous use of reinforcement could be counter-productive, since its excessive use would devalue its effect. This may be the case but there is little evidence about this effect at the moment. The main problem, it seems to me, is more likely to arise from the uninformed use of reinforcers. My observations of classrooms and examination of many transcripts of lessons lead me to conclude that few teachers are likely to overdo reinforce-ment in the present state of practical teaching.

In the extract little provision is made for pupil responses and what there is is the familiar phenomenon of the children ostensibly playing guessing games in reply to the teacher's questioning. Note that in utterance 17 the question gives very little clue as to what the teacher is getting at. Not surprisingly the pupils make intelligent guesses. The teacher's rejoinder, 'Yes, disease', confirms the pupil's reply as acceptable, but utterance 20 qualifies it immediate-ly and indicates that although 'disease' has been accepted it is not really what is wanted. It may perhaps be best looked upon as a quasi-reinforcer, that is, an apparent reinforcer. It is impossible to say how it is interpreted by the child who makes the answer. It could possibly be a weak reinforcer, or it could be analagous to being damned with faint praise. Certainly it is difficult to regard this kind of comment as being particularly reinforcing. It is an important classroom phenomenon, if only because of its ubiquity, as utterances 26, 27 and 44 suggest.

The passage illustrates another ubiquitous phenomenon that clearly increases the likelihood of teachers' using quasi-rein-forcers. I am referring to the inexorable grind to the 'correct' answer: that is, the answer that the teacher has in his mind. In the passage in question I identify three unqualified reinforcers – 3, 15, and 50. Pupil's comment 49 attracts the most positive

Sustaining learning 307

reinforcer. Not only does teacher say, 'That's a very good answer', but she also takes up the pupil's contribution and gives a gloss on it. We might ask, however, why some of the other pupils' answers were greeted with less enthusiasm: utterance 18, 'disease', in the context seems very reasonable but it only attracts a quasi-reinforcer. The answer is, of course, as I have already suggested: that reinforcement in this extract is earned not for useful and plausible contributions to a joint exploration of phenomena, but for coming to the same conclusion as the teacher.

This very common problem is one about which we have little information, even at the descriptive level. It is thus not possible to say anything with certainty about its effect on classroom affective climate. On the face of it, however, it would seem reasonable to take the view that replacing quasi-reinforcers by genuine reinforcers in situations such as I have been discussing would be a desirable thing and would have increased the overall level of pupil involvement.

Accepting it as desirable is one thing, putting it into practice is another. However, as with other aspects of psychopedagogy, recognizing the problem is just a first step. Planning and analysis before the event can then give a helpful orientation. The occasional look back over a lesson by the use of a tape recorder can increase one's understanding of the problem and give some indication about solving it.

This kind of self-monitoring is probably of particular significance in developing the type of skills discussed in this chapter. There seem to be good grounds for believing that most teachers reinforce far less than they would intuitively think. The fear commonly expressed – that too much praise or commendation would become fulsome and self-defeating – seems to be rather irrelevant in view of its present sparseness. The subject is virtually unexplored, and yet it is clearly of vital importance and may well hold the key to a radical change in classroom atmosphere if it were better understood. I hope that the guide to reinforcement included in this chapter and similar instruments devised by workers such as Good and Brophy will be helpful to teachers wishing to explore the question. Possibly such explorations would add to our information about the process of classroom reinforcement.

13

A pattern of teaching skills

Socrates was one of the earliest practitioners of what is probably the currently most fashionable specific skill of teaching, the art of questioning. But he didn't invent it. Probably the very first question was asked by the serpent in the garden of Eden, with results that certainly underline the power of this form of verbal communication (Genesis 3:1). Socrates obviously swore by it since he used little other in the way of pedagogic aids. And it may be that his faith in the technique was justified. Since men have been trying to teach others for thousands of years, it would be surprising if no useful ideas related to that and other teaching skills had been developed.

But while we may have acquired some very useful insights about teaching skills from earlier distinguished educationists in different cultures throughout the world, and also from general pedagogic folklore, the venerableness of those skills should not deter us from appraising them and reappraising them in the light of knowledge we construct about the way people learn. Only in this way are we

A pattern of teaching skills 309

likely to be able to refine the concepts and weed out ideas that are deleterious or unproductive.

In some fields of the study and practice of teaching this critical scrutiny is frequently lacking. For example, much work in micro-teaching makes use of a basic corpus of skills that vary little from those proposed by the original begetters in Stanford in the sixties. Such uses involve student teachers practising skills such as questioning, beginning and ending lessons, varying the stimuli, reinforcement, and so on, while teaching small groups of children for short periods of time, commonly about half a dozen children for about ten minutes, frequently with the use of video-recording. The practice in itself is with little doubt of great value for the improvement of teaching skills; the main problem to be guarded against, it seems to me, is conceiving of the skills being practised as ends in themselves, barely related to each other and with no overall theoretical rationale. (Allen and Ryan, 1969)

I discussed these problems earlier (pp. 196 ff.) and suggested that some of them might be overcome by relating them to the body of general teaching skills I have been discussing in the last few chapters. With this sort of approach it becomes possible to establish relationships among the various skills according to the extent to which they may be thought to contribute to overall skills of a general nature. Many of the skills commonly included in microteaching programmes seem to me to be second-order skills; second-order in the sense that they are more specific than the ones I have been discussing. These second-order or sub-skills are relatable to the general skills of concept teaching, reinforcing, teaching of psychomotor skills and teaching problem solving in much the same way as the more specific teaching objectives are related to the overall aims of one's teaching: relatable but currently rarely related. But if we are to get maximum benefit from the deployment of these skills we need to appraise them in the light of pedagogical principles and apply them in an orderly, disciplined and systematic way that will help us to make more rapid and reliable progress than we would be likely to make if we were not to put these ideas under such detailed scrutiny.

Our scrutiny of existing ideas about teaching will be helped by relating them to the key higher-order skills I have referred to.

310 *Psychopedagogy*

Unless they can be seen to relate directly to them and to be useful in achieving those objectives, then we would query their value. This would follow, since we could assess the validity of the claim of any skill for consideration as an important and non-trivial component of teaching by referring to the main skills which are themselves related to a body of theory concerned with human learning. But more than that: we do not merely assess the value of skills already recognized; we are in a position to propose other skills on the basis of our analysis. Thus some of the items in the schedules I have produced could themselves form the basis for sub-schedules for the evaluation of second-order skills. In the concept-teaching schedule, for example, the item relating to increasing the salience of the criterial attributes could form the basis for a subordinate or second-order schedule to act as a guide to the most effective ways of doing this. This schedule would comprise items focusing on that particular activity in greater detail. It would be concerned with such things as the varying of the intensity of physical stimuli – visual, aural, olfactory, tactile and possibly gustatory – in various ways so as to make the attributes of the concept on which we wish the learners to focus stand out more than they would normally. The use of simplified diagrams in science and engineering, the use of different colours on maps and charts to draw attention to specific features, are examples of increasing the salience in the field of visual perception. Speaking particular letter combinations deliberately or with emphasis in teaching beginning reading would be an example of increasing salience in the auditory field. The fact that such devices are commonplace in teaching that owes nothing directly to systematic approaches does not imply that the study of this particular element in the concept-teaching schedule is trivial. Many of the methods referred to are much open to question since teachers often misuse them, for example, by not distinguishing clearly between criterial and non-criterial attributes in their placing of emphasis.

The same kind of approach can be applied to items in the schedule of teacher's use of reinforcement. Take the item relating to the avoidance of punishers. A sub-schedule dealing with this item would need to focus on the teacher's actions when faced

A pattern of teaching skills 311

with learning failure or perhaps antisocial behaviour. The schedule would pick out commonly observed aspects of teachers' behaviour that may be considered punishers, so as to guide the teacher to specific examples of the genre and thus increase his sensitivity in this field. Items on the schedule might refer to such things as the avoidance of disappointed (and disappointing) comment on work returned to pupils that had not come up to scratch or to the avoidance of comment that impugned the integrity of the pupils, perhaps expressed in the form of sarcastic remarks.

The latter example, I suggest, indicates that in some cases the individual items on the general schedules would probably be advantageously combined with other items to form sub-schedules. Thus it would probably be better to introduce into the sub-schedule I have just considered items relating to the positive as well as to the negative reactions to undesirable pupil activities, whether these be unsatisfactory classroom behaviour or inadequate learning. Items 9 and 10 in the reinforcement schedule (p. 295) could well be linked with the item discussed above.

Some second-order skills

A slight acquaintance with the field of classroom studies will be enough to reveal that several skills are currently the object of study and use, especially in connection with microteaching. Some of them have been subjected to a great deal of investigation, particularly those selected for inclusion in minicourse programmes in the USA (Borg *et al.* 1970). Minicourses are self-instructional packages designed to help teachers improve their teaching skill using approaches akin to microteaching. The courses focus on particular skills. In Great Britain a research project has focused on the questioning minicourse in an attempt to apply it to British conditions and to test its efficacy (Perrot 1975).

I have indicated above that I think that to produce isolated specific skills is to put the cart before the horse. There is a great danger that methods of training in quite trivial skills could be devised and there could be a proliferation of skills bearing little or no relation to each other. Although I do not suggest that questioning is trivial skill, I think to focus on it as an end in itself

312 *Psychopedagogy*

is misguided. Nevertheless, since people are actually working with these skills and some experience has been gathered about them, it would be obtuse not to consider them in order to see to what extent they can make a contribution to a teacher's understanding of how best to help pupils' learning and how these skills relate to the general approach outlined above.

Questioning

There is little doubt that this is one of the most popular skills. Most probably this is a consequence of its ubiquity as a pedagogical technique. It is also extremely difficult to pin down. The question 'What is a question?' is not merely facetious, but reflects the ambiguity at the heart of teachers' use of questions. The serpent spoke with a forked tongue when it asked the first question and the consequences have been with us ever since. Sometimes teachers ask questions in a genuine search for information: 'What is your date of birth'? Sometimes to order: 'Can you open the window?' Sometimes to chide (punish): 'Is that the best you can do?' But by and large, in teaching and learning interactions, the staple form of question is akin to the Socratic dialogue conducted with a crowd. Teachers rarely ask questions because they want information.

Two approaches to the study of questioning may help to make the point I am concerned with. In one of these Taba (Taba and Elzey 1964) followed a method similar to the one described here. She started from the processes of concept learning and deduced from them the questions likely to enhance concept learning in children. Thus, for example, a question aimed at helping the pupils to abstract the common properties of phenomena in concept learning would be of the type: 'What belongs together? On what criterion?' On the other hand the British work on the minicourse takes questioning as the point of departure, with no theoretical orientation of this type. As a consequence the training programme comprises a heterogeneous collection of teacher activities some of which might well enhance concept formation, for example, asking the pupil for further clarification of the answer he has given. This could demand more complex thinking on the part of the pupil and

A pattern of teaching skills 313

also by the teacher. Other teacher activities dealt with, however, are of a completely different order: for example, avoiding repetitions of pupils' answers; calling on non-volunteers. The first of these examples aims to eliminate habits (the teacher's) that interfere with discussion, the second to increase pupil participation. A case might be made for the inclusion of these two items on the grounds of enhancing motivation, but the case is not made explicit. The upshot is that we have a set of activities related to the teacher's questioning that have no real conceptual unity. There is a real danger that, lacking a theoretical rationale and merely acquiring the skills in an unquestioning way, a teacher could employ the techniques mechanically and sometimes quite inappropriately. For example, sometimes it is probably helpful to repeat a pupil's answer. The decision as to whether it is or not cannot be made on the basis of practice of that activity. It can be made only on the basis of a more general theoretical perspective. In this particular case, ideas about reinforcement could be very useful in helping a teacher decide whether or not to repeat an answer.

In order to put some flesh on the bones of this discussion, I should like to consider another short extract from the 'rabbit' lesson referred to in an earlier chapter (p. 191). Recall that I inferred that the teacher's objective was to try to get the pupils to observe different things about the rabbit in order for them to write a poem about it later. She is not necessarily trying to teach them what a rabbit *is* so much as to heighten their sensitivity to aspects of its appearance. Consider the nature of the cognitive demands made on the children in this extract.

LESSON FROM LIFE: 12

    1 (T) What about his colour? What colour is he?

    2 (P) His face is black.

    3 (T) He's grey with a black face. What sort of grey is it? Is it grey – what other things are grey? Grey like a – what? Let's have some from this side. Grey like a – what?

    4 (P) Elephant.

314 *Psychopedagogy*

5 (T) Grey like an elephant. Are elephants that colour?

6 (P) No.

7 (T) OK, but it's not far off.

8 (T) What else is grey? What's grey that comes out of chimneys?
[No prizes for guessing what answer the children gave to the last question.]

9 (T) What about his fur? Would you say it was long?

10 (P) No.

11 (T) What would you say about it then?

12 (P) It's very short.

13 (T) Well, that'll do.

14 (P) Soft. We've got soft.

15 (P) [Whispering] I'd say soft.

16 (T) Anything else about his fur?

17 (P) Hard.

18 (T) Eh?

19 (P) Very soft.

20 (T) Hurrah. We've got the colour. We've got soft. He's sort of – do you think he's shy a bit?

21 (P) Yes.

22 (T) Do you think he's fairly soft?

23 (P) Yes.

In this short passage are several commonly observed types of teacher question apparently aimed at getting the children to think about the subject under discussion but which in reality scarcely demand any thought from the children at all. The reasons for this failure are several. Take utterance 1. The teacher asks a question, the answer to which can be derived simply by looking at the rabbit. Provided a child has a previous grasp of colour names, all he has to do is to look. If he doesn't have this grasp, then the

A pattern of teaching skills 315

question is really illegitimate. Utterance 3, asking for the type of grey, exemplifies the 'guess what I'm thinking about' type of question, and the children do the same kind of thing as the younger children in Bruner's twenty-question-type experiment (p. 91): they guess. But they don't guess what's in the teacher's mind, and this near-miss evokes another type of question. Utterance 5, 'Are elephants that colour?', really means 'No' and, young though the pupil is, he has been in the game long enough to know by the tone of the teacher's voice what reply is expected. Note, however, that this question has only two possible answers and the amount of information a child can get from it is minimal unless the teacher expands on the subject. Utterance 8 is a question so heavily cued that only pupils fast asleep could fail to respond correctly. Question 9 directs the children's attention to the rabbit again, but cueing is heavy and the subsequent response again demands little if any thought. It is not possible to be sure about the effect of the tone of the teacher's voice, but it is very likely that this was cueing the children very strongly in addition to the cueing from the way the questions are phrased.

This example of teacher's questioning was taken at random from a collection of transcripts of lessons recorded in ordinary classrooms. It is not specially 'posed' or scripted. I am not, here, attempting to evaluate the extract as good or bad teaching. I merely concerned to draw it to your attention as a typical piece of classroom questioning. It illustrates the difficult problem that a very large proportion of questions asked by teachers demands a very low level of thought by pupils. Naturally, there is no suggestion that pupils and teachers should be operating at cognitive top speed all the time, but, since one of the most important aims of teaching is to help pupils to acquire more complex modes of thinking, there is very good reason for attempting to increase the proportion of questions that demand more complex modes of thought than those observed in the extract. Insight into methods of doing this could be obtained by the methods adopted by Taba and by those suggested above – that is, by relating the questions to the theories of concept learning. On the other hand, no enlightenment can be expected by considering such things as whether the teacher repeats a question, or whether he pauses for

316 *Psychopedagogy*

pupils to reply, which are items found in some approaches to the skill of questioning.

Sometimes approaches to questioning make use of the Bloom taxonomy to give insight into questioning. The idea is that teachers learn to classify questions according to the various levels of the taxonomy of cognitive objectives. Lower-order questions are those that ask recall questions, middle-range questions are those that ask for application of knowledge, and a third level asks for analysis and synthesis. Clearly it is useful for a teacher to know about this form of classification. There is, however, the point mentioned when I discussed concept formation: that the way in which a question is classified can be determined only when the whole of the relevant instruction is taken into account. Questions asked about matter that has already been used in any exposition can only be classified as recall, even though on the face of it it looks complex. Knowledge about concept learning will help a teacher to classify such questions accurately and help him to frame them appropriately for the aim he has in mind.

To conclude this discussion of questioning I would suggest that it is probably justifiable for teachers to use it as one of the most important teaching devices. It makes use of language, which is the most powerful instrument in human learning, and it is potentially extremely flexible in its use. I would argue, however, that it is a mistake to try to develop teachers' questioning skills without a general frame of reference such as I have tried to provide. With that frame of reference it becomes possible to plan, identify and practise questioning more insightfully than would otherwise be possible. Merely learning that higher-order questions are 'a good thing' could well blind a teacher to the desirability of using simple questions to draw attention to the criterial attributes of concepts and thereby increase their salience, or to the value of using simple questions at the early stages in a learning gradient to enhance motivation. Working from principles of pedagogy would suggest to a teacher which circumstances would be appropriate for the use of the different types of questions.

Set induction

I turn now to another specific skill popular with afficionados of skill training. I mentioned it in passing earlier in this chapter under the title of beginning a lesson. Set induction is somewhat more than that since it can be deployed not just at the beginning of lessons but at any point when new lines are to be taken or new subjects are to be raised. In essence, set induction is in the nature of an attention-gaining device that relies on notions from the psychology of attention and principles of arousal and what Pavlov called 'the what-is-it reflex'. The general principle underlying arousal is that organisms maintain a state of equilibrium with their environment that is steady but dynamic. The steady flow of stimulation is monitored at a very low level of awareness. When new forms of stimuli appear, the pattern of the stimulation changes, the organism attends to the new stimuli, and the level of awareness is raised sharply. The sense mode by which the new stimulation is perceived serves to alert the whole organism, so that a new sound does not alert merely the hearing apparatus but all the senses.

Clearly, by itself, inducing attention can contribute only indirectly to learning. A teacher would use the principles in order to enable him to bring into play other skills that will help him to achieve his teaching objectives. It thus seems reasonable to look upon this skill as a second-order skill and, since it refers to the affective state of the learner, it is relatable to the use of reinforcement schedule, particularly item 4, reinforcing by satisfaction of curiosity. In order for curiosity to be satisfied, it first has to be aroused. This naturally should be planned for in the pre-active stage of the lesson when methods of presentation are being planned. These are referred to in the concept-teaching schedule which underlines the fact that the cognitive and affective are inseparable and also serves to guard against gimmicky openings, unconnected with the substance of the teaching, that could well be counterproductive to the aim of the lesson while still arousing the pupils. In fact, in some of the schedules that have been produced to check on set induction, notice has been taken of the twin aspects of set, and items relating to cognitive matters

318 *Psychopedagogy*

are included. The point to note here is that 'set' is used not only in the sense of arousal but also in a sense of orientation to the conceptual nature of the learning about to be undertaken. In order to examine the processes involved in set, let us now consider one or two real-life examples.

LESSON FROM LIFE: 13

The first extract comes from a lesson given to twelve-year-old pupils.

> Well, I'm going to explain to you what phyla are. Now if I were to ask you all to think of all the different animals and plants that you could that lived on the earth today, I'm sure that we would soon fill this blackboard full. But I think it might surprise you to know that there's nine hundred and fifty thousand different kinds of animals and three hundred and forty thousand different kinds of plants that live on the earth today.
>
> Now because of this very large number biologists decided that they'd like to put different animals into different groups and different plants into different groups so that they get more idea, sort of, where they fitted into the pattern of life.
>
> Now you might ask why they bothered with this. How many of you have got a stamp collection? Anybody? Right, well, if I was to walk in here and put down on the table hundreds of different kinds of stamps and ask you to add them to your collection how would you go about it? What would you do?

The first thing to note about this extract is that it consists entirely of the most familiar of all classroom stimuli: the teacher's voice. Not much here in the way of unusual stimulation to attract attention or stimulate arousal. In addition the teacher introduces a strange word in the very first sentence and then continues talking without relating his opening gambit to the explanation following. True, the use of the strange word might have aroused the curiosity of some pupils, but it could also have confused others. Would it not have been more effective to take up his

A pattern of teaching skills **319**

stamp idea earlier, even presenting the pupils with a sorting problem right at the beginning?

LESSON FROM LIFE: 14

The second extract takes a different tack. The pupils are twelve-year-olds.

1 (T) Right. Can you pass this round. Does anyone know what it is? Can you pass it round. Do you know what it is? What is it?

2 (P) It's a fossil.

3 (T) She thinks it's a fossil. It is a fossil. Can you have a look and see. Has anyone ever found a fossil? . . .

In this extract an unusual stimulus is introduced into the classroom and the teacher's language is used to focus the children's attention on it and to direct their thinking towards identification of the object. This is a very different thing from the questions asked in the 'rabbit' lesson. The answer is not 'there' for the pupils to see and the unusual nature of the object is likely to arouse their curiosity, thus producing the heightened state of arousal referred to as 'set'. The questions in the 'rabbit' lesson, of course, did not come at the beginning and their purpose was different. In fact in that lesson the teacher used an attention-gaining ploy by bringing the rabbit into the classroom in a box and asking the children to guess what she had in the box. There is a considerable difference between the two approaches, however. The 'fossil' opening was directly related to the subject to be elaborated later, and the children's attention was focused on attributes of the object that would single it out as a fossil, whereas the rabbit in a box could only give rise to guessing games to discover what was in it. This is not to suggest that this particular gambit was 'wrong'. It probably served to alert the children and this is clearly a positive effect. Perhaps you can think of a way in which the teacher could have achieved a similar result and at the same time focused the pupils' attention in the way she wanted – that is, on the physical appearance of the animal.

320 *Psychopedagogy*

These two examples of openings are extremely common. Here are a few more of the same types: 'Well, I'm going to explain . . .'; 'Right, I'm going to talk to you about . . .'; 'Right. Well today I am going to talk to you about . . .'; 'Can you tell me what this is?'; 'Right, can you pass this round.' As before, these extracts are taken from transcripts of lessons. This is the way real lessons frequently start. Almost certainly the questioning openings are more likely to stimulate arousal than the 'Right: today we're going to . . .' openings. But neither type is in the same category as the type of activity designed to induce concept learning, although clearly until attention is secured no learning of any sort can take place.

There is very little that is startling about the methods of beginning lessons so far mentioned. But this is life. Most lessons start in similar ways so far as arousal is concerned. There are limitations as to what one can do, of course. It would take considerable ingenuity and energy to produce high-key introductions to every lesson one taught during the course of a week. I also guess that one would be forced into somewhat bizarre openings if one wished to produce something different and startling every time. Having said this, I think there is little doubt that many teachers and most student teachers could profit greatly from considering carefully the question of how best to start a lesson and how best to introduce new topics. If one bears in mind the general idea of arousal, this will help. Introducing into the classroom unusual stimuli in any of the sense modalities will evoke arousal and orienting activity. But also unusual, intriguing or unexpected teacher activity will have a similar effect. And, as in all teaching, language is a powerful instrument. Posing questions that present familiar phenomena in an unusual light arouses curiosity and, if the subject for discussion is related to the phenomena, then the cognitive set is productively aligned with the arousing stimuli. From the psychological point of view it is important to realize that it is not merely a question of *attracting* attention, it is a question of *raising the level* of attention so that the pupils will be more receptive to the continuing stimuli connected with the learning activities planned by the teacher.

A pattern of teaching skills 321

Closure

'Closure' refers to the way lessons are ended. However, it should not be interpreted too literally. The lessons may come to a close but the intention should not be to say the last word on the subject. Indeed, one of the key aspects of effective closure is that the learners leave in a highly motivated state, either to continue the learning independently, or to be enthusiastically looking forward to the next lesson on the subject. A tall order, no doubt. But is anyone likely to disagree with it as an aim?

I referred to the skill in terms of its motivating effect on students. Thus we would expect the teacher activities that contribute to it to be related particularly to those set out on the reinforcement schedule (p. 295). But in most cases there will also be a cognitive element. Recapitulation by the teacher will consolidate the concepts that have been taught and orient the pupils to the continuation of the work in the next session. The evaluative section of the schedules, however, will give a framework for closing activities. The teacher will be concerned to establish whether he has achieved his teaching objectives by observing his pupils' learning. He will be concerned to establish that the pupils have enjoyed the learning, and this will, one could reasonably expect, lead to enhanced motivation and the enthusiastic looking-forward mentioned above. In the psychomotor field, the evaluation would be concerned to encourage the learner to continue practising and this item would imply the consolidation of the new skill. Providing feedback (as mentioned in the schedules) appropriately at the end of the lesson will also help to consolidate the points made in most existing schedules related to closure.

Other skills

Questioning, set and closure are just three of a number of specific skills commonly discussed in connection with an analytical approach to practical teaching. Others include varying the stimulus, the use of silence, the use of non-verbal cues, reinforcement, illustration and use of examples, and lecturing (Allen and

322 Psychopedagogy

Ryan 1969). I hope the discussion in this chapter has made clear the reason I believe the collection of skills commonly in use is heterogeneous and lacking a unifying rationale. If you consider the list you will notice that many of the items may be seen as instrumental in concept teaching or constructing a positive affective atmosphere in the classroom. However, they could be practised quite pointlessly unless the teacher understood the reasons for using them. Varying the stimulus is another example of maintaining arousal and is fine if the teacher is aware of the purpose. Relating the skill to ideas of motivation through reinforcement and the ideas of concept learning will help him avoid ritual variation of the stimuli at times when it would hinder rather than help learning. The key difference between these skills and those of reinforcement, concept teaching and teaching for psychomotor learning is that the three proposed first-order skills are pervasive. They apply to all teaching once the objectives have been specified. I believe that the subordinate items in the four schedules (pp. 206, 242, 268 and 295) provide checklists of activities that would ensure that these specific skills would be developed as and when necessary, contributing to the pupils' learning according to a unified set of principles.

A master skill?

The approach to teaching skills that I have outlined in the last few chapters has been based on the assumption that it is possible to analyse teaching objectives and thereby identify specific teaching skills. There has been some criticism of this approach on the grounds that any attempt to analyse teaching in this way dismantles the teacher into an arbitrary collection of separate skills that destroys the very thing that is the object of study. I believe this view is mistaken, and I hope that the discussion of the various skills, their interrelationships and the unifying principles has helped to explain why. In addition, it is not possible actually to practise only one skill at a time. Thus, in the same way that the various items on the four suggested schedules tend to interrelate, so do the skills a teacher practises in actual teaching.

There is one skill I have not mentioned so far which is some-

A pattern of teaching skills 323

times proposed as *the* teaching skill. It is the skill of knowing what to do in order to achieve the objectives of the teaching, sometimes referred to as 'decision making' (Shavelson 1976). This superordinate skill is much the same as the one proposed in my model of objectives in educational psychology (Stones and Anderson 1972). The objective related to the teaching of concepts reads: '*decide* on the types of pupil learning most appropriate to the objective and specify the teaching and learning activities most likely to optimize the pupils' learning'. This is the most general objective. Analysis produces demands for more specific decisions. These objectives were not related to practical teaching directly. To make that connection we should specify that the objective would ask the teacher not only to *specify* the relevant teaching activities, but to carry them out. At this stage we are talking directly about the teacher's decision making in the classroom. I suggest, therefore, that the approach to skills I have been taking knits in with the ideas of decision making very closely. The scheme as a whole provides a conceptual framework unifying the specific skills and decision making. There are, however, factors influencing a teacher's decision making that are not dealt with in this scheme, and I should like to touch upon these now.

Obviously one of the key influences on a teacher's decision making is his view of society and other people, particularly children. If he believes that children are the same as adults only smaller, he is likely to make decisions that take no account of the findings we have discussed in earlier chapters about the nature of cognitive development. If he accepts the Jensen thesis (see Chapter 17) that white children are well endowed with the type of intellectual functioning that stresses concept learning but that black children are poorly endowed with the basic ability to think conceptually (although, fortunately, better at rote learning), he is likely to decide on one kind of teaching for the blacks and one for the whites, even if he does know a lot about the cognitive development of children. He may, on the other hand, believe that children have the same qualities of thought no matter what their colour but think that they are all basically evil, as Golding appears to do in his book *Lord of the Flies*. Other personal factors

324 *Psychopedagogy*

will influence a teacher's decision making: the state of his health; whether he is relaxed or tense, kind or cruel, patient or impatient, or quick or slow in his perceptions.

Some writers take the view that personal factors such as these are the key factors in teaching effectiveness, and if you examine the literature in educational psychology you will find a plethora of studies examining teaching performance in the light of personality. Smith (1969) discusses the role of personality and attitude in teaching and makes the point which I accept that, while such factors are important, they are not decisive. Teachers with a variety of outlooks and personalities will all be equally incompetent if they know nothing about theory related to teaching and about teaching skills. With a knowledge of such theory and practice they will be more competent but will express their competencies in different individual ways. If any of the ways of implementing the teacher's knowledge of theory and practice grossly transgresses currently approved norms of professional conduct, the remedy will have to be outside the field of psychopedagogy. Smith suggests counselling and the discussion of issues in an analytical way in order to change attitudes. Obviously the value judgements involved in this kind of activity are open to the criticism that the process is one enforcing conformity to the currently dominant ideology. This may be true, but the same must be said about any of the curriculum decisions or the philosophical outlooks that inform the selection of the original objectives of teaching. But as with those there is nothing in the approach I have been discussing that dictates the way an individual teacher must operate.

In addition to the personal qualities of the teacher – and this includes his knowledge of pupils and theories and practices in teaching – other factors will influence the way a teacher operates. One of the main influences is the actual teaching environment. In classrooms, size, position in the school, lighting, facilities and other physical factors are bound to influence the teacher's thinking as he decides on the teaching strategies and tactics he hopes to employ. Thus in deciding which approach to adopt, which teaching skills to employ, how best to evaluate his teaching, a teacher is performing a complex task of information processing. He is

A pattern of teaching skills 325

receiving information from the environment about classroom conditions, the state of the pupils – that is, their level of current understanding and their motivation – he is drawing on his knowledge of the theory and practice of teaching; and all the while his interpretation of the information is influenced by his own physical and mental state.

A further, and particularly important, factor that cannot but influence a teacher's decision making is the fact that he is so personally involved in the process that his very involvement may distort his assessment of the situation and lead to wrong decisions (Shavelson 1977, 1978). For example, if he takes the credit when the children learn but considers their failure to learn to be due to deficiencies within the pupils, his pedagogical decisions are bound to be wrong.

In view of the extreme complexity of classroom events and the interplay of factors affecting those events, any teacher's decision making is bound to be problematic. In his endeavours to cope with this type of complexity he will be much aided if he can give it thought in relative tranquillity when preparing the lesson, that is, in the pre-active stage of teaching. This preparation will help to cope with the complexities of the interactive stage of teaching but will not solve all the problems. Decisions have to be made continually in the flow of classroom interactions, and at this stage the deeper the teacher's grasp of the skills and sub-skills of teaching discussed above, the more prepared he will be to make satisfactory pedagogical decisions. But not *the* most satisfactory decision. In my view the concept of a most satisfactory or ideal lesson is utopian and chimerical besides being static and conservative. This follows from the view of teaching as experimentation seeking continuous refinement.

Currently there is little explanatory value in regarding the overall teaching skill as decision making. There is, however, some descriptive and heuristic value. It may help us to look in the right place for explanations. In fact some information from the general field of the study of decision making could well be helpful in teaching. These studies try to identify general factors that influence human decision making and, if and when they are seen to have general utility, they could help us to acquire insights into

326 *Psychopedagogy*

how teachers make decisions and then help them to make them more accurately and effectively (Shavelson 1977).

Synthesis

We have now looked fairly closely in the last few chapters at the important aspects of the application of psychological principles to the practice of teaching. I have discussed at some length the skills I believe to be of particular importance, and I have looked at the way in which some of the specific skills currently used in some programmes of teacher preparation relate to the more general skills. The line I have taken is that in attempting to apply ideas from the psychology of learning to the practice of teaching, with the intention of helping pupils to learn, a teacher will enhance his insight into theory and practice. It seems to me that this approach has potential not only for improving the theoretical understanding and practical expertise of individual teachers but also to make a genuine addition to knowledge in both spheres. This approach sees teachers as experimenters working with principles related to human learning and bodies of concepts about subject matter, testing and trying both in teaching/learning encounters. The application of inert bodies of subject matter or the mechanical application of received bodies of principles has no place in this scheme. But, naturally, the more information a teacher has of the factors involved in human learning and the greater his knowledge of the factors that influence his decision making when he is teaching, the more likely he is to make correct decisions and be a better experimenter.

The schedules I have produced to evaluate different aspects of teaching should be viewed in the same spirit. They are not tablets from on high to be followed slavishly, but are guides to action and open to improvement in the light of that action. Since they are to be used in evaluating and guiding individual teachers, since those individual teachers are operating in areas related to all the aspects covered by the schedules and making decisions in the same fields at much the same time, and since, in any case, many of the items within and between the schedules relate to each other, I have attempted to bring the key aspects of the schedules together in a unified and simplified form which I hope will be more readily usable in the actual evaluating of practical teaching. Like the other schedules from which it is derived, its central focus is on pupils' learning. This schedule is set out in Figure 13.1.

Figure 13.1 *Schedule for evaluating teaching (SET)*

This schedule may be used by supervisors and student teachers to identify strengths and weaknesses in student practical teaching. Its main focus is on pupils' learning. It only attempts to cover practical teaching. Matters relating to professional attitudes, etc., are not dealt with.

Not all items will apply to all lessons but when appropriate the student and/or supervisor should rate the performance in some way; for example, as weak, satisfactory or good. The student will then have an idea of those aspects of his teaching that need improvement and those areas where he is competent.

A PREPARATION

1 State the aims of the lesson in terms of pupils' learning.
2 Analyse the lesson aim to establish the key constituent elements.
3 Identify key characteristics of concepts and skills to be learned.
4 Check pupils' present level of competence in the subject to be taught.
5 Decide how to provide a learning gradient to ensure a high level of pupil success.
6 Decide on type of pupil activities, nature of feedback to be provided, nature of presentation and evaluation.

B TEACHING

7 Explain nature of new learning to be taught at beginning of lesson.
8 Provide examples that cover the whole range of key characteristics of the concepts to be learned.
9 Sequence examples so as to teach concepts economically and effectively.
10 Contrast examples with non-examples to clarify concepts.

328 *Psychopedagogy*

Figure 13.1 – continued

11 Introduce new examples to extend the understanding of concepts.

12 Help students a lot in early phases of learning and gradually withdraw help until pupils can demonstrate learning unaided.

13 Encourage pupils in a variety of ways to give them good experience of success and maintain enthusiasm.

14 Encourage pupils to explain the new concepts by questions, cues, suggestions, etc.

15 Enhance pupil motivation by providing for a high level of successful learning by all the children.

16 Provide feedback about pupils' activity at each stage of their learning.

17 In teaching motor skills, arrange monitored practice in a variety of situations.

18 In teaching motor skills, ensure smooth transition between sub-skills.

19 Encourage pupils to take an independent, analytical and open-minded approach to problem solving.

C EVALUATION

20 Check pupils' ability to apply learning in new situations (transfer).

21 Attempt to assess pupils' enthusiasm for subject being taught.

22 Compare success of pupils with the aims set for the lesson.

In this figure the categories and the language describing them are simplified in an attempt to increase the utility of the instrument in classroom conditions. There is a hidden category that could be expressed as 'Establish an atmosphere of mutual trust and respect in the classroom'. Apart from the extremely high level of inference involved in this item, which makes it difficult to assess, it also depends on aspects of a teacher's personality that may be difficult to influence. However, it seems reasonable to suppose that, if the items on the schedule are followed, then the hidden category would stand a good chance of being complied with.

The 'Schedule for evaluating teaching' would be used as a

A pattern of teaching skills 329

first guide to a teacher or student teacher, either in connection with a short piece of microteaching or in a longer conventional lesson. The teaching would be rated on the appropriate individual items in the schedule and the ratings would give diagnostic clues indicating strengths and weaknesses relating to the various items. The pattern of these ratings would suggest those aspects of the teaching that would benefit from particular attention and possible remedial action.

It may be that, having located one or two weak points in the teaching, the teacher wishes to get more detailed information about the problematic items. At this stage, one of the more detailed schedules could be employed. If the lesson is recorded, the schedule could be used to reappraise it and so bring the troublesome items into finer focus and facilitate the identifying of possible remedial measures. If there were still problems it might be necessary to take the separate categories on the schedules and analyse them still further. At this stage some of the specific-skill schedules, such as questioning and varying the stimulus, might be useful.

The complete operation using the schedules would resemble a filtering device. First of all a wide mesh, the general schedule, would pick out any major problems. These would be put through the finer filters of the more specific schedules relating to concept teaching, etc. Any remaining problems would need to be examined by using finer filters devised by the analysis of specific items on the second-line schedules or any specific-skill schedules from the microteaching stable at the appropriate level of generality.

Whether or not the schedules proposed in these chapters are acceptable in whole or in part does not affect the general approach. It is unlikely that all the items on all the schedules would be widely rejected by psychopedagogues. Some of them are, indeed, commonly used in various ways at present. Any that are of doubtful efficacy will be exposed by the act of putting them into practice. Most of the items have, in fact, been exposed to this type of test at least as much as items on many other schedules. But, as I suggest, it is the approach which is important. Individual teachers might well get more mileage out of instruments of their own and this would be an outcome entirely to be applauded.

330 *Psychopedagogy*

It would be perfectly possible for a student to use this system to evaluate his own teaching. He can do this by attempting to assess his performance at the end of the lesson using one of the schedules as a guide. Or he could record his lesson in some way and then examine his teaching at leisure and possibly several times. He could also, when using recorded material, examine his teaching from different angles using different schedules. The object in each case would be to scrutinize his own performance in the light of his understanding of the principles of human learning. He would, in fact, be using his own activity as the material for examination in practising type-B skills.

While there is much to be said for assuming responsibility for one's own learning, there are problems. One of them is the fact that one is so personally involved in the process that one is likely to be biased and therefore make erroneous diagnoses and decisions. Knowing of this danger will help, of course, but it will not entirely solve the problem. This is where a supervisor can be extremely helpful, as can other students or teachers because of their more objective analysis. But it is not only the greater objectivity of others that can help in evaluating one's teaching. Obviously a supervisor's greater experience and understanding of theory will provide information and observation not otherwise available. It is important, however, to remember that the supervisor's overall objective is to help student teachers attain pedagogical autonomy in order that they become capable of evaluating their own teaching.

14
Programming teaching

In the early 1960s a star appeared in the west. To some educationists it was a dreadful omen, warning of the impending collapse of all that was civilized in our society. In the words of one terrified observer:

> Away with everything, then, say the flame-gunners of . . . progressive educationalism. But since these destroyers have no concrete alternative themselves that works, a frightening tribe is waiting to take over: the tribe of teaching machines. And here, perhaps, is our nemesis. Here may be the price we shall pay for encouraging the flame-gunners of recent years. Into the vacuum left by their eager destroying may come electronic science-fiction hordes, lights flashing and tapes spinning, taking over the education we have been pressed to neglect. (Gagg 1966)

To others the transatlantic illumination was the harbinger of our educational salvation, its instrument, B. F. Skinner; its faith, programmed instruction – the universal pedagogical panacea.

332 *Psychopedagogy*

As it turned out our pupils did not walk off into a shining future hand in hand with their teaching machines. Nor were they hurled into Skinnerian darkness. The supernova has burnt out but the memory lingers on and teaching will never be quite the same again.

To which thousands of teachers who have never heard of programmed learning will no doubt make suitably sceptical comments. Nevertheless, despite the slow rate of percolation through the system, many of the ideas sparked off by programmed learning appear in different forms in many current approaches to teaching. Like an individual faced with a phenomenon radically different from his existing cognitive structures, the system as a whole had a big problem of accommodation rather than a relatively minor reaction of assimilation. But the system has changed, perhaps not as much as some ardent programmers would have wished; and some of the effects are embodied in the approach to teaching taken in this book.

Among the several aspects of programmed learning that have influenced teaching it seems to me reasonable to single out a very general one for special mention. It is the attempt to systematize teaching. We can reasonably take 'systematize' in two senses. The first one, applying more pervasively to teaching, is the sense of taking a systematic approach: attempting to do things in logical ways, as in stating objectives and analysing teaching tasks. The other sense is that of creating teaching systems. I shall consider both in this chapter.

Origins

Programmed learning as we came to know it in the early sixties was largely the brainchild of B. F. Skinner whose work in the field of animal learning I have discussed earlier. He was not the sole and true begetter, however. Pressey in the twenties had developed a machine which he said taught students by giving answers at once to questions posed. Skinner's seminal contribution was his development of step-by-step teaching via the medium of a machine that, like Pressey's, gave students immediate feedback related to their learning activities.

Programming teaching 333

Skinner took his ideas from his work with animals which involved the process of shaping. As you will recall, this involved the careful programming of reinforcement so as to produce patterns of activity preplanned by the programmer. When this was applied to human learning, first of all gobbets of information were presented to students; then, to assess their learning immediately, a question was asked; this was followed by feedback telling them whether they were right or wrong. For Skinner, feedback had also to be reinforcing: in other words, the student had to be right. In his work with pigeons Skinner had rapidly come to the conclusion that he would wait for ever if he withheld reinforcement until the pigeon had performed the full activity he had in mind for it. He thus reinforced its every move in the right direction by throwing corn to it until it finally did what he wanted it to do. Instead of throwing corn to students he arranged his programme so that they would get nearly all the answers right and be reinforced by knowing they were right.

He also carried over to his approach to teaching humans some of the gadgetry he had used with birds. His pigeons and rats were housed in special cages connected up to electrically controlled devices that arranged reinforcement according to precise programmes. He closeted his students in learning carrels with teaching machines that looked a bit like ancient gramophones with the turntable concealed. The tune they played was *The Analysis of Behaviour*, Skinner's exposition of the all-pervading power of reinforcement in the affairs of humans and infra-humans (see below). The activity of the students, like the activity of the pigeons, controlled the delivery of reinforcement not by electrical means but through the careful sequencing of the information presented to them. The students had to read the information, construct a response and then move on to the next section to find out how they had fared. Ninety-five times out of a hundred they were likely to be right, as Skinner had preordained when he had constructed the sequence of information. The machine controlled the flow of information so that the students saw only a sentence or so at once and did not see the correct answer until they had constructed and written their own answer. The machine, that is, prevented 'cheating'. It did this because the programme (American

334 *Psychopedagogy*

'program'), which is what the sequenced flow of information came to be called, was presented on the concealed turntable and only a bit was revealed to the student at a time through a transparent window. First the student sees the information and the question related to it, he makes his reply, then moves on the disc by moving a lever and exposes the correct answer to the previous question and the next gobbet of information plus related question. By that time, his written answer has gone beyond recall into the maw of the machine so that his second thoughts (or urge to cheat) are quite futile.

The individual sections of the programme became known as 'frames'; here are a few from the archetypical *Analysis of Behaviour* (Holland and Skinner 1961).

1 A stimulus which follows a response is called a . . . if the rate at which similar responses are emitted is observed to increase. (Answer: reinforcer.)

2 A hungry pigeon pecks a key and is immediately given food. The . . . of pecking will increase since presenting food . . . a reinforcement. (Answers: rate; is.)

3 If, instead of presenting food after the pigeon pecks the key, a loud noise is turned *on*, the rate of pecking will *not* increase. Presenting a loud noise . . . a reinforcement. (Answer: is not.)

4 When pecking a key *turns off* a very loud noise for a few moments, the frequency of pecking in the presence of the noise is observed to *increase*. Ending the loud noise . . . a reinforcement. (Answer: is.)

5 Reinforcement which consists of *presenting* stimuli (e.g. food) is called positive reinforcement. In contrast, reinforcement which consists of terminating stimuli (e.g. painful stimuli) is called . . . reinforcement. (Answer: negative.)

These frames could almost be regarded as museum pieces. Some later programmes were much more subtle in construction. Frames grew in length, became more challenging to the student. The level of reinforcement often dropped below the 95 per cent correct answers prescribed by Skinner. Machines of the type used by

Programming teaching 335

Skinner to present his programme fell into disuse when it became clear that they added little if anything to the level of learning, whereupon programmes appeared in the form of books. At first the books were designed to all sorts of ingenious specifications to prevent cheating, some reminiscent of youngster's thriller magazines complete with disappearing and reappearing print, others like puzzle books with coded answers, with answers printed upside down or with frames distributed randomly through the text. Travellers in railway trains began to be intrigued at the sight of people apparently reading books upside down, not realizing that they were struggling with programmed texts – frequently, the book version of *The Analysis of Behaviour.*

None of the departures from the original Skinnerian formula made much difference to the efficacy of the programmes. Length of frame, level of reinforcement and the prevention of cheating were all investigated and found to make little significant difference to student learning – a fact that suggested strongly that these matters were less important than Skinner had believed and that the effectiveness of programmed learning was to be found in other attributes.

N. G. Crowder was an American who had thought this all along. He took a pragmatic approach and wrote programmes that more resembled traditional books with check questions cropping up every page or so. True, on occasions the information presented on an individual page looked pretty meagre compared with the blank space surrounding it, and it often bore a suspicious resemblance to a frame in the Skinnerian mode. Nevertheless Crowder quite explicitly rejected the Skinnerian approach, averring that we did not know enough about human learning to be dogmatic about the way this kind of teaching should be designed. He attempted to present his teaching material in small logical units and then tested the student's grasp of the material by asking check questions straight away. If the student is correct he is presented with the next piece of information; if he is not he is given further information explaining his error and then retested. The test questions are of the multiple-choice type (see pp. 384 ff.), and there is a separate set of information for each alternative answer in the question. Thus, whereas in the Skinnerian mode of

336 *Psychopedagogy*

programming, the student moves from frame 1 to frame 2 and then frame 3, and so on, in Crowder's mode the student starts on frame 1 but then, depending upon his answer to the related question, goes on to frame X, Y or Z. It was claimed that this approach catered more effectively for individual student differences, enabling bright students to go more quickly than the others since they would get all the answers right and not have to make detours through the remedial material related to the wrong answers. This remedial material is intended to explain difficult points more thoroughly to equip the student to cope more adequately with the test questions when he tries the frame again. To illustrate the approach in this type of programming, here is a section from the Crowder programme *The Arithmetic of Computers* (Crowder 1962). Like Skinner's *Analysis of Behaviour*, this programme is of historical interest rather than practical utility to current programmers. At the same time it is important to anyone who wishes to acquire a comprehensive concept of programmed learning.

Electronic digital computers perform complicated logical and arithmetical operations in thousandths or even millionths of a second. Inside the computer, numbers are represented by sequences of electrical pulses. But the number system used usually differs considerably from that commonly employed in pen-and-paper arithmetic.

To understand how a computer uses its peculiar number system, we shall have to spend some time discussing and examining closely the number system we already know.

Our familiar number system uses ten different numerals: 0, 1, 2, 3, 4, 5, 6, 7, 8, 9. Each single numeral is called a digit. Because the system uses ten different numerals or digits it is called the *decimal* system (latin *decem* = ten). The arithmetic we learned at school is decimal arithmetic.

We are so familiar with the decimal system and decimal arithmetic that the decimal system may seem to us the 'natural' system. Actually it is only one of many systems of writing numbers.

Now here is a question on the material you have just read.

Programming teaching 337

Select what you believe to be the correct answer and turn to the page number indicated to the right of the answer you chose.

Would you say that the two numbers 492 and 0·29 are both written in the decimal system?

ANSWER

Both 492 and 0.29 are written in the decimal system. Page 4
Only 0.29 is written in the decimal system. Page 8

Turning to page 4 we have:
Your answer: Both 429 and 0.29 are written in the decimal system.

You are correct. The word 'decimal' refers simply to the fact that our common number system uses only ten different numerals, or digits. With these ten single digits (0, 1, 2, . . . 9), we can count up to 9. Beyond 9 we must use combinations of these numerals, such as 1 and 0 for ten (10), and 1 and 1 for eleven (11), etc.

Turning to page 8 we have:
Your answer: Only 0.29 is written in the decimal system.

Well, let's see.
You once learned that 0.29 = 29/100
and   0.4 = 4/10
and   1.333 = 333/1000

Fractional quantities such as 0.29 and 0.4 and 0.333 written with the aid of the decimal point are called decimal fractions. You probably were thinking about this use of the word 'decimal' when you decided that the decimal fraction 0.29 is written in the decimal system and the whole number 492 is not.

The fact that no decimal point is shown does not exclude the number 492 from the decimal system. The word 'decimal' means 'ten'. The decimal system is a number system which uses ten different digits. Both whole and fractional numbers may be written with decimal system digits.

The number 492 and the number 0.29 are both written in the decimal system because they both use the decimal system digits which are 0, 1, 2, 3, 4, 5, 6, 7, 8, 9. Please return to page 1 and choose another answer.

338 *Psychopedagogy*

This example illustrates not only the approach to the type of programming that came to be known as 'intrinsic' (since it was held that the student's own actions determined his route through the instructional material, unlike the Skinnerian, or linear, approach which laid down the same sequence for all students) but also some of its weaknesses. The key weaknesses lies in the nature of the question-and-answer section. Although in theory there may be very many alternative answers to each question, in practice the difficulty of providing such a variety is immense. Further, it is important that the incorrect answers should relate to genuine problems of understanding and not merely catch questions or irrelevant distractors. Many programmes of this genre fell far short of this criterion. The upshot of this particular difficulty was that intrinsic programmes often suffered from trivial and irrelevant alternative answers which in no way fulfilled the aim of coping with genuine student learning difficulties. A glance at the specimen of intrinsic programming given above will reveal another aspect of this difficulty. The problem facing the student who makes a mistake, goes to the remedial section and is then referred back to the main line of the programme is very often a non-problem. In the example above there is only one other alternative for him to choose: the correct one. Although he may still not have grasped the point, he gets the answer right willy-nilly and goes on to the next frame. If he has not understood he could have trouble with later frames and build up a cumulative learning deficit. The way to avoid this is by the process of validation, or trying out the programme. This process applies to linear and branching programmes and I will discuss this more fully below. In the meantime, see Figure 14.1 for some diagrammatic representations of different approaches to programming which may help you to see their general lines of procedure.

Anyone handy with a pencil and ruler can draw diagrams like this. It is a different matter when one comes to devise programmes with flexible structures that really can take account of individual differences in responding. And, in fact, few people working in the intrinsic mode have done more than produce the herringbone type of programme.

In fact, I believe, linear and intrinsic, or branching programmes

Figure 14.1

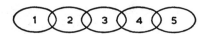

(a) *Diagrammatic representation of linear programme*
   Note the chaining. The items are linked by a certain amount of common content. (Taken from Stones (1966a), p. 234.)

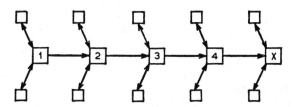

(b) *Diagrammatic representation of branching programme*
   Shows the common type of the genre, the herringbone type with only two choices per frame.

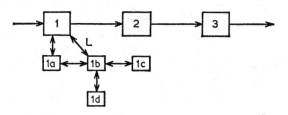

(c) *Diagrammatic representation of branching programme with subsequences*
   A mistake at 1 could lead to 1a; a mistake at 1a could lead to 1b; a mistake here could lead to 1c. A correct response at 1a, 1b, or 1c could lead back to the main sequence by the branch lines or via a special return line L. (Taken from Stones (1970), p. 239.)

340 *Psychopedagogy*

as they are now more commonly known for obvious reasons, are more alike than different. In fact, I would argue, they are both linear in the sense that they both have what their authors see as a best path through the learning material. In the case of orthodox linear programmes this is obvious, in the case of branching programmes the programmer provides what is essentially a linear sequence of main frames with remedial appendages. Later developments blurred the edges between the prototypical programmes, and there are now few purists who would resist programmes that combined features of both approaches. I believe that this is a desirable development and think that the best conception of programmed learning is one that encourages the maximum flexibility and openmindedness of approach, without owing dogmatic allegiance to one camp or the other.

Flexible programming

Seized with the idea that programming should be flexible in conception, I aimed to produce a programme that exemplified that flexibility. I was also taken with the relevance of the work of Mager when he found that students, told what their learning objectives were, would work towards them on their own and only ask for help from their instructor when they had difficulty. They learned as much as students following traditional courses, despite the fact that they required much less attention from the tutor. Other factors that interested me were the possibility of giving pupils some say in the way they worked through the teaching material, omitting that which they did not need, as with Mager's students, but also tackling things in the order that seemed best to them.

I had other considerations in mind. Skinner's position seems to me to be vulnerable in that he could be doing nothing more than shaping students' verbal behaviour and that this acquired verbal behaviour could be conceptually empty, that is, it could be rote learning. Seeking to avoid this problem, I would take an approach that attempted to take into consideration what we know about the learning of concepts, which could involve the use of material other than verbal. The way I worked out this approach and the

Programming teaching 341

programme exemplifying it are described more fully elsewhere (Stones 1968, 1970, 1971). Here I will outline the programme to give an idea of a method of programming that illustrates how flexible approaches may be developed.

The programme in question was designed for children around the age of eleven. It was intended to discuss a small part of English history, the Great Fire of London. I wished to give the children freedom to move through the programme as I have outlined above; I also wished to give them the idea of the simultaneous occurrence of a multitude of events; further, I wished to provoke them into thinking in a variety of ways about the events of the fire, the way people behaved and the way the authorities tackled the disaster. I also wished to provide some flavour of life at the time and to avoid the dry recital of 'facts'. A tall order, possibly, but it seemed to me to be a necessary attempt at the time, since I believed that there was potential in this approach to teaching and that the strictures levelled by some against programmed learning as being essentially rote teaching, or a rather dull, unimaginative form of brainwashing, were mistaken. Only the pupils working through the programme can tell me whether the attempt succeeded or not.

Figure 14.2 provides a schematic outline of the programme. The key to the programme is the Master Card which presents the main concept areas of the programme. Pupils starting work on the programme decide which of the subjects they wish to tackle first by consulting the Master Card. This card gives them a reference number that tells them which place in the programme to find the information. This will begin on a Main Concept Card. To find out the information they are interested in they will work through that section of the programme. Working through the sections involves the pupils in more than merely reading and learning responses; it involves them in looking at accompanying material resembling archive material that demands of them that they scrutinize it and answer questions. The material is functional and integral with the teaching, not just decorative. At the end of the section pupils tackle a worksheet that tests their understanding of that section. This completed, they check their performance against a model answer, the Comparator. Finally the worksheet tells them to return to the Master Card to make another choice. Pupils can, if they feel confident, tackle the worksheet related to any section *before* tackling the teaching material in that section. If they can cope with the worksheet there is no need for them to work through the section.

Thus the programme provides for a variety of paths through

Figure 14.2 *Schematic layout of a programme for relatively unstructured material*

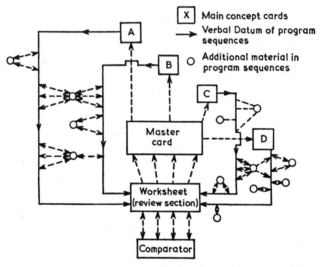

(Taken from Stones (1970), p. 352.)

the instructional material, it demands that pupils interact with accompanying material and think about it, and it allows them to go at their own pace and tackle only those aspects of the programme they feel are necessary. In addition, while they are working through the various sections, they are invited at times to take up questions with their teacher or with other members of the class. The questions are related not just to factual matter in the programme, but also to questions of values and ethics. An example of the latter is the frame that invites them to discuss the

Programming teaching **343**

actions of those Londoners who refused to allow *their* houses to be pulled down to form firebreaks, thus allowing the further spread of the fire.

Frame A21
> Unfortunately many Londoners objected to firebreaks and would not allow houses to be pulled down. Why do you think these people objected?
>
> ....
>
> Because they didn't want *their* houses to be pulled down.

Frame A22
> But it made no difference whether their houses were pulled down or not. In the end they were destroyed. How were the houses destroyed if they weren't pulled down or blown up?
>
> ....
>
> They were burned by the fire.

Frame A23
> I think we can understand why they didn't want their houses pulled down. But some people think they were being selfish and were not thinking about other people. What do you think?
>
> ....
>
> There is no right answer to this question and you might not agree with me. Talk to your teacher or your friends about this and see if you can agree.

This example, I hope, illustrates my point that programmes can be flexible and can cope with some of the criticisms sometimes levelled at them. The method can be applied to many fields of teaching and learning, given sufficient ingenuity and application.

Framing

The frames that form the teaching element in a programme can vary not only in size but also in design. While the only real indicator of a programme's usefulness is its validation history,

344 *Psychopedagogy*

which I discuss below, a good idea of its quality can be obtained by inspection of the frames. The key thing to look for is the way the reader's learning is developed by the instructional discourse in the frames. Each frame should present some information and by skilful discussion build up a teaching theme, the logic of which will enable the learner to answer the questions posed by the programmer. Unsatisfactory frames will do little, if any, teaching and may well consist of nothing more than long strings of questions. Others will help the learner by use of formal prompts, that is, prompts that make use of things other than the logic of the instructional discussion. For instance, formal prompts can be given by providing some of the letters of missing words in answers, or by indicating how many letters there are in the missing word, or words in the missing phrase. Some frames make no demands at all on the learner beyond the ability to copy. This type of frame could well provide quite nonsensical information but, since there is nothing to do except copy, the person using the programme would have no difficulty at all in getting the correct but incomprehensible answer. Here is an example.

Frame

To constint the proolop you must first deconk the balat.
(The learner then has to complete the following)
Before constinting the proolop it is necessary to —— the balat.
Answer is 'deconk'.

This frame illustrates a very real problem. It is all too easy for a pupil to get an answer right without having understood the question. This danger is particularly likely when formal prompts are relied on excessively. There is probably little to be said for ever using formal prompts unless one is trying to drill the learners in rote learning of material. By and large it is best to avoid them.

A tested product

The approach to programming that I have just outlined is a reasonable indication of current views on programmed learning.

Programming teaching 345

The common factor in all programmes, it is now generally considered, is not the size of frame, the level of successful responding, or whatever. The key characteristic is that a programme is an empirically validated product. That is, it is instruction that has been prepared and tried out repeatedly until sufficient data have been accumulated for the programmer to be able to say that, given students for whom the programme was written and given appropriate working conditions, the programmer can *guarantee* a given level of successful learning. Thus the various aspects of the programme on the Great Fire are all perfectly legitimate elements in any programme as, indeed, are those of Skinner and Crowder. There is thus no limit to experimentation in the way that the information is presented to the students. There is, however, a very stringent expectation that a programme shall be validated and in this way the emphasis is shifted from the product, i.e. the actual programme, to the process, i.e. the way in which the teaching material is prepared.

Any reader who has persevered so far in this book will already be very familiar with much of the process of programming. It is, after all, the same as the approach to any systematic attempt to teach. Programmers will start with a clear idea of the pupils for whom the programmed material is intended. They will then delineate clearly the objectives of the teaching and produce a test instrument to assess the extent of their success in that teaching. They will conduct a task analysis of the teaching task and construct a sequence of learning experiences planned so as to take into account as far as is possible the logic of the subject matter and the psychological factors involved in the learning. In many respects they will be following procedures outlined in the chapters on teaching skills, and indeed the schedules produced in connection with these chapters could well form checklists for much of the preparatory work of the programmers.

Validating the programmed material is the one aspect of programming that I have so far not touched on; but it is the crucial element. In the process of validation the teaching material is prepared through the processes of task analysis I have mentioned and the material is then tried out with the pupils for whom it was written and refined until it is demonstrated to teach those pupils

346 *Psychopedagogy*

up to given levels of competence. Only when it has been demonstrated that the programme teaches consistently to set levels of student performance can it be seen as fulfilling the key criteria of programmed material. It goes without saying, of course, that the programme a teacher is interested in must be in line with his own objectives. It is no good providing a programme that is one hundred per cent effective if it doesn't teach what he wants to teach. Here I should like to exemplify the process of validation by reference to the validation history of a programme I published in 1968 related to the psychology of learning and teaching (Stones 1968).

Before publication this programme was tried out and revised on several occasions and with several hundreds of students. It was written for students with no previous knowledge of educational psychology but with the level of competence in English demanded of students entering initial teacher training in Britain. As a result of the tryouts and revisions the levels of student achievement rose until the programme produced consistently average scores of around 75 per cent on the programme test. At this stage I decided against further attempts at refinement in view of the fact that the *average* score was well within the range that would gain a student a distinction in any examination in British colleges. Since publication thousands of students with the minimum entry qualifications have worked through the programme and the results of the original validation have been borne out repeatedly, so that it is now possible to guarantee given levels of success to different groups of students.

Which is all very well, but there are other factors one needs to bear in mind. There is the crucial matter of the test of learning, usually referred to as the 'criterion test'. If this is worthless then nobody is going to be impressed by a brilliant score. As far as my programme is concerned the potential user is invited to examine the test in order to assess its suitability as a measure of learning that would be worth the while of his students, and also its adequacy as a test of learning related to the programme's objectives. For my part, I have produced a programme test that implements the approach advanced in this book. All the test items make use of novel examples of the principles taught in the

Programming teaching 347

programme. None asks for recall-type answers. Whether the test items are good items is for the potential user to judge, but he can only do this by examining the programme and probably, to be sure, trying it out with some students. However, once a potential user has decided to use the programme and is satisfied that competence on the criterion test is a worthwhile goal for his students to attain, then he can rest assured that they will attain that level of competence when they work through the programme.

All the information relating to validation and previous tryouts is provided for the potential user in a tutor's handbook and the programme criterion test is available to him on request. All the provisions made in connection with this programme are in accord with the suggestions made by an American committee on procedures for describing programmed materials (Joint Committee on Programmed Instruction and Teaching Machines 1966). They illuminate the difference between programmed materials and other teaching devices such as books. A programmer really undertakes to teach students; the author of a book can at best hope that his readers will learn from what he has to say. In view of the fact that very few teachers are likely to have the time and opportunity to construct their own programmes, it behoves them to pay close attention to the validation data of any programme they happen to consider. There are, in fact, very many products that are programmes in name only, not having been validated.

Monitoring

I should like to mention one further aspect of the programme *Learning and Teaching* that was useful in its validation but which, additionally, is of considerable value in enhancing the usefulness of programmed material as self-instructional devices. This is the technique of linking the teaching and testing systematically and explicitly. I refer to this procedure as 'keying'. Keying, within the programme, enables a student to monitor his own performance as he works through the material. As he completes each section of the programme he is presented with 'review frames'. These frames do not attempt to teach anything, but are basically test

348 *Psychopedagogy*

questions that seek to assess the student's understanding of the teaching in that part of the programme. Each of these review frames attempts to assess the learning of the major elements in the section. Should a student be unable to answer one of these questions or make a response that does not agree with the one in the programme, he consults the key within the frame that tells him which teaching frames deal with the problem he has had difficulty with. He is thus in a position to monitor his performance as he works through the programme and take remedial action wherever necessary. It should be noted that the items in reviews of this kind should not merely test recall of material taught in the teaching frames, but should demand that the student apply the learned principles to new problems. The provision of review sections like this also enables students to use the programme more flexibly than starting at frame 1 and working to the end. A student entering the programme with some prior knowledge of the subject could attempt some of the review sections before reading the programme. If he coped he would not need to read the part of the programme keyed to the particular items in the review frames.

The internal keying of review frames to teaching frames is paralleled by the keying of the criterion-test items to the appropriate sections of the programme. Thus a student having difficulty with any of the questions on the test would be able to identify those aspects of the programme that were related to those difficulties and take remedial action.

The value of the technique of keying in programme validation lies in the feedback it provides the programme writer. As he tries out the programme he will be able to identify those areas of the teaching that seem to be unsatisfactory in that a large proportion of students seem to have difficulty. His keying of those review frames and criterion-test items that are giving difficulty will direct him to the corresponding sections of the programme so that he can revise it in order to teach more effectively. This is another facet of the programmer's responsibility. He does not take refuge from student failure by blaming their unsatisfactory heredity, their low intelligence, their colour or any of the other afflictions the flesh is heir to. Instead he, the teacher/programmer, takes responsibility, examines his teaching and tries to do better.

Programming teaching 349

In this respect, as in many of the others described above, he is doing no more than a conscientious teacher ought to do.

Programming today

And this is where programmed learning stands today. Should you consult other books on this subject, make sure you get an up-to-date version or you will find a whole variety of criteria for identifying programmes. (You may, indeed, find these in some recent versions of texts over whose authors the new waves have washed unnoticed.) Among these criteria you will find most of the attributes I have mentioned above. Some authors still equate programmed learning with operant conditioning in spite of a fair body of work involving the deliberate programming for concept teaching. Some still aver that the frames need to be very short, even though there are effective programmes around with quite lengthy frames. This point is, of course, connected with the point about operant conditioning. Other one-time dogmas in relation to programming that you may still encounter are such things as the drawing of strict distinctions between linear and branching programmes, and the need for a very high level of success in working through the programme. One other aspect of programming, which more or less sank without trace after the first decade of electronic euphoria, was the view that machines were a necessary part of programmed learning. In fact, all machines of whatever level of sophistication were nothing but elaborate page turners. Even when computers were invoked they added little more. The reason? Gadgetry was no substitute for hard thinking and pedagogical skill in constructing the teaching programme. Designing machines to present programmes, and writing programmes for computers to present programmes, is child's play compared with writing the programmes to be presented. Should the day dawn when a computer is able to generate a teaching programme in the way a human teacher does, things will be different. There is no sign of this happening at the moment. Should this state of affairs come to pass it will be through the involvement of psycho-pedagogues more than writers of computer programmes.

These, then, are the non-criterial attributes of programmed

350 *Psychopedagogy*

learning, all at one time thought to be vital. What then remains? Only feedback and the process of validation. And this is the justification for the discussion in this chapter. The fact that the teaching material works and can be guaranteed to work is the crucial thing. You may think other things desirable and look for programmes that embody those things. But the first thing to look for is whether what the programme claims to teach is worth teaching and then, if it is, whether there is reliable evidence that the programme does in fact teach according to explicit criteria.

If I were looking for a programme I should look for this evidence first. I should then look for some form of self-diagnostic device such as keying. I should look for this because I should want the programme to be independent of other teaching agencies for the direction of the pupils' learning. Note, I am not saying that other things should not be involved. There is on the contrary every reason to encourage the linkage of programmes to other teaching resources including the teacher. The point is that the programme provides a datum which the pupil uses as a basis for, and guide in, his learning activities. The use of programmed materials in this way may, indeed, involve the use of machines. But they would not be general-purpose machines suitable for the presentation of all types of programmes. They would be devices specifically intended for a particular purpose, perhaps in the presentation of stimuli, as in some forms of programming the teaching of reading which make use of printed or film-projected visual material in conjunction with recorded auditory stimuli. Other devices and teaching aids would also be used in conjunction with the programmed material. Slides, tape recordings and films can all be linked to the programme. But virtually anything is grist to the programmer's mill, as it is to the teacher's. Thus the programme becomes part of a teaching *system* which involves all resources available to a teacher including himself and his colleagues. The unifying element that ensures we have a system and not a collection of unrelated parts is the prior analysis of the learning and teaching task and the planning decisions that determine how the parts of the system shall be related. The programmed aspect of the system will be the validation of the whole system or perhaps some of the key elements.

A teaching system

Any teaching system after this fashion is likely to make use of various instructional gadgets such as tape recorders, film strips, etc. I do not propose, here, to go into fine detail about these devices. Sometimes considerable mystique is generated about the so-called 'new media', which can get in the way of efficient teaching. A little pedagogical reflection, however, will in the main help one to get a sensible perspective on these devices. The approach to task analysis discussed earlier (pp. 176 ff.) should help here. Checking each aspect of the teaching task will help to indicate which equipment will be of use. Most devices, other than teaching programmes, are presenters of stimuli only, since they do not provide feedback. The stimuli may be relatively simple as in a two-dimensional chart or map, or could be more complicated as in a film loop providing a model of a motor activity – for example, planing a piece of wood. Most of these devices can hardly be said to teach by themselves, but need to be integrated into the teaching system in accordance with a plan of instruction. The case of film and television, sound radio or specially recorded taped material is different. These devices can undoubtedly teach but they will almost certainly function more efficiently if the teacher is familiar with them and has dovetailed them into his own teaching according to his own objectives. But it is no good his expecting the film or television programme to achieve his objectives for him, since even if the programme producers were excellent pedagogues they could hardly be expected to know what his objectives were. In fact many producers of educational television programmes and films are quite innocent of pedagogical knowhow and it frequently shows. All too often such films labour long to make simple points in visually spectacular ways, attempting to capitalize on their strong point. Too many such producers take as an act of faith the saying 'One picture is worth a thousand words', not realizing that far more frequently one word is worth an infinite number of pictures. As I argued earlier in this book, man lives in a world of symbols and, paradoxical as it may seem, it is likely that more learning will be induced by the words in a sound film or a television production than by the visual images.

352   *Psychopedagogy*

The implications of the last point take us back to the beginning of this discussion on teaching media, since the most appropriate source of relevant symbols to the pupils' learning is the teacher. This is another argument for trying to integrate any use of such programmes into one's own lessons, and this may involve at times turning off the sound and adding one's own words. The system-making use of media in this way will have the teacher's own planned pupil activities and provision of feedback. As with all the approaches to teaching discussed above, such procedures will involve the elements of planning, of taking account of pupil capabilities, and of weighing the pros and cons of different methods of proceeding; this will involve making decisions about the use of educational media. Decisions in this connection, that is, must be pedagogical, not related to gimmickry or faddism induced by uncritical 'experts' or commercial pressures. And, as I said earlier, decision making is one of a teacher's key tasks.

Teachers, programmes, programming

Few teachers are likely to write programmes for publication or for general use in schools. But, then, few teachers write books. On the other hand, all teachers at some time interact with pupils and try to teach them something. Most of these teachers will also attempt to carry out some form of lesson preparation. Few authors will do either but all programme writers *must* do both. This is one of the main reasons I have felt it useful to devote a fair amount of space to discussion of the subject.

Apart from the guidance I hope I have provided the teacher who wishes to select a programme for a specific job, I have tried to give you an idea of the *process* of programming, not only because I believe it to be the important aspect of programmed learning, but because it is a paradigm of teaching that can be of value to any teacher. The point is this: it is well worth while attempting to write a short programme even if its likely scope of application is limited. If you do this you would practise most of the elements in a complete teaching task. The emphasis in the planning of the programme would relate to the pre-active stages in the schedules discussed in previous chapters, and validation would provide

Programming teaching **353**

practice for some of the skills in the interactive and evaluative stages of teaching. While you would not get the practice directly related to the personal teaching of groups of pupils, the process of preparing and trying out instructional materials brings teaching into a very fine focus which is rarely otherwise obtained. The careful systematic approach provides feedback to the teacher in the form of a record of pupil responses to specific parts of the teaching. Sitting with a few pupils, working through the preliminary versions of a programme and discussing their difficulties with them, will give him an insight into teaching that would hardly be possible in any other way (Stones 1966a).

15
Evaluating teaching and learning

In the last chapter I suggested that one of the most important aspects of the processes of programming teaching lay in the way it can provide feedback to the programmer or teacher about the efficacy of his teaching. I also argued that a well-wrought teaching programme would have stages on the way that would give the learner information about his performance as he proceeds, and an end stage that would give him information about his overall level of success as well as diagnostic information relating to weaknesses which would pinpoint those aspects of his learning that would benefit from more attention.

My argument was for evaluation to be seen as part of a system of teaching, integrated with it and related to the same objectives. There is little doubt that present usage of testing rarely has my first point as an important consideration. Informing a teacher about his success or failure in teaching is probably the least-considered of all the uses suggested for the tests. The suggestion that some teachers take the credit when their pupils succeed in tests and let the pupils take the blame when they fail is perhaps

Evaluating teaching and learning   355

not too cynical an observation. Certainly, in textbooks that comment on the uses of tests, feedback is mentioned, if at all, in relation to pupils rather than the teacher. That is, it is suggested that the pupils learn of their strengths and weaknesses by the results of tests, whereas the strengths and weaknesses of the teacher are rarely mentioned.

It is my view that lack of integration of testing with teaching is an important factor that frequently renders the use of tests of doubtful value to teachers, often harmful to pupils and misleading to the public. Students have sometimes damned examinations outright because of uses which have seemed to them to be anti-educational (Fawthrop 1968). On the other hand there is no shortage of supporters of testing and examining who write and speak with fervour about the virtues of these devices for maintaining standards in an educational system which is going to the dogs. I suspect that alienated students and fervent test fans see examinations in much the same light, but I believe that the latter misconceive the way in which most current approaches to testing operate and that the former do not appreciate the possibilities for enhancing learning inherent in different approaches to evaluation. In this chapter I hope to explain why I think many current practices are of doubtful validity but also to make some positive suggestions which I hope will be of help to teachers and will also persuade sceptical students of all ages not to throw the pedagogical baby out with the examination bathwater (see also, Rowntree 1977).

Evaluation and guidance

Countless thousands of pigeons, rats, chimpanzees, flat worms and other lowly creatures in psychological laboratories the world over have learned all sorts of fancy tricks largely because they have received knowledge of the results of their activity, signalling to them that they are on the right lines. Not that they are likely to have seen it like that; but they learned nevertheless. So have millions of human beings: in just the same way. This is learning at its simplest: the making of stimulus-response connections that are likely to be quite arbitrary. In nature such connections are

356 *Psychopedagogy*

usually non-arbitrary, because there is a real causal link between given stimuli or responses and events in the environment. A predator learning to stalk its prey in the wild acquires a pattern of behaviour that makes sense according to various laws of physics, for example. If you approach from up wind, the prey smells you and is off. If you make a din, it hears and again escapes. And the same with sight. Thus behaviour patterns develop in recognition of a reality that is stable and based on unvarying natural laws. A pigeon dancing to a psychologist's tune is engaging in superstitious behaviour because there is no natural causal link between learning the steps and the appearance of the corn. If the psychologist has a bad night he might change the schedule and the pigeon would dance in vain. More likely, perhaps, he completes his experiments, goes off to write his paper and comes back with more schemes in mind which call for different steps altogether. The pigeon's erstwhile successful performance now produces no corn and he has to start all over again. Nature is much less unkind.

Kinder, perhaps, but no more informative. A fox catching a rabbit after a complex piece of stalking is not consciously calculating his line of action on the basis of the physical laws involved. All that happens is that reinforcement, the successful outcome of the activity producing food, makes the activity likely to recur. The fox will never know why he should set about things in the way that pays off; all he knows – if you will forgive the anthropomorphism – is that it works.

Some human learning is of this nature. The most basic processes in language learning involve the learning of stimulus-response connections that have no basis in logic or natural laws. Learning that one animal is called 'fox' and another 'rabbit' is a case of purely arbitrary learning. There is no *logical* reason why we should have one sound to symbolize one animal and a different one for the other. Speakers of other languages make different noises when they see these animals but we do not dispute their right to do so, nor they ours. When we are learning our native language we receive feedback from others that the noise we make when referring to this thing or that is correct or incorrect. We do not stop to ask the reason why; it is enough to learn that this is

Evaluating teaching and learning 357

the correct or incorrect combination, and there is no more to it. There is no explanation, nor can there be: we are either right or wrong purely for arbitrary reasons. Thus the feedback we receive is nothing more than reinforcement if we are right and non-reinforcement if we are wrong. The rewarded connections will recur and become part of our repertoire; the others will die away and be forgotten. Examples of this type of learning are learning the sounds letters symbolize when we first start to learn to read, or that *lapin* stands for 'rabbit' when we first learn French.

The only way to test learning of this nature exhaustively would be to ask a learner to provide the correct responses to all the stimuli for which he had learned the connections. In testing knowledge of the alphabet this would be conceivable; in learning vocabulary in a foreign language this is clearly impossible, and the best one can do is to sample; unless, that is, one is concerned only with checking short lists of words learned in one lesson or for homework. The results of testing would tell the teacher whether his teaching had been successful or not and the pupil whether he had learned satisfactorily. They would not tell the pupil any more than that. The reason he is right or wrong is that we all agree that these are the correct connections. There is no other justification.

There is nothing wrong in this. Learning of this simple type is inevitably arbitrary and, as I have discussed earlier in looking at the role of language in human learning, arbitrariness is a very powerful force in human learning because it makes symbolic learning possible and by that agency brings conceptual learning into the grasp of human beings, thus transforming learning in man.

Teachers are pre-eminently concerned with learning involving language and the acquisition of concepts. In the learning of concepts it is much more economical of time to provide knowledge of results that cues the progressive stages of learning than merely to provide the minimum feedback saying 'right' or 'wrong' as is often the case in concept learning experiments in the laboratory. In practical classroom testing, giving a mark out of ten for a piece of work indicates to a pupil roughly the value a teacher ascribes to his work, usually as compared to that of the rest of the class,

358 *Psychopedagogy*

but it tells him nothing about his strengths and weaknesses. A high mark may confirm his notion of an acceptable answer upon which he could model subsequent effort, but a low mark leaves him in a fog, not knowing which of an almost unlimited number of corrective measures he should adopt.

In classroom tests the piece of work being evaluated is a test piece, the concrete expression of the operation of complicated, mainly cognitive, skills upon complex bodies of concepts. Often the skills deployed and the concepts upon which they operate are newly acquired so that the teacher's evaluation of his product gives some guidance to the learner's future efforts. However, more precise and informative feedback than is usually found, which focuses on the key aspects of the work, would be much more valuable.

The least helpful procedure for guiding learning is when global assessment and summed mark (e.g. so many out of ten) are combined with test administration which is removed in time from the original learning. End-of-course examinations exemplify this type, of assessment, and such examinations may be defended on the grounds that they exercise a quality-control function. However, they do imply a division, if not a divorce between learning and evaluation, which is being increasingly questioned.

The sampling of behaviour

Tests and examinations may be divorced from learning for another, more fundamental reason. Presumably almost all tests are given to assess capabilities in a given field. Rarely, if at all, is a test likely to cover all aspects of the field under scrutiny. But, more important, there is almost always an assumption, usually implicit, that the ability to achieve high marks in an examination at the end of term, year or course is a valid indicator of ability in the fields covered by the various test papers. What is meant by 'ability' in this context is often not made clear, thus making it extremely difficult to decide whether the assumptions are justified or not.

At the heart of the problem is the general lack of clearly specified aims and objectives. Presumably in most tests we have

Evaluating teaching and learning 359

in mind the assessment of some end result of teaching. We may be thinking about goals related to the pupils' future lives, or we may have more immediate goals in mind related to performance soon after learning. But tests purporting to assess the attainment of either immediate or long-term goals have validity only to the extent to which they can be accepted as genuine samples of the behaviour related to the goals of instruction. Where goals are not specified, it is virtually impossible to establish such validity. Even when goals are clearly specified, care is needed when preparing test material that the demands made on the candidates do genuinely tap skills related to the objectives in mind.

In relatively simple learning – for example, in learning the alphabet – a test which asks for the alphabet to be repeated tests the learning completely. But when testing the grasp of complex concepts it is impossible to sample the learning exhaustively. All one can do is to take test samples. In many cases what is being taught cannot be fully assessed by pencil-and-paper tests anyway, but recourse is made to such tests because of the impossibility of testing the skills in the situations in which the skills would be manifested naturally. Here, for example, is a question from a public examination geology paper: 'How would you differentiate (a) in a hand specimen, (b) in the field between continental and oceanic volcanic products?' The examiners who set this question make the assumption that the ability to write a short essay in reply to the question is a valid test of the candidate's ability to distinguish between the two phenomena in real life. The written answer, that is, is taken as a legitimate surrogate sample of the candidate's competence in a practical task. A less obvious example may be taken from another field, this time from English Literature: 'Discuss the nature and effect of the humour of *Gulliver's Travels*, illustrating your answer from at least three of the Books.' Although this question does not relate to a practical skill in the same way as the geology question, presumably the examiners take the ability to answer such questions to their satisfaction as an indication of an enhanced sensitivity to irony and a general heightening of aesthetic understanding. Whether, in fact, this assumption is justified is a matter for conjecture; it would certainly be difficult to demonstrate that it is in such a complex and ill-defined field.

360 *Psychopedagogy*

The important point is to realize that test answers are very often substitute behaviours being taken as accurate indicators of the abilities we are trying to test. If there is any doubt that the test question does, in fact, sample the ability accurately, the question is likely to be invalid. The trouble is that questions like this have no relevance outside themselves. All that we test if we use such questions is the ability to answer that kind of question. We learn nothing about the ability we are seeking to assess. I do not suggest that we should, therefore, restrict our evaluation to those areas where it can be unequivocally demonstrated that the questions we ask are valid surrogates of the criterion behaviour we have in mind, rather that we be constantly alert to the possibility that we may be asking questions for the sake of asking questions instead of asking them to evaluate the achievement of our long- or short-term objectives.

An approach to teaching which employs the ideas of the specification of objectives and the analysis of teaching tasks helps to avoid the asking of sterile questions. For example, applying this approach to the teaching of map reading would involve our analysing the task of teaching for the achievement of this objective. Our analysis would most likely produce statements of skills needed, such as the skill of discriminating between different types of map symbols and the knowledge of concepts such as scale and orientation. Our pencil-and-paper tests drawn from such an analysis would ask pupils to make discriminations on material in the classroom and solve problems involving orientation. We should be assuming, not unreasonably, that the ability to perform satisfactorily on such questions is a valid indication of their ability to read maps. We would make this assumption because our analysis had indicated that these concepts and skills are prerequisite to competence in this field.

This approach helps us to avoid sterility in our questions but does not thereby guarantee that our questions are effective measures of the criterion behaviour. Thus it is quite conceivable that we might merely demand that the pupil answer questions about the various elements on which we have focused in our teaching and, as we have seen in previous chapters, it is not unlikely that questions of this type could be answered purely at the

Evaluating teaching and learning 361

level of rote learning and so have no bearing on the skill we are trying to teach. In the final analysis the only unequivocally valid test of the ability to read a map is whether the pupil can cope with problems in the field that are dependent upon that ability. Between this type of test and the entirely verbal question-and-answer test is a range of possible approaches likely to have different degrees of correlation with competence in map reading. For example, recognizing symbols and matching them with descriptions of the features they refer to, or building up three-dimensional models to demonstrate knowledge of contours.

When we test abilities such as these we assume not only that they provide an indication of a pupil's likely competence in a given field, but that the tests themselves are worthwhile tests of subordinate skills prerequisite to the overall skill we are trying to teach. Whether the skills are genuinely contributory depends on the efficiency of our task analysis. We need, therefore, to exercise care in at least two major directions: we need to check carefully that our subordinate skills are genuine sub-skills of our criterion behaviour, and, if we are so convinced, we need to ensure to the best of our ability that our test questions genuinely evaluate the pupil's performance in the sub-skills.

Nature of skills tested

One of the problems experienced by teachers and examiners when they subject tests to analysis, using the concepts from teaching and learning I have discussed in earlier chapters, is that they find that few of the test items actually assess the higher-level skills. Even in the British Advanced Level of the General Certificate of Education – essentially an entry test for university – questions are often at the level of remembering facts. An attempt has been made in recent years by some examining boards to use the ideas of the classifying of objectives, to so systematize the production of test questions that different levels of demands are made on the candidates by different questions covering the more complex types of objectives.

If we follow an approach to teaching and learning like the one expounded in earlier chapters, test questions will fall naturally

362 *Psychopedagogy*

into different levels of difficulty according to the initial specification of objectives and task analysis. According to the model of diagnosis-prescription-evaluation, testing and teaching mesh with each other; so that, if you have in fact been attempting to teach problem-solving skills according to your analyses, then the test items you produce should, because of their relationship to the original objectives, themselves be related to problem solving. The incompetent framing of test questions, could, of course, lead to inadequate evaluation if tested at inappropriate levels.

One of the most common pitfalls in the production of test questions intended to evaluate learning at the higher cognitive levels – such as problem solving or the grasp of principles – is that they do not go beyond the examples provided in the teaching phase. Thus, if you ask questions making use of the same examples you used when you were teaching, all the children would have to do to perform satisfactorily would be to remember just what you had told them earlier. As I suggested in an earlier chapter, when you have learned a concept or a principle you should be able to recognize new exemplars of the concept and apply the principle to situations you had not previously encountered. To be quite certain that the children are not merely remembering what you told them earlier, it is therefore important that you present them with new material. Test questions that do this are sometimes referred to as *transfer* questions because they ask the pupil to apply or transfer the skill or knowledge to a new situation.

Transfer questions help to guard against rote learning and are, therefore, essential when we are interested in testing most school learning. In some circumstances, however, transfer questions are inappropriate because the learning, if not rote, is of a simple nature essentially demanding merely the remembering of facts previously imparted. Examples of this type of learning and evaluation would be questions such as 'What is the capital of China?', 'How long is the river Ganges?' or 'Which horse won the Derby in 1933?' Whether, in fact, such gobbets are worth learning or testing is another question, but there seems to be little scope in this type of material for transfer questions.

Evaluating teaching and learning **363**

Test reference

My emphasis on the developing of tests related to pre-specified objectives has assumed an approach to teaching involving what is being increasingly referred to as *mastery learning*. This means that the criterion behaviour entails the learning of skills and concepts related to the achievement of the objectives. Tests linked to this approach to learning are generally referred to as *criterion-referenced* tests, and are designed to evaluate mastery learning. Such tests inform the teacher whether or not he has achieved his objectives. That is, has he, in fact, taught his pupils what he set out to teach them? If the results of his testing indicate that the children have not, in the main, mastered the learning, then he will scrutinize his teaching procedures to locate the weak spots and then try to improve his teaching sequences. This approach is clearly very much in line with that outlined in the discussion on programmed learning.

Few tests or examinations in current use in Britain are criterion-referenced. In the main, classroom tests and public examinations are what is referred to as *norm-referenced* tests, which are aimed at producing a rank order of students' test scores. An individual's performance is assessed in such tests in relation to the performance of the group. A candidate may be described as average, or above or below average. When finer scales are used it is common to grade candidates as A, B, C, D or E; this is the so-called five-point scale. Fifteen-point scales are common, and there is the widely used mark out of ten or out of a hundred. All these scales have the common property that they rank the candidates and report the ranking with varying degrees of discrimination. Note that this approach says nothing at all about the competence of the pupils in relation to the mastery of a learning task or the achievement of any objectives. It would, in theory, be possible to get an A in such a test and have learned merely the rudiments of the subject being taught. This would follow if the group being tested all showed a similar lack of understanding. Conversely it would be possible to demonstrate a good grasp of a subject and obtain a C merely because others had done better. An A in the first case might well be awarded for a lower level of understanding than a

364 *Psychopedagogy*

C or a D in the other subject. This question will be raised again later when I discuss the way in which test scores may be handled: it is raised here to bring out the difference between criterion-referenced tests and norm-referenced tests.

In criterion-referenced tests the individual questions are selected according to their efficacy in evaluating the candidate's learning of given skills and concepts. If the questions are judged to be good indicators of such learning, they are chosen even if all the candidates in a particular administration of the test arrive at the correct answer. In norm-referenced testing, such questions would probably be dropped. This is because the test of a good question using this approach is the extent to which it discriminates between the candidates. Discrimination is of crucial importance in providing a rank order of candidates, and the more clear-cut the differences among candidates the more useful the test.

Norm-referenced tests have been used extensively for selection in many different fields. In Britain they have been used particularly to select children for secondary education. Although it was suggested at one time that these tests distinguished between children with two or three different types of mental ability corresponding to different types of schools, most psychologists would now accept that this is pure fiction. A convenient fiction, the cynic might add, for administrators who had a limited number of secondary grammar school places to ration out.

The way in which the marks from secondary-selection tests were used not only illustrates the dubious value of the claim to distinguish between different types of children but also exemplifies the way in which selection-test scores are often handled. After the test has been taken the scores are arranged in rank order. A line is then drawn across the list to cut off the number of children for whom there are selective places. The scores of candidates on the border line are given special attention to make sure that the rank order at this point is accurate and justice done to the candidates. However, the key step in the operation is clearly not the sophisticated preparation of the test by consultant psychologists, but the drawing of the line across the list of scores, an activity that can hardly be classified as psychological or educational. (Indeed the *Times Educational Supplement* reported some years

Evaluating teaching and learning 365

ago on the case of the unfortunate action of a clerk in the education office of one local authority who by error drew the cut-off line lower than it should have been and selected some children 'by clerical error'.)

In public examinations such as the General Certificate of Education similar principles operate although they are more complicated in their operation. The grades reported by the different examining boards refer to the performance of candidates in relation to the performance of the whole group and not the degree of achievement of learning objectives. Lines are drawn across the pass lists according to a notional percentage in the heads of the examiners about what the 'right' percentage of passes should be. By and large this percentage remains stable in most subjects, but it is prone to fluctuation as examiners' attitudes change. With such an approach, every year will inevitably bring its crop of successes and failures. It is impossible for all to succeed. A criterion-referenced approach would make it possible for all to succeed; and, of course, the opposite – all could fail. Success or failure in this case would be related to a standard of achievement and not to the performance of the other candidates.

Standardized tests

Norm-referenced tests are used in other fields. In many British schools reading tests of this description are common. The most widely used tests are probably the graded-word tests. In these tests the child is presented with a card on which is printed a series of words arranged in order of difficulty; for example, in one such test the first two words are *tree* and *little* and the last two are *bibliography* and *idiosyncrasy* (Schonell and Schonell 1960). A child reads as many words as he can and his performance is then compared with the average score for children of his age. If his score is lower than his peers he will be taken to be behind in reading and if higher he will be regarded as ahead. Generally the teacher notes the age for which the score made would be average and records this as the child's *reading age*. Tests of spelling and arithmetic employing the same rationale are also sometimes used. Such tests are often referred to as *standardized tests*. In these

366 *Psychopedagogy*

tests the levels of performance or *norms* that form the basis for determining the levels of ability of individual children are determined by trying out the test on large numbers of the population for which the test is intended. From these tryouts, or standardization procedures, the appropriate norms are derived.

It should be noted that tests of this kind tell us little if anything about the strengths and weaknesses of children in the subjects being tested. If we wish to find out whether a child is deficient in some of the subordinate skills of reading, we need a criterion-referenced test which gives us information about performance related to the possession of specific abilities such as the ability to discriminate between printed letters or spoken sounds. Some tests of this type are used in schools (e.g. Daniels and Diack 1958) but not to the same extent as the norm-referenced tests.

Clearly criterion-referenced tests of basic skills such as reading are much more valuable to a teacher than norm-referenced tests. The latter merely indicate to him that there may be a problem (if a child scores below the norm for his age) but they do not tell him anything about the nature of the problem. The former, being related to the achievement of the sub-skills in reading, provide information to the teacher about the specific difficulties the child is experiencing so that he is able to take remedial action to help the child over his difficulties.

There is a similarity between norm-referenced tests of this type and the global mark in a class test referred to earlier. In both cases the testing procedures tend to be viewed separately from the teaching. In neither case does the teacher gain information that will help him take remedial action to help improve the pupils' learning or his own teaching. It thus seems likely that the widespread use of norm-referenced tests of the basic skills is of limited value.

Diagnostic evaluation

A diagnostic approach similar to that used in criterion-referenced tests of the basic skills may be used generally in the classroom. I have already given details of an approach to this type of evaluation when I discussed programming teaching. In that approach the

Evaluating teaching and learning 367

student working through the teaching programme is given information as to which part of the programme he has not understood perfectly by the test given when he has finished. The test guides him to those parts of the teaching that need more attention so that he can correct his misunderstandings. This is an example of a test with diagnostic feedback geared to the same objectives as the teaching and criterion-referenced test.

This example is taken from self-instructional teaching, but it is an approach that is applicable in any structured teaching. Whenever a teacher sets out to assess his pupils' learning, he has the option of adopting an approach like this – the main problem being that of constructing good test questions which are clearly related to identifiable aspects of the teaching they evaluate.

The use of this type of approach to testing de-emphasizes the global score and lays stress on the pattern of replies to the questions. Thus, instead of a test yielding an inscrutable percentage mark, it provides a profile of a pupil's strengths and weaknesses in the field under scrutiny. When the teaching task and the preparation of test questions are approached analytically the test questions may be considered almost individually with no attempt to add them together. An intermediate stage between this extremely analytical approach and the global one is the method that adds the number of correct items on the subsections of the tests which are related to specific aspects of learning, as in the example of the programme test referred to above. This approach gives diagnostic information not supplied by the global approach. However, even this modest adding together of a few test questions makes assumptions that are probably unjustified in terms of the theory of measurement.

Problems of measurement

The assumption made as soon as one adds one mark to another is that they are of exactly the same value as, for example, would be the case if one gramme were added to another gramme, or one metre added to another metre. With measurement of this nature we can say with some degree of confidence that two grammes is twice as much in weight as one gramme. With test scores the

368 *Psychopedagogy*

situation is different. Consider, again, the example of the graded-word reading test. A child's score is obtained by adding together the number of words he reads correctly, and each word is awarded one mark. Can we really say with confidence that the ability to read 'tree' is exactly the same as the ability to read 'little'? Or 'bibliography' the same as 'idiosyncrasy'? Or even 'tree' as 'idiosyncrasy'? All words get the same mark. In fact, of course, there is no question of the level of difficulty being the same. The words are arranged in ascending order of difficulty according to the results of tryouts with large numbers of children. The basal age is taken to be five years so that each word read correctly adds 0.1 of a year to reading age five. All that any reading age tells us is that the reader is able to read the same *number* of words, not necessarily exactly the same words, as the average child of that chronological age. Thus two children of the same reading age could have different patterns of correct and incorrect responses. The score tells us they are the same; the pattern of responses tells us they are not the same. The rationale of *reading age* gives us no guidance at all as to where to bend our efforts to help the pupils improve their reading abilities.

This example can be paralleled by an infinite number of examples taken from classroom tests. Few teachers ever stop to question the time-honoured procedures of totting up marks and arriving at a global total, so that the average classroom test is likely to embody the flaw of this essentially illegitimate procedure.

In much of school learning, however, there is every reason to ask questions that are deliberately not the same. Our discussion of concept learning made the point more than once that the acid test of concept learning was whether the learner could identify new instances of the concept. The test of the concept would be more searching if it demanded the identification of several exemplars, each of which included different non-essential attributes of the concept. Thus the best test would be one which presented the learner with sets of stimuli that were deliberately different. Treating each task in such a test as being equal in value and then adding would clearly be rather pointless and could lead to the waste of valuable information about the nature of the responses.

It is very likely that in many tests there will be questions

Evaluating teaching and learning **369**

relating to different types of skills. Some questions may be tests of concept learning while others may be tests of simple response learning. Pupils who answer correctly different proportions of these types of questions will clearly have different levels of competence which would be revealed by a profile of scores but obscured by a global total.

There is a further complicating problem attached to the question of reporting test scores in global terms. Teachers often add the marks from an examination in one subject to the marks from another subject. If you consider the assumptions that underlie this practice you will see that they are of considerably less validity than adding marks within a subject, a practice which itself is suspect. The assumption is made in such situations that adding a mark of, say, 50 per cent in arithmetic to 60 per cent in geography is the same as adding 50 per cent in geography to 60 per cent in arithmetic or 40 per cent in English to 70 per cent in biology. The contemplation of such disparate disciplines, each of which makes demands on the pupil of a completely different nature from those made by the others, is enough to expose the meaninglessness of aggregating the marks and arriving at a class order, as is often done in schools.

The adding of marks in school subjects and then reporting global totals is all of a piece with the practice I refer to later (p. 411) in relation to the sub-tests on the Wechsler Intelligence Scale for Children. In this test greatly different educational capabilities are liable to be obscured by a global total, and only fine scrutiny of sub-test scores can give an indication of the nature of these differences. Ironically, these sub-tests are limited in scope since they have to fit into the whole test and thus do an inferior job to a well-designed test of a specific school subject.

Validity

Validity is the Achilles' heel of testing. In fact I have been discussing the problem throughout this chapter. I have referred to the prime need to make sure that the tests we use really do test the skills and knowledge we intend them to. If they don't they are invalid. I know of no way in which the validity of any test

370 *Psychopedagogy*

of complex abilities can be established beyond doubt. The best we can do is to make tests that will gain the approval of experts in the field being tested. If they all agree that the test is a good test of clearly delineated skills established by analysis of the nature of the learning being tested, then we can accept the test as being as valid as it is currently possible to make it. But it is essential to be humble about this: the test that you write today will probably look less than perfect in ten years' time as your knowledge of teaching and learning matures.

The validity obtained by the consensus of experts is often referred to as *content validity*, or sometimes *face validity*. All this means is that it is a test of what has been taught. This form of validity is the most important form for teachers. Other types mentioned in texts on the subject are likely to be such forms as *predictive validity*, meaning the ability of a test to forecast performance on other tests at a later time or the ability to cope in other situations after testing. Tests used for selection or guidance are of this type, intelligence tests being the prime example. Those used for secondary school selection were very well designed according to the criteria and methods generally recognized for norm-referenced testing, but their predictive validity was always a source of bitter controversy; this as well as other reasons led to their gradual phasing out as instruments of selection in British schools, although they have not faded away completely. It should be noted that tests of this type are very different from the tests of prerequisite competence to which I have referred from time to time. The tests of readiness inform a teacher whether a pupil is ready to go on to the next stage of learning, but the predictive tests were not related to specific new learning at all, being intended, rather, as general-purpose predictors. For reasons that I discuss later, I am sceptical of the use of such tests to teachers and think that in practice they would be better off without them.

Reliability

Reliability means the extent to which a test will produce the same kind of results with the same examinees on different occasions. This measure is usually applied to norm-referenced tests and,

Evaluating teaching and learning 371

indeed, we still await the development of a generally agreed theory of reliability for criterion-referenced tests. All that is meant usually is that the test with complete reliability would produce the same rank order of testee scores from one administration to the other. If we are not interested in ranking our pupils, this type of reliability is of little interest.

Of more interest is the type of reliability better known as marker consistency. This alludes to the desirability for a test to produce the same score when marked by different markers or by the same marker on different occasions. Obviously if an answer paper is given different marks by different people it is not very useful. Unfortunately there is abundant evidence that many tests used in schools and in public examinations suffer from the complaint of marker inconsistency. One way of coping with this problem is by having the work marked by more than one marker and thus arriving at a consensus mark. Another, more practical method for a teacher is to try to devise tests that reduce the problem. Objective tests can help here, since most of the problems of unreliability or marker inconsistency arise in the marking of essay-type tests. I shall return to this question later. However, it is important to note that consistency and reliability are all in vain if the test is not demonstrably a valid test of the learning it purports to test.

Problems of ranking

I have already referred to problems connected with ranking. I have also pointed out that much of our test theory and practice is based squarely on ranking procedures that emphasize the way people can be sorted out. In this chapter I have de-emphasized the summing of scores over broad areas of study but there is a further difficulty not yet mentioned. Adding scores on tests of different subjects is virtually meaningless but could lead to most unfortunate conclusions being drawn about a child's current competence in specific fields. Even within distinct fields of study it behoves the teacher to be extremely cautious about adding marks obtained on different questions. The logic of these arguments leads to a very important point, namely, that it is difficult ever to

372 Psychopedagogy

justify the preparing of lists of scores from different individuals for the purpose of comparison or ranking.

Currently most writers on the theory and practice of tests and testing acknowledge the difficulties associated with the practice of treating marks for correct answers as if they were equivalent. While generally agreeing that the most common current practice transgresses the theoretical premisses of measurement, they commonly go on to explain how to deal with marks based on such practices. Thus explanations are given of such subjects as calculating averages and spread of marks and correlation which are all, strictly speaking, illegitimate in view of the dubious nature of the prior assumption of equivalence of the questions and answers.

Apart from the doubtful validity of the practice of summing scores from the point of view of measurement theory and the virtual total lack of feedback from such tests, there is one other compelling reason for exercising considerable restraint in ranking pupils. Any rank order obviously must produce more losers than winners, especially in current classroom climates where only the first half-dozen or so get much attention. Since all the rest of the class have failed to 'come top', the publication of a rank order cannot but act as a punisher to those pupils. It is sometimes argued that the experience of failure acts as an incentive but the experimental evidence suggests that in fact the opposite is the case. Pupils who experience failure in learning do less well in later learning, lose confidence in themselves, and are more vulnerable to emotional illness (Glidewell and Stringer 1967; in Kirkland 1971).

Aspects of evaluation

In this discussion of evaluation I have put forward ideas about the nature of tests and the way in which they may influence learning. I have also made suggestions about what I conceive to be the most useful ways of approaching evaluations which are based on the view of human learning and teaching put forward in earlier chapters. Supporting evidence for these suggestions may be found in research into human learning generally, but there is also a body of experimental work providing important information

Evaluating teaching and learning **373**

about the use and effects of tests specifically in classroom situations. Brief mention is made of this work here, largely based on the useful review by Kirkland (1971). More detailed information may be obtained from the specific references mentioned.

A number of studies bears out the contention that feedback from tests promotes learning. Page (1958) found that the type of feedback provided to pupils influenced their subsequent learning. Pupils who were given detailed feedback scored highest, those given global scores only scored the lowest; pupils given global scores and comments such as 'B. Good work. Keep at it' or 'A. Excellent: Keep it up' were intermediate. Panlasigui and Knight (1930) found that pupils encouraged to compare their achievements with a set of standards gained substantially higher scores than those who were not. This experiment had some of the elements of a criterion-referenced approach to testing. In addition, since the pupils compared their performance on units of learning leading up to a final test, the situation resembled the monitoring of learning referred to earlier.

Kirkland reports several studies which found that pupils who experienced failure had lower motivation. Even being told they had failed when objectively they had not has been found to correlate with impaired learning. Failure, or the belief that he has failed, influences the pupil's self-concept (the way he sees himself); so it is important to realize that it is not only the objective fact of success or failure but the pupil's perceptions of the outcomes of his learning which can influence his later motivation and performance.

The level of competence to which pupils aspire, or their level of aspiration, is much related to their experience of success or failure. A typical finding is that of Moss and Kagan (1961) which concluded that 'the child who attains scholastic honours is rewarded by those around him and that this experience frequently leads to an expectancy of future success for similar behaviour thus increasing the probability that the child will continue in such tasks. Failure would result in the opposite behaviour, i.e. avoidance or withdrawal' (Kirkland 1971).

Findings from investigations such as these provide the evidence from classroom experiments indicating clearly that quite common

374 *Psychopedagogy*

practices such as the reporting of global scores, the drawing up of rank orders and the predominance of norm-referenced testing may be deleterious for pupils' learning and also for their emotional adjustment. This is not to say that evaluation of pupils' learning should be ended. The need is rather for more informed use of evaluative instruments which provide informative feedback to the learner and do not build into every evaluative situation the certainty that large proportions of learners will experience failure. Fortunately there is hope. It lies in the approaches to testing that I discuss in the next chapter.

16
Making
a test

Earlier sections of this book have covered many of the preliminary aspects of test making. The specification of objectives, the analysis of the teaching task, the discussion of the relation of evaluation to teaching are all vital components in any test procedures. That is, if you take my view that the important aspect of testing is to find out whether what you have been trying to teach has in fact been learned. In much classroom practice, I suspect, the activities recommended above are honoured more in the breach than in the observance. To some extent this is because the tests are hard to construct. But in the main I believe the key reasons are the lack of acquaintance with test techniques by teachers and also the fact that norm-referenced testing has dominated test theory and practice unchallenged until quite recently. The consequences of the dominance of norm-referenced testing are many, but two of the most important ones are the preoccupation with discriminating among pupils instead of focusing upon the learning of the whole class, and, flowing from this preoccupation, the rather off-putting statistical devices for determining whether a test

376 *Psychopedagogy*

question is a good one or not. I am referring here to problems of item analysis in the construction of objective tests.

Taking a criterion-referenced approach does not make the job of test construction easier but it does focus attention on the nature of the test questions as samples of desired behaviour rather than on their ability to discriminate among pupils. The former is a pedagogical scrutiny while the latter is purely psychometric and could be done without ever looking at the test questions. Far better, it seems to me, to do our hard thinking about the former than the latter.

The skills tested

I suggest that having in mind the threefold division of skills I discussed earlier (Chapter 7) can be helpful in clarifying the nature of the skills to be tested and thus give an appropriate indication of the nature of the test items. Recall that type-A skills demand the demonstration by the learner that he can actually *do* something, not just write about it. My example of map reading is an illustration of this type of skill. If the aim of instruction is to get pupils to read maps in the field (type-A skill) then the only way to test that ability is to go out into the field and set problems. Orienteering is a good example of an activity that sets problems to test the ability to read maps effectively. All too often, however, assumptions are made that type-A skills in all subjects are tested adequately by pencil-and-paper tests that are really inappropriate. But type-A skills do not necessarily involve practical activity. Any type of problem solving requiring the application of learning to new situations is a type-A skill and could involve the learner in mainly cognitive activity. Type-B skills can also be regarded as problem-solving skills, the difference being that, instead of the problem requiring the pupil to demonstrate the skill himself, he is asked to assess examples of activity to see to what extent they exemplify the principles he has learned. Type-C skills require that the learner has grasped the concepts on which the activities involved in type-A and type-B skills are based.

In most pencil-and-paper tests the level of testing rarely goes

Making a test 377

above the level of type-C skills, the testing of learned concepts. Even at this level the tests frequently fall short of assessing conceptual learning. Merely asking a pupil to remember what the teacher has told him earlier is no guarantee that he has learned anything more than a stimulus-response connection. There is nothing wrong with this if one is concerned to test only basic simple learning that is prerequisite for future learning, but if it is intended to assess the learning of concepts it just won't do. Questions that aim to test concept learning must go beyond the information given in the teaching; they have to test transfer. It is impossible by looking at a test item to tell whether it tests transfer – that is, the ability to apply existing learning to new situations. To do that one needs to know the nature of the teaching to which the test is related. Again we are reminded of the crucial nature of the link between learning and the assessment of learning. If the test uses exactly the same examples or problems the teacher used in the teaching or interactive phase of learning, then there is no sure guarantee that success in the test indicates conceptual learning.

Tests attempting to test learning of the three types of skill will take somewhat different forms. For example, tests of type-A skills might demand that the learner speak French at a given level of fluency, or analyse a chemical substance, or write a poem in sonnet form, or analyse a soil sample, or read a sentence not seen before, or work out a long-division sum, and so on. All these could be assessed by the evaluation of some end product produced as a result of the application by the learner of principles learned earlier. The last two of the examples given may be fairly simple to assess, but some of the others would be more difficult and would demand the exercise of judgement on the part of the assessor. If more than one judge can be involved and if the criteria of assessment can be made explicit and agreed by others, so much the better. Tests of type-B skills would demand that the learner recognize, on the basis of his grasp of oral French, a speaker speaking French at a given level of fluency, or a competent example of soil analysis, or a chemical sample, or a sonnet, or an adequately read sentence or accurately worked-out long division. And the tests of type-C skills would involve a demonstration by

378   *Psychopedagogy*

the learner that he knew what principles were involved in the type of activity under consideration.

Essay-type tests

Of all these skills type-C skills are the ones most amenable to orthodox approaches to testing. These are the tests with which most readers will be familiar. In Britain it is most likely that the tests will be of the essay type, with the pupil given so much time to write about so and so with various instructions as to the kind of treatment expected. By their late teens most British pupils are thoroughly familiar with the traditional three-hour, four- or five-question examination paper. Since there is good reason to think that this type of test has a number of deficiencies, it is highly likely that methods of assessment relying on this approach give a very unclear picture of pupil capabilities. Apart from well-documented deficiencies of essay tests, which I shall discuss shortly, there is an additional one rarely mentioned but of considerable importance. Consider: the only kind of type-A skill that writing an essay can assess is writing an essay. Equivalent type-B skills would demand some form of critical comment on existing writing. Equivalent type-C skills would demand a knowledge of the attributes of 'good' essay writing. It is true that there are forms of writing resembling essays that could be tested at level A; for example, writing reports or writing papers for discussion relating to a course of action. But if it is hoped to test knowledge in a given field, or ability in a skill, writing an essay is only a vehicle, and all it can do, even if the writer is fluent, is to test at level C, or possibly, with special arrangements, at level B. This follows, since all that can be done in reply to an essay question is to write about the concepts and principles in a given field. It is even likely that the answer would demonstrate nothing more than recall if what was called for was merely a rehearsal of information previously imparted at the teaching stage. Nobody is more convinced than I that fluency in writing is an attribute to be cultivated, but I cannot support its indiscriminate use as an all-purpose medium for the evaluation of learning. I carry with me still a vivid memory of teaching young plumbing apprentices how to

Making a test 379

write reasonable English so that they could answer questions about how to make joints in pipes and similar literary activities. Year after year examiners in many technical subjects complained that candidates failed because they could not express themselves in their replies to questions of a technical or craft nature. It seemed then, and it seems to me now, that attempts to assess technical competence should have employed different methods to ascertain the students' understanding of technical processes and principles. If it were thought necessary to assess proficiency in English, then that should have been a specific objective of the course and provided for accordingly, thus avoiding fouling up the testing of other subjects.

Apart from the fact that the essay question has a limited scope of application because of its inherent limitations as a testing medium, there are other problems. Among the best known is the high level of marker inconsistency. It is common knowledge that different markers will award different marks for the same piece of work even though they are all 'experts' in the field. And the mark one gives an essay answer today will almost certainly be different next week. Other problems are that these tests, consisting as they do of only a few questions, can cover only a small part of most courses. The examiner has the task of making a judgement about the most useful areas to cover, tempered by the recollections of what areas were covered last year or the year before. The teacher, if he is a different person from the examiner, will have the obverse problem of trying to spot the questions the examiner is likely to ask.

But even if his teacher's track record for question spotting is of Olympic standard, the candidate's problems are not solved. He has to decide which of the questions to answer. He will naturally choose those that seem the least difficult to him. The trouble is, his subjective appraisal may mislead, since *post hoc* decisions by boards of examiners when they scrutinize the papers from candidates may influence the final level of difficulty of the question in comparison with others. Add to this the fact that there are 252 possible combinations of questions when a candidate has to answer five questions out of ten, and a picture emerges of candidates ostensibly taking the same examination but in reality taking

380 *Psychopedagogy*

different ones which may or may not be comparable in level of difficulty.

Another problem a teacher must face in using essay-type tests is the fact that extraneous factors, such as the quantity written and the handwriting, influence the marker even though neither of these is the subject of the test. A further vexing point is the problem of the halo effect. This phenomenon is observed when the rosy glow suffusing the examiner as he reads an answer that he likes spreads through the whole answer paper, so that other answers tend to be seen in the same light and gain higher marks than they would have done otherwise. Or, on the contrary, when a sulphurous cloud of disapproval obscures the merits of answers that follow a first misguided step.

The obvious main advantage of essay-type tests is that they assess a person's ability to write continuous prose. At its best this approach would give evidence of a pupil's ability to develop lines of argument, marshall ideas, demonstrate facility in organizing and presenting in his own words information from his own background knowledge, as well as providing him with the opportunity to demonstrate his skill in literary forms and such things as grasp of spelling and punctuation. The best demonstration of many of these skills, I fear, is rarely to be found in the answers to essay questions, except perhaps at the relatively high levels of working as in literary courses in higher education or in the upper reaches of the secondary school. But this kind of test does provide a teacher or an examiner with some evidence about the current level of operation of the pupil in those skills – provided, that is, they are constantly alive to the problems I have already discussed concerning the fallibility of markers and the impossibility of achieving a 'true' mark for any given piece of work.

As far as the mechanics of preparing essay-type tests are concerned, there are apparently no problems. All one has to do is to think of a limited number of questions, doing one's best to avoid ambiguity and unnecessary complication. But it is often a case of repenting at leisure when the time comes to mark the test. If more than one marker is involved and if an analytical method of marking is to be employed, the markers have to devise a mark scheme and then apply it to mark the questions which are likely

Making a test 381

to be written in multitudinously different handwritings, layouts and modes of argument. If only one marker is involved it may be less trouble to agree a marking scheme but the difficulties of applying it will remain.

To cope with these problems, multiple-impression marking has occasionally been adopted. This approach takes the view – for which there is some empirical support – that impression marking, in which the marker reads the answer quickly making no attempt to be analytical and then awards a mark, is virtually as reliable as careful analytical marking. Bringing in other markers and aggregating or averaging the scores awarded to each answer is a reasonable device that acknowledges the subjective nature of the operation and probably affords a more just solution to the problem than most other approaches.

In normal day-to-day classroom practice you may not consciously encounter the problems I have been rehearsing. But that does not mean that they don't exist. They do. And not realizing they exist may keep from you vital information about how different children are coping with the work you set them. The problems of dealing with language may obscure the feedback from the pupil's learning attempts, so that you get little diagnostic information and are thus less able to help than if you were able to get a clearer picture of the pupil's strengths and weaknesses. It is possible, however, to devise tests that are more helpful in diagnosing learners' difficulties and in overcoming some of the other problems referred to above. Let us now turn to consider them.

Objective tests

For want of a better term I shall refer to the tests I am about to discuss as *objective tests*; they are sometimes known as short-answer tests. The word 'objective' should be interpreted with caution. The days are gone when test constructors would claim confidently that these tests were completely objective. Some are more objective than others. In some cases there would be no argument about the correct answer, but the more complex the reasoning demanded in the answering of the questions, or the nearer they approach to questions of values, the more likely are

382 *Psychopedagogy*

we to find their objectivity becoming fuzzy. Much depends on the test constructor. As in many pedagogical processes, the method is neutral, and the worth of the product depends on the maker. With this caveat let us consider the virtues of objective tests.

Perhaps their main virtue is that the way they are constructed compels one to think before one tests. It is true that it is useful to think before setting any test. But in the case of essay tests the main concern of the test writer is largely in the couching of the questions, looking out for ambiguities of language, and solecisms of grammar or punctuation. Rarely is much thought given to the *answers* when the questions are being written. When writing an objective test the nature of the answer is determined in the writing of the test question. Instead of asking a general question to see what comes out, one writes a number of specific questions, having specific answers in mind that one believes will reveal the extent of the pupils' knowledge in specific parts of the matter being tested. Taking this type of approach enables one to iron out many problems before actually setting the test. If a tryout is carried out this is a further aid to improving the test: trying out an essay-type test would provide very little feedback as to its value for later use, but careful testing of an objective test can be most useful.

Since it is possible that some readers may be unclear about what an objective test comprises, I will explain this before I go on to discuss other characteristics and the construction and use of these tests.

Very briefly, objective tests are composed of a number of questions which normally demand fairly short answers to which there is (again, 'normally') only one correct answer. To explain my use of 'normally' and to illustrate the need for caution in asserting the 'objectivity' of test items, as the questions are usually called, here is an example of an item from a test by one of the most eminent of British writers in the field. You have to answer 'True' or 'False'.

Intelligence may be defined as inborn all-round mental efficiency. (Vernon 1955.)

The 'correct' answer is 'False'. But let us consider. Some eminent

Making a test 383

psychologists would probably not agree with this – Eysenck and Jensen, for instance (see Chapter 17). But there is another problem. The framing of the question is sloppy. Intelligence *may* be defined as anything you like. If I wish to define intelligence as the ability to ride a bicycle backwards, that is my privilege. Possibly few people will agree with me, but no one can say that I *may* not use this definition and 'may' or 'may not' imply that permission is granted or withheld. This is a second reason why the answer could be 'True'. There is one further point. The item as it stands is an example of the type of question that almost certainly tests very simple learning. Students could well have learned this definition from lecture notes or psychology texts without engaging in much thought about it but, having learned it quite effectively by rote, would get the answer 'right' according to the scoring key and be very little the wiser. The tester would be very misguided to take the answer as an indication that the student had thought deeply about the problem. With this awful warning of the pitfalls into which even the 'experts' can fall, let us continue our discussion of the nature of these tests.

Despite reservations about the possible spuriousness of the objectivity of some tests, I have little doubt that this type of test can avoid subjectivity if constructed with care and tried out. In simple factual learning this is quite obvious. There is only one answer to the question 'What is the capital of England?' Testing more complex forms of learning with objectivity is much more difficult but not impossible. I discuss some of the methods of testing this type of learning below.

The fact that objective tests demand short answers enables the test writer to cover much more ground than the tester using essay-type questions. He can usually sample the whole domain that has been studied. In addition, since the answers are determined before the test is given, extraneous factors such as handwriting or grammatical shortcomings do not influence the score in tests that are not intended to judge these abilities. Similarly, the halo effect is removed. The nature of the answers to the first few questions does not predispose the marker to look benevolently or malevolently on the remaining answers and influence the marks he gives. That option is not open because the answers are pre-

384 *Psychopedagogy*

specified and unequivocal. The same point applies to the question of standards between papers. Marker inconsistency virtually disappears; in a good test it should disappear altogether. A final very important point is that all pupils take the same test since there is no choice of questions.

ITEM TYPES

I have already mentioned two kinds of items used in objective tests – the true/false item and the straightforward question. Other types are multiple-choice, matching and completion items. Here is an example of a multiple-choice item from a general science paper of the Ordinary Level of the British General Certificate of Education, usually taken at about age sixteen. You must choose one of the five alternatives.

An illuminated object is placed on the axis of and nearer to a converging lens than its focal point.
The image obtained is
   A real, erect and magnified
   B real, inverted and magnified
   C virtual, erect and magnified
   D real, inverted and diminished
   E virtual, inverted and diminished.

(JMB, O-Level, Summer 1971)

Here is another example that you might find more congenial:

Here are a few items from a test designed to evaluate the results of teaching aspects of botany. Pick out the two items which are technically poor. Say why they are poor.
   A From the collection of leaves given, pick out the oak leaf, the chestnut leaf and the beech leaf.
   B What is an ovary?
   C What is the difference between the root and the stem of a plant?
   D Sketch the flower provided and on your sketch label the following parts. (Parts then specified.)

(Stones 1968)

This item is intended to test the understanding of testing practice.

Making a test 385

It may, therefore, be used to explore some aspects of this type of item. The two faulty items are held to be B and C because both could be rote learning. If the student has learned only the verbal chains, he could satisfy the demands of these items by parrot-fashion responses. Choice A can be taken as evidence of a learned ability to discriminate and to name leaves. We can be certain that it tests more than parrot-fashion learning since the pupil is asked to demonstrate his ability to name and discriminate. We cannot, however, presume to glean anything from the correct reply about *how* he got the answer right. We must therefore presume no more than the demonstration of the simplest type of learning that would be able to account for the correct response, in this case, stimulus discrimination. It may be that the reason the pupil was able to get the right answer was because of his understanding of leaf structure which would depend upon conceptual learning; the point is that that kind of ability is *not necessary* in order to answer that type of item. As long as we are clear about this, there is no harm done. The great danger is always that we assume we have tested more than we have done in actuality.

Answer D would probably be the best alternative for assessing conceptual learning; that is, assuming the pupil had never been instructed in naming the parts of that particular plant previously. Here he would have to apply his knowledge of concepts and principles in identifying the various parts.

You will notice the different approaches to objective-test items adopted by the two examples. As is often the case with other things, it is misleading to use the definite article when referring to multiple-choice items. There is no such thing as *the* multiple-choice item; there are different sorts of multiple-choice items. You are quite likely, therefore, to encounter a variety of exemplars of the concept *multiple-choice item*. There is no reason at all why a teacher should not experiment with the genre. Taking this line may help him to avoid the worst excesses of some tests which consist of countless items, all more or less the same length, all with the same number of choices, written in the same style and boring in the extreme. Sometimes the style is adopted so that the tests can be scored by machine. When tests are designed to fit the machine and not the learner that is the time to stop testing.

386 *Psychopedagogy*

MATCHING

Matching items ask the learner to match items from one source with items from another source. Often the two sources are lists, as in this example.

Read the statements below, carefully paying attention to their relation to one another. Then next to each statement mark A, B, C, or D as indicated,

A If the statement contains the *central* idea around which most of the statements can be grouped.

B If the statement contains a main *supporting* idea of the central idea.

C If the statement contains an *illustrative* fact or detailed statement relating to a main supporting idea.

D If the statement contains an idea or ideas which are irrelevant.

1 The Roman roads connected all parts of the Empire with Rome.

2 The Roman roads were so well built that some of them remain today.

3 One of the greatest achievements of the Romans was their extensive and durable system of roads.

4 Wealthy travellers in Roman times used horse-drawn coaches.

5 Along Roman roads caravans would bring to Rome luxuries from Alexandria and the East.

6 In present day Italy some of the roads used are original Roman roads.

(ANSWERS 1-B, 2-B, 3-A, 4-D, 5-C, 6-C.)

(Educational Testing Service 1961)

Other approaches to matching items make use of material other than lists. Diagrams or pictures are possible sources with which one would match statements. Figure 16.1, for example, gives an item where the pupil is asked to match the curve with the equation.

Figure 16.1 Example of matching item using a diagram

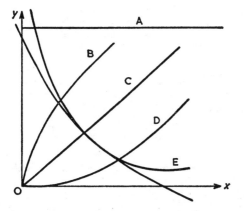

Of the five curves in the figure, choose the one which best represents each of the following relations between x and y (k is an arbitrary constant). Write the letter of the correct answer in the blank to the left of the relation.

..........................$y=kx^2$ ....$y=x$
..........................$y=k\sqrt{x}$ ....$xy=k$

COMPLETION ITEMS

Sometimes instead of asking a straight question the item presents an incomplete statement which the pupil has to complete. For example:

> If people's eyes were not sensitive to blue light, objects which now appear blue would appear ...
> (ANSWER: black)
>
> (Educational Testing Service 1961)

Items of this type are satisfactory as long as they deal with unambiguous matter that demands answers of no more than one or two words. Should the item demand complex reasoning that takes longer to explain, there is every chance that it would attract a bewildering variety of answers that would be very difficult to

388 *Psychopedagogy*

assess and equate. In this respect this type of question resembles the straight question referred to earlier which, unless it is very carefully controlled, can suffer from some of the difficulties of essay-type tests. A similar criticism can be levelled at questions like the one mentioned above where I gave an example of an item to test knowledge of the assessment of learning. Here I asked for explanations to back up the choice of answer. However, the context of this specific question has a very important influence on the matter. The item is one in a number in the review section of a teaching programme and the student sees the answer at once. The student himself has to decide whether his answer is the same as the one given in the text. In a different context, with a teacher marking the students' answers, difficulties of interpretation could quite easily arise.

INTERPRETATIVE ITEMS

Sometimes referred to as structured questions, these items are particularly suitable for testing higher-level learning. Basically they present an array of data and one or a series of problems, the solution to which can be derived by study of the data. Properly constructed, an item of this type could be answered only by someone who had a good grasp of the field being assessed. In a way they resemble the problems one encounters in everyday life. The weather forecaster bringing to bear his knowledge of meteorology to analyse the data provided by weather stations to predict weather in various localities is operating in the way one should be asked to operate in answering interpretative items.

In fact, the meteorologist is exhibiting a type-A skill in terms of the categories I discussed earlier (pp. 376ff). The test items that are normally used rarely attempt to test this level of skill. The problem is thoroughly to test the grasp of concepts and principles in a given field of knowledge and to avoid the danger of assessing only simple paired associate learning masquerading as concept learning. Figure 16.2 gives an example of a question that demonstrates this approach in an interesting way.

This item is taken from a set of questions given to pupils who had taken one year of high school physics, and is based on fundamental concepts from the field of mathematics. The pupils had to apply the principles they had learned in a novel situation.

Figure 16.2 Example of interpretative item (1)

One method of obtaining 'artificial gravity' in a space station is to have the station rotating about axis AA' as it revolves around Earth.

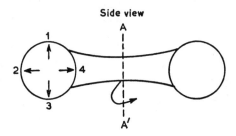

The inhabitants of the space station would call which direction 'down'?

A Direction 1
B Direction 2
C Direction 3
D Direction 4
E Any one of the four depending on speed of rotation.

(From Education Testing Service 1963)

Figure 16.3 exemplifies another question of this type with a different slant but making the same type of cognitive demands on pupils.

The multiple-type item that depends on interpretation is one of the most satisfactory of the items available to testers. The other types of items suffer from the key problem of being difficult to employ in the testing of complex learning and other problems quite extraneous to the business in hand such as the tendency towards a response 'set' where people tend systematically to choose 'True' or 'False' in a true/false question when they do not know the answer.

Figure 16.3   *Example of interpretative item (2)*

In the following questions you are asked to make inferences from the data which are given you on the map of the imaginary country, Serendip. *The answers in most instances must be probabilities rather than certainties.* The relative size of towns and cities is not shown. To assist you in the location of the places mentioned in the questions, the map is divided into squares lettered vertically from A to E and numbered horizontally from 1 to 5.

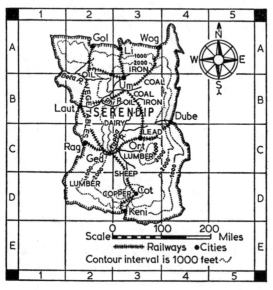

Which of the following cities would be the best location for a steel mill?

   A Li   (3A)
   B Um (3B)
   C Cot (3D)
   D Dube (4B)

(From Education Testing Service, 1963)

Making a test 391

Teachers and tests

When talking to teachers, I have sometimes found that they view objective tests with suspicion. I believe that this suspicion arises from a lack of knowledge about these tests, being based on the idea that such tests tend to assess very low-level abilities, in the main, rote learning. They may have good reason to think so, since many objective tests are of this nature. But the depressingly trivial and boring format is inherent not in the nature of objective tests but in the nature of the test constructor. Constructing objective-test items is an interesting and challenging activity. Though it rarely comes naturally, and demands time, care, patience and training or some form of tutelage, it is not impossible for a teacher to teach himself objective-test writing provided he applies himself to the literature and gets sympathetic feedback from his colleagues and informative feedback from his pupils. (See the Educational Testing Service Tests and Measurement Kit for a very useful source of information on this subject. See various Schools Council Examination Bulletins for specific aspects of testing; also Wiseman and Pidgeon 1970.)

On the other hand, I believe that there is a good deal of misunderstanding about the nature of essay-type tests, which are often attributed with qualities they do not possess. They may give opportunity for the demonstration of original thinking and the ability to marshall arguments, but the trouble is that pupils, with depressing frequency, fail to take advantage of the opportunity. It is difficult to *make* pupils demonstrate this type of cognitive ability when they have a free rein in their answer. In order to channel the pupils' thinking and writing into the type of response you are looking for, it is necessary to move some way towards the objective-test approach and give more specific and precise directions to candidates than is usually the case: try to explain precisely what you mean when you ask them to *discuss* something; give them some guidance. To cope with one other problem of essay-type tests you must ask all the pupils to answer all the questions. If you allow choice then you introduce error if you are trying to assess the pupils' competence in relation to each other or, as I would prefer, against some external criterion. You should also

392 *Psychopedagogy*

strive so far as is possible to avoid the pitfalls I outlined in my discussion of essay-type tests

My counsel to a teacher on the subject of evaluation, assessment or testing would be to urge that he become acquainted with objective tests, practise the art of item construction and integrate them into his teaching. All the processes I discussed earlier – such as the specification of objectives, the analysis of teaching tasks, the identification of the types of learning involved – lead in natural progression to the construction of tests to assess the achievement of the intended learning outcomes. A good objective test will give a teacher the information he seeks. Moreover, it will tell him what the strengths and weaknesses of his teaching have been. If all the pupils show ignorance in various parts of his test, it will be a signal to him to examine his teaching and try to do something about it, so that the failing pupils will succeed. I would say the same with regard to the use of essay tests. Be alive to their pitfalls and don't expect them to do more than their nature allows. In the main they will be used for assessing pupils' ability to express themselves and to bring together ideas in a coherent fashion. They are by no means satisfactory as a general medium for tapping high-level abilities in various fields of knowledge.

The curious view of testing that sees the teacher as the one on trial is, of course, a consequence of my attitude towards criterion-referenced testing. Embracing, as I do, the idea that testing and teaching are different aspects of the same process and therefore being much more interested in methods of teaching that increase the understanding of the whole group of pupils rather than teaching that increases the differences among them, I do not think that there is much need for a practising teacher to become acquainted with the stock-in-trade of many test constructors which helps them to write items that discriminate among pupils. I am referring to the practice of item analysis in norm-referenced tests, which you are bound to find in any book on test construction.

Item analysis in norm-referenced testing involves the trying out of an objective test on a group of pupils followed by the inspection of each item to discover which pupils got it right and which got it wrong. A good item is considered to be one that most of those who score highly on the test as a whole get right and the

Making a test 393

low scorers get wrong. The main criterion for the selection of items for the final test then becomes the effectiveness of the item to discriminate between the highs and the lows. Since quite often the discrimination value of an item takes precedence over its content validity as a test of what has been taught, I would prefer not to use this criterion for selecting items.

Item analysis in criterion-referenced testing involves the inspection of score patterns of items by pupils who have had instruction and those who have not. If most of the pupils who have had instruction get the item right and most of those who have not get it wrong, it is an indication that the item is satisfactory. But not a guarantee. The correct answers may indicate nothing more than that you have taught a particular piece of jargon which would be meaningless to those who had not come across it but which was not a very effective test of conceptual learning at all, merely a test of the simple ability to remember words. Thus item analysis needs to be tempered with the careful inspection of the item using other criteria of a less precise and mathematical nature, but criteria that keep a firm focus on the pedagogical nature of the item rather than its statistical characteristics.

Tests, institutions, teachers

This chapter has discussed some of the key issues related to the evaluation of pupils' learning. In the process I have raised some of the problems concerned with the use of tests and examinations which are almost always ignored or unappreciated in schools and other educational institutions. What are the implications for teachers, especially beginning teachers, of this discordance between current practice and the approach recommended in this chapter? It is obviously essential to take full account of the fact that current practices of grading and norm-referenced testing are strongly institutionalized, hallowed by tradition, and have served a useful function in terms of the demands of schools and society. (That the premises upon which the practices were based may well have been fallacious does not invalidate the fact that the practices were perceived as being useful.) However, within the constraints of a system which may well be operating other

394 *Psychopedagogy*

procedures, it is possible for a teacher to have an approach to his own teaching that stresses the unity of evaluation with the processes of learning.

Taking such an approach, a teacher would attempt to develop test instruments that could be used to monitor pupils' learning as they moved from stage to stage. He would do his best to ensure that they received the maximum possible feedback from the results of testing and involve the pupils themselves in the analysis and evaluation of their own work. He would seek to enhance reinforcement and thereby increase motivation by using criterion-referenced tests which make it possible for all the class to do well, provided that his teaching is related to the achievement of objectives matched with the pupils' existing competence. He will be assisted in diagnosing competence by the very act of developing diagnostic-test instruments such as have been discussed earlier. There is no implication in this approach that the achievement of all pupils is to be reduced to uniformly low standards. Instead, although the rationale of the approach is one that emphasizes the cognitive and affective growth of all the pupils, the diagnostic nature of the instruments makes it possible to cater more effectively for individual differences in learning.

It is possible that the school may demand that the teacher produce a rank order of pupils' scores, even though he has avoided doing this himself. It will probably be politic in such circumstances to produce the summed scores on his criterion-referenced tests while at the same time making the point that this is not the way he would want the scores treated. However, I think that the process of adding raw scores from tests of different subjects is so obviously indefensible that a teacher should resist any attempt to carry out such an operation.

So far as his own teaching is concerned, should he adopt the suggestions made above, a teacher would develop tests as a natural outcome of the planning of his teaching. The tests would be related to the same objectives, the same item analysis and the same view of the nature of the learning to be assessed. Should he develop his own objective tests in relation to the objectives he sets himself, he will soon have a bank of items that he will be able to use without having to construct new items every time he wishes to assess the

Making a test 395

learning of any particular group of pupils. Selecting the appropriate items as pupils complete a unit of a course will give them an indication of the way they are progressing as well as giving the teacher diagnostic feedback on his own efforts. If he uses this feedback to eliminate the weaknesses in his teaching, there should be a continuous process of improvement in the average level of score of the class. There would be no question of the average being 50 per cent in such a system; 70 per cent, 80 per cent or 90 per cent would be possible, although I obviously recognize that not all teachers will be able to achieve such levels of success. That fact that even the suggestion may seem rather bizarre in our present pedagogical climate is, I believe, a reflection more on our present preoccupation with sorting people out rather than on any inherent crankiness in the idea.

Standardized tests

I have commented on standardized tests briefly earlier in this chapter, but now I shall say just a word on how I perceive them in relation to the task of individual teachers: the word is *caution*. Recall that standardized tests are not devised with *your* pupils in mind but for a larger population, perhaps the complete pupil population of a geographical area or even a whole country. The test compilers cannot possibly know your objectives when they devise the test, so it is impossible to marry that test with your teaching as I have suggested earlier. Far better, it seems to me, to make a study of test construction along the lines suggested here and try your hand yourself with the aid of feedback from colleagues, 'experts' if you can find any, but, above all, from the pupils.

It might be suggested that in some fields – for example, in the teaching of reading and number – standardized tests would be useful. Again, caution. It depends on your purposes. The commonly used graded-word reading tests to which I have already alluded are easy to administer and yield reading ages in no time. And this, I think, is the danger. All too readily you have the measure of your pupils expressed in tidy rows of numbers looking all neat and efficient but concealing all the problems of pupils with

396 *Psychopedagogy*

difficulties. This is because this type of test is norm-referenced and constructed without any consideration of the essential sub-skills of reading. A score on this type of test provides the reading age of a pupil but gives no clue as to what to do with this information. If he gets the words all right, there is probably no problem. The trouble starts when you want to help a pupil with difficulties. All that the reading age tells you is that the pupil has scored the average for a person of that particular age on that particular test. There is nothing objective or absolute about these scores and they offer no diagnostic information about pupils. If you can find a test based on a skills analysis of basic subjects such as reading and arithmetic you may well be able to use these to provide diagnostic feedback, which will give you guidance about the action to take with regard to particular pupils. These tests will be some help; the others, hardly any. Indeed, in the hands of a teacher who is ignorant of their rationale and has not thought about skills analysis in relation to teaching reading, norm-referenced tests could be very harmful.

Public examinations

Public examinations in Great Britain that come at the end of certain stages in secondary education suffer from some of the difficulties that arise in standardized tests. As with standardized tests there is the difficult problem of objectives. In recent years there has been a move towards the provision of objectives rather than lists of syllabus content, but the objectives sometimes provided leave much to be desired, frequently lack precision and are too general to be much guide to a teacher. There also seems to be an undue focusing on the Bloom taxonomy as a model for the specification of objectives. This focus has had a welcome effect of bringing about an enhanced emphasis on the testing of higher-level cognitive abilities, but the problem still remains that it is impossible to tell by looking at an actual test item whether or not the answer calls for the exercise of high-level cognitive skills or not; only by comparing the substance of the teaching with the substance of the testing can one determine the level of test item.

One other point seems to me of some importance. The over-

Making a test   397

whelming emphasis in these examinations is on the type of skills I describe as type-C skills. As I have suggested, there are more complex skills which demand the application of learned concepts and principles in what might be described as practical situations. In some fields there have been interesting developments along these lines – particularly in the science-related subjects, perhaps because these have traditionally included a practical element. The Schools Council report on assessment in the secondary school (Schools Council 1975) refers to skills closely resembling the ones I discussed in Chapter 7, except that the author has reversed the labels. For him the knowledge of content is at level A, *Knowledge*. Level B, *Identification*, is the use of knowledge in the analysis of phenomena, materials, activities, etc., to discover to what extent they exemplify the learned concepts. Finally, *Performance* (level C) demands that the person being tested actually does something. The report of the Schools Council research programme into the proposals for new secondary examinations, N and F level, also includes ideas related to the notion of three types of skill (Schools Council 1977). These are: (1) recall of basic facts and principles (recall of specific terms and principles); (2) understanding, handling and application of information (using numerical and non-numerical data, translation of information from one form to another, critical assessment of data); and (3) communication abilities (construction of hypotheses, design of experiments, logical and coherent communication of ideas) (pp. 13 and 14, report of biology group).

These are all interesting and encouraging developments which could be usefully applied to most, if not all, of the fields of assessment. The crucial point, however, still remains that the examiner can never know what level is being tested unless he knows the way the candidates have been taught. One candidate's responses could be evidence of level C (A in my hierarchy), and yet be nothing more than a demonstration of rote learning by another candidate who had been drilled in the kind of activity related to the specific question. There is also the other problem that in the main public examinations are norm-referenced, and in addition the embarrassing question of the validity of adding marks on the assumption that all items are equally difficult is largely ignored.

398 Psychopedagogy

Of course the last two problems apply to all tests, whether external or not, but they are much more tractable, and the rote learning difficulty is soluble by internal tests, or tests developed with the cooperation of the teachers who taught the candidates.

All of which suggests that external testing is in principle less satisfactory than testing by the candidates' own institution. Certainly this is the case if the purpose of the examination is to assess the achievement by a school of its pedagogical goals. External examining by its nature serves different ends. Rather than providing information about the degree of achievement of objectives as a monitoring function for the school, it acts as a quality control mediating between the school and other aspects of society such as higher education and the professions. There is no reason why there should be this functional schism between the two approaches. A marriage could be arranged. There are practical problems in that schools in the main lack the staff with the necessary time and expertise to carry out testing programmes related to the goals of the school and the pedagogical objectives of the different disciplines. The adoption of approaches such as the ones permissible in the Certificate of Secondary Education – whereby the school either decides on the objectives and syllabus which is externally assessed, or is allowed to do the assessing itself subject to the moderation of an outside body – would go far to solve these problems.

Continuous assessment

Although the term has not so far been used, much of the discussion of testing has been related to what is commonly known as *continuous assessment*. Like many things I have already discussed, this label has different connotations for different people. To many it suggests tests at the end of each week or similar period of time, where the tests could well be short-answer-type quizzes, probably norm-referenced, and probably the scores will be added, both within the individual tests and among tests. This is not what I mean. I would advocate a form of continuous assessment such as I have described above: evaluation that monitors the teacher's teaching and provides feedback to teacher and pupils at key points

Making a test 399

in a subject of study. It would be diagnostically related to the objectives which would be explained to the pupils, and the tests would be criterion-referenced and of the short-answer type in the main, with items that tested the pupils' learning in scope and in depth and stressed problem-solving skills of type A. External moderation would help to ensure that the objectives were realistic and that the tests were genuine tests of those objectives. The essential thing is that the testing and the teaching should be intimately related.

17
Made to measure?

Until fairly recently the most influential body of opinion in educational psychology was little concerned with relating teaching and testing. Its object was rather to divorce the two. The dream of the constructors of these tests was that one day they would design a test that would pierce the skin of experience and culture and reveal the 'true ability' of the individual. I refer, of course, to the constructors of intelligence tests. The psychologists concerned seem intent on demonstrating the truth of Hogben's (1955) title, *Man Must Measure*, and seem to have an irresistible urge to measure the minds of their fellow human beings. The hope was that their tests would enable psychologists to classify pupils according to their 'basic innate ability' and then prescribe the most appropriate ways of educating and teaching them.

This book takes a different view, but one that has received an increasing amount of support in recent years (e.g. Bloom 1976; Stott 1978). It is not merely that the two approaches differ but that they are mutually exclusive. This is a different position from that of some who have written critically of testing. Hegarty (1977)

Made to measure? 401

for example, in a critical appraisal of intelligence tests, describes those who would dispense with them altogether as the 'Luddites of educational measurement' (p. 39). He justifies continued work on them on the grounds that '. . . we have an education system where people are going to use tests whether they are good or bad, so it makes sense to try to make the range of available tests as good as possible'. The kindest thing one can say about this type of argument is that if applied generally it would be a recipe for intellectual stagnation. The opposite point of view embodied in this book is that the processes associated with intelligence testing are deleterious to learning and teaching and their continued use can only hinder progress in pedagogy. Because of this view, I have devoted little of this book to questions of intelligence and its measurement. However, in view of the important influence it has had on the development of education over the past twenty or thirty years, I think it necessary to consider the work of the mental testers. At the same time I also devote some attention to a similar phenomenon associated with measuring and classifying allegedly basic attributes of human beings. To introduce the subject you might like to see what you can make of this question and ponder which cognitive or affective traits it relates to. Answer in the space provided.

> Once upon a time some clever men invented a way of distinguishing between children who were good at learning (type A) and those who weren't so good (type B). The education authorities used the method to decide which children should have more money spent on them to provide such things as well-qualified teachers, small classes and lots of equipment. Which type had more money spent on them?
> *TYPE . . . children had more money spent on them.*

And thereby hangs a tale.

And a very long and involved tale too. Whatever answer you gave to the question can be checked against historical fact. But if your knowledge of recent educational history is cloudy and you were tempted to work the answer out from your own understanding of and feelings about teaching and children you might well have come to a different conclusion. Certainly there was

402   Psychopedagogy

never, nor is there likely to be, a consensus of opinion about what the education authorities *should* have done. The decision could never have been taken on psychological or educational grounds but on the basis of political or philosophical outlook, or as a result of economic considerations or probably a complex combination of all these and other factors.

Label and liquidate

Intelligence testing is probably the most spectacularly ubiquitous example of the tendency to set up categories into which we can slot people so that on encountering the label we have a reaction all ready. This is a very useful thing, as anyone who has had any classification job to do will attest. The cognitive strain involved in examining individual phenomena and deciding on the most appropriate treatment is considerable. How handy to have a simple ready-made device that tells us quickly which kind of person or thing we are dealing with. Labelling solves our problems.

Many years of labour and large sums of money have been expended in devising methods of allocating people to categories in the way that intelligence tests purported to do. In the main the work has been related to the field of mainstream psychology and has provided intriguing problems for many generations of students. Often the results have been descriptive in the sense that the researcher will tell us what people with a certain label did in one circumstance in contrast to what people with a different label did. Often the labels are dichotomous: you are either bright or dim, creative or not creative (although, I suppose, the label here should logically be 'destructive'), gifted or not gifted. It is true that in most cases the dichotomies are derived from scales of scores on appropriate tests that were never intended by psychologists to be dichotomized, but, in general, usage concentrates on the division between those who score high and those who score low. But although most of the work has been done, as I have said, in mainstream psychology, it has often been imported into educational psychology, and attempts have been made to relate it to teaching. In the case of intelligence testing the attempt at importation was eminently successful, and for many years intelli-

Made to measure? 403

gence testing was what educational psychology was all about. In other fields there has been nothing comparable, but a glance at the literature in educational psychology will be enough to demonstrate that dichotomous categories are fairly well entrenched.

Categorization has usually been applied to what is known as *individual differences*. In particular, intelligence tests have been used for many years to allocate people to categories according to their scores in these tests. Although for purposes of selection for secondary education in Britain the key categories were pass and fail (i.e. dichotomous), the tests have been widely used to set up many more categories, especially in connection with the ascertainment of pupils with learning difficulties. Several categories of mental handicap were identified until recently, mainly by the score on an intelligence test, and educational decisions were made on the strength of that classification. Recent developments are more in line with the approach taken in this book in respect of learning and teaching generally. Instead of allocating to broad categories such as feeble-minded, dull or educationally subnormal, and treating those so designated as homogeneous groups, there is increasingly a focus on specific learning difficulties with an attempt to identify the nature of those difficulties. Unfortunately, the method of categorizing pupils in the broad groups, and treating them in a conventional mode according to the category identified, is still with us in many schools and colleges. Its worst manifestations may be seen in cases where teachers take the imputed limitations of the global classification as indicating that there is little one can do for a child in that category in an ordinary school.

This problem highlights the possibly deleterious effects of the practice of classifying people rather than problems, especially in the fields of intelligence testing. I shall return to the question of intelligence later. I should now like to consider the other manifestations of the practice of labelling and, in particular, its connection with the question of personality and its testing.

404 *Psychopedagogy*

Salami theories of personality

There are many definitions of personality and many different views as to what are its most important aspects. Perhaps one of its most common contemporary usages is in such phrases as 'a TV personality'. Here it merely refers to somebody who is widely known. The word applied generally to individuals – that is, when referring to someone's personality – sometimes means those aspects of the whole human being that distinguish him from other people: such traits as honesty, dependableness, cheerfulness, kindness, and so on. Sometimes the word is used to describe a person's outward aspects, as in such expressions as 'a colourless personality' or 'he has lots of personality'. The connotations of the term you are likely to encounter in psychology texts belong to none of these usages.

Current psychological usage focuses on those aspects of the ways in which individuals are thought to differ other than the cognitive. Thus intelligence is often largely excluded. However, like intelligence, personality tends to be defined in terms of test scores. Unlike intelligence, however, there are a large number of tests examining different phenomena all held to be aspects of personality. My title 'Salami theories of personality' refers to this tendency to slice people up in various ways in order to describe the personalities of groups of people. Different psychologists espouse different views about the various ways of slicing up the person, and there is no reason why additional methods should not be developed *ad lib*, except, perhaps, the lack of imagination in finding names for the various attributes. In fact, workers in the field of personality testing have been very ingenious in finding dimensions along which to measure human beings. A list of some of the more popular ones will give you a flavour. In most of the categories a linear scale provides the basis for the classification, but very frequently the main focus of attention is the two extremes of the particular scale, so that very often the discussion of the trait is conducted in terms of the way in which individuals scoring particularly high or particularly low behave in certain circumstances.

Made to measure? 405

A sample of categories

Introvert	Extrovert
Divergent thinker	Convergent thinker
Neurotic	Stable
Radical	Conservative
Tough-minded	Tender-minded
Gifted	Giftless?
Creative	Not creative

These categories do not, in principle, overlap. All of us, it would be held, can be described in different ways by them. It is, therefore, perfectly possible to conceive of two people who would differ in all the attributes, and there is a very large number of possible combinations and permutations of the categories.

In practice psychologists of a statistical bent have found mathematical relationships between the test scores relating to some of the categories and would assert that certain combinations of categories are more likely than others. In addition, other categorizers may not be within the psychology camp. And, among the categories favoured by psychologists, different workers find different categories of interest. It would, therefore, be difficult to produce an order of importance among the various dichotomies. It is also important to remember that this is just a *sample* of the variety of ways of describing individuals, so the possible permutations and combinations of attributes is even greater than appears from a scrutiny of the list. Thus the picture emerging from an inspection of the current scene in this approach to describing individuals is at best complex or, perhaps more accurately, confused, or even chaotic.

There is one other very important factor that bears on the question. All the categories are *constructs*. In other words they are hypothetical phenomena inferred from the way in which people respond to certain contrived situations, usually by answering questions on test inventories. It is important to understand the method of operating. It is not that investigators devise ways of assessing phenomena that we agree actually exist, such as height, weight and colour, but that they invent the measuring instruments first and then describe what they measure in terms

406 Psychopedagogy

of their measuring instrument. Naturally the individual investigator has his own ideas as to what he is interested in before he constructs his measure, but all discussion of the attribute takes place with reference to the scores produced by the application of the instrument. Nevertheless we find that the discussion very quickly assumes the character of a debate about genuine entities, and their entirely subjective origins become lost to sight. This tendency may be innocuous when experimentalists converse among themselves, but it is nothing short of alarming when this type of discourse finds its way into discussion about factors influencing the practice of teaching and the processes of learning.

I find the tendency alarming because I believe that it is bound to lead to the neglect of the learning difficulties of individual children. This would seem paradoxical to the enthusiastic classifier, who argues that the reason he interests himself in the subject is so that he can get a better idea of the way the hypothesized qualities affect individual pupils' learning. He is likely to produce findings from his experiments that indicate such things as that introverts do better on this or that type of learning task than do extroverts. An example of one of the more tentative statements of this nature should give you an idea of the genre (Entwistle 1975).

> Many apparent contradictions in the literature [on personality and achievement] can be resolved by the recognition that stable extroverts *tend* to be successful in primary schools, while introverts, and *possibly* even neurotic introverts, predominate among outstanding students. *It is not clear, however, to what extent personality, rather than attainment, is changing over this period.* [My italics throughout]

And later.

> . . . it may be salutary to look for practical, rather than theoretical importance in the research findings. It still requires considerable faith and imagination to see where these results may lead.

No need for italics here. Other authors are less tentative, but the drift of the first quotation is typical. The search is for types of

Made to measure? 407

people, or people with certain characteristics, and for the way they perform in different situations. The second quotation raises one of the crucial issues leading me to believe that the urge to slice people up is no help to teachers. So what if you do find that extroverts do better than introverts in primary schools but worse in higher education? Do we try to make students in higher education more introvert and possibly neurotic in order to increase their chances of a good degree? The reply to this would probably be that the idea is eventually to identify the types of learning environment most helpful to the different types of people. Attempts would then be made to match the environment to the individual.

I have already hinted that such ambitions are likely to be difficult to fulfil in view of the large variety of ways in which pupils may be categorized using even the few dichotomies I have listed. If you then consider the implications of adding to that list other categories in common usage such as high/low intelligence, working/middle class, black/white and male/female you will get some idea of the enormity of the task of finding the optimum learning environment for each pupil. Add to that complexity the assertion by some psychologists that the characteristics of pupils interact so that pupils with different labels interact in different ways with other pupils. And don't forget that the teacher's characteristics come in too. Different pupils will react differently to the same teacher depending upon which particular combination of the categories he possesses. By now we are dealing with possible combinations of circumstances of astronomical proportions.

Thus it seems to me that this approach to individual differences has no practical utility for teachers. Even if the categories represented real phenomena, which they do not, and even if the tests employed to allocate people to categories were demonstrably valid, which they are not, we would be better off without them (Buros 1977). It would be completely impossible to provide for different learning environments on such a scale, even if the constructs and the tests were universally accepted and even if we could be guaranteed that nobody else would invent new categories, neither of which is the case.

I said earlier that I found the tendency to label people in the way I have been describing as likely to achieve the opposite of

408 *Psychopedagogy*

what many of the categorizers aver is their intention, and instead of helping to cope with individual learning problems it is likely to hinder. This would follow in the event of the serious adoption of categorization because it would deflect attention away from a pupil's actual performance in a learning task to factors not connected directly with the process of learning. There would be a great possibility that in the case of a pupil having a learning problem, a solution would be sought in terms of the imputed qualities of the categories that happened to fit him. This is a completely different approach from the one advanced in this book, which advocates diagnostic analysis of the learning task and the pupil and teacher activities that led to the problem. Any consideration of pupil characteristics taking this approach would be concerned with his level of cognitive capability in relation to the task and his affective state in relation to the learning situation.

Focusing attention on a pupil's personality when one evaluates one's teaching has an additional hazard, apart from distracting one from analysing the teaching/learning encounter. By its nature it is defeatist. What *can* a teacher do to help a failing pupil if the pupil's personality is the wrong kind for a particular learning situation? In thousands of cases involving categorization by intelligence tests the answer has been 'nothing'. Subsequent research and practical experience has proved this to be a very mistaken view, but in the meantime many teachers have neglected many pupils unlucky enough to have been given a low IQ label. Fortunately, so far, personality tests have not penetrated the schools in the way intelligence tests did in the past – otherwise we might have a similar phenomenon with them.

Intelligence?

The biggest slice taken so far to reduce people to predetermined Procrustean dimensions is without doubt 'intelligence'. Like the other qualities discussed earlier, *intelligence* is a construct. Like many of the other constructs, its nature is the subject of argument. There is no consensus as to what intelligence is, and there is no law against anyone inventing his own brand of *intelligence*.

In Anglo-Saxon cultures it has tended to connote the ability

Made to measure? 409

to do well in traditional school learning. To be sure, it is frequently claimed that intelligence tests measure abstraction or relational thinking, but in fact the items in such tests are almost invariably chosen because they are useful in predicting school performance. In the same way that the various traits in personality are inferred from scores on personality tests devised according to the personal predilection of the tester, intelligence is inferred from the scores on tests devised according to the views of testers on the nature of intelligence. In no time, however, in discussion, the subject of debate shifts from scores on these tests to *intelligence* as a thing in itself. What starts off as an idea in the mind of a tester becomes an independent entity through various magical statistical manipulations. So potent is the magic that serious debate and controversy is conducted about the amount of intelligence inherited and the amount due to environment. A somewhat pointless exercise, one might imagine, in view of the fact that there is no general agreement as to what the nature of intelligence is. However, since *intelligence* has loomed large in the study of educational psychology and has exerted an enormous influence on schooling in Britain in recent years, I think it important to devote some time to discussing it because I think an uncritical acceptance of some of the assertions on the subject in a multitude of texts could seriously undermine a teacher's effectiveness.

Testing, testing

The first person to attempt to assess intelligence was a French psychologist, Alfred Binet, in the first decade of the twentieth century. He had a specific purpose in mind which was very much in the spirit of this book. He wanted to carry out diagnostic procedures in a systematic way so that he could identify those children in Paris schools who were below the normal standards of education, in order to provide them with remedial education in special schools. It is important to note this approach. He was trying to identify *existing learning deficits*, and *not* attempting to *predict* what the *future* might hold for children making particular scores on his tests. On the one hand we are trying to establish what is the current case, so as to try to change it; on the other

410 *Psychopedagogy*

we are trying to forecast the future. All too often the latter use has been the excuse for not trying to do anything. Binet himself had sharp words for people of that persuasion:

> Some recent philosophers appear to have given their moral support to the deplorable verdict that the intelligence of an individual is a fixed quantity which cannot be augmented. We must protest and act against this brutal pessimism. We shall endeavour to show that it has no foundation whatsoever. . . . A child's mind is like a field for which an expert farmer has advised a change in the method of cultivation, with the result that in place of desert land we now have a harvest. It is in this particular sense, the only one that is significant, that we say the intelligence of children may be increased. One increases that which constitutes the intelligence of a school child; namely the capacity to learn, to improve with instruction.
>
> (Clark and Clark 1966)

My great concern is that the brutal pessimism Binet mentions is still abroad and exerting a baleful influence in far too many fields of education and society at large.

Paradoxically, the key characteristic of intelligence tests that recommends them to many educationists and psychologists is one of their potentially most misleading qualities for teachers. The tests strive to give us an indication of the general cognitive ability of individuals and, indeed, many white Anglo-Saxon psychologists would agree that they probably do this. But it is this very claim to generality that is liable to create difficulties. The point is this. Most tests aimed at assessing this all-round cognitive ability comprise a variety of sub-tests. The final score is the summated standard scores of the various sub-tests. So long as we consider only the global score we could be constructing a veil of ignorance for ourselves in relation to the different capabilities of the testees. To illustrate. Many tests of intelligence make use of clusters of items that attempt to assess different capabilities – some cognitive, some non-cognitive. It is quite possible for two individuals to obtain the same composite score on the whole test and yet have very different patterns of scores on the clusters of test items. Figure 17.1 sets out the score patterns of three individuals on a commonly used, individually administered intelligence test, the Wechsler Intelligence Scale for Children. The three children scored the same overall total but their patterns of scores were very different. Anyone making an educational recommendation purely on the strength of the overall score might well treat the three pupils in the same way. It is only by examining the patterns of scores that one gets a picture of the various strengths and weaknesses of the different pupils. Tests that do not have the subdivisions do not allow of this approach, and consequently the differential abilities remain obscured.

Figure 17.1 Pupil scores on a selection of sub-tests from an intelligence test

(Pupils all have the same composite score but very different patterns of sub-test scores.)

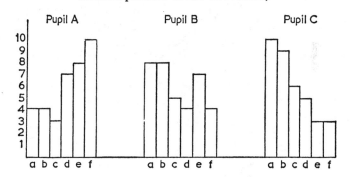

Titles of sub-tests

- (a) Information
- (b) Comprehension
- (c) Vocabulary
- (d) Block design
- (e) Object assembly
- (f) Picture completion

The WISC test, as I have indicated, is a test that is administered by a psychologist to a child on an individual basis. When many children are to be tested in schools, recourse is made to group tests of intelligence. These tests resemble the individual tests except that they tend to concentrate on clusters of items that

412 Psychopedagogy

relate particularly to cognitive activities. The same problems apply to these tests as apply to the individual tests; that is, the overall score obscures the constituent differential abilities.

The paradoxical aspect of these tests is that, although their main claim to attention lies in their status as the best all-round predictors of school learning, we learn more that is pedagogically useful by looking at the sub-test scores, many of which, in the group intelligence tests, resemble tests in traditional school subjects. Provided we keep this fact to the front of our minds when using such tests, they may provide preliminary indicators of a person's current capabilities, but for useful pedagogical information we need to scrutinize the sub-test score patterns and then, for information of a diagnostic nature, we need to employ tests specifically constructed to give us an indication of the pupil's current strengths and weaknesses in the area of study we are interested in.

To describe this procedure is to reveal the basic weakness of these global tests intended to reveal to us basic ability. Like the standardized tests discussed in Chapter 15, they are norm-referenced and not related to the learning objectives of specific groups of pupils. Thus even the sub-test scores will not be very informative to individual teachers about the nature of pupils' abilities in relation to the teachers' own teaching objectives. They will tell us nothing of a diagnostic nature about the pupils. All they will do is give us a rank order of pupils on that particular test. The tests are designed to discriminate among children according to the ideas in the minds of the compilers concerning the nature of 'intelligence', not to yield information about the levels of competence achieved by children in relation to specified learning tasks. They are thus prone to the disadvantages discussed in Chapter 15, particularly the fact that the actual level of achievement of the standardization group could be quite low, since the aim of the test is satisfied if it discriminates among pupils somehow or other.

It seems to me, then, that although professional educational psychologists might find occasional use for individual intelligence tests paying particular attention to the pattern of sub-test scores, group tests are of no practical use in school. Since their main

Made to measure? 413

virtue lies in their claim to indicate all-round ability, their most useful application would seem to be in making all-round educational decisions. Since in real life *pedagogical* decisions are hardly ever global, their value *to teachers* is dubious in the extreme. To *administrators* faced with a problem of distributing scarce resources they could well be appealing, but that is a very different matter. Similar comments may be made about the use of tests of general ability to allocate pupils to different *streams* or *tracks* in schools. Apart from the problems of differential abilities currently under discussion, there are the factors discussed earlier in this chapter that make it quite impossible ever to achieve grouping that is really homogeneous.

In fact the use of group intelligence tests to make global decisions of an administrative or educational nature has declined considerably in recent years in Britain. The current main use of individual tests is probably in the field of clinical psychology when children are referred to a child guidance clinic in connection with educational or psychological problems. Traditionally in such referrals use would be made of tests administered on an individual basis as part of a battery of other tests and techniques for assessing the nature of children's difficulties. However, attitudes and practices are changing in the field of clinical psychology and this procedure is being questioned. Mittler (1970) sums up the situation.

> ... the classical global test approach makes the assumption that constructs such as 'intelligence' and 'personality' are in themselves relevant in helping the individual patient; thus if systematic information can be collected under these headings, it is assumed that this must be of value in treatment. But it frequently happens that the psychologists' findings play no significant part in deciding how an individual can be helped. Reports couched in the most general terms and confined to global descriptive statements about intelligence or personality are duly filed away, together with routine investigation such as skull X-ray, haemoglobin counts and urine analysis which are carried out for the sake of clinical thoroughness, *and not because there is anything in the patient's symptoms or problems*

414 Psychopedagogy

> which specifically calls for these investigations rather than for
> any others. [My italics]

(p. 819)

This comment is made under the heading 'Linking assessment with treatment'. This is clearly the clinical equivalent of my thesis that diagnosis of learning status and teaching should be viewed as two aspects of the same process. Mittler also argues the case for specific tests, as I have done in relation to learning, and concludes: 'Diagnosis divorced from treatment is a mere intellectual exercise, and sometimes hardly that.'

This kind of thinking is being reflected in changes in the role of professional educational psychologists in some institutions. However, it is still likely that in many places the clinical report on a child with learning difficulties would be of the global type and unrelated to the child's current learning status in specific areas of school learning. I suggest to the teacher who receives such a report to remember Binet's words and not succumb to the 'brutal pessimism' of which he spoke and which still persists in some places. It is not impossible for a teacher to receive a report that pronounces an upper limit on a pupil's possible level of achievement, as if the score on an intelligence test gave a true indication of his future performance no matter what steps a teacher might take. I suggest that a teacher should not accept this pessimistic view. Rather he should take the report as a challenge for action, not an excuse for inaction.

Colour and complex learning

One of the most serious examples of the brutal pessimism that Binet describes may be observed in the current discussions about the alleged difference in the intelligence of people of different ethnic groups. I do not wish to engage in the controversy about the relative contribution to measured intelligence of inheritance and environment which has occupied a central place in the argument. I do wish to examine the nature of the proposed differences that are claimed to exist between different ethnic groups. Jensen (1973) is the main propounder of the thesis that the *type of intelligence* between ethnic groups differs. His thesis is that white

Made to measure? 415

children and non-white children are about the same when it comes to rote learning. When it comes to higher-level learning he avers that whites are better. He bases his arguments on scores from two types of tests. The tests of rote learning are standard psychological laboratory tests where the subject often has to memorize arbitrary connections between symbols. The tests of higher levels of learning use the Raven's Progressive Matrices test, which is a test of intellectual ability making use of non-verbal test items to derive a score of ability. Jensen argues that this test is 'status free'; that is, scores are not affected by the socio-economic circumstances of a child's upbringing or by his race.

The tests that provide the data for Jensen's assertions will give an indication of the type of learning ability they purport to assess. The test of rote learning is reasonably straightforward. It is completely arbitrary. The experimenter decides, for example, that a given nonsense syllable will be paired with another nonsense syllable and the person taking the test has to memorize a number of such arbitrary connections. There is no principle which a learner could learn and then apply to new arbitrary connections. On the other hand, the Raven's Matrices test makes use of logical principles. It is a non-verbal test that requires a learner to examine an incomplete array of patterns and to select from a number of alternatives the one that completes the array. The person taking the test thus has to induce the principle determining the pattern and then identify the correct alternative by deduction.

As I have already indicated, there is no general consensus as to what 'intelligence' is. Further, there is no general agreement that the Raven's test is 'status free'. Discussion about ethnic differences, therefore, can legitimately make reference only to Raven's test scores, *not to differences in intelligence*. This point cannot be stressed too much when we are considering the pedagogical implications of the debate in this field.

There is another very important factor that we need to note. The rote-learning tasks are direct measures of simple learning. What is being assessed is how quickly and efficiently children learn new connections between arbitrarily paired stimuli. A good learner will make the connections quickly and accurately as

416   Psychopedagogy

compared with a poor learner. If we have results from many such tests and one child invariably copes better than another, we can reasonably say that his rote-learning ability seems to be better than that of the other child. Note, however, the crucial difference when we consider the case of complex learning, the one that in Jensen's view is the prerogative of white people. The rote-learning problems were direct learning *tasks*, but the Raven's matrices are *tests* of conceptual learning ability. That is, they do not sample actual new learning of a complex kind, but sample *existing competence* in coping with the Raven's test, and *no provision is made for learning*. Any argument that the score indicates a level of competence in complex learning is an inference only. In order to assess complex learning ability in any reasonable way, it would be necessary to give the learners the chance to learn the skills related to the test material. In the case of the Raven's Matrices, it is quite conceivable that some children would be better at the beginning than others at the kind of operations necessary for successful completion of the task and would therefore do better. A true test of conceptual learning ability should examine the performance of learners in learning the skills appropriate to the solving of problems dependent upon conceptual learning. From previous discussions, you will remember that the acid test of this kind of learning is the ability to transfer existing principles to new materials that embody the same principles and solve *new* problems embodying those principles; the Raven's Matrices makes no provision for this kind of approach.

LEARNING AND TESTING

I have looked at two important aspects of the use of the Matrices test. One investigation explored the claim that the test could penetrate the skin of acquired ability and give a true indication of complex learning ability unaffected by culture or practice as Jensen asserts. In this investigation (Renhard 1971) we examined the extent to which the principles underlying the Raven's Matrices test could be learned and taught. I should stress that the aim was not to coach for the test but to teach the principles using materials of a quite different nature. Pupils were taught

Made to measure? 417

the principles using some materials of a pictorial nature; some were abstract and some made use of numbers. The Raven's material was at no time introduced to the pupils. The teaching was accomplished by a self-instructional teaching programme making use of the principles of concept formation discussed in this book. The Raven's Matrices were then given to the pupils as a test. We found that pupils aged about twelve who had two and a half hours' instruction using the teaching programme scored higher on the Raven's test than pupils who did not, thus suggesting that the principles underlying the test could indeed be taught and learned.

Naturally this one small-scale investigation does not prove conclusively that the principles underlying the Raven's test are affected by learning, but there is no more conclusive evidence that competence in the test is not so affected. The onus of proof, it seems to me, lies on those who claim it is not affected by learning.

The second investigation looked at the performances of three ethnic groups on a complex learning *task* (Stones 1975). This involved the use of the Vigotsky material and the tests of transfer described in Chapter 4.

In the investigation the performances of pupils of West Indian, Pakistani and English ethnic groups on the learning task and transfer test were compared. There was no significant difference between the groups. The same groups were given a rote-learning task of a similar nature to those reported by Jensen. Again there were no significant differences. From these results I conclude that much more convincing evidence is needed before Jensen's thesis about the different types of ability in different ethnic groups can be accepted.

BLACK AND WHITE PEDAGOGIES?

I have questioned the argument that the colour of one's skin determines the type of learning one is capable of on several grounds, but there is one more aspect of Jensen's views that bears directly on our study of pedagogy. On the basis of his proposition that there are two kinds of ability, he proposes that the blacks should have different kinds of pedagogies from those of the whites.

418 *Psychopedagogy*

Whites, being able to learn conceptually, should be taught by conceptual methods; blacks, being good at rote learning and bad at conceptual learning, should be taught by rote methods. Here we have a crude example of Binet's 'brutal pessimism'. Instead of seeking ways to help those who are not capable of complex learning (according to this thesis) we are urged to give up the attempt *for the good of the pupils*. Further, there is an assumption that we know more or less all there is to know about teaching for conceptual learning. If this assumption were not being made, presumably Jensen would offer hope of future advances making it possible for us to help the unfortunates condemned to a life of rote learning. The pedagogical naïvety of this point of view is matched only by the brutal inhumanity of its pessimism.

It seems to me that this view of children is one of the worst forms of labelling. Merely looking at a child, it would seem, is enough to determine his capacity for learning. Instead of taking the approach outlined in this book and espoused by many educationists – of finding out as accurately as possible the existing capabilities of a pupil prior to specific learning activities and then prescribing those activities, having in mind the pupil's demonstrated prior and relevant knowledge – one applies the crudest visual criterion to delimit the learning activities. The whole field of complex learning I have discussed is virtually ruled out by this view. All that is essentially human in the field of learning – the acquiring of complex bodies of concepts, the development of abstract thinking, of inference, of classification, analysis and synthesis – are allegedly virtually beyond the grasp of people with black faces. Whatever the final outcome of the esoteric debates about the exact proportion of 'intelligence' that is 'heritable', the simplest observation of children of different colour in schools will give the lie to this extraordinary argument.

Expectations great and small

Prescribing different pedagogies for different coloured pupils is not only withholding from those pupils access to learning experiences that are characteristically human, it also sets up in teachers and pupils affective ripples that deeply influence the

Made to measure? 419

overall learning of the pupils. Such a course of action is just the extreme case of treating differentially various categories of children. The effects are the same in kind but they will probably differ in degree. The point is this. By treating groups of pupils differently from other pupils, the teacher signals these differences to all the pupils. Since in almost every case the differences will involve an evaluative element – that is, group A is *better* than group B at this, that or the other – the signals from the teacher will be saying to many of the children: 'You are not as good or as worthy as the other children.' The effect of such action on pupils is naturally to depress the levels of self-esteem.

A graphic illustration of the effects of this treatment is to be found in the film *The Eye of the Storm* (Community Relations Commission 1970). This film recounts the experiences of a class of children which was divided up by the teacher into those with brown eyes and those with blue eyes. She agreed with the whole class that the brown-eyed children were to be considered less able learners than the blue-eyed children. The blue-eyed children and the teacher then proceeded to treat the brown-eyed children as if they were of lower ability; for example, the teacher's not addressing questions to the brown eyes since she was sure they would not be able to answer. Basically, she and the blue eyes *expected* the brown eyes to be dull and treated them accordingly. Although all the children were party to the initial decision to segregate the two colours, in the space of a few weeks the differences began to be real. Tensions arose in the class, the brown eyes stopped trying, felt resentful and were generally very negative in attitude to the work of the class. It was a classic case of the self-fulfilling prophecy.

The self-fulfilling prophecy is the term applied to the phenomenon of 'living up to expectations'. If a teacher *expects* pupils to behave in a certain way, or to be capable of certain levels of achievement, there is a good chance that his expectations will be fulfilled. The reasons for this are complex but essentially are of the type described above: the way in which teacher and other pupils treat children with certain *given* expectations influences the whole pedagogical climate of the classroom. In particular, it influences the motivation of the pupils. The phenomenon works in a variety of ways. If a teacher believes a child is bright and

420 *Psychopedagogy*

treats him accordingly, the chances are that this treatment will affect his level of motivation and thereby influence his attitude to learning and enhance his performance.

I came across a very interesting example of the self-fulfilling prophecy many years ago which illustrates the power of the teacher's expectations in quite unusual ways. The teacher was an early nineteenth-century pedagogue, the Rev. D. G. Goyder. Goyder taught at schools in several parts of Britain in the first few decades of the century. He was an enlightened man in many ways and studied the work of the contemporary leaders of pedagogical thought such as Wilderspin, Owen and Pestalozzi. He was also a phrenologist. That is, he believed that a person's character and abilities could be ascertained by the shape of his head. This was a widely held view at the time and Goyder applied it to his work as a schoolteacher. In his school he selected pupils for a variety of duties according to the shapes of their heads. In his words: 'I drew my monitors from the ranks of my pupils for different duties according to their [phrenological] organization, and was always successful. I had a music master, a teacher of geography, and a reading master all from my pupils, and all turned out to be good teachers. Phrenology, therefore, I thought must be true' (Goyder 1862). Not many would agree with him today. However, hundreds would recognize the phenomenon. In many ways it is a prototype of the various means we have today of sorting pupils out, be it intelligence-test score, personality profile or skin colour. Few would disagree that in general the convictions a teacher holds about the capabilities of his pupils is one of the most potent factors in determining the nature of their performance (Baker and Crist 1971; Insel and Jacobson 1975).

Labelling language

I have discussed the way in which use of language and thinking interact and influence each other. I have also discussed the dangers for learning of empty verbalism where the use of the word conceals the fact that there is no conceptual content to it. And in the last few pages I have drawn attention to the way in which language

Made to measure? 421

used for labelling can deflect attention from serious discussion or investigation of children's learning, by setting up dubious connections between various characteristics of learners and their learning capabilities. The work of one writer contributes in a curious and complicated way to all of these; I refer to the work of Bernstein.

Bernstein is a sociologist who has excursed into various fields including linguistics, and in his time he has made a creditable contribution to the body of labels in circulation. From a study of the language of different social classes in England he has developed a hypothesis suggesting that children from working-class homes are brought up in a linguistic environment that differs in important ways from that in middle-class homes (Bernstein 1973). The essential difference in language usage is said to be that in working-class homes speech tends to be abbreviated, short on syntactical complexity, and very much context-bound. This type of language usage he calls a *restricted code*.

On the other hand, he believes, middle-class speech tends to be much more flexible, more complex syntactically and not so dependent upon the physical environment as is the speech in working-class homes. This type of language usage is called an *elaborated* code. I have been at pains to avoid the use of the expressions *the* restricted and *the* elaborated codes, since to discuss the proposed codes in that way would be to give the impression that their existence has been 'proved' and generally accepted. This is not so. Unfortunately the labels 'restricted' and 'elaborated' are used with the assumption that they refer to real identifiable phenomena, and the fact that they are challenged strongly by some researchers is overlooked.

The misunderstandings that may flow from an uncritical acceptance of the codes hypothesis are exacerbated by Bernstein's concomitant study of the intelligence-test scores of the two linguistic groups. He found that working-class boys scored lower on verbal-intelligence tests than a comparable group of middle-class boys with the same non-verbal test scores. He believes that this discrepancy may be linguistically induced. 'Such children's low performance on verbal IQ tests, their difficulty with "abstract" concepts, their failures within the language area, their general

422 *Psychopedagogy*

inability to profit from the school, all may result from the limitations of a restricted code' (Bernstein 1973, p. 175). All too readily the two hypothetical entities, linguistic code and intelligence, become linked themselves and with the common connection: social class. All too readily the labelling effects in respect of the use of the terms 'restricted' and 'elaborated' codes come into operation, and the danger arises that teachers' expectations will differ in regard to the users of the two hypothesized codes.

I have no wish to attempt a sociological or linguistic critique of the thesis advanced by Bernstein. Various people have developed such critiques on a variety of grounds. Coulthard (1969) found the evidence unconvincing, Labov (1972) and Rosen (1972) argue that the speech of working-class children is in its own way just as powerful and associated with levels of thinking equal to those of middle-class children. Jackson (1974) argues that the whole conception of the two codes is a myth and points out that all that empirical work has shown is minor differences in relative frequency of some grammatical elements between middle-class and working-class groups. However, even this, he points out, has been questioned by Labov who produces evidence that the results are an artefact of the experimental method.

From the psychological point of view, the paucity of empirical evidence is crucial. No link has actually been demonstrated between code and intelligence. What was discovered is quite unexceptional: that middle-class children in general score higher on verbal tests of intelligence than do working-class children. This is unexceptional because it is a fairly commonplace finding (Butcher 1968). The problem arises when an attempt is made to establish a *causal* link between one hypothesized variable, intelligence, and another hypothesized variable, linguistic code. Bernstein is cautious in his discussion of the discrepancy between the scores made by the working-class children on the non-verbal tests and the scores on the verbal tests. He says they *may* result from the limitations of the restricted code. They *may*, but many other factors *may* be responsible for the effect. One very important factor, which *may* have nothing to do with codes at all, may be the fact that the intelligence tests on which the hypothesis is founded are constructed with a bias in favour of middle-class

Made to measure? 423

children. In other words, they are not instruments that can give us a true measure of intellectual functioning or ability to deal with abstract concepts, as Bernstein suggests. A different test designed according to different criteria might well produce very different patterns of test scores.

Bernstein did his early work in this field in the early sixties when ideas about intelligence tests were very different from what they are now. The validity of the construct 'intelligence' is widely challenged today and the validity of the tests that purport to test this construct is even more challenged.

The dubious nature of the construct intelligence, and the disputed existence of the construct linguistic code, leads to a highly speculative enterprise if one seeks to explain the one by the other. Of course Bernstein has not done this. And he has been cautious in his claims, as was pointed out above. Nevertheless there is, in his discussions of these possible connections, an apparent underestimation of the complexity of establishing causal relationships between the two highly problematic constructs.

The reader may well think that this discussion of these contentious issues is somewhat esoteric and wonder how it relates to pedagogy. As I see it, the problem is that the uncritical acceptance of the Bernstein formulations may unwittingly saddle working-class children with a double handicap. They are labelled with a low IQ and with a restricted code. Bernstein makes a plea for an understanding of the problems of working-class children trying to learn in schools pervaded with middle-class mores and for increased help to those children. Ironically his promulgation of the codes hypothesis could have the opposite effect by imposing another label on the children at a time when the disrepute of IQ scores is making them less potent.

The key thing, it seems to me, in the labelling by code, like other labels, is that it attributes failure to deficiencies within children. An alternative interpretation of the low verbal scores of working-class children, which I think is far more plausible than Bernstein's, is to do with deficits in teaching and not in children. A systematic approach to pedagogy will go a long way to cope with problems of learning of all children from whatever class.

424 Psychopedagogy

Although the ideas enunciated by Bernstein have formed part of many college syllabuses, the lack of connection between the theoretical and practical sides of the courses has probably diluted the effects of the uncritical promulgation of notions about code and intelligence. However, to the extent that it has set up low expectancies in student teachers about the ability of pupils speaking in a restricted code, it is likely to have had damaging effect.

I am not suggesting in these remarks that language is not important in the development of thinking. In fact the argument throughout this book has been precisely the opposite. What I am urging is determined resistance to the application of dubious labels to language itself, with the associated expectations that lead to the imputing to individuals, because of their membership of this (hypothetical) group or the other, advantages or disadvantages they may or may not possess. By avoiding these labels we are more likely to take a child as we find him, an individual, and try to help him with his particular learning strengths and weaknesses.

Streaming

Goyder read their heads, Jensen looks to see what colour they are, Bernstein codifies, and there are many other devices for separating the geese from the swans. One teacher did it by body odour (Rist 1970, quoted by Leach and Raybould 1977). Until quite recently British education authorities did it according to score on intelligence tests. Within schools that are allegedly non-selective, similar processes are at work. Assigning pupils to different streams or tracks sets in motion the same kind of processes that produced the differences between the blue-eyed children and the brown-eyed children and the dancing masters for Goyder. A moment's reflection will suffice to indicate that any measure attempting to do this is bound to miss the mark. Given the number of ways in which psychologists and others have attempted to classify human beings, any attempt to sort out an intake of, say, one hundred children into three homogeneous groups is doomed to failure. This is not to say that teachers innocent of such refined approaches to segregation will not *think* the groups are homogeneous. There is every reason to believe they will, as all the

Made to measure? 425

literature on expectancy suggests. But even if one assumes that there are *no other differences among pupils* than differences in scores on intelligence tests or standardized mathematics tests or reading tests, the possible combinations of score levels is high enough to make segregation into classroom-sized groups impossible If to this we add the differences in personality and the undoubted differences obtaining *within* the scores of pupils on individual tests – namely, the fact that some pupils do well on some parts of the tests and others do better on others – the situation is made even worse.

It is ironic that one of the main reasons advanced for the practice of streaming is that it helps teachers to cater for individual differences; ironic, because it produces exactly the opposite effect. Any global measure of ability in any subject that we have at the moment is primitive and a very blunt instrument. Rather than catering for individual differences, it produces them. This iron law of segregation is pathetically but strikingly epitomized by the illustration of the teacher who sorted by smell. The smelly children were sent to the back and received less teacher attention than the nice clean ones at the front, and within days of starting school the vicious circle of initial disadvantage compounded by teacher neglect was set up.

In previous chapters I have discussed various approaches to individual differences that attempt to cope with this kind of problem. I do not for one moment suggest that they cope entirely satisfactorily, but at least they make possible a more realistic and more pedagogically just approach to the question of individual differences. Instead of looking for some hypothetical universal touchstone to tell us which pupil is better than which, we focus on the *actual* differences in coping with specific learning tasks. The approach discussed makes it more possible to take into account the variety of ways in which pupils differ in their learning for whatever reason, and gives us some insight into how to help them do better. I do not attempt to hide the fact that this approach is much more difficult than the segregation method which purports to produce packaged pupils stamped appropriately A, B or C. A teacher who believes that a child stamped 'C' is a C is a C is a C will not lie awake at night wondering how he is going to

426   *Psychopedagogy*

cope with the differences among all those thirty-odd complicated human beings next day. Nor will he cope, no matter how his day seems to go for him. His presuppositions will get between him and the individual needs of his pupils.

There is another factor which may seem paradoxical in this discussion. While taking into account as best we can the fact of individual differences, we must make an assumption that human beings are more alike than they are different. The unique characteristics of all of us are built on the foundation of our common humanity. Thus the basic features of learning that I discuss in this book are relevant not only for the blue eyes but also for the brown eyes, not only the roundheads but also the oval heads, the black and the white, the dim and the bright. The fact that pupils are capable of different things is largely a function of their history of learning experiences. Different learning biographies produce different levels of competence. A teacher with this in mind will have a very different approach from that of the teacher who thinks that such differences are in our stars and therefore beyond influence. Such a teacher will do his best to ascertain the present capabilities of the pupils in relation to the demands of any new learning and then, using the same fundamental processes of teaching, but ones geared to the needs of the individual, do his best to advance the pupils to fulfil the teaching goals he set for himself and his pupils at the outset.

Which differences?

This chapter has taken a somewhat negative view of some things that are given prominence in texts on educational psychology. Indeed, until fairly recently much of educational psychology was concerned entirely with the topic of individual differences. In the main, however, discussions in this field tended to be concerned with rather esoteric distinctions between different levels of intelligence-test scores. In my critique, I do not claim that individual differences are not important; indeed, a major thesis of this book is that we need to be much more systematic in our study of these differences when planning teaching. The important point, however, is that the differences I am concerned with are

Made to measure? 427

those relating to specific teaching tasks. They are diagnostic of present capabilities, which in turn are related in a systematic way to the teaching to be undertaken. Clearly levels of development in the Piagetian sense will be important, clearly competence in language will be important, and obviously emotional state will bear on a pupil's learning. However, at no time should a teacher use the highly dubious devices discussed above in making his diagnosis prior to teaching. In seeking to provide general all-purpose methods of sorting out children, these devices almost invariably end up by producing side effects of unknown but probably devastating proportions. I know of no way in which the methods of labelling discussed above can be of any help to any child in school. Since there is no *demonstrated validity* for any of them, it seems to me time to consign them to the pedagogical dustbin. I am greatly encouraged in this opinion by the fact that the training of professional educational psychologists is also taking a similar line in some places, where intelligence tests are now being consigned to a 'museum' (Wedell 1978a).

I believe that the answer to the question I asked at the beginning of this chapter adds weight to my point of view. In fact more money was spent on the children who were already doing well at school. But there is a twist to the story. It frequently turned out that girls did better on intelligence tests than boys and therefore, in equity, there should have been more girls in grammar schools than boys. Since this clearly flew in the face of all reason, a 'correction factor' was applied to the test scores to bring the percentage of boys in grammar schools at least up to that of the girls. This is a mild example of a phenomenon described by Kamin (1977) in an exhaustive account of how intelligence tests have been used throughout their history to discriminate against various groups of people. Moral? Before using the prescription, examine the motives of the labeller.

Learning difficulties

Intelligence tests were used not only to select children for grammar schools but also to allocate them to categories that allegedly corresponded to certain levels of learning ability. The

428 Psychopedagogy

lower the level of intelligence (IQ) the greater the difficulties a child would have in learning. In the extreme case the child would be deemed 'ineducable' and would be denied access to formal education on the grounds that his low intelligence precluded him from benefiting from any form of schooling. In England such children were the responsibility of the Department of Health and Social Security until 1971 and no attempt was made to educate them in the usual sense. Having the greatest learning difficulties of all, they were the most deprived of all by the kind of brutal pessimism that Binet talked about. The staff of the institutions they were housed in were not teachers, the level of provision of equipment and expert assistance was very much lower than in schools, and in general the treatment accorded them was an extreme form of that accorded the children who failed the selection examination for grammar schools.

In recent years changes have taken place that indicate moves away from this method of dealing with pupils with severe learning problems. These moves are of the same basic type as those that have led to the gradual phasing out of selection for secondary education. They are based on the crumbling of the case that IQ scores can define with a fair degree of precision the level of learning of which a person is capable.

In the case of the severely subnormal pupils, defined as IQ under 50, this change has been signalled by their translation from the Department of Health to the Department of Education in 1971 and the recognition that the categorization once thought so precise and definite is spurious. Even more recently the DES Report on Special Education (DES 1978) has recommended the abolition of the present system of classifying children by types of disability, on the grounds that such labels stigmatize and in fact create problems for the pupils concerned. This report also recognizes that there is a worldwide trend to integrate handicapped children into normal schools so that they shall have as far as possible the same advantages as other children. This recommendation applies to children with physical handicaps as well as those with learning or behavioural problems. There is little doubt, however, that the recommendations are influenced by the general change of opinion that is beginning to see children with learning

Made to measure? 429

difficulties, not as different kinds of beings to be accorded different treatment from that given to 'normal' children, but as children with problems who need special help and effort and greater resources than other children but along similar lines to those that should underpin all teaching of human beings.

The DES report also recommends that a special education element be included in all courses of teacher training. In my view this recommendation is a recognition of general deficiencies in current courses of initial training which very often pay little attention to psychopedagogy and much attention to hypothetical constructs that allegedly distinguish among pupils. The effect of this in the past, in training institutions as in schools and all too often in clinics, has been to divert attention from the problems of failing children. If a 'scientific' measure such as IQ tells you that the child is ineducable, the problem is removed, as happened when Pinel pronounced Victor an 'idiot'. If attention in training institutions can be turned away from such preoccupations towards a systematic approach to psychopedagogy, all teachers would be helped to cope with children with learning problems, not the least because they would have to confront the problems rather than avoid them.

It is because of reasoning like this that I have not provided a separate chapter on backwardness and its treatment as is sometimes the case in books of this type. To do so tacitly accepts the validity of categorization. But, more important, the view is that the whole of the book is about the teaching of pupils with problems as much as it is about pupils without problems, if there are such fortunate beings. Recent work in this field supports this point of view. The concern of many workers with children having learning problems is precisely with such topics as achieving clarity in objectives, analysing learning and teaching tasks, careful scheduling of reinforcement, criterion-referencing of any tests that are used and the rejection of the classification of pupils (e.g. Stott 1978; Wedell 1978b; Leach and Raybould 1977). The British Psychological Society, in its evidence to the DES Enquiry into Special Education (BPS 1976), takes a similar view: 'Special education is special in so far as it pays particular attention to the match between learner and curriculum. It is not merely a matter

430 *Psychopedagogy*

of aids and prosthetic devices, but of arranging the learning environment to suit the needs of the individual.' There is no difference between this view and the general argument of this book. The contribution of special education is that it is likely to be better able to pay the particular attention because of the higher concentration of resources on pupils with learning problems. The development of teaching skills outlined earlier should go a long way to helping *any* teacher cope with children with learning difficulties.

I do not suggest, given our present state of knowledge about learning and teaching, that the implementation of the suggestions advanced in earlier chapters will remove all problems. As I have argued repeatedly, teaching should be informed experimentation, and experimentation presupposes the possibility of failure. But the failure to achieve one's objectives is not entirely negative. It provides one with information that may be of use in later experiments. However, the difficulties that particular pupils may have with learning may be too gross for a teacher in a normal classroom to surmount. It is difficult enough to implement a systematic approach to teaching in such classrooms at all. Children with particularly gross learning problems may need the special attention, time and resources that can only be provided by taking them from the normal classroom and giving them the special treatment they need – for example, massive reinforcement and teacher attention (Wedell 1978b).

But the withdrawal should not be permanent. The idea is generally to get the withdrawn pupil back to the mainstream as soon as possible. To this end varied types of provision are made, from part-time withdrawal from class for specific teaching to full-time withdrawal for teaching across the whole curriculum. At present there is insufficient provision for such treatment of children with learning problems. It is insufficient in amount and flexibility. Possibly as a result of changing attitudes, as exemplified in the DES report, this situation may improve.

One type of provision that could well prove useful is the basing of provision in ordinary schools on a 'resource room' (Raybould and Leach 1977; Hamill and Wiederholt 1972). The overall operation of such resource rooms is to give specialized and well-

Made to measure? 431

supported assistance to *any* child, whatever his problem, to help him learn more effectively in his normal class. The teachers in these resource rooms liaise with the pupils' ordinary teachers, so maintaining the continuity of normal schooling.

Diagnosis

The ascertainment of pupils in need of special educational provision was at one time almost entirely done by the use of intelligence tests. In many places such tests still play an important part. Some current thinking and practice, however, takes a very different approach, making use of methods such as discussed throughout this book and leaning heavily on the systematic and structured observation of the teacher in the process of trying to help the pupil to learn. Of relevance here are the ideas relating to the use of baseline techniques and the monitoring of the pupil's approach to learning, together with diagnostic criterion-referenced tests that give information about the nature of the specific learning problems the pupil is experiencing. The psychologist goes to the school, confers with the teacher and makes suggestions for the better identification of the nature of the pupil's difficulties and their treatment. The most fruitful source of diagnostic information is seen as the teacher's monitoring of the pupil's work over a period using systematic techniques such as those discussed in earlier chapters. The evidence of the British Psychological Society considers that psychologists 'should be closely involved in diagnostic teaching and in planning for the child's development. They should not be seen merely as people who pay brief visits to schools to administer intelligence tests' (BPS 1976, p. 2). The same report also considers that the demands made on the child by teachers should be a little over his achievement. 'When he has achieved what is required of him, he should be enabled to enjoy his achievement for a while before moving on to the next stage. The dangers of the self-fulfilling prophecy are particularly hard to avoid for handicapped children who have in the past sometimes suffered as much from the underexpectation of parents, teachers and of society as a whole, as from their own disabilities. *The teacher's task is to beat prediction*' (p. 3, my italics). This approach

432 Psychopedagogy

resembles that advocated by Vigotsky when he proposed the zone of potential development (p. 101), and in fact some recent work has explicitly drawn on this idea in work with children with learning difficulties (Sutton 1977). Only in the most difficult cases should children be taken from the school for treatment in special schools. Decisions about withdrawals are taken on the basis of an in-depth appraisal by the child's teacher and the educational psychologist of the pupil's strengths and weaknesses in coping with school work.

The practical application of these ideas by clinical educational psychologists profoundly changes their methods of operating with pupils who are failing. Wedell (1978b) points out the key difference: the fact that the 'battery' approach where the psychologist administers tests to investigate all conceivable underlying processes is largely a waste of time. Instead the psychologist takes the child backwards from the target task down the task hierarchy to the point where he reaches the component skill which the child has mastered. 'The target task will be defined in terms of the teacher's curricular objectives and the hierarchy will be determined *both* by the psychologist's analysis of the teacher's method of instruction, and by the child's performance on the elements of this analysis.' Readers will notice at once the similarity between this and the general line of argument of this book, in particular the sections on objectives, task analysis, and the diagnostic backtracking mentioned in the sections on programming teaching and testing. Diagnosis, seen as the continuous monitoring of pupils' developing capabilities rather than one-shot assessments, brings it within the competence of most teachers. This, combined with the adoption of systematic techniques for the creation of opportunities for children to learn using notions from psychopedagogy, will ensure that fewer 'hard-to-teach' children are produced (Stott 1978).

Specific disabilities

There is one further factor that may handicap children with learning problems and the teachers who try to help them, and that is the tendency to use labels for particular learning problems

Made to measure? 433

in a similar way to the way in which intelligence labels were used with children who had learning problems of a more general nature. One particular label in this genre is dyslexia. Dyslexia, commonly known as 'word blindness', is a term applied by some to characterize people with learning difficulties specific to reading. There is a school of thought which holds that the condition is different from other forms of difficulty in learning to read, in that it is a consequence of neurological impairment. This is an extremely high-level inference and there is no general agreement that there is really such a condition. It is suggested sometimes that the term has appeal because it is much less of a stigma to suffer from dyslexia than not to be able to read. Although it may console some, it may have adverse effects on teachers who may see it as a condition that rules out treatment or remediation in the same way as a low IQ was regarded by some. Although there is disagreement about the existence of a condition called 'dyslexia', there is general agreement about its treatment which follows the lines proposed above and in other parts of this book in respect of learning problems in general. There seems, therefore, little point in perpetuating its use, although there is little doubt that it will be with us for some time yet. Nor is it impossible that other conditions will appear – not excluding *dyspedeutia*, which I interpret as inability to teach!

18
Learning teaching

As I predicted in the early part of this book, a very large number of symbols have passed before your eyes since you read the first word. I hope that many of those symbols that were then strange and unfamiliar to you now appear less odd and more meaningful. If they do, it will be a small indication of success of the enterprise that started on that first page. It will also be another illustration of the power of language in human learning.

In those early pages I suggested that this lengthy procession of symbols, although following willy-nilly a linear sequence, does not produce a corresponding linear sequence of concepts in the reader's mind. Human learning is not like that. Human learning copes with the complexity inherent in the eternal parade of abstractions in linguistic attire by a process of reduction and concentration. Concentration in two senses: in the sense of active attention and in the sense of distillation. Distillation proceeds by bringing together the multitudinous abstractions in basic cognitive structures that change according to the experiences one has, in ways I have discussed in this book. Thus, although every

Learning teaching 435

reader has read the same words, every reader takes his personal message from his reading since this reading is coloured by what he brings to it in the way of his hopes, expectations, attitudes and other predispositions. All interact in complex ways with what one reads, to create a unique quintessential understanding.

I welcome this variety, since without it there can be no change or development. Teachers attempting to implement the same approaches will produce their own applications of theoretical principles, which will in their turn react on theory to enrich it, as I have argued at various places in the book.

Further, in their experimentation they will be learning what no book can teach – namely, how to teach. This follows because the best book can only develop understanding of theoretical principles and not show how to apply them. In the terms I have used in the book, the best a book can do is to help a reader develop type-C skills. To expand his competence he needs different types of experience. My suggestion would be that through the practising of type-B skills he would acquire the entry capability to tackle the learning of the type-A skills he wishes to deploy in actual teaching.

In my 'lessons from life' I have tried to help the reader in approaching the learning of type-B skills. In fact the intention was quite complex. I wished to put into practice the principles of teaching concepts that I preach by providing a variety of exemplars. At the same time I tried to demonstrate how protocol material, in these cases transcripts of classroom discourse, can be used to practise type-B skills. Beyond this, it seems to me, a book can do little if anything. Further and fuller practice of type-B skills using material taken from teaching situations of various kinds is probably the most helpful next step and, following that, to take the plunge into the practice of type-A skills and try to implement the principles in one's own practice.

Illusion and reality

I am conscious that my prescription is honoured almost entirely in the breach by most teacher-training institutions. Student teachers are invited to make the most prodigious leaps from

436 *Psychopedagogy*

lectures on theory to action in the classroom. Frequently they are expected to start by a brief skirmish with the realities of the classroom before encountering any theory at all. Often theory and practice are institutionally segregated, a practice that probably reflects a division in the minds of the providers as well as signalling to the student consumers the fact that theory is theory and practice is practice and never the twain shall meet.

Institutional signals such as these, amplified by theoretical studies often remote from reality, not surprisingly engender attitudes that see theoretical studies as peripheral to the real business of practical teaching. It is my hope that focusing on psychopedagogy as distinct from educational psychology and practical teaching will engender an attitude that makes the distinction between the two meaningless.

Mastering the model

One of the main consequences of the divorce between theory and practice is that neophyte teachers have little option but to turn to experienced practitioners for models of the practical skills of teaching. From our discussion about the learning of skills you may remember the problems inherent in the 'show and tell' method, not to mention the difficulties of looking and imitating. No matter how expert the teacher, he can only provide a limited range of exemplars of this most complex skill and can be of even more limited help in passing his skill to the learner teacher. In fact the deficiencies of the approaches that seek to model the master teacher are the obverse of those that seek to transmute the dross of lectures on recherché aspects of educational psychology into the gold of competent practice (Stones and Morris 1972).

The resolution of the opposition of the two unsatisfactory procedures is not to be found in a middle-road compromise but in form of synthesis that changes both and produces a new method of operation. This approach is of the type that Stolurow (1965) characterized as 'mastering the model'. It is the type of approach I have tried to expound in these pages, and involves the systematic practical analysis of the job of teaching in order to identify its key

Learning teaching 437

characteristics and then the attempt to master the type of activities the analysis identifies. This approach takes the view that there is little profit in trying to analyse teachers or pupils to identify their key characteristics in order to allocate them to appropriate treatments. Knowing that 'research shows' that good teachers are informal, reactionary, extrovert, democratic, white, right-handed, short females, especially when they teach introverted neurotic Anglo-Saxon pupils brimming over with nAch and communicating like mad by means of the elaborated code is of little help to the aspirant teacher who happens to be formal, progressive, introvert, authoritarian, black, left-handed, tall and male, and asked to teach pupils who are extroverted, stable, negroid, low on nAch but full of the restricted code. The mere contemplation of this *ignis fatuus* is, I hope, sufficient to convince us of its futility and to return us to our enterprise of identifying what makes good teaching rather than what makes good teachers.

This is your style

Curiously the single characteristic that one might reasonably expect to be a criterial attribute of a teacher has received little attention in the research literature. I refer to the teacher's attitude towards pupils. The question is: 'Does he like children and young people?' I do not mean this in any sloppy sense but in the sense of being respectful of them, concerned about them, interested in them and the things that interest them, and genuinely desirous of helping them to the best of one's ability. The characteristic sketched out by these attributes seems to me to be a *sine qua non* of being a teacher, and a person without it ought never to enter the profession.

On this essential foundation it is possible for most persons entering the profession to express the skills of teaching in their own way. The delineation of aspects of skills such as may be found in the various schedules provide heuristic devices that will help to guide one's steps without laying down exactly what one must do.

You may have heard talk about 'styles' of teaching, implying that there are readily identifiable approaches to the job that everyone can observe and agree on. Democratic, autocratic, expository,

438 *Psychopedagogy*

discovery-oriented, formal, informal, are all labels that have been applied at times to teaching. And like most dichotomous labels they are very misleading – in the first place because it is very difficult to reach a consensus on how they may be identified, and also because at different times teachers are likely to adopt different approaches. The open and inquiring conception of teaching I have been advocating should guide a teacher into varied ways of organizing children's learning. It is unlikely that he will adopt an entirely didactic expository approach because such an approach would make experiment very difficult.

Naturally the way one expresses the skills of teaching will be influenced by factors outside the scope of psychopedagogy. It is to be hoped that other aspects of courses of teacher preparation will help here in identifying and inculcating attitudes towards children and teaching which complement the work in psychopedagogy.

Cooperative diagnosis

Armed with a grasp of the principles of psychopedagogy and energized by a sense of vocation and a concern for your pupils, you will be well placed to master the teaching model. It will be of enormous value, however, if you can enlist the aid of others to help you acquire the various skills. If you are taking a course in teacher preparation your first appeal will naturally be to your teaching supervisor and/or the cooperating teacher in the school you happen to be in. But there are different ways of making use of your supervisor, and a little thought and planning will help you to get the maximum benefit from his cooperation.

In the first place you will want to know a little more about your teaching than that the observer thinks it good, bad or indifferent. Such global comments are of little use for two main reasons. One is that people's perceptions of what constitutes good teaching often do not coincide and the comments you receive might not be very reliable. The other reason is that such a comment is very coarse feedback. It may be reassuring to be told that your teaching is very good, or even perhaps satisfactory. But if there are weaknesses you need more information than that it is weak. Probably

Learning teaching 439

even the good and certainly the satisfactory performer would benefit from knowing his particular strengths and weaknesses. Allied to this is the fact that being more analytical informs you about the relative importance of the criteria by which your performance is being judged. Obviously the discovery that your main failing is your untidy appearance has different implications from being told that your reinforcing technique is weak or that the pupils aren't learning anything.

To help obtain this focus, the best thing to do is to discuss with the observer the objectives of the teaching before the event. Make some sort of analysis of the skills you expect to be involved, perhaps using some of the categories in the schedules. This will provide the necessary specific focus for you to receive maximum benefit from the post-teaching discussion as well as increasing the usefulness of any feedback you might get. Discussing these matters before the event permits a very important process of clarification. Having even a limited set of objectives or categories of observation will facilitate this clarification so that you will be in a position to arrive at some mutual understanding, not only about what are the things to be considered important and given particular attention, but also what each of you thinks is involved in the exercise of the activities listed in the schedules. You will also be able to come to some agreement as to what would be reasonable to consider satisfactory performance along the various dimensions on which you chose to concentrate. Ideally, in addition, you would be able to discuss the links between what you hoped to do in the teaching with the theory that you had previously discussed and tried to apply in different circumstances before actually coming to the practice of type-A teaching skills.

Having prepared the ground before the event, you should be able to discuss the teaching afterwards with reasonable chance of genuine communication. But in the complexities of the classroom your perceptions of what happened are unlikely to be the same as those of the observer, so that you may not agree about what actually took place, let alone about what the events signify. Some form of recording of the teaching can be of great assistance here. Video-recording techniques would be particularly useful but less obtrusive audio-recording could be of considerable help. The

440 *Psychopedagogy*

ability to replay the relevant parts of the teaching to establish what happened, and then to negotiate as to the significance of what you agree happened, is a very enlightening learning experience not only for the student teacher but also frequently for the observer.

It is unlikely that even if you are a student teacher you will have unlimited access to a supervisor to consult as I have suggested. But there are other ways of acquiring the feedback you need, and to those not in training who wish to appraise and improve their own performance these are particularly useful. The first possibility is to cooperate with colleagues by taking in each other's pedagogic washing. The procedures are the same as suggested in connection with working with a supervisor, except that you benefit not only from another person's appraisal of your performance but also from having to bring an analytical focus to bear on another person's performance. On the one hand you will get feedback about your performance implementing a type-A skill, actually teaching with the principles of psychopedagogy in mind; on the other hand you will be practising type-B skills in bringing to bear your understanding of psychopedagogical principles to appraise your colleague's teaching. In both instances the operation will be enhanced if some form of recording is made and use made of some device such as a schedule for focusing attention on crucial issues.

The principles of mutual assistance discussed here can be extended in a very useful way by involving other colleagues, with or without a supervisor. Small-group discussion of specific teaching episodes, focusing on specific key elements, combines some of the principles of concept teaching with the practice of type-B skills. If a small group of people meet to examine recordings of examples of each other's teaching, they are all practising type-B skills – that is, striving to apply theoretical principles to the appraisal of a practical activity, and at the same time encountering a variety of exemplars of the very complex concept of focused teaching. An additional benefit can frequently accrue from this type of activity. After a little experience of exposing oneself in public in this way, the critical appraisal of one's performance becomes less threatening and less personally felt. The comments of colleagues become to some extent objectified, so that it be-

Learning teaching 441

comes possible to accept criticism of your performance more as *a* piece of teaching than as *your* teaching, a phenomenon that holds considerable promise for group development of pedagogical skills.

In the absence of cooperative colleagues and supervisor all is not lost. It is possible with the use of simple recording devices to obtain a fair amount of feedback about one's performance if one uses a structured analytical instrument. Though it is true that this type of feedback may be less informative than when other people are involved, it can still be very helpful.

One other source of feedback is available but seldom considered. Pupils experience a great deal of teaching and it would not be unreasonable to suppose that they learn something about it through their experience. The question is whether their views about teaching can be of any help to a teacher anxious to improve his effectiveness. There is evidence that it can, indeed, be helpful (Meighan 1977, 1978; Veldman and Peck 1963). When the possibility of their comments being taken seriously is raised, pupils' reactions have been for them to take the matter seriously and do their best to make helpful comments. The feedback obtained is likely to be in somewhat different form from that obtained from colleagues using an analytical schedule, but it can be related to similar aspects of teaching. The interesting thing is that, when compared with comments and evaluations from peers, supervisors and cooperating teachers, and student teachers' self-assessments, the pupils' evaluations show a fair amount of agreement. This is a very interesting and suggestive source of feedback about teaching that offers far-reaching possibilities for the development of teaching, not the least for the impact it could have on the relationship between teacher and taught.

The acid test of teaching, as I have argued all along, is that the pupils learn something and like learning it. This final assessment of the extent of your success is something you may ascertain yourself. Whether or not you are able to do this will depend upon your understanding of modes of assessment and competence in implementing assessment techniques. This is where the evaluative sections in the schedules come in. They can guide your scrutiny to some extent, but of course the actual implementation of their suggestions will call for techniques based on the principles discussed

442 Psychopedagogy

in Chapters 16 and 17. A crucial thing in this connection is that you cannot get helpful feedback by using norm-referenced tests. The main type of feedback that these tests will provide is that A seems to be better than B at this or that and that the average mark of the class is so and so, a piece of information that may or may not signify that your teaching has been particularly successful if we assume that the touchstone of success is pupils' learning. Thus in order to get useful informative feedback that helps you to diagnose the strengths and weaknesses of your teaching you need criterion-referenced modes of assessment relating explicitly to the objectives you set for your teaching. Links of this type will emerge in the process of task analysis discussed in Chapter 10.

Helping

Throughout this discussion the assumption has been that the supervisor of a student teacher or the colleagues he cooperates with are helpers and not merely assessors. This assumption may not accord with practice in some institutions for teacher preparation. But in the same way as I would urge an inversion of the usual view of the assessment of pupils' learning – that is, seeing it as an indication of the success of the teacher's efforts rather than, or at least as well as, the pupils' – so I would urge a view of supervision as a form of teaching with the same basic rationale. With an approach like this, supervisor and student would be more in a counselling relationship than in one of assessment. The interview between supervisor and student teacher is a piece of teaching, in the course of which the supervisor could well be practising teaching skills appropriate to that type of teaching situation. I have already suggested one aspect of psychopedagogy common to teaching and to advisory sessions on teaching, namely, the value of presenting various exemplars of concepts. There is another important element: reinforcement. Beginning teachers need at least as much encouragement as pupils in their learning. Feedback and reinforcement do not always coincide but both are necessary.

I should now like to introduce my last 'lesson from life' which takes up the points about supervision being a form of teaching.

Learning teaching **443**

This extract is taken from a supervisory interview following a student teacher's practising of reinforcement with a small group of pupils. It is as genuine an example of counselling as can be expected from a recorded session.

LESSON FROM LIFE: 15*

The context for the extract is supplied by the supervisor who was a teacher in the school where the student was practising. The student had had some instruction about reinforcement and had discussed it with his supervisor and had read some literature about it. He had also been given an instrument to assist him to make an appraisal of his performance. The supervisor who had worked closely with the student teacher for over a month failed to detect any evidence in that time that he had any sense of humour. The lesson under scrutiny was taught, in the words of the supervisor, 'with grim determination'. Just before the extract begins, the supervisor had tried to set the student at ease by a jocular remark which produced no response, and in fact the supervisor felt he was on a sticky wicket, but eventually the dialogue started.

In the extract the supervisor's remarks are identified by S, the student teacher's by T.

1 (S) Of course you prepared a lesson and you had certain objectives in the lesson itself. You may say sort of behavioural objectives. What did you hope that the children would learn from the lesson itself?

2 (T) Well I hope that they would sort of pick up questions which would follow in and – what points I was looking for, and most of all respond to the questions.

3 (S) What were the objectives for that particular lesson that you taught there?

4 (T) As regards the pupils, I think to pick up the ideas of why castles very vaguely were built in the places they were like on top of the hill rather than underneath the hill, and judging from my point of view it was trying

* A. Selkirk (1976) *Microteaching*. Liverpool University. Mimeo.

444 *Psychopedagogy*

to get them to answer questions where I could try and respond.

5 (S) So you were as much aware of the fact that you were trying to reinforce as you were that you were teaching a lesson about castles?

6 (T) That's in fact one of the things that puts me most uneasy, that you sometimes think, well, exactly what word should I use there, and then I tend to find that if I deliberately think like that I end up by using words that sound false anyway.

7 (S) So you sort of use your natural reactions? You would say that you are a natural reinforcer anyway, would you?

8 (T) Not exactly a classic example of how to reinforce but I generally do try to encourage pupils – even if the answer is wrong.

9 (S) Did you predetermine what types of reinforcement you were going to use in the lesson and say 'I must make a point of reinforcing this way, that way and the other way?'

10 (T) Not really – going back again – I found – eh – that means I'm concentrating more on that than on the lesson and it tends to sound a little false the second I say it.

11 (S) So in a sense the lesson wasn't any different from any other lesson you might have taught? You weren't consciously thinking 'I must reinforce with the right word?'

12 (T) Only on the odd occasion.

13 (S) Well you would expect in a situation like this. In a sense it is a false situation and you are trying to highlight that particular skill. Do you think you taught a good reinforcing lesson?

14 (T) Eh –

15 (S) What is your own appraisal of the lesson?

Learning teaching 445

16 (T) I would say a little above average. I wouldn't say it was really good in that perhaps, as we noticed afterwards, I had left one pupil almost completely out of the lesson which wouldn't obviously have done his – eh – enthusiasm much good really.

17 (S) So you think that as well as reinforcing you must try to get participation going as well? I thought you succeeded very well in that really.

18 (T) Yes, as I say, it was just that one lad and I think that, rather than reinforce his enthusiasm, it just deadened it really.

19 (S) Actually, there was one particular instance when you could have pulled him in. Perhaps we'll find it in a moment. In this one instance there was a classic opportunity, as it were, when I thought you reinforced all of them very well. We'll look at that and see if we can see where the place is where you might have brought Steve in. One of the things I liked was that there was a quick succession of reinforcements with a lot of children early on which I felt set them at ease. I could see that right at the beginning of the tape. Maybe we could have a look at that first and you'll be able to see just what I mean there.
[There follows the first run back of the tape. S points out the quick succession of reinforcements, verbal, 'good', 'that's good', etc., and commends T for them.]

20 (S) You said 'Good', 'That's good' and then a sort of variation, 'Oh yes, that's good' which maybe added a little weight to the reinforcement. I suppose you feel that you have to watch out that it doesn't become stereotype (T: Yes) because otherwise, well, it doesn't really reinforce any more, it just becomes a stock reply to the answer to the question. I suppose the only real way that you feel it is reinforcing is if the children respond more spontaneously and accept what you have to say and obviously are the better for it. You felt that the lesson was good in that respect really?

446 *Psychopedagogy*

21 (T) With my personality I've got to hope that even if I'm saying the same phrases like 'Good' the kids will accept it sincerely.

22 (S) But did you not feel that, perhaps, in the lesson, there was nothing that required that extra little bit. I wondered whether there was the odd occasion . . .

23 (T) There was perhaps, it's again the fact that I don't sort of go overboard for praise and perhaps I missed out.

24 (S) That's possible but a point I was particularly interested in was when you saw the opportunity to reinforce the whole group rather than an individual pupil. I think I can find that and show you the point at which you did this very well.
[Second run back of the tape. The picture is held at the spot where T says 'Oh, good, everybody's in'. This was when in response to a question every hand shot up.]

25 (S) And that was just the moment – look at Steve sitting up in the corner there – when you might have said: 'Right, we'll have you, Steve', seeing as every hand was up.

26 (T) Yes, and there was another time when I noticed his hand was up there as well and I missed him.

27 (S) Yes, it's quite important that you should see that. But I did like that when you said 'Oh, good, everybody's in' and you grasped the opportunity of reinforcing the group and saying 'well it looks as if we're all together now' – I liked that. There is a point where I wondered whether you might just have put in a little extra reinforcement into an answer – an answer I thought was particularly good. Can you recall what it might have been?

28 (T) Eh . . . I think it was the one where, on the question of the siege when one side might have more food than the other.

29 (S) I think that was good but that wasn't the one I particularly had in mind. Let me just find the one that I

Learning teaching 447

thought perhaps might have benefited from a little extra word of praise.

[Run back to an instance where a child describes the windows of castles as slits 'to prevent arrows from going in'.]

30 (S) I thought that was a particularly good reply and instead of saying 'that's good' you might have said 'Now that's a *very good* answer' or something of the sort. The pupil has obviously thought about it – but still, it was there and you did say it was good. Do you think that your reinforcement might be a bit limited?

31 (T) Yes, but as I said before, I'm sort of trusting to luck, I don't know, I would rather that, if it is possible, the kids would get to realize that it is sincere rather than using a wide variety of phrases which, I must admit, as I say, sound false.

32 (S) Do you not feel that, perhaps, your emphasis was, on the whole, on verbal reinforcement? Because, it may be that you could consider that, by a smile and a look, not necessarily even a word, that you can reinforce, so perhaps it's worth looking at the odd other area of reinforcement that could be used. As I say, the non-verbal one, the nod, the obvious sign of pleasure on your part or the mmm or grunt, the sort of extra-verbal on top of the more usual ones but, on the whole I thought it was a good reinforcing lesson and I hope you felt it worthwhile coming along and worthwhile having a look at it and being able to see for yourself.

Before the counselling interview both supervisor and teacher had completed the schedule evaluating the lesson for the teacher's use of reinforcing techniques. The reinforcement was almost entirely verbal. The teacher rated his performance here fairly highly, the supervisor's rating was low to average (3 on a scale 1–7). Extra-verbal and non-verbal reinforcement were rated low to average by the teacher and the supervisor. In the interview the supervisor did his best to encourage as far as possible that which

448 *Psychopedagogy*

was commendable and tried to draw from the teacher any suggestions he could make to improve his performance for the future. Indications of this are to be seen in the transcript, but in addition to this the supervisor made use of very many non-verbal and extra-verbal reinforcers in order to encourage the teacher and draw him out. As the transcript attests, he had a difficult task.

The most striking overall impression that I receive from this transcript is the supervisor's extremely sensitive approach to the problem of helping the teacher to see that his technique of reinforcement was rather indifferent. Note how the supervisor tries to get the teacher to make his own appraisal of his efforts rather than giving him a list of strengths and weaknesses. A good example is the exchange beginning at 27 where S builds on a positive comment about T's use of reinforcement to introduce the suggestion in 30 that he could have been more commendatory of the pupils. Then again, in the final comment 32, even though S has failed to educe from T the recognition that he could have made use of non-verbal reinforcers, S makes a suggestion for T to consider, rather than telling him what he should have done. The last utterance raises important and interesting questions about the use of reinforcement that gives many people pause to think, including the teacher in this exchange. He was very afraid of insincere praise, see 31. As I suggested in my earlier consideration of reinforcement, this is a question that needs much more investigation. But there seems to me a fairly high probability that an important issue in teaching as it is now is the dearth of explicit encouragement. Perhaps we are making the price of our approbation too high and our fear of being hypocritical is an unfortunate consequence of that. Perhaps it is possible to be commendatory much more than most of us seem to be without being false and insincere. Perhaps a greater effort with non-verbal reinforcers would help us to cope with this unease. Perhaps a better understanding of the pupils' task when they come to learn what we try to teach might make us more appreciative of their efforts. I hope that some of the topics discussed earlier will facilitate such a reappraisal.

There is one other aspect of utterance 32 that raises an im-

Learning teaching **449**

portant question. What the supervisor says is at variance with what he thinks is the reality of the teacher's use of reinforcement. The question raised by the statement is to what extent we should give misleading feedback to learners, be they teachers or pupils, in our anxiety to be encouraging. In the case of this counselling encounter I would think myself that it would have been better had the supervisor not said that he thought the lesson was a good one from the point of view of reinforcement, since the teacher might have gone away thinking that there was little that he needed to do. On the other hand I must admit that many of the short-comings of the teaching had been pointed out, even if somewhat gently, and perhaps as much had been done at the one time as was possible. It is difficult to be sure about this and the reason for this difficulty is the extreme complexity of the situation. My own feeling is that in his zeal to be supportive the supervisor probably went too far and may have misled the teacher. I freely admit, however, that this is a question for conjecture: perhaps you might find it an interesting topic for discussion with colleagues. But I do not think that the problem is a very prevalent one. In my experience the overdoing of reinforcement is as rare in supervisory interviews as it seems to be in classrooms.

I should like to comment on one further aspect of the transcript. Note the use of the recording of the lesson. Had this recording not been available, the points relating to the brief excerpts could not have been made with the same effect as was possible using the recording. It is possible that it could not have been done at all since the supervisor had the use of the recording when he was evaluating the lesson before meeting the teacher. Without the recording he might never have picked up the points in the first place.

Utterance 26 provides a particularly interesting illustration. In the course of the lesson T had not noticed the boy was not partici-pating. On looking at the recording he notices it and S uses the point for specific focus. I suggest this is particularly interesting because it bears on the question of the scanning of the classroom (discussed in Chapter 12) to monitor what is happening. A person having difficulty doing this would almost certainly have difficulty realizing that there was a problem. The supervisor's focused

450 Psychopedagogy

commentary helps him to see the problem, which is the first step to doing something about it.

Much of the discussion of this transcript clearly relates more closely to the work of the supervisor than to that of the teacher. However, I hope that teachers and intending teachers will find the discussion of interest and profit. It is useful to remember that many of the points made would be applicable if you were involved as a person practising teaching in discussions with colleagues about aspects of their teaching. It may also be useful to try to open up lines of communication with your supervisor to bring out into the open some of the problems that both of you face. Teaching is a complex job; how much more complex is teaching teachers? All too little is known about either at present. A cooperative approach among teachers at all levels is more likely to extend our knowledge than maintaining barriers.

Teaching experiments

The same is true of the attitude that each venture into teaching is an experiment, even if only in a very small way. As I suggested in the first chapter, no lesson is ever the same as another, no matter how hard a teacher might try to make it so. This is not to say that every lesson should be entirely different from anything you have done before. If it were, it would be very difficult to ascertain which aspects of your teaching were likely to prove of abiding utility.

By the same token it is impossible to provide specific teaching prescriptions for all seasons and subjects. This is why I have tried to expound ideas that may be of some general utility rather than elucidate specifics appropriate to particular subjects or age groups. I hope that some indication of the mode of application of these general principles will have been obtained from the various examinations of their manifestations in the examples from different fields of learning and teaching and the 'lessons from life'. Your personal attempts to apply the principles to your own 'lessons from life' with an experimental cast of mind is likely to be the most effective way of clarifying and consolidating your understanding of the theory and practice of teaching.

The experimental cast of mind I referred to will, I hope, help

Learning teaching 451

you develop a habit of critically appraising not only your own practice but the preaching and practice of others. I am not recommending a cynical detachment, but a habit of examining on their merits the many nostrums and enthusiasms that teaching is prone to, and of not accepting pronouncements as truth without convincing evidence. Putting interesting hypotheses to the test in your own way may help to provide some of the evidence.

Envoi

If, dear reader, you have read this book because you are to become a teacher, it is highly likely that at some time you will meet the cynic with a poor opinion of theory ·who will tell you to put behind you all that childish stuff and come out into the real world.

You may find it difficult to resist social pressures like these. However, I hope you do, because it is only through the work of real teachers with some theoretical insight in real schools that there can be any substantial progress in the theory and practice of teaching.

BON VOYAGE

Summary

Chapter 1

The theme of the book is foreshadowed by a consideration of the crucial effect of a social environment and the use of language on human learning. Learning is observed when a more or less permanent change in behaviour caused by experience takes place. Teaching is seen as arranging suitable conditions for learning, and to optimize learning a systematic and analytic approach to teaching is recommended. Examples to illustrate the theme are taken from the work of Itard on socializing a feral child, the 'Wild Boy', and from attempts to teach chimpanzees to communicate through the use of sign language.

The thesis is developed that work such as this and also that of all the most important students of learning such as Pavlov and Skinner involves teaching as well as experimenting and that teaching itself is a form of experimentation. Both teachers and experimenters create problems for learners and study the way learners solve them. Teaching creates problems for learners that would never otherwise exist. This results in the developing of far more complex activities by learners, human or non-human, than

Summary 453

would otherwise be the case. Human beings acquire very much more complex behaviour than other species. Within the human species the view is taken that except in pathological cases learning capability among individuals is similar, so that it is possible to envisage a body of general principles of teaching that would be useful for most individual pupils. If pupils fail to learn, the principles must be scrutinized: this is a vital part of an experimental approach to pedagogy.

Chapter 2

Aspects of learning are now considered in more detail. Reinforcement is seen as a powerful determinant of human behaviour, but its effects are modified considerably by the influence of language and the influence of the social environment. Reinforcing every time is seen as most effective in establishing new learning, with intermittent reinforcement maintaining it in strength. Punishment is seen as of limited value in teaching, with various problems attached to its use. One of the problems is recognizing when a teacher is punishing a pupil by rejection of work. The use of extinction rather than punishment as a technique for reducing undesirable behaviour, in connection with either school work or conduct in the classroom, is suggested.

Reinforcement is instrumental in establishing patterns of discrimination and generalization but, as with other aspects of human learning, the processes are greatly affected by human use of language. Reinforcement and positive feedback often coincide, but sometimes in teaching it may be necessary to reinforce when the feedback is negative and would act as a punisher. The careful arranging of feedback and reinforcing in teaching is important in setting up complex patterns of behaviour as in learning sets. The work of Harlow in research on learning sets is seen as an example of an experimenter teaching in order to obtain information about learning.

Learning by imitation is seen as a useful form of learning but there are limitations that are not always appreciated. Particularly difficult is imitating complex skills such as teaching.

Affective or emotional factors are crucially important in learn-

454 *Summary*

ing. These factors are much influenced by reinforcement and punishment and express themselves in the motivation of the learner. Motivators relevant to school learning such as curiosity, success in learning, and the steps a teacher can take to enhance motivation in failing pupils are considered.

Chapter 3

Language transforms human learning in several ways. Teachers can tell learners what to do but in addition language makes possible human knowledge. The use of words as symbols transforms the processes of learning found in other animals so that humans can respond to categories of things, not just to individual items, and also to things that are not physically present and abstractions. Abstractions, referred to as *concepts*, are built on experience, and the main element in most teachers' jobs is the arranging of experiences for the pupils to build up complex bodies of concepts. Because words symbolize concepts, language enables us to juxtapose concepts in an infinite variety of ways, thus creating an enormously complex environment of abstractions to which humans have to learn to adapt.

Language enables learning to pass down the generations as well as from one person to another. This is achieved by the accretion of human artefacts, customs and skills that make the environment ever-increasingly complex. Schooling intensifies these effects and itself depends very much on language. Language is not merely used to label concepts; its process function is crucial in concept learning. Labels can hinder learning, as when the word is learned but not the concept it symbolizes. Labels are sometimes used as if they have explanatory power, which deflects attention from basic learning difficulties.

Chapter 4

Language and thinking are closely connected. Through experience, the use of their own language and the influence of adult language, children gradually acquire a view of the world resembling that of adults. Piaget has examined this process closely and

Summary 455

has advanced an explanatory scheme that sees the development as a succession of stages. This view has implications for teaching in view of suggestions about particular sequences and timing of development. Other people are critical of some of the formulations of Piaget and have advanced evidence contrary to his theses.

Soviet psychologists have made a particular study of the effects of language on human actions. They see the development of children's self-regulatory activity as initially mediated by the language of adults and gradually becoming independent. In the progress towards independence children's own speech aids their self-regulatory activity and their development of concepts of different levels of complexity. Overt speech gradually becomes internalized and ever more closely identified with thinking.

Bruner has argued that human learning is mediated by different modes of internal representation related to motor activity, imagery and symbolization. Criticism of this view hinges particularly on the role of imagery.

Some workers argue that cognitive development depends much more on active intervention by teachers than is usually believed. With an approach that analyses the learning task, the rate and sequence of development could be affected.

Chapter 5

Teachers use language to guide learning by cueing learners at crucial points in the learning of tasks. By its use they are also able to share their thoughts with learners. In teaching, oral exchanges between teacher and pupils fulfil many complex functions – monitoring and cueing learning, heightening salience in key aspects of concepts, prompting, and functions connected with managerial activities.

There is a good deal of evidence that much teacher talk presents difficulties to pupils because of misapprehension by teachers of the level of conceptual development of pupils. Pupils learn words but misunderstand the concept or do not learn the concept at all. Analysing classroom discourse can give useful insights into problems such as these.

456 *Summary*

Chapter 6

Various methods of analysing classroom discourse have been developed. Many categorize the discourse in different ways such as talk by the teacher and by pupils: questioning, answering, volunteering information, giving instructions, commending, and so on. Different systems have different purposes. Some focus on the pedagogical significance of the discourse; others are more interested in it from a social, psychological or anthropological viewpoint. Some critics of verbal-interaction analysis argue that it gives a very distorted picture of the reality of classroom life. Naturally this method of analysis cannot catch non-verbal elements, which are sometimes of crucial importance. Sometimes non-verbal interaction negates the ostensible message of the verbal.

Chapter 7

Analysis of learning problems is seen as crucial not only for efficient teaching but for the development of pedagogical theory. Setting aims and arranging teaching to achieve them will enable teachers to obtain feedback about their teaching by assessing their success in achieving the objectives. *Objectives* is a more precise term than *aims*, and the suggestion is that these should be expressed in very explicit and unambiguous terms stating what the end state of the learner should be.

Deciding on appropriate objectives is likely to be a question of reaching consensus among colleagues. Meaningful agreement will be more likely if the objectives are specified analytically. Methods of analysing objectives usually involve a hierarchical approach. The most widely known method is the Bloom taxonomy originally intended to aid the classification of test questions. Cognitive operations are classified hierarchically according to complexity. Similar taxonomies have been produced in the affective domain and in the psychomotor domain. The taxonomies are of limited use in the production of objectives. I have outlined a method of producing objectives by a process of analysis of the types of skills involved in a given learning task and the types of concepts a

Summary 457

learner needs to master in order to deploy the skills effectively. In addition to the cognitive objectives there are affective objectives in any field of learning which may be summed up by a statement such as the learner should like the experience sufficiently for him to wish to continue or come back for more.

There is a problem in producing objectives. The operation is potentially very time-consuming and also difficult. Establishing objectives for a whole field of study would produce very large numbers of objectives that might end by being counterproductive. A commonsense approach that tackles a limited field is likely to be more productive. However, the task does not have to be repeated in total every time the teaching recurs, but will stand for some time subject to renewal of aspects that are seen as obsolescent.

Some people do not care for this approach to objectives and fear that it might have a stultifying influence on teaching. I do not agree and argue that stultifying influences are produced by stultifying teachers, not the objectives, which are neutral in that respect.

Chapter 8

Objectives determine the goals of teaching; to establish the method of achieving them involves the examination of the related teaching. This can be done by analysing the teaching task to establish the nature of the skills the learner has to acquire and then deciding on the type of learning necessary to acquire them. Similarly the nature of the concepts to be learned needs to be established, and approaches to teaching them decided. The act of teaching will reveal the extent of the effectiveness of the analysis and the suitability of the objectives, as well as suggesting to us methods of improving both these and the teaching.

Chapter 9

Implementing teaching plans involves the deployment of certain key teaching skills. Currently teaching skills are not conceived as having any particular conceptual relationships. Some form of classification of skills is desirable to establish interrelationships

458 *Summary*

and to help establish a theoretical basis for them. Teaching skills can be conceived of according to the scheme proposed for the production of objectives. The most complex skill would be the application of psychological principles in actual teaching. The next most complex would be the skill of evaluating a piece of teaching or a representation of it according to psychological principles. The least complex skill would be knowing the psychological principles relevant to particular teaching skills.

Probably the most important application of these aspects of skill teaching is in teaching concepts. Effective concept teaching needs to take into account what is known about concept learning and to apply it systematically. Guidance can be obtained from a schedule of teacher activities in relation to concept teaching. Examination of transcripts of classroom discourse reveals little evidence of the systematic application of knowledge about concept learning to teaching. However, it would be very difficult to spend the whole of the time implementing suitable procedures for teaching concepts. Management activities take up a good deal of the time of a teacher. This is not entirely a bad thing. Time out from concentrated teaching and learning is essential for both teacher and learners. What constitutes a reasonable balance between the two is unknown at present.

Chapter 10

The teaching of psychomotor skills is a task not only for craft and physical education teachers but also for most other teachers, since they are likely to be faced at times with problems of teaching such skills. Although, basically, such skills depend upon less complex learning than concept learning, concept learning is often involved as well as motor activity. Similar approaches to task analysis as are employed in other forms of teaching are appropriate. Showing and telling and then expecting pupils to be able to copy the skill is not likely to be very successful. Explanation of the nature of the task, cueing, guiding, providing guided practice with consistent feedback are all crucial elements in teaching these skills. The teaching of many psychomotor skills is handicapped by the lack of analysis of the constituent elements.

Summary 459

Chapter 11

Ideally most of the teaching we engage in should prepare pupils to solve problems. Basically this involves them in applying what they have learned to novel situations. In addition to teaching pupils skills and bodies of concepts relating to learning in specific fields, it is also useful to give them some idea about ways of tackling problems. One approach is through applying algorithms, an approach that has great potential for the application of straightforward logical procedures to solve problems. This method can be taught, but it is important to ensure that the users of algorithms have the necessary prerequisite skills and concepts or the learner will have problems.

Heuristic approaches are less clearly structured than algorithms and are applicable to problems that are not susceptible of logical analysis by an algorithmic method. Teaching methods of attacking problem solving resemble the approaches to teaching skills mentioned earlier. Creativity seems to be a special case of problem solving and might profitably be cultivated in the same way as problem solving.

Chapter 12

The skill of using reinforcement is very important. Learning gradients should be arranged so as to provide maximum opportunity for the learner to succeed as he proceeds. There are serious problems in arranging reinforcement for a whole class of pupils. Careful analysis of tasks and pre-planning with the provision of reinforcers not dependent upon the teacher can help. Vicarious reinforcement is possible by reinforcing the whole class and by encouraging cooperative working.

Undesirable behaviour, whether related to learning or to class conduct, is best ignored where possible in order to extinguish it. Punishing to stop unwanted behaviour is rarely effective and can create other problems, not least by creating a negative affective atmosphere in the classroom if used overmuch. There are serious problems of identifying punishers and in being consistent in

460 *Summary*

applying extinction techniques that need constant and careful observation by the teacher.

Problems may arise when feedback and reinforcement are discordant. In such cases it is desirable to reinforce the effort and to exercise one's judgement as to the way feedback involving knowledge or lack of success should be presented.

An individual's history of reinforcement is very important in the development of motivation. Intrinsic motivation related to learning tasks is to be desired and can be influenced by careful organizing of learning experiences including ample opportunity for the reinforcement of success and teacher approval.

Examination of transcripts of classroom discourse suggest that rather little verbal reinforcement takes place in the average classroom. This is not the whole story, since non-verbal reinforcers are important too. Much more information is needed about this aspect of classroom interaction.

Chapter 13

Many of the teaching skills used in approaches to teaching such as microteaching are seen as second-order skills to the ones discussed above. The method of analysis adopted in relation to those skills enables us to establish relationships among the various skills and lays the foundations for some form of taxonomy. It may be that there is a superordinate skill of decision making. This possibility accords with the suggestions made earlier in the book that teaching should be conceived as experimentation, even if only in a modest way. A teacher having an outlook like this will not take the schedules proposed in these chapters as writ from on high to be followed unquestioningly, but as guides to action to be tested empirically. In other words, to be used as heuristic devices.

Chapter 14

Programmed learning is a carefully structured approach to teaching which raised great passions in the early sixties. Different approaches to programming were proposed but there seems very little basic difference among them. Teaching programmes can be

Summary 461

constructed in very many different ways and do not have to be entirely verbal. They can be designed to make use of adjunctive material and involve the learner in activities away from the programme. Such programmes may be seen as control centres in a system of learning. Various methods of construction are possible, but the basic features are the careful preparation of the teaching material and the empirical validation. Potential users of teaching programmes should insist on seeing validation data and make decisions about using the programme only after scrutinizing these data and the criterion test that should go with the programme. Although the difficulty in preparing programmes has led to there being very few around, the exercise of programme writing is very valuable and worth the attention of all teachers.

Chapter 15

The key aspect of programme validation is whether it achieves its objectives or not. That is, it is a paradigm of good teaching. The objective is almost invariably that the person using it will learn something. Thus the instrument used to assess learning in connection with the programme is of crucial importance. The test should therefore be geared to the same objectives as the programme. The same should apply to tests in general, but very often the connections are rather tenuous; this could well be a consequence of vague objectives.

A great problem in testing is the avoidance of superficial testing. Tests frequently assess learning at the lowest level of understanding, but they should be valid test pieces of the behaviour which the teaching is intended to develop. All aspects of the learning should be sampled.

Simple skills can be tested directly by getting the learner to perform. More complex skills and concept learning frequently cannot. In such testing it is essential to go beyond the teaching and test the learner's competence in applying the learning in new circumstances.

Many tests in current use are not directly related to the achievement of objectives related to teaching, but are designed to discriminate among pupils to produce rank orders according to test

462 *Summary*

score (norm-referenced tests). There are problems in this approach to testing, one of which is that the global score does not provide diagnostic feedback to teacher and learner in the way that tests designed to assess the achievement of objectives do (criterion-referenced tests). Sometimes tests comprise sub-tests. Similar global scores on such tests could be made up of very different patterns of sub-test scores and could, therefore, be misleading. In fact there is a serious problem connected with adding any scores together, since we can never be certain that the test items are of equivalent difficulty. (In fact, in many approaches to testing, items of different levels of difficulty are deliberately selected.)

Deciding whether a test is valid is a very difficult task. The most appropriate approach at present seems to be by the consensus of experts in the field. This is a form of face or content validity. Other methods are open to various criticism. Statistical methods used in connection with testing are almost exclusively related to norm-referenced testing and are not relevant to criterion-referenced testing. The effects of tests on pupils and students, and their attitudes to them, is an under-researched field, but it is probable that some effects are undesirable. More consideration needs to be given to this feature of testing and the other problems discussed than is at present.

Chapter 16

Test construction is more difficult than is often acknowledged. Essay-type tests, which are largely in use in English education, often fail to do what they are thought to do because of a number of deficiencies of this kind of test. Objective or short-answer-type tests can cope with many of the problems of essay tests but they are also prone to defects. Both kinds of tests may actually test rote learning when they are intended to test the grasp of concepts and abilities in skills. Different types of objective-test items may be used in the construction of versatile tests. The key consideration in the construction of these tests is that they test transfer of learning. Having in mind the suggested three types of skill when constructing items can help to ensure this.

Summary 463

Criterion-referenced tests can be fitted into systems of teaching more effectively than norm-referenced tests. This is because they are more useful in monitoring the learning of the pupils and the teaching of the teachers. They are useful for the diagnosis of learning. For these reasons, among others, there is much to be said for the adoption by schools and other institutions of externally moderated but internally produced tests integrated with the teaching and the institutional objectives.

Chapter 17

Many attempts are made to categorize pupils. Some of them are not explicitly intended to apply to teaching but they often do impinge on it. Intelligence and aspects of personality are the most common attributes used in classification. There are so many ways of categorizing pupils that the hope of providing optimum learning environments for each category of child is probably impossible to achieve, even if the theoretical bases for the various categories were sound. In fact there is a substantial body of opinion that considers the foundation to be unsound. Another serious problem with the various methods of categorizing pupils is that the category labels frequently influence teachers' attitudes towards pupils to create expectations that may be deleterious. Some authors impute to categories of people qualities that could bear on the type of teaching appropriate to their capabilities. Jensen believes that black people are inferior at conceptual learning than white and recommends a different pedagogy. This position is a dubious one and the pedagogical recommendation is inappropriate, whatever the validity of his basic premises. Bernstein argues that middle-class children use a linguistic 'code' that differs from that of working-class children, and that there is a connection between the code used and verbal intelligence. The hypothesis has been strongly challenged and seems insecure.

The acceptance of labelling hypotheses such as those mentioned as verified theory can have serious consequences if it leads teachers to develop attitudes towards pupils based on them.

The search for methods of differentiating among children may have the opposite effect from the one usually intended. Instead

464 *Summary*

of helping individual learners to learn more effectively by examining the pedagogical principles and practices employed, it focuses attention on dubious personal qualities. The most fruitful approach to the study of individual differences is as diagnostic assessment of a learner's existing capabilities relating to specific learning tasks.

Intelligence tests, which were once the main instruments used in identifying learning difficulties, are now being replaced by a form of experimental investigation in which teachers and psychologists diagnose learning problems by systematic observation of the child in school. The DES report on special education recommends the discontinuance of labelling disabilities and that special attention should be given to the subject of special education in teacher training. The view is expressed that the approach to teaching proposed in this book is in line with proposals for remedial teaching. Reference is made to the fact that the work of professional educational psychologists and teachers has much in common and is, in fact, in some cases, developing along similar lines.

Chapter 18

The complexity of the skill of teaching ensures that any constituent body of knowledge or sub-skills will be expressed in ways personal to individual teachers. It is therefore more likely to be helpful to teaching if the overall task is analysed and studied to find out what are the important things in the job rather than merely observing individual teachers at work. This approach is consistent with the one outlined in Chapter 1, of teachers as experimenters.

Improvement in teaching can be assisted by the comments of others. It is important to clarify the objectives of teaching and criteria of effectiveness before teaching if maximum benefit is to be obtained. The level of success of the pupils in achieving the objectives set is the key criterion that informs a teacher of his success. In any process of supervision of teaching, the relationship of supervisor and teacher should be seen as a helping one rather than an evaluatory one. Recordings of teaching can be very useful in identifying strengths and weaknesses in teaching.

Summary 465

Since all lessons are unique, it is not possible to give teaching prescriptions suitable to all conditions. In working out in his own way general principles thought to be relevant, a teacher will deepen his understanding of both the principles and his practice. Theory-informed practice of this type should help teachers to cultivate a critical cast of mind that will enable them to test hypotheses from psychology themselves rather than accepting them as received truths.

References

ALLEN, E. A., and RYAN, K. (1969) *Microteaching.* Addison Wesley.

ARGYLE, M. (1969) *Social Interaction.* Methuen.

AUSUBEL, D. P. (1963) *The Psychology of Meaningful Verbal Learning.* Grune and Stratton.

AUSUBEL, D. P. (1968) *Educational Psychology: A Cognitive View.* Holt, Rinehart and Winston.

AUSUBEL, D. P., and ROBINSON, F. G. (1969) *School Learning: An Introduction to Educational Psychology.* Holt, Rinehart and Winston.

AXELROD, S. (1977) *Behavior Modification in the Classroom.* McGraw-Hill.

AZRIN, N. H., and HOLTZ, W. C. (1966) 'Punishment'. In W. K. Honig (ed.), *Operant Behaviour: Areas of Research and Application.* Appleton-Century-Crofts, 1966. 380–47.

BAKER, J. P., and CRIST, J. L. (1971) 'Teacher Expectancies: A Review of the Literature'. In Elashoff and Snow (1971), 48–64.

BARNES, D. (1969) *Language, the Learner and the School.* Penguin.

BENJAMIN, H. (1939) In J. A. Peddiwell, *The Saber-Tooth Curriculum.* McGraw-Hill, 1939.

BERNSTEIN, B. (1973) *Class, Codes and Control.* Paladin.

References 467

BINET, A. (1911) 'A Study of the Effects of Differential Stimulation on the Mentally Retarded'. Quoted by Clark, A. N. and Clark, A. D. (1966), 145.

BJORSTEDT, A. (1968) *Preparation Process and Product in Teacher Pupil Interaction*. Malmo School of Education. Mimeo.

BLOOM, B. S. (1976) *Human Characteristics and School Learning*. McGraw-Hill.

BLOOM, B. S. (ed.) *et al.* (1956) *A Taxonomy of Educational Objectives: Handbook I: The Cognitive Domain*. Longmans, Green.

BLYTH, W. A. L. (1976) 'Non-Verbal Elements in Education: Some New Perspectives'. *British Journal of Educational Studies*, XXIV, 2, 109–26.

BORG, W. R., LANGER, P., and KELLEY, M. L. (1970) 'The Minicourse: A New Tool for the Education of Teachers'. *Education*. February–March, 1–7.

BRACKBILL, Y. (1962) In R. A. Bauer (ed.), *Some Views on Soviet Psychology*. American Psychological Association, 1962.

BRITISH PSYCHOLOGICAL SOCIETY (1976) 'Summary of Evidence Presented by the BPS to the Enquiry into Special Education set up by the Department of Education and Science'. *Bulletin of the British Psychological Society*, 29, 1, 1–6.

BROWN, R. (1973) *A First Language*. Allen and Unwin.

BROWN, R. and HERRNSTEIN, R. J. (1975) *Psychology*. Methuen.

BRUNER, J. S. (1964) 'The Course of Cognitive Growth'. *American Psychologist*, 19, 1–9.

BRUNER, J. S. (1966) *Toward a Theory of Instruction*. Belknap Press, Harvard University Press.

BRUNER, J. S., GOODNOW, J. J., and AUSTIN, G. A. (1956) *A Study of Thinking*. Wiley.

BRUNER, J. S., OLVER, R. R., and GREENFIELD, P. M. (1966) *Studies in Cognitive Growth*. Wiley.

BRYANT, P. (1974) *Perception and Understanding in Young Children*. Methuen.

BUROS, O. K. (1977) 'Fifty Years of Testing. Some Reminiscences, Criticisms, and Suggestions'. *Educational Researcher*, 6, 7, July–August.

BUTCHER, H. J. (1968) *Human Intelligence: Its Nature and Assessment*. Methuen.

468 References

CHOMSKY, N. (1965) *Aspects of the Theory of Syntax*. MIT Press.

CLARK, A. N., and CLARK, A. D. (eds) (1966) *Mental Deficiency: The Changing Outlook*. Methuen.

COLE, M., GAY, J., GLICK, J. A., and SHARP, D. W. (1971) *The Cultural Context of Learning and Thinking*. Methuen.

COLE, M., and SCRIBNER, S. (1974) *Culture and Thought*. Wiley.

COLLEGES OF EDUCATION RESEARCH GROUP (1969) *Objectives in the Teaching of the Philosophy of Education*. University of Birmingham School of Education. Mimeo.

COMMUNITY RELATIONS COMMISSION/ABC NEWS USA (1970) *The Eye of the Storm*. 35 minutes, colour.

COULTHARD, M. (1969) 'A Discussion of Restricted and Elaborated Code'. *Educational Review*, 22, 1, 38–50.

CROWDER, N. A. (1962) *The Arithmetic of Computers: An Introduction to Binary and Octal Mathematics*. English Universities Press.

DANIELS, J. C., and DIACK, H. (1958) *The Standard Reading Tests*. Chatto and Windus.

DAVIES, I. K. (1976) *Objectives in Curriculum Design*. McGraw-Hill.

DELAMONT, S. (1975) 'Participant Observation and Educational Anthropology'. *Research Intelligence*, 1, 1, 13–21. British Educational Research Association.

DEPARTMENT OF EDUCATION AND SCIENCE (1975) *A Language for Life*. HMSO.

DEPARTMENT OF EDUCATION AND SCIENCE (1978) *Warnock Report*. HMSO.

DONALDSON, M. (1978) *Children's Minds*. Fontana.

DOWNING, J. (n.d.) *Children's Developing Concepts of Spoken and Written Language*. University of Victoria, BC. Mimeo.

DOWNING, J. (1970) 'Children's Concepts of Language in Learning to Read'. *Educational Research*, 12, 106–12.

DRABMAN, R. S., JARVIE, G. J., and ARCHBOLD, J. (1976) 'The Use of Extinction in Classroom Behavioural Programs'. *Psychology in the Schools*, 13, 4, 470–6.

DUNKIN, M. J., and BIDDLE, B. J. (1974) *The Study of Teaching*. Holt, Rinehart and Winston.

References 469

DUTHIE, J. H. (1970) *Primary School Survey: A Study of the Teacher's Day*. Scottish Education Department. HMSO (Edinburgh).

EBEL, R. L. (ed.) (1969) *Encyclopaedia of Educational Research*. American Educational Research Association.

EDUCATION TESTING SERVICE (1961) *Making the Classroom Test*. Evaluation and Advisory Service Series Number 4. Princeton, New Jersey.

ELASHOFF, J. O., and SNOW, R. E. (1971) *Pygmalion Reconsidered*. C. A. Jones.

ENTWISTLE, N. J. (1975) 'Personality and Academic Attainment'. In *Personality and Learning* (1). Open University.

FAWTHROP, T. (1968) *Education or Examination*. Radical Student Alliance.

FINEMAN, S. (1977) 'The Achievement Motive Construct and its Measurement: Where are we now?' *British Journal of Psychology*, 68, 1–22.

FLANDERS, N. (1963) *Teacher and Classroom Influence on Individual Learning*. Paper presented at the Seventh Annual Curriculum Research Institute, Eastern Section, Association for Supervision and Curriculum Development, USA.

FLANDERS, N. (1970) *Analyzing Teacher Behaviour*. Addison Wesley.

FLAVELL, J. H. (1963) *The Developmental Psychology of Jean Piaget*. Van Nostrand.

FLESHNER, E. A. (1963) 'The Mastery by Children of Some Concepts in Physics'. In Simon and Simon (1963). Also reprinted in Stones (1970a).

FODOR, J. A. (1972) 'Some Reflections on L. S. Vigotsky's "Thought and Language"'. *Cognition*, 1, 1, 83–95.

FODOR, J. A. (1976) *The Language of Thought*. Harvester.

FORD TEACHING PROJECT UNIT 4 (n.d.) *The Castles Group*, Ken Forsyth. Centre for Applied Research in Education, University of East-Anglia.

FORD TEACHING PROJECT UNIT 3 (n.d.) *Implementing the Principles of Inquiry/Discovery Teaching: Some Hypotheses*, Compiled by C. Adelman *et al*. Centre for Applied Research in Education, University of East Anglia.

470 *References*

FORD TEACHING PROJECT UNIT I (n.d.) *Primary School Elective Tasks*. Centre for Applied Research in Education, University of East Anglia.

GAGG, J. C. (1966) 'The Age of the Flame Gunners'. *Times Educational Supplement*, 1 April, 1013.

GAGNÉ, R. M. (1977) *The Conditions of Learning*. Holt, Rinehart and Winston.

GALPERIN, P. Y. (1957) In Simon (1957).

GLASER, R. (1972) 'Individuals and Learning: The New Aptitudes'. *Educational Researcher*, June.

GLIDEWELL, J. C., and STRINGER, L. A. (1967) *Early Detection of Emotional Illness in School Children*. St Louis, Mo., County Health Department, Division of Research and Development, USA. In Kirkland (1971).

GOOD, T. L., and BROPHY, J. E. (1973) *Looking in Classrooms*. Harper and Row.

GOYDER, D. G. (1862) *Autobiography of a Phrenologist*. London.

GREENFIELD, P. M. (1966). In Bruner *et al.* (1966).

GUILFORD, J. P. (1967) *The Nature of Human Intellect*. McGraw-Hill.

GULLIFORD, R. (1971) *Special Educational Needs*. Routledge and Kegan Paul.

HAMILL, D., and WIEDERHOLT, J. L. (1972) *The Resource Room: Rationale and Implementation*. Pennsylvania, Journal of Special Education Press.

HANSEN, S., and JENSEN, J. (1971) *The Little Red School-Book*. Stage 1.

HARLOW, H. F. (1949) 'The Formation of Learning Sets'. *Psychological Review*, 56, 51–65.

HARROW, A. J. (1972) *A Taxonomy of the Motor Domain*. McKay.

HAYES, K. J., and HAYES, C. (1951) 'Intellectual Development of a Home-Raised Chimpanzee'. *Proceedings of the American Philosophical Society*, 95, 105–9.

HEGARTY, S. (1977) 'Fair Play in Assessment'. *Times Educational Supplement*, 13, May, 39–40.

HERRIOT, P. (1970) *An Introduction to the Psychology of Language*. Methuen.

References 471

HILL, B. (1972) 'Piaget now'. *Times Educational Supplement*, 18 November.

HILSUM, S., and CANE, B. (1971) *The Teacher's Day*. National Foundation for Educational Research.

HOGBEN, L. (1955) *Man Must Measure: The Wonderful World of Mathematics*. Rathbone.

HOLLAND, J. G., and SKINNER, R. F. (1961) *The Analysis of Behaviour*. McGraw-Hill.

HUNT, W. A., and MATARAZZO, J. D. (1973) 'Three Years Later: Recent Developments in the Experimental Modification of Smoking Behaviour'. *J. Abnorm. Psychol.*, 81, 107–14.

INSEL, S. A., and JACOBSON, L. F. (1975) *What Do You Expect?* Cummings.

ITARD, J. M. G. (1801) *The Wild Boy of Aveyron*. Trans. G. and M. Humphrey. Appleton-Century-Crofts, 1962.

JACKSON, L. A. (1974) 'The Myth of the Elaborated and Restricted Code'. *Higher Education Review*, 6, 2, 65–81.

JENSEN, A. R. (1973) 'Level I and Level II Abilities in Three Ethnic Groups'. *American Education Research Journal*, 4, 10, 263–76.

JOINT COMMITTEE ON PROGRAMMED INSTRUCTION AND TEACHING MACHINES (1966) *Recommendations for Reporting the Effectiveness of Programmed Instructional Materials*. Washington, DC, Division of Audiovisual Instruction, National Education Association.

KAMIN, L. J. (1977) *The Science and Politics of IQ*. Penguin.

KIRKLAND, M. C. (1971) 'The Effects of Tests on Students and Schools'. *Review of Educational Research*, 41, 4, October.

KOHL, H. (1969) *The Open Classroom*. New York Review.

KOHL, H. (1977) *On Teaching*. Methuen.

KOUNIN, J. (1970) *Discipline and Group Management in Schools*. Holt, Rinehart and Winston.

KRATHWOHL, D. R., BLOOM, B. S., and MASIA, B. B. (1964) *Taxonomy of Educational Objectives: Handbook II: The Effective Domain*. McKay.

LABOV, W. (1972) 'The Logic of Non-Standard English'. In Giglioli P. P. (ed.), *Language and Social Context*. Penguin.

LANDA, L. N. (1976) 'The Ability to Think – How Can it be Taught?' *Soviet Education*, March, 4–66.

472 References

LANE, H. (1977) *The Wild Boy of Aveyron*. Allen and Unwin.

LANGE, M., and HORA, F. B. (1963) *Collins Guide to Mushrooms and Toadstools*. Collins.

LEACH, D. J., and RAYBOULD, E. C. (1977) *Learning and Behavioural Difficulties in Schools*. Open Books.

LINDEN, E. (1976) *Apes, Men and Language*. Penguin.

LIUBLINSKAYA, A. A. (1957) 'The Development of Children's Speech and Thought'. In Simon (1957). Reprinted in Stones (1970).

LUCHINS, A. (1942) 'Mechanization in Problem Solving: The Effect of Einstellung'. *Psychol. Monogr.*, 54, 6.

LUNZER, E. A. (1968) *Development in Learning 1: The Regulation of Behaviour*. Staples.

LURIA, A. R. (1960) *The Role of Speech in the Formation of Temporary Connexions and the Regulation of Behaviour in the Normal and Oligophrenic Child*. Department of Psychology, Moscow University. In Simon and Simon (1963).

LURIA, A. R. (1961) *The Role of Speech in the Regulation of Normal and Abnormal Behaviour*. Pergamon Press.

LURIA, A. R., and YUDOVICH, F. Y. (1959) *Speech and the Development of Mental Processes in the Child*. Staples.

MCCLELLAND, D. C., ATKINSON, J. W., CLARK, R. A., and LOWELL, E. L. (1953) *The Achievement Motive*. Appleton-Century-Crofts.

MCLEISH, J. (1976) 'Learning in Groups: Facilitation and Inhibition Processes'. *British Psychological Society Bulletin*, 29, 1, 7–15.

MAGER, R. F. (1975) *Preparing Instructional Objectives*. 2nd ed. Fearon.

MAGER, R. F., and CLARK, C. (1963) 'Explorations in Student Controlled Instruction'. *Psychological Reports*, 13, 71–6.

MEIGHAN, R. (1977) 'Pupils' Perceptions of Classroom Techniques'. *British Journal of Teacher Education*, 3, 2, 139–48.

MEIGHAN, R. (ed.) (1978) 'The Learner's Viewpoint'. *Educational Review*, Special Number (10), 30, 2.

MERRIT, J. (1969) 'Reading Skills Re-Examined'. *Special Education*, 58, 1, 18–21.

References 473

MINISTRY OF EDUCATION (1955) *Report of the Committee on Maladjusted Children*. (The Underwood Report.) HMSO.

MITTLER, P. J. (1970) *The Psychological Assessment of Mental and Physical Handicap*. Tavistock.

MORRIS, D. (1967) *The Naked Ape*. Penguin.

MOSS, R. W., and KAGAN, J. (1961) 'Stability of Achievement and Recognition Seeking Behaviors from Early Childhood through Adulthood'. *Journal of Abnormal and Social Psychology*, 62, 504–13.

O'CONNOR, N., and HERMELIN, B. (1963) *Speech and Thought in Severe Subnormality*. Pergamon.

O'LEARY, K. D., and O'LEARY, S. G. (1977) *Classroom Management: The Successful Use of Behaviour Modification*. Pergamon.

OLERON, P. (1957) *Research on the Mental Development of Deaf Mutes*. National Centre for Scientific Research, Paris.

PAGE, E. B. (1958) 'Teacher Comments and Student Perfomances: A Seventy-Four Classroom Experiment in School Motivation'. *Journal of Educational Psychology*, 49, 173–81.

PANLASIGUI, I., and KNIGHT, F. B. (1930) 'The Effect of Awareness of Success or Failure'. In F. B. Knight (ed.), *Twentyninth Yearbook of the National Society for the Study of Education: Report of the Society's Committee on Arithmetic*. University of Chicago.

PAVLOV, I. P. (1941) *Selected Works*. Foreign Languages Publishing House, Moscow.

PAVLOV, I. P. (1955) *Lectures on Conditioned Reflexes*. Trans. W. H. Gantt. Lawrence and Wishart.

PEEL, E. A. (1967) 'Some Problems in the Psychology of History Teaching: Historical Ideas and Concepts'. In W. H. Burston and D. Thompson (eds), *Studies in the Nature and Teaching of History*. Routledge and Kegan Paul, 1967. 159–71.

PERROT, E., APPLEBEE, A. N., WATSON, E., and HEAP, B. (1975) 'Changes in Teaching Behaviour after Completing a Self-Instructional Microteaching Course'. *Programmed Learning and Educational Technology*, 12, 6, 348–62.

PETERS, R. S. (1977) 'Education as a Specific Preparation for Teaching'. In *Education and the Education of Teachers*. Routledge and Kegan Paul, 1977. 51–66.

474 References

PHILLIPS, J. L. (1969) *The Origins of Intellect: Piaget's Theory.* Freeman.

PIAGET, J. (1961) 'The Genetic Approach to the Psychology of Thought'. *Journal of Educational Psychology*, 52, 1941, 151–61. Reprinted in Stones (1970a).

PIAGET, J. (1962) '*Comments on Vigotsky's Critical Remarks Concerning The Language and Thought of the Child and Judgement and Reasoning in the Child*'. MIT Press.

RAVEN, J. C. (1969) *Coloured Progressive Matrices.* Lewis.

REID, J. F. (1966) 'Learning to Think about Reading'. *Educational Research*, 9, 1, November, 56–62.

RENHARD, D. H. (1971) 'An Attempt to Increase Nonverbal Intelligence Test Scores by the Programming of the Principles of Inductive Reasoning'. Unpublished M.Ed. dissertation, University of Birmingham.

RIST, R. C. (1970) 'Student Social Class and Teacher Expectations: The Self Fulfilling Prophecy in Ghetto Education'. *Harvard Educational Review*, 40, 41–51.

ROSEN, H. (1972) *Language and Class: A Critical Look at the Theories of Basil Bernstein.* Falling Wall Press.

ROSENSHINE, B., and FURST, N. (1971) 'Research on Teacher Performance Criteria'. In B. O. Smith (ed.), *Research on Teacher Education: A Symposium.* Prentice Hall, 1971.

ROWNTREE, D. (1975) *Educational Technology in Curriculum Development.* Harper and Row.

ROWNTREE, D. (1977) *Assessing Students, How Shall We Know Them?* Harper and Row.

SAPIR, E. (1963) *Language.* Hart-Davis.

SCHONELL, F. J., and SCHONELL, F. E. (1960) 'The Graded Word Reading Test'. In *Diagnostic and Attainment Testing Including a Manual of Tests, their Nature, Use, Recording and Preparation.* Oliver and Boyd, 1960.

SCHOOL OF BARBIANA (1970) *A Letter to a Teacher.* Penguin.

SCHOOLS COUNCIL (1975) *Examinations Bulletin 32.* Evans/ Methuen Educational.

SCHOOLS COUNCIL (1977) *18+ Research Programme Studies Based on the N and F Proposals.*

References 475

SEMEONOFF, B., and SKINNER, D. J. M. (1971) 'Equivalence of Alternative Forms in a Concept Formation Task'. *British Journal of Educational Psychology*, 41, 3, 332–4.

SHAVELSON, R. J. (1976) 'Teachers' Decision Making'. In N. C. Gage (ed.), *The Psychology of Teaching Methods*. Yearbook of the National Society for the Study of Education, 1976.

SHAVELSON, R. J. (1977) 'Teachers' Estimates of Student "States of Mind"'. *British Journal of Teacher Education*, 3, 2, 131–8.

SIMON, A., and BOYER, E. G. (1967) *Mirrors for Behaviour: An Anthology of Classroom Observation Instruments*. 6 vols. Research for Better Schools.

SIMON, B. (1957) *Psychology in the Soviet Union*. Routledge and Kegan Paul.

SIMON, B., and SIMON, J. (1963) *Educational Psychology in the USSR*. Routledge and Kegan Paul.

SINCLAIR, J. MCH., FORSYTH, I. J., COULTHARD, R. M., and ASHBY, M. C. (1972) *The English Used by Teachers and Pupils*. Final report to SSRC, September 1970 to August 1972. University of Birmingham.

SKINNER, B. F. (1948) *Walden Two*. Macmillan.

SKINNER, B. F. (1954) 'The Science of Learning and the Art of Teaching'. *Harvard Educational Review*, 24, 86–97.

SKINNER, B. F. (1962) *Cumulative Record*. Methuen.

SMITH, B. O. (1969) *Teachers for the Real World*. American Association of Colleges for Teacher Education.

SOLOMON, R. L. (1964) 'Punishment'. *American Psychologist*, 19, 239–53.

STOLUROW, L. M. (1965) 'Model the Master Teacher or Master the Teaching Model'. In J. D. Krumboltz (ed.), *Learning and the Educational Process*. Rand McNally, 1965.

STONES, E. (1966a) *Introduction to Educational Psychology*. Methuen.

STONES, E. (1966b) 'The Use of Programming Techniques in Teacher Education'. *Education for Teaching*, February, 31–7.

STONES, E. (1968) *Learning and Teaching: A Programmed Introduction*. Wiley.

STONES, E. (1970) *Readings in Educational Psychology*. Methuen.

476 References

STONES, E. (1971) 'Verbal Labelling and Concept Formation in Primary School Children'. *British Journal of Educational Psychology*, November.

STONES, E. (1975) 'The Colour of Complex Learning. Concept Formation in Three Ethnic Groups'. *Research Intelligence*, 2, 5–10. British Educational Research Association.

STONES, E., and ANDERSON, D. (1972) *Educational Objectives and the Teaching of Educational Psychology*. Methuen.

STONES, E., and HESLOP, J. R. (1968) 'The Formation of Class Concepts in British Primary School Children'. *British Journal of Educational Psychology*, November.

STONES, E., and MORRIS, S. (1972) *Teaching Practice: Problems and Perspectives*. Methuen.

STOTT, D. H. (1978) *Helping Children with Learning Difficulties*. Ward Lock Educational.

STUBBS, M. (1976) *Language Schools and Classrooms*. Methuen.

SUTTON, A. (1977) 'Defects in Defectology'. *Times Educational Supplement*, 13 May.

TABA, H., and ELZEY, F. F. (1964) 'Teaching Strategies and Thought Processes'. *Teachers College Record*, 65, 6, 524–34.

THORNDIKE, E. L. (1921) *The Psychology of Learning*. Kegan Paul, Trench, Tubner and Co.

TRAVERS, R. M. W. (1973) *Second Handbook of Research on Teaching*. Rand McNally (AERA).

VELDMAN, D. J., and PECK, R. F. (1963) 'Student Teacher Characteristics from the Pupils' Viewpoint'. *Journal of Educational Psychology*, 54, 346–55.

VERNON, J. (1963) *Inside the Black Room*. Penguin.

VERNON, P. E. (1955) *The Bearings of Recent Advances in Psychology on Educational Problems*. Evans.

VIGOTSKY, L. S. (1962) *Thought and Language*. MIT Press.

WEDELL, K. (1973) *Learning and Perceptuo-Motor Disabilities in Children*. Wiley.

WEDELL, K. (1978a) 'Personal Communication'. Unpublished.

WEDELL, K. (1978b) *Investigation Strategies for Helping Children with Learning Difficulties*. Paper presented at 75th Conference of the Dutch Special Education Association 1978. Mimeo.

References 477

WELFORD, A. T. (1968) *Fundamentals of Skill.* Methuen.
WHITE, R. W. (1959) 'Motivation Reconsidered: The Concept of Competence'. *Psychological Review*, 66, 297–333.
WISEMAN, S., and PIDGEON, D. (1970) *Curriculum Evaluation.* NFER.

Index

abstractions, 20, 21
aims, 143, 156, 298; importance of systematic approach, 143; and objectives, 156; in teaching, 143
accommodation, 72, 73, 74; and adaptation, 72; and assimilation, 72; and schemas, 74
action, 69, 85
adaptation, 54, 72; and accommodation, 72; and assimilation, 72; and cultural accretion, 54; and learning, 54; and meaning, 54; Piaget's view, 72; and species, 54; and syntax, 54
affect, 40, 45, 111; in classrooms, 111; and learning, 40, 45; and motivation, 45; and speech, 111
algorithms, 182, 254–60, 265; in arithmetic, 256; and

botany, 258; and heuristics, 257, 259, 260; and problem solving, 254, 260, 458; and psychopedagogy, 260; and teaching, 256
Allen, E. A., 309, 321, 466
Amerslan, 5
Anderson, D., 150, 154, 155, 170, 323
anxiety, 26
Applebee, A. N., 473
Argyle, M., 140, 466
arousal, 317
Ashby, M. C., 475
aspiration: level of and tests, 373
assimilation, 72, 73, 74
Atkinson, J. W., 472
attention, 317–20
attitudes, 24; of teachers, 324
Austin, G. A., 467
Ausubel, D. P., 64, 188, 466
Axelrod, S., 287, 466
Azrin, N. H., 26, 466

Index 479

Baker, J. P., 420, 466
Barnes, D., 116, 117, 466
baseline, 431
Bauer, R. A., 467
Bellack, 133, 134
Benjamin, H., 295, 466
Bernstein, B., 421, 422, 423, 463, 466
Biddle, B. J., 468
Binet, A., 409, 410, 418, 428, 467
Bjorstedt, A., 133, 467
Blake, W., 150
Bloom, B. S., 44, 45, 149, 150, 151, 152, 400, 467, 471
Bloom taxonomies, 150, 151, 152, 153, 154, 316, 456; and test items, 153, 154
Blyth, W. A. L., 139, 467
Books: learning from, 109; as learning environment, 109, 110; limitations of in learning, 252; in teaching, 252
Borg, W. R., 311, 467
Boyer, E. G., 123, 475
Brackbill, Y., 94, 467
British Psychological Society, 429, 431, 464, 467
Brophy, J. E., 292, 307, 470
Brown, R., 66, 467
Bruner, J. S., 15, 89, 90, 91, 97, 100, 107, 180, 237, 315, 455, 467; critique of, 97; and representation, 180
Bryant, P., 96, 99, 467
Buros, O. K., 407, 467
Butcher, H. J., 422, 467

Cane, B., 133, 222
chaining, 228
chimpanzees, 5, 66
Chomsky, N., 53, 468
Clark, A. N. and A. D., 410, 468
Clark, C., 472
Clark, R. A., 472
classroom: climate, 277, 278, 282, 290; and reinforcement, 303, 460; discourse, 122, 123, 125, 126, 130, 455; analysis of, 123, 456; management activities, 114, 115, 222, 225, 226, 284, 285, 458; teacher/pupil ratio, 126, 130
classrooms, 105, 110; language in, 105; as learning environments, 110
cognitive skills, 108
Cole, M., 57, 468
Colleges of Education Research Group (Birmingham University), 177, 468
communication, 139; non-verbal, 139
Community Relations Commission, 419, 468
competence and motivation, 43
concept of concept teaching, 225
concept labelling, 58; and language, 58
concept learning, 15, 34, 50, 73, 76, 87, 88, 99, 100, 101, 117, 162, 163; and counterpositioning, 100; and discrimination, 34; and experience, 50, 101; and generalization, 34; and knowing, 162, 165; and language, 88, 107; and levels of generality, 162; and phasing out of guidance, 101; and principle learning, 163; and schooling, 54; and symbolling, 100; and teaching, 100, 101; and tests of transfer, 87, 88, 377
concept teaching, 60, 61, 62, 131, 197, 199, 200, 201, 202, 203, 204, 205, 206, 207, 221, 279, 458; and cueing, 202, 204, 312; and counterpositioning, 203; and definitions, 61; and entry competence, 200, 201,

480 *Index*

concept teaching – *contd.*
202; as feedback, 204; and
increasing salience, 203; as
a key teaching skill, 196,
199; and language, 60, 61,
199, 204; and presentation
of exemplars, 203, 221, 279;
and prior knowledge, 61;
and sensory experience, 202;
a schedule for guidance,
205, 206, 207; and
structure, 60; and task
analysis, 201; and transfer
as acid test of, 205; use of
exemplars in, 131; and
variations of attributes, 60;
and verbal learning, 62
concepts, 49, 50, 51, 52, 54,
63, 82, 94, 117, 118, 119,
120, 163, 169, 225; analysis
of, 163, 169; as
complicating the
environment, 54; defined
concepts, 63; in history,
117, 118, 119; and
language, 54, 454; and
learning, 82, 454; mismatch
by teachers and learners,
118, 119, 120; and
misunderstandings, 118; and
symbols, 82, 454; and
syntax, 52; and systems of,
163; and teaching, 50, 94;
of time, 54; uniqueness of,
51; and words, 5
conditioning, 12, 13, 14, 356;
classical, 14; instrumental, 14
conservation, 77, 78, 90
Coulthard, M., 422, 468, 475
counselling; and use of
recordings, 449; and
reinforcement, 448, 449
counterpositioning, 100, 203;
in concept learning, 100, 203
creativity, 267, 268, 269, 270,
459; criteria of, 270;
critique of, 268, 270; tests
of, 269, 270
Crist, J. L., 420, 466

Crowder, N. A., 335, 468
cueing, 40, 107, 108, 114, 202,
204, 233, 261, 273, 315;
and concept teaching, 202,
204; an example of, 273;
and explaining, 114; fading
of, 108; as feedback, 204,
357; and guiding, 233; and
language, 107, 455; as
modelling, 40; in problem
solving, 261; and
psychomotor skills, 233;
and structuring, 114; and
teaching, 114
culture, 55, 69; and the
environment, 55; and
evolution, 55, 454; and
language, 55; and learning,
69; and skills, 55; and
species adaptation, 55; and
technology, 55
cultural accretion, 54; and
adaptation, 54; and learning,
54; and meaning, 54; and
species, 54; and syntax, 54
cultural evolution, 5, 65; in
chimpanzees, 5
curiosity and motivation, 42,
43, 76, 297; and
reinforcement, 76
curriculum, 10

Daniels, J. C., 168, 368, 468
Davies, I. K., 231, 468
Decision making: as key
teaching skill, 323, 325; and
teacher attitudes, 323, 324
definitions in learning, 202
Delamont, S., 136, 468
demonstrating, and modelling,
108
Department of Education and
Science, 165, 428, 429, 430,
464, 468
development, 75, 76, 80, 81,
95; Piaget's views on, 75, 80;
and teaching, 80, 81, 95, 455
Diack, H., 168, 368, 468
diagnosis, 3, 431, 432, 438, 464

Index 481

discovery learning, 263
discipline, 292
discrimination, 28, 29, 31, 32, 34; among stimuli, 28, 29, 30; and concept learning, 34; and distress, 32; and generalization, 32, 33; and teaching, 29, 31
Donaldson, M., 71, 92, 94, 468
Downing, J., 169, 468
Drabman, R. S., 286, 287, 468
Dunkin, M. J., 17, 468
Duthie, J. H., 222, 469
dyslexia, 433
dyspedeutia, 433

Ebel, R. L., 469
Educational Testing Service, 389, 390, 391, 469
egocentricity, 76, 77, 83, 92; and development, 76; and speech, 83
Elashoff, J. O., 469
Elzey, F. F., 312, 476
empty verbalism, 62, 64, 101, 117
entry competence, 280, 464
Entwistle, N. J., 406, 469
evaluation, 9, 194, 230; of learning, 194, 354; objectives of, 230; of psychomotor skills, 230; and task analysis, 230; of teaching, 354; taxonomy of, 230
evolution, 55
expectancy, 419, 424, 425
experimenters as teachers, 8, 38
experimenting and teaching, xix, 435, 450, 460
explaining, 114
exploratory activity, 11
extinction, 27, 28, 286, 287, 460

facts, 48
failure, 41, 45

Fawthrop, T., 335, 469
feedback, 34, 35, 36, 45, 108, 115, 194, 195, 204, 236, 237, 266, 332, 348; and attitudes, 45; and concept teaching, 204; and cueing, 204, 357; and failure, 45; instrumentation for, 237; kinesthetic, 238; and language, 204; and learning, 196; from peers, 283; and psychomotor skills, 236; and practice, 266; and punishment, 35; and reinforcement, 35, 36, 293, 294, 460; and success, 45; to teachers, 116, 194, 354; and teaching, 35, 36, 358, 438, 439, 464; and tests, 373, 442
feral child, 2
Fineman, S., 44, 469
Flanders, N., 104, 134, 469
Flanders Interaction Analysis Categories (FIAC), 123, 124, 125, 126, 131, 132, 133, 135, 136, 139; an example of, 127–30; and self appraisal, 139; teaching of, 139
Flavell, J. H., 71, 469
Fleshner, E. A., 203, 469
Fodor, J. A., 97, 98, 100, 469
Ford Teaching Project, 272, 273, 276, 469
Forsyth, I. J., 475
Frank, F., 90, 95
Furst, N., 27, 474

Gagg, J. C., 331, 470
Gagné, R. M., 63, 470
Galperin, P. Y., 94, 95, 99, 100, 102, 103, 188, 235, 261, 470
Gardner, A. and B., 5
generalization, 32, 33, 34, 50; and concept learning, 34; and discrimination, 32, 33; and reinforcement, 34;

482 *Index*

generalization – *contd.*
 semantic, 50; and teaching,
 33
Glaser, R., 17, 470
Glidewell, J. C., 372, 470
Good, T. L., 292, 307, 470
Goodnow, J. J., 467
Goyder, D. G., 420, 470
Greenfield, P. M., 57, 467, 470
grouping, 57, 58; and
 taxonomic class, 57, 58;
 and teaching, 57
growth, 7
guidance, 15, 93, 106, 108,
 194, 263, 458; and feedback,
 106; and language, 106,
 194; and learning, 15, 93,
 106, 194; and punishment,
 106; and reinforcement, 106
guided learning, 10
guiding, 233; and cueing, 233;
 and psychomotor skills, 233
Guilford, J. P., 269, 470
Gulliford, R., 470

Hamill, D., 430, 470
handicap: ascertainment of,
 468; and psychopedagogy,
 429
Hansen, S., 37, 470
Harlow, H. F., 37, 38, 453, 470
Harrow, A. J., 230, 231, 470
Harrow taxonomy, 232
Hayes, K. J. and C., 4, 470
Heap, B., 473
Hegarty, S., 400, 470
Hermelin, B., 49, 473
Herriot, P., 65, 470
Herrnstein, R. J., 66, 467
heuristics, 182, 232, 254, 257,
 259, 260, 265, 267, 275;
 and algorithms, 257, 259,
 260; and problem solving,
 257, 260, 458
Heslop, J., 87
Hill, B., 71, 471
Hilsum, S., 133, 222, 471
Hogben, L., 400, 471
Holland, J. G., 334, 471

Holtz, W. C., 26, 466
Honig, W. K., 466
Hora, F. B., 258, 472
Hughes, M., 92, 93, 99
Hunt, W. A., 25, 471
hypotheses; and practice, 143;
 and theory, 143; in teaching,
 143

imitation, 39, 40, 109, 453,
 458
individual differences, 426, 427
individualization of learning,
 177
individualized instruction, 178
Insel, S. A., 420, 471
intelligence, 408, 409, 416,
 423, 463; and race, 414, 415,
 416
interaction analysis, 133, 134,
 135, 136, 137; a linguistic
 approach, 135, 136;
 unstructured approach, 136,
 137; varied approaches, 133
internal speech, 103
Itard, J. M. G., 1, 2, 8, 452,
 471

Jackson, L. A., 422, 471
Jacobson, L. F., 420, 471
Jensen, A. R., 414, 415, 416,
 417, 463, 471
Jensen, J., 37, 470
Joint Committee on
 Programmed Instruction
 and Teaching Machines,
 347, 471

Kagan, J., 373, 473
Kamin, L. J., 427, 471
Kelley, M. L., 467
Kirkland, M. C., 372, 373,
 471
Knight, F. B., 373, 473
knowing, 162, 163
knowledge, 48
Kohl, H., 272, 471
Kounin, J., 292, 471
Krathwohl, D. R., 471

Index 483

labelling, 2, 3, 401, 408, 418,
421, 424, 427, 429, 432, 433,
463, 464
Labov, W., 422, 471
Landa, L. N., 254, 255, 256,
257, 261, 471
Lane, H., 1, 4, 5, 472
Lange, M., 258, 467, 472
language, 4, 11, 47, 48, 49,
53, 54, 55, 58, 59, 61, 65,
69, 81, 85, 86, 88, 89, 99,
104–9, 117, 120, 121, 194,
199, 204, 264, 266; and
action, 69, 85, 455; in
classroom, 104, 105; and
concept labelling, 58; and
concept learning, 59, 88, 89,
117; and concept teaching,
60, 61, 199, 204; and
concepts, 54; and context of
learning, 54, 109; and
cueing, 107, 204, 455; and
culture, 55; and definitions,
61; and environment, 54,
55; and evolution, 55; and
exploratory activity, 11;
and feedback, 106, 204;
and guidance, 106, 194;
and increasing salience, 108;
and knowledge, 48; and
labelling, 59, 454; and
learning, 4, 11, 47, 106, 107,
454; Pavlov's views of, 81;
and pedagogy, 4; and
practice, 107; and prior
knowledge, 61; and problem
solving, 464; problems of, in
teaching, 120, 121; process
function of, 59, 61, 86, 88,
454; and prompting, 266;
and punishment, 106; and
reinforcement, 106, 107,
453; and remote reference,
54, 54; and signing, 2; and
skills, 55; and species
adaptation, 55; and speech,
4; and symbolling, 4, 49,
454; and task analysis, 264;
and teaching, 99, 105; and

technology, 55; and thinking,
65, 69, 81, 85, 99, 105, 454;
and time, 54; Vigotsky's
views of, 81
law of effect, 14
Leach, D. J., 424, 429, 430, 472
learning, 7, 10, 11, 12, 13, 15,
20, 24, 26, 35, 37, 39, 40,
45, 47, 53, 54, 57, 60, 64,
66, 67, 69, 73, 74, 81, 83,
89, 95, 105, 106, 107, 108,
109, 194, 196, 228, 262, 280,
452, 461; and abstraction,
20; and adaptation, 54; and
affect, 40, 45; and anxiety,
26; arbitrary, 356, 357; of
attitudes, 24; books and,
109; and chaining, 228; and
change, 7; in chimpanzees,
5, 66; of cognitive skills,
108; and concepts, 82; and
culture, 69; and cultural
accretion, 54; effects of
culture on, 66; effects of
environment on, 67;
errorless, 293, 294;
evaluation of, 194, 354, 461;
of facts, 64; and feedback,
106, 355; and growth, 7;
and guidance, 13, 14, 15,
60, 93, 106, 194; and
individual differences, 16;
and initiation, 39, 107;
and language, 4, 49, 106,
107; and lesion, 7;
mastery, 363; and meaning,
54; and motivation, 45;
non-verbal, 105; Piaget's
views, 73; and pedagogy, 4;
and practice, 107; and
problem solving, 262; and
psychomotor skills, 228;
and punishment, 26, 106;
and reinforcement, 106, 107;
and representation, 89; of
schemas, 74; and schooling,
57; and signing, 4, 5; and
social behaviour, 24; and
social environment, 24;

484 *Index*

learning – *contd.*
  social influences on, 105;
  and society, 20, 47; and
  species, 54; and species
  differences, 6, 16; and
  speech, 4, 5, 20; structuring
  for, 280, 282, 294; and
  success, 11; superstitions, 35;
  and symbols, 83; and
  symbolling, 4, 82; and
  symbolic environment, 20;
  and symbol system, 5; and
  syntax, 53, 54; and teaching,
  8, 26; and thinking, 5;
  transfer of, 37, 39
learning: ability, and race, 417,
  463; environment, 109, 110;
  gradient, 280; sets, 36, 37,
  38, 60, 453; tasks, 23, 24;
  to learn, 38
Linden, E., 4, 472
linguistic codes, 421, 422, 423,
  424, 463
linguistic register, 117
Little Red School Book, 37
Liublinskaya, A. A., 88, 472
Lowell, F. L., 472
Luchins, A., 264, 472
Lunzer, E. A., 24, 472
Luria, A. R., 58, 67, 84, 102,
  130, 472

McClelland, D. C., 43, 472
McLeish, J., 24, 472
Mager, R. F., 146, 178, 472
marking scales, 363
Masia, B. B., 471
Matarazzo, J. D., 25, 471
meaning, 54
meaningful learning, 64
Meighan, R., 441, 472
mental actions, 102
Merrit, J., 169, 473
Metfessel, L., 154
microteaching, 196, 309, 311,
  460
minicourse, 311, 312
Ministry of Education, 473
Mittler, P. J., 413, 414, 473

modelling, 40, 108, 109, 236;
  and cueing, 40; and
  demonstrating, 108; and
  psychomotor skills, 236
Morris, D., 2, 473
Morris, S., 123, 125, 476
Mosher, F. A., 91
Moss, R. W., 373, 473
motivation, 41, 42, 43, 44, 45,
  46, 76, 266, 454; and
  competence, 43; and
  curiosity, 42, 43, 76, 297,
  454; enhancement of, 46;
  extrinsic, 295, 297; and
  failure, 41, 373; intrinsic,
  295, 297, 298, 460; as
  learned, 44; and
  reinforcement, 76, 460; and
  success, 43, 44, 45, 454

need to achieve, 43, 44
non-verbal communication,
  139, 140
norms, 240, 241
norms, critique of, 240, 241

Objectives, 145, 146, 147, 148,
  149, 155, 156, 157, 158, 161,
  162, 164, 166, 170, 171, 172,
  173, 174, 177, 178, 230, 263,
  345, 456, 457; and aims,
  156; analyses of, 162, 164,
  172; analysis of taxonomies,
  of, 149; concepts in, 170;
  and concensus on, 148, 149,
  161; criticisms of, 171, 173,
  174; and different specificity
  of, 171; and evaluation, 230,
  461; hidden, 157; imprecise,
  173; instrumental, 159;
  and performance, 158, 159;
  in performance terms, 155;
  need for precision in, 147;
  problem solving, 263; skills
  in, 170; specifying as
  neutral activity, 174;
  problems in specifying, 158,
  170; spurious accuracy in,
  173; for students, 178; and

Index 485

task analysis, 230, 345;
taxonomy of, 230; a
taxonomic system, 155; for
teaching reading, 166; and
tests, 360; types A, B, C,
161, 162; vagueness in, 145,
146; values of, 171; and
value judgements, 161, 164;
for whom?, 177
O'Connor, N., 49, 473
O'Leary, K. D. and S. G., 22,
287, 289, 473
Oleron, P., 65, 473
Olver, R. R., 467
operations, 78, 79; concrete,
78; mental, 78, 79
overlearning, 229

Page, E. B., 313, 473
Panlasigui, I., 373, 473
Pavlov, I. P., 11, 12, 13, 14,
24, 31, 42, 81, 317, 452, 473;
and language, views of, 11,
81; and thinking, 81
Peck, R. F., 441, 476
Peel, E. A., 119, 473
permanent object, 75, 76
Perrot, E., 311, 473
personality: categories of, 405,
463; tests of, 404, 407
Peters, R. S., 473
Phillips, J. L., 474
Piaget, J., 71, 72, 75, 78, 79,
80, 81, 86, 89, 90, 92, 93,
94, 96, 97, 98, 99, 454, 474;
critique of, 80, 81, 92, 93,
94, 96, 97, 98; and
development, 80; and
teaching, 79, 80
Pidgeon, D., 391, 477
Priel, P., 2, 429
practice, 98, 229, 238, 239,
266; and feedback, 266;
graded, 239; instrumental,
229; and overlearning, 229;
and psychomotor skills, 229;
status of, 98; and theory,
98, 436
Pressey, S., 332

principle learning, 163; and
concept learning, 163; and
knowing, 163
principles, 63
problem solving, 17, 37, 103,
237, 261, 262, 263, 264, 265,
266, 275, 458; and
algorithms, 237; and
cueing, 261; and heuristics,
237; and language, 264;
and learning, 262; objectives
in, 263; prerequisites for,
264; and prompted practice,
266; and task analysis, 264,
265, 275; and teacher, 17;
and teaching, 17, 103; and
theory, 17; and thinking,
103; and transfer, 262
programmed learning, 282,
331, 332, 333, 334, 347, 348,
349, 352, 460; criterial
attributes of, 350; sequence
in, 333
prompted practice, 266
prompting, 108, 266, 273; an
example of, 273
prophecy: self fulfilling, 419,
420, 431
psychology and teachers, 97
psychomotor skills, 227, 228,
229, 230, 233, 235, 236, 240,
241; and chaining, 228;
and cueing, 233; and
evaluation, 230; and
feedback, 236; and guiding,
233; as instrumental, 229;
and learning, 228, 240;
and modelling, 236;
objectives of, 230; and
overlearning, 229; and
practice, 229; as prerequisite,
227; and self monitoring,
240, 241; sequence in, 235;
types A, B, C, 233; and
task analysis, 230, 232;
taxonomy, 230; teaching of,
235, 236
psychopedagogy, xviii, 31,
260; and algorithms, 260;

486 *Index*

psychopedagogy – *contd.*
  explained, xviii;
  respondance, 31
punishment, 25, 26, 27, 35,
  286, 459; as feedback, 35;
  and habituation, 25;
  identification of, 26, 290;
  and learning, 26, 454; and
  management, 26; problems
  of, 27, 290, 291, 453; as
  reinforcer, 26, 35; side
  effects of, 26; and teaching,
  26, 27, 35, 289, 291

questioning, 131, 132, 197,
  308, 312, 314, 315, 316;
  and probing, 132

race: and intelligence, 414,
  415, 416; and learning
  ability, 417, 463
Raven, J. C., 417, 474
Raven's matrices, 417
Raybauld, E. C., 424, 429,
  430, 472
reading, 164, 165, 168, 169,
  190; analysis of skills in,
  169; concepts in, 169;
  definitions of, 165, 168;
  knowledge about, 169;
  skills in, 169; task analysis
  in, 190; teaching of, 164
Reid, J. F., 169, 263, 474
reinforcement, 11, 19, 22, 23,
  24, 34, 35, 36, 76, 278, 279,
  283, 288, 289, 454; and
  classroom climate, 278, 284;
  and classroom discourse,
  303; and counselling, 448;
  and curiosity, 76; and
  error, 24; and feedback, 35,
  36, 293, 294, 460; and
  generalization, 34;
  intermittent, 285, 286, 453;
  and language, 453; and
  management activities, 285;
  and motivation, 76; by
  peers, 283; planning for,
  281, 459; in programmed
  learning, 333; as

punishment, 35; schedules
  of, 22, 23, 279; and
  success, 23; in teaching, 22,
  35, 287, 288; and teaching
  skills, 278; and victor, 19
reinforcers, 21, 307
remote reference, 53, 54, 91, 132
Renhard, D. H., 416, 474
representation, 89, 90, 91, 97,
  102, 107, 181, 455; and
  learning, 89, 90; and
  thinking, 97
rewards, 9, 11
ripple effect, 292
Rist, R. C., 424, 474
Robinson, F. G., 188, 466
Rosen, H., 422, 474
Rosenshine, B., 27, 474
rote learning, 14, 361
Rowntree, D., 355, 474
Ryan, K., 309, 321, 466

Sapir, E., 51, 52, 474
schemas, 74, 75, 89; and
  accommodation, 74; and
  assimilation, 74; cognitive,
  74; motor, 74
Schonnell, F. J., 365, 474
School of Barbiana, 277, 474
schooling, effects of, 57, 454
Schools Council, 391, 397, 474,
  475
Scribner, S., 57, 468
segregation, 424, 425
self appraisal, 139, 294, 295,
  307, 330, 441
self concept, 45
self evaluation, 237
self perceptions, 45
self regulation, 83, 84, 85, 92,
  130; and speech, 85, 455;
  and symbolling, 83, 455
Semeonoff, B., 89, 475
sequence: in learning, 188; in
  programmed learning, 333,
  345; in psychomotor skills,
  235; teaching in, 235; in
  teaching number, 189; in
  teaching reading, 189

Index 487

Shavelson, R. J., 323, 325, 326, 475
shaping, 9, 203
signing, 4, 5, 65, 452; in chimpanzees, 5; and language, 4; and learning, 4, 5
Simon, B. and J., 475
Simon, A., 123, 475
Sinclair, J. McH., 135, 475
skills, 55, 56, 160, 169, 196, 205, 235, 236, 252; and culture, 55; knowledge about, 169; psychomotor, 236; in reading, 169; sequence in, 235; and species adaptation, 55, 56; taxonomy of, 169; and teachers, 56; teaching of, 196, 235, 236; and technology, 55; types A, B, C, 160, 205, 252
Skinner, B. F., 8, 11, 22, 24, 35, 47, 281, 331, 332, 333, 334, 335, 452, 471, 475; criticism of, 282
Skinner, D. J. M., 89, 475
Smith, B. O., 324, 475
Snow, R. E., 469
social environment, effects of, 5, 24
socialization of feral child, 3
society and abstractions, 20; and cultural accretion, 68; effects on humans, 1; and learning, 10, 20, 47; and speech, 20, 68; and thinking, 68
Solomon, R. C., 25, 475
species adaptation, 55, 56
species differences, 16
speech, 5, 20, 68, 83, 84, 85, 102, 103, 111; and abstractions, 20; and activity, 68; and affect, 111; in chimpanzees, 5; in classrooms, 111; and cultural accretion, 68; and egocentricity, 83; inner, 83, 84; and learning, 4, 5, 20,

68; and pedagogy, 4; and self regulation, 85, 102, 105, 455; and signing, 4, 5; and society, 68; and symbolic environment, 20, 68; and teaching, 6; and thinking, 68
stimulus deprivation, 42
Stolurow, L. M., 436, 475
Stones, E., 87, 88, 123, 125, 150, 154, 155, 170, 323, 341, 346, 353, 417, 436, 475, 476
Stott, D. H., 400, 429, 432, 476
Stringer, L. A., 372, 470
structuring, 114
Stubbs, M., 476
success, 11, 20, 23, 43, 45; and attitudes, 45, 454; and feedback, 45; and learning, 11, 454; and motivation, 43, 44, 45, 454; as reinforcement, 20, 23, 454
successive approximation, 198, 279, 333
superstitious behaviour, 356
supervision as teaching, 442, 450
supervisors, 139, 330; and appraisal, 139, 295; and teaching, 139
Sutton, A., 432, 476
symbols, 82, 83; and concepts, 82, 454; and learning, 82, 83, 454
symbol system, 5
symbolic environment, 20
symbolling, 4, 65, 66, 76, 83, 91, 100, 455; and concept learning, 100; and deafness, 65; and language, 4; and learning, 4; and remote reference, 91; and self regulation, 83; and teaching, 100
syntax, 52, 53, 54

Taba, H., 312, 315, 476
task, the learners and the teachers, 179

488 *Index*

task analysis, 9, 179, 180, 181, 183, 186, 187, 190, 196, 201, 230, 232, 234, 264, 265, 275, 280, 457, 458, 464; and concept teaching, 201; and entry competence, 280; and evaluation, 230; an example of, 180, 182; of handwriting, 234; and language, 264; and learners, 181; and learning gradient, 280, 459; objectives of, 230; and practical teaching, 126; and problem solving, 264, 265, 275; and programmed learning, 345; and psychomotor skills, 230, 232; of reading, 190; a systematic approach, 182; and teachers, 181; of teaching reading, 180, 182, 186, 187; and testing, 360

taxonomies: of objectives, 149, 150, 151, 152, 230, 231, 232; and task analysis, 230; for teaching psychomotor skills, 231, 232

taxonomic class, 57, 58

teachers, 8, 17, 70, 96, 97, 143, 144, 194; as experimenters, 8, 70, 96; feedback to, 194; as practitioners, 144; as reinforcing agents, 281; and problem solving, 17; and psychologists, 97; and teaching, 17; and theory, 17, 143; as theorists, 144

teachers': questions, 115; talk, 115

teaching, 8, 9, 17, 26, 28, 29, 31, 33, 36, 38, 40, 48, 50, 51, 57, 64, 79, 80, 81, 94, 95, 100, 101, 102, 103, 104, 105, 114, 121, 130, 132, 137, 138, 139, 143, 144, 164, 189, 196, 198, 199, 235, 236, 252, 256, 416; aims in, 143; and algorithms, 256; and

anxiety, 26; appraisal of, 139, 354, 439; appraisal of by peers, 137, 438, 440; appraisal and psychopedagogy, 440; appraisal of by pupils, 441; appraisal using recordings, 439, 441; appraisal by supervisors, 139, 438, 440; and objectives, 439; and books, 252; and concept learning, 100, 101; of concepts, 50, 51, 94; conventional views of, 104; and cueing, 114; and development, 81, 95, 455; direct, 130; and discrimination, 29, 31, 33; as enhancing learning, 138, 441; and experience, 101; as experimenting, xix, 435, 450, 460; and explaining, 114; by exposition, 64; and extinction, 28; of facts, 48; and feedback, 36, 355, 438, 439, 464; and generalization, 33; and grouping, 57; and guidance, phasing out of, 101, 102; and imitation, 40, 453; indirect, 130; of knowledge, 48, 63; and language, 105; and learning, 8, 26; machines, 282, 333, 349; method, 207; and objectives, 439; a paradigm, 3; and Piaget, 79, 80; of principles, 63; as problem solving, 9, 17, 103, 452; of psychomotor skills, 233, 236, 458; punishment in, 26, 27, 35, 289; and race, 417, 418; of reading, 164, 166, 167, 168, 180, 189; recordings of, 121, 137, 138, 464; and reinforcement, 23, 35, 287, 288; remedial, 430; and remote reference, 132; and self appraisal, 137, 138;

Index 489

sequences in, 189, 235; of skills, 196, and speech, 6; and structure, 38, 114; and symbolizing 100; and taxonomic classification, 57; as test of theory, 144; and testing, 355, 391, 392, 394, 397; and theory, 17, 18; and thinking, 103, 105; transcripts of, 137; types of, 17

teaching objectives, 155, 156, 157; generalizing of, 156, 157

teaching programmes, 335, 336, 337, 340, 341, 342, 343, 344, 345, 346, 347; in teaching system, 350

teaching schedules, as guides to action, 326, 327, 330

teaching skills, 196, 197, 199, 205, 208, 278, 308, 309, 310, 311, 313, 457, 458, 460; critiques of, 322; decision making as key skill, 323; as of general application, 197; types A, B, C, 198, 199; and reinforcement, 278; styles, 437; systems, 350, 351, 352; task, 178

technology, effects on learning and teaching, 55

testing, and teaching, 355, 360, 391, 392, 394, 397

test items, 153, 154, 364, 376, 384, 386, 387, 389, 390, 393; and Bloom taxonomy, 153, 154, 396

tests: of concept learning, 377; construction of, 391; criterion referenced, 325, 363, 364, 368, 393, 442, 462, 463; diagnostic, 368, 392, 394, 398, 431, 462; discrimination in, 375; essay type, 378, 379, 380, 381; and feedback, 373, 394, 442; of intelligence, 370, 401, 402, 403, 410, 412, 413, 427, 464; and monitoring of

learning, 394; and motivation, 373; norm referenced, 363, 364, 368, 393, 442, 463; objective, 381, 382, 383, 384, 385, 386, 387, 388, 389, 390; and objectives, 360, 362, 394; of personality, 404; profiles in, 367, 368, 369; problems of, 367, 368, 369, 372, 374, 394; of readiness, 370; of reading, 368; reliability of, 370, 371; and rote learning, 361, 362, 398; as samples of abilities, 359, 360; in selection, 364, 370, 403; of simple learning, 377, 397; and skills types A, B, C, 376; standardized, 365, 368, 395, 396; as surrogates, 359, 360; and task analysis, 360, of transfer, 362; validity of, 358, 369, 370, 462

theories, xix, 18, 69, 70, 98, 143, 144; as hypotheses, 69; as laws, 70; as problematic, xix; and teaching, 18, 143

theory and practice, 98, 144, 195, 326, 436

thinking, 5, 65, 68, 69, 72, 79, 81, 82, 85, 97, 99, 103, 105, 261, 269, 270; and action, 69, 82, 85; and activity, 68; and algorithms, 261; convergent, 269; and cultural accretion, 55, 56; divergent, 269, 270; formal, 79; and heuristics, 261; and language, 65, 69, 81, 85, 99, 105; and learning, 5; Pavlov's view of, 81; Piaget's view of, 72; and problem solving, 103; and psychopedagogy, 72; and representation, 97, and society, 68; and speech, 68; and symbol system, 5; and teaching, 99, 103; Vigotsky's views, 81

490 *Index*

Thorndike, E. L., 13, 14, 476
time, 54
time out, 287, 289, 458
transfer, 262, 362
Travers, R. M. W., 123, 476

validity of tests, 359, 462
Veldman, D. J., 441, 476
verbal learning, 62
Vernon, J., 42, 476
Vernon, P. E., 382, 476
victor, 2, 19, 66, 429
Vigotsky, L. S., 67, 68, 81, 83, 84, 85, 86, 87, 88, 93, 94, 97, 98, 101, 117, 130, 432, 476; blocks, 86; critique of, 97, 98; and language, 81; and thinking, 81

Viki, 4, 65

Washoe, 4, 65, 66
Watson, E., 473
Wedell, K., 427, 429, 430, 432, 476
Welford, A. T., 230
Wechsler Intelligence Scale for Children, 411
White, R. W., 43, 477
Wiederholt, J. L., 430, 470
Wiseman, S., 391, 477

Yerkes, R. M., 5
Yudovich, F. Y., 472

zone of potential development, 101